PERSONALITY IN THE MAKING

The Midcentury White House Conference on Children and Youth

Honorary Chairman

THE PRESIDENT OF THE UNITED STATES

HONORABLE HARRY S. TRUMAN

Chairman

HONORABLE OSCAR R. EWING

Vice Chairmen

LEONARD W. MAYO

ELEANOR ROOSEVELT

BENJAMIN SPOCK, M.D.

GEORGE D. STODDARD

KATHARINE F. LENROOT, *Secretary*

MELVIN A. GLASSER, *Executive Director*

PERSONALITY

IN THE MAKING

THE FACT-FINDING REPORT OF THE
MIDCENTURY WHITE HOUSE CONFERENCE
ON CHILDREN AND YOUTH

Edited by

HELEN LELAND WITMER
RUTH KOTINSKY

HARPER & BROTHERS, PUBLISHERS

New York

THE NATIONAL COMMITTEE *

Raymond B. Allen, M.D.

Francis Bacon

Charline Banks

Harvie Branscomb

A. J. Brumbaugh

Lyman Bryson

Mrs. J. L. Blair Buck

James Carey

Christ L. Christensen

Mrs. Jerome Evanson

Oscar R. Ewing

Katherine E. Faville

Lawrence K. Frank

Rabbi Solomon Goldman

Shelby M. Harrison

Mrs. John E. Hayes

Charles Janeway, M.D.

Rev. Raymond B. Johnson

T. Duckett Jones, M.D.

Flemmie P. Kittrell

Rev. C. E. Krumbholz

Mary Leeper

Mrs. David M. Levy

Eduard C. Lindeman

Very Rev. Msgr. John J. McClafferty

Chauncey McCormick

Leonard W. Mayo

Benjamin E. Mays

William C. Menninger, M.D.

Mrs. Agnes E. Meyer

Mabel Newcomer

Herman Neusch

Pauline Newman

Emma C. Puschner

Walter Reuther

Max Rheinstein

Mrs. Eleanor Roosevelt

Helen Ross

Ruth Schaffer

Edward B. Shaw, M.D.

G. Howland Shaw

Boris Shishkin

Benjamin Spock, M.D.

George D. Stoddard

Donald F. Sullivan

Gerard Swope

Mrs. Phyllis Jones Tilley

Edward M. M. Warburg

Mrs. Roy C. F. Weagly

Rev. Luther Weigle

John Wood

Benjamin E. Youngdahl

* Appointed by the President of the United States.

The Technical Committee on Fact Finding

Benjamin E. Youngdahl, *Chairman*
Leo H. Bartemeier, M.D.
Leroy E. Burney, M.D.
Mrs. Eveline M. Burns
Jules V. Coleman, M.D.
Fred DelliQuadri
Oscar Dombrow
Honorable Harry L. Eastman
Abraham N. Franzblau, M.D.
E. Franklin Frazier
Ruth Freeman
Robert J. Havighurst
Donald S. Howard
Reverend Reuel L. Howe
T. Duckett Jones, M.D.
Philip Klein
Otto Klineberg
William H. Lemmel
David M. Levy, M.D.
Alain Locke

Grace Marcus
The Very Reverend Monsignor
 John J. McClafferty
Margaret Mead
Henry B. Mulholland, M.D.
Mabel Newcomer
The Right Reverend Monsignor
 John O'Grady
Willard C. Olson
Catherine J. Personius
Louis E. Raths
Helen Ross
Robert Sears
Benjamin Spock, M.D.
George D. Stoddard
Julius J. Teller
Ruth Updegraff
Lois Wildy
Ellen Winston
Donald Young

The Fact-finding Staff
Full-time

Helen L. Witmer, *Director*
Ruth Kotinsky, *Assistant Director*
Dale C. Cameron, M.D.

Howard R. Cummings
Dorothy Lee
Elizabeth Healy Ross

Part-time or short-term

Millie Almy
Herbert W. Beaser
Muriel W. Brown
Kenneth B. Clark
Norris Class
Donald Dukelow, M.D.
Sibylle Escalona
Roma Gans
Regina F. Herzfeld
Eleanor P. Hunt
Alice Scott Hyatt
Mary Alice Jones

Moses Jung
Leonard T. Kurland, M.D.
William S. Langford, M.D.
Sol Markoff
Maryland Y. Pennell
Ruth Reed
Duane Robinson
Sophia Robison
Edward E. Schwartz
Morton A. Seidenfeld
A. Delafield Smith
Ruth Taylor

CONTENTS

PREFACE

This report is a benchmark in the upward and forward movement of our useful knowledge about children and youth.

The information and points of view about the development of healthy personality in children and young people it sets forth are regarded as basic and essentially valid by large numbers of people who work directly with children in a professional capacity or who engage in studies in relevant fields.

This is where we stand at the moment in our knowledge of personality and how it develops. Much of this knowledge, the authors of this report have said, is still tentative, but it is probably the best that we now have at hand. Even so, what we do know is still far from being put adequately to use. Therefore, an attempt has been made to point up as sharply as possible the usefulness of established information for all those who are concerned with the lives of the young in the home, the church, the school, the community—wherever children are to be found.

Limitations of time and resources made treatment of all relevant subjects or of all facets of the subjects impossible. They precluded, also, both exhaustive review of literature and full documentation of all generalizations. It was therefore necessary in preparing this report to rely in large measure on the authors' competence in their professional fields and on expert judgment brought to bear by various consultants and advisers.

In reviewing the materials assembled for the Conference, the Technical Committee on Fact Finding shared a widespread feeling that there is great need for tested knowledge in the social and psychological sciences. The report presents much information that should be helpful in the guidance of children and youth, but much more research remains to be done before practice can be said to rest upon a firm scientific foundation.

For example, a generation ago the advent of dynamic psychology challenged extant theory of the manner in which personality develops. To many this new approach has seemed basically sound, though still requiring refinement of techniques and expansion of insights. For them, the usefulness of this approach has been demonstrated not only in clinic and hospital, where it was first used in the treatment of personalities already disturbed or distorted, but also in its later application in the home and school. Others have questioned the scientific grounding of this approach, feeling that its findings have been largely subjective rather than supported by quantifying investigation. All agree as to the importance of proving or disproving what dynamic psychology holds to be true, for example, concerning personality development during the early years of life, and its implications for the subsequent years.

All who work in the fields pertaining to child life and child development are acutely aware of great chasms of ignorance. We still do not know the complete answers to questions like: What are the real roots of character? What experiences in home and school are most conducive to the attainment of "the good life" in maturity? What configuration of events in the life history leads to the making of a bigot? What is the effect of economic insufficiency upon developing personality? What are the effects upon personality of cultural variations?

Because of such gaps in knowledge, the practitioner often must improvise, relying on evidence that is empirical rather than scientific; he must frequently depend solely upon reasonable assumption. The Technical Committee on Fact Finding has prepared a separate document to delineate some of the areas which must become more fully known to us before we may proceed with certainty. Only with renewed dedication to this search for knowledge, its dissemination through education, and its intelligent application may we help the next generation, and the next, to grow more healthy and to live more abundantly.

We commend this book to all those concerned with human well-being. The best now known in this field is far too seldom put to fruitful use. And the best now known is still known so tentatively that by its very nature it challenges us to search for more inclusive, more extensive, and more fully tested knowledge, resting on widely accepted and incontrovertible research.

The Members of the Technical
Committee on Fact Finding

ACKNOWLEDGMENTS

The *Fact-finding Report to the Midcentury White House Conference on Children and Youth* is the product of many minds and hands, the outcome of the generosity of numerous universities, agencies, and organizations, including those of the Federal government. Before listing the individuals and organizations to whom we are indebted, we want, however, to explain briefly how the contributions of many persons were used to make this present volume.

The *Report* is the result of the joint work of the Technical Committee on Fact Finding, appointed by the National Committee of the Conference, and the fact-finding staff. The members of the Committee were drawn from the fields of education, health, law, philosophy, psychology, religion, social work, and the social sciences. The Committee met five times during the period of a year and discussed with the fact-finding staff the general scope and direction of the fact-finding work. Within the limits of time and circumstances, the Committee acted generally in an advisory and consultative capacity. In addition, individual members of the Committee were frequently called upon by the staff for special consultation within their respective fields. Needless to say, no one Committee member is in complete agreement with every detail, emphasis, or conclusion of the *Report,* but the material includes points of view which the Committee believes important to bring to the attention to the American people.

The members of the fact-finding staff, recruited from universities, national professional organizations, governmental and voluntary agencies, worked constantly together and learned much from each other. Each member of the staff carried primary responsibility for a particular portion of the *Report.* In that capacity he solicited "working papers" from experts in his field of competence, as well as developing materials himself. These products of the staff members and the contributors were pooled and drawn upon when the final *Report* was prepared, so every part of the *Report* reflects in general a composite of the thinking of the whole staff.

It is obvious that this book cannot contain within its covers all that the many contributors to the fact-finding work of the Conference wrote. Less clear, however, is the fact that the gist of what many of them said in their working papers is set forth here. Nevertheless, there is much that had to be passed by in preparing the present document. We are pleased, therefore, to be able to report that many of the original papers—both those drawn upon in preparing this report and those that lay outside the scope of this effort—have been or will be published separately, in book or monograph form or as articles in professional journals. By these means a wider audience will be reached than this single volume can attract, and the work of the Midcentury White House Conference will be the further advanced.

As to the present report, the list of parts and chapters parallels the over-all plan of fact finding and demonstrates its logic. To some chapters many individuals made contributions; to others, few. On some subjects many facts and opinions were stated; on others, less was said, perhaps less could be said. Implications for practice were rather fully considered by some writers, less so by others. On some topics there was much scientific documentation and much consideration of research needs; on others, experts, well versed in theory or methods of practice, gave us the fruit of their reflections. This variation in quantity and nature of data we on the fact-finding staff did not find regrettable, in the light of the Conference's aim. It seemed to us that, for a consideration by many people of how the development of more healthy personalities can be made possible, facts and opinions of many kinds, presented in many forms, are needed.

The reader will soon note that this book is neither a complete rewriting of the contributed materials to form a unitary whole nor yet is it a collection of individual reports and essays. In preparing each chapter, the editors started from the working papers, used the most pertinent ones as the base, combined, elaborated, sometimes added new information or raised new questions, and finally arrived at the present product, which is so much a synthesis that no names of authors can be signed. Nevertheless, the differences in the original material still remain, a tribute, we think, to the sturdiness of conception of the authors and evidence of the complexity and unevenness of development of this new field.

The *Fact-finding Report to the Midcentury White House Conference on Children and Youth* could not have been brought to completion without the generosity of the following universities, agencies, and organizations:

The American Jewish Committee
The American Library Association
The American Medical Association
The Field Foundation

The Food and Agricultural Organization of the United Nations
The Josiah Macy, Jr., Foundation
The Menninger Foundation
The National Catholic Welfare Conference
The National Child Labor Committee
The National Conference of Christians and Jews
The National Foundation for Infantile Paralysis
Rand McNally and Company
The University of California at Los Angeles
The University of Cincinnati

It is impossible to estimate the contributions of the many agencies and bureaus of the Federal government that turned to in various needed ways to make the *Fact-finding Report* well rounded. Some lent personnel, others provided essential information, and still others prepared basic materials for incorporation in the report. The separate report of the Advisory Council on Federal Government Participation gives only partial indication of all that the government has done. Here we would mention, as a minimum, the following contributing departments:

The Bureau of Human Nutrition and Home Economics, Department of Agriculture

The Bureau of the Budget
The Bureau of the Census, Department of Commerce
The Children's Bureau, Federal Security Agency
The Department of Labor
The Office of Education, Federal Security Agency
The Office of the General Counsel, Federal Security Agency
The U. S. Public Health Service, Federal Security Agency

In addition, numerous individuals contributed one or more "working papers" of substance—papers designed as source material for the fact-finding staff. The list is long, the gratitude of the staff and of the Technical Committee on Fact Finding unbounded:

W. R. Ackroyd, M.D.
Margaret Adams
Frederick H. Allen, M.D.
Edna P. Amidon
Virgil A. Anderson
M. Corinne Bancroft
Felix S. Barker
Harriet M. Bartlett
Mary C. Bentley
Grete L. Bibring, M.D

Francis V. Bishop
Elizabeth Bixler
Opal Boston
Donald J. Bourg, M.D.
Roy Butler, M.D.
E. Jane Carlin
Isabel G. Carter
Mamie P. Clark
Collie Mae Coons
Hazel Corbin

Grace L. Coyle
Marion M. Crane, M.D.
Margaret Creech
Jane Culbert
Edwin F. Daily, M.D.
Anna Engel
Erik H. Erikson
Raymond Fisher
Franklin M. Foote, M.D.
Lawrence K. Frank
Abraham M. Franzblau, M.D.
John T. Fulton, D.D.S.
Ben Humphries Gray
Elizabeth J. Hall
William G. Hardy
Mary L. Hemmy
Marjorie Heseltine
Seward Hiltner
Betty Huse, M.D.
Marie Jahoda
Reynold A. Jensen, M.D.
Wendell Johnson
Joseph A. Johnston, M.D.
Leo Kanner, M.D.
John W. Keltner
Ruth Knee
George Kopp
John W. Knutson, D.D.S.
Leonard T. Kurland, M.D.
Stanley Lebergott
William G. Lennox, M.D.
Arthur J. Lesser, M.D.
Reginald S. Lourie, M.D.
Viktor Lowenfield
Martha W. MacDonald, M.D.
Romaine P. Mackie
Darrel J. Mase
Dorothy McKay
Florence L. McKay, M.D.
M. F. Ashley Montagu
Maud Morlock
Margaret Mudgett
Marian Nicholson
Henry B. Ollendorf
Genevieve Owings

Benjamin Pasamanick, M.D.
Meyer A. Perlstein, M.D.
Elisabeth C. Phillips
Esther F. Phipard
Judah Pilch
Carl L. Plack
Louis E. Raths
E. R. Regnier
Leon H. Richman
Julius Richmond, M.D.
J. Franklin Robinson, M.D.
John Romano, M.D.
Helen Ross
Helen Rowe
Joseph Rudolph, M.D.
W. Carson Ryan
Harold R. Sandstead, M.D.
William M. Schmidt, M.D.
Hildred Schuell
Milton J. E. Senn, M.D.
Jane Shover
Doris Siegel
I. Evelyn Smith
Helen F. Spaulding
Helen R. Stacey
Hazel Stiebling
Fred L. Stricker, M.D.
Marie Swanson
John W. Tenny
James J. Thorpe, M.D.
Phyllis Treusch
Warren T. Vaughan, Jr., M.D.
LeRoy Voris, M.D.
Catherine Lee Wahlstrom
Howard C. Walser, M.D.
Allen E. Weatherford
Charles R. Webb, M.D.
Wilma L. West
Margaret Williamson
Eunice W. Wilson
Gertrude Wilson
James R. Wilson, M.D.
William G. Wolfe
Harley Wooden

INTRODUCTION

This volume constitutes the final version of the *Fact-finding Report to the Midcentury White House Conference on Children and Youth.* In it are set forth the chief facts and theories, as currently conceived by many competent scientists and professional workers, regarding what is required for the healthy development of personality in childhood and youth. The chapters embodying these ideas are followed by others in which detailed consideration is given to their implications for the conduct of the various social institutions important to children's welfare and for professional practice in relation to these institutions.

That the Midcentury White House Conference on Children and Youth should have taken the healthy personality as its theme is a consequence both of recent scientific developments and of the traditional interest of the White House Conferences. The Midcentury Conference was the fifth in a decennial series that began in 1909, when President Theodore Roosevelt called together a group of experts and laymen to consider what might be done to better the lot of children whose families were financially unable to support them.

The first two conferences were concerned chiefly with the problems of particular groups of socially disadvantaged children in the United States; the next two gave major attention to certain social and economic aspects of the well-being of all American children. Through the work of these four conferences the welfare of children was considerably advanced.

In the meantime a new conception of children's needs developed, and we now know that even if the recommendations of the previous conferences were fully carried out it would not be enough. The new ideas, which are still in the making, have to do with the qualitative aspects of human relations. As research proceeds, it becomes increasingly apparent that all who have to do with serving children must work in a way that takes children's feelings into account if they are fully to accomplish their purposes.

This new way of looking at children's needs leads to the conclusion that the conditions discussed by previous conferences—demeaning poverty, inadequate school and health services, racial and ethnical discrimination, and the like—are handicapping to children not only in and of themselves but also because they are contrary to the democratic tenet that every person is of precious and equal worth. The presence of these conditions arouses feelings of uncertainty and inferiority, envy and resentment. Quite aside from the individual, humanitarian aspects of the matter, these are serious consequences for a society that now more than ever stands in need of efficient workers, clear thinkers, loyal citizens, who are strong enough to protect its way of life and flexible enough to cooperate with those whose ways are different.

To say that some of the chief ills of the present day are psychological is not to imply that their causes are necessarily of the same nature. Emotional ill health may have economic, sociological, physical, psychological, and spiritual causes. A child's personality development may be handicapped by inadequate food and housing, racial discrimination, physiological malfunctioning, lack of spiritual values, as well as by insufficient love from his parents. Nor are these various explanations of personality maladjustment to be regarded as secondary to the psychological. While scientists are still far from knowing the whole answer, it is increasingly evident that many factors are involved, no one of which is dominant.

One reason previous conferences paid rather little attention to personality is that knowledge about it was, and still is, very much in the making. In recent years, considerable advance has been made, however, and various professions are discovering that the new findings in psychology, sociology, and physiology have important implications for their work. Parents, too, are learning about (some might say, are being engulfed by) the new ideas, and the general public regards them as matters of interest and concern. In all this there is some danger that the new ideas will be misunderstood and misused, for they are neither easily communicated nor easily put into practice.

In undertaking to examine the situation of American children with respect to their personality development and to consider measures that might be undertaken to improve it, many ideas and practices have to be taken into account. Such diverse matters as economic resources, law, custom, the insights of religion (to mention only a few topics) have to be considered, and the work of all the social institutions that received the attention of previous conferences has to be reviewed.

In all these matters there is still much to be learned. We are far from knowing exactly how personality development proceeds and exactly what influence various factors have upon it. Nevertheless, there is much that is known that is basic to health and happiness. The challenge is to put this knowledge to work—for the benefit of our children and ourselves and all people everywhere.

In accordance with this reasoning, the National Committee of the Midcentury White House Conference on Children and Youth drew up the following statement to guide the fact-finding effort:

The Midcentury White House Conference on Children and Youth bases its concern for children on the primacy of spiritual values, democratic practice and the dignity and worth of every individual. Accordingly, the purpose of the Conference shall be to consider how we can develop in children the mental, emotional, and spiritual qualities essential to individual happiness and to responsible citizenship, and what physical, economic, and social conditions are deemed necessary to this development.

To do this the Conference shall:

1. bring together in usable form pertinent knowledge related to the development of children and indicate areas in which further knowledge is needed;
2. examine the environment in which children are growing up, with a view to determining its influence upon them;
3. study the ways in which the home, the school, the church, the law, health and welfare agencies, and other social institutions, individually and cooperatively, are serving the needs of children;
4. formulate, through cooperative efforts of laymen and specialists, proposals for the improvement of parental, environmental, and institutional influences on children;
5. suggest means whereby these proposals may be communicated to the people and put into action.

Following this directive, the national fact-finding staff, with the advice of the Technical Committee on Fact Finding, gathered material for the Conference's consideration. A digest of their findings was prepared for use at the Conference.[1] The present volume offers a more comprehensive statement of facts and well-considered opinions regarding the healthy development of personality and the factors involved in it.

It will be noted that in this report the expression "healthy personality" has been substituted for the National Committee's phrase "in-

[1] *A Healthy Personality for Every Child,* Health Publications Institute, Inc., Raleigh, North Carolina, 1951. In addition, many papers contributed to the fact-finding effort have been or will be published in scientific and professional journals or as books or monographs.

dividual happiness and responsible citizenship." In this substitution there are various implications.

First and most obviously, we imply that to be happy and responsible is to be healthy in personality. If so unscientific a statement can be allowed at all, it is surely only if the emphasis is on the "and." Many people are apparently happy without being particularly responsible as citizens, and perhaps without being healthy in personality. Many are responsible citizens but clearly far from happy—and certainly not healthy, as their stomach ulcers and even suicide attest. What we desire in these days of strain and crisis is that young people shall have both of these qualities, so that, among other things, they may produce a social order in which the chance for happiness will be greatly improved.

In stating the matter this way we imply, too, that happiness is something other than a lighthearted, frivolous pleasure in one's own well-being. The happiness that characterizes a healthy personality, the happiness that endures in spite of the individual's and society's vicissitudes, is made of sterner stuff. It is an equanimity indicative of personal integrity. It encompasses the possibility of both anger and tears.

There is an implication, also, of American values in this equating of happiness and responsibility with health of personality. There are societies in which civic responsibility is a slight thing, where allegiance and duty lie along family or other lines and the wider responsibilities of citizenship, the responsibilities of each for all, are almost unknown. And there are societies in which individual happiness is accounted a foolish optimism, and those in which so personal a value is frowned upon. In such societies, health of personality produces feelings and behavior other than those we prize. We are speaking as Americans, then, and perhaps not for all the rest of the world when we say that the healthy personality is one in which individual happiness and responsible citizenship are combined.

So much, then, for the words we are using. In a sense, the equation of terms is made lightly, without solemn, scientific documentation. In another sense, it is made in very earnest. For it is the thesis of this report that by putting to use what is currently known about conditions favoring or obstructing the healthy development of personality we can rear a generation of happy, responsible individuals who will be better able to "take" modern life and, therefore, to produce such changes in it as will improve the circumstances of later generations. To do this, to learn how to do it, we regard as the prime challenge of our times.

PART I

THE DEVELOPMENT OF THE

HEALTHY PERSONALITY

⟋ I ⟍

The Making of
a Healthy Personality

"PERSONALITY" is a word of such varied usage, in scientific as well as in popular language, that we must make clear at the start just what is meant by it in this report. Obviously, we are not using the word in the advertiser's sense: something that some people have and others ought to acquire. Nor do we refer only to what the man-on-the-street is talking about when he says that John's personality, his combination of psychological characteristics, is different from Joe's.

We have, instead, a bit of the philosopher's definition in our concept: the notion that personality is an inward awareness of the self as permanent and unchanging. We take from the physiologist and the psychologist the idea that personality is the organism itself in its most complex functioning, a system of reactions, physical and emotional, that has continuity but is indefinitely variable. We add the sociologist's dictum that personality is the individual's peculiar embodiment of the ideas and customs of the culture to which he belongs. We cap it with the psychiatrist's finding that through all the flux of behavior and feeling there is consistency and that there are depths to the personality of which the conscious mind is not aware.

Throughout this report, then, we mean by personality the thinking, feeling, acting human being, who, for the most part, conceives of himself as an individual separate from other individuals and objects. This human being does not *have* a personality; he *is* a personality.

This intellectually, emotionally, socially functioning human being, this personality, varies in his behavior from time to time and from situation to situation. He develops and changes throughout life, in accordance with a pattern that is set biologically for the human species and culturally for the group to which he belongs, and in accordance with myriadfold particular circumstances. Nevertheless, from an early age, perhaps even from birth, there is continuity in his behavior. Physical

3

and intellectual factors set limits to his variation. Responses to new experiences are in part conditioned by what has gone before. In his conception of himself and in his relations with others the individual comes to behave in a way that is peculiarly his own.

This core mode of thinking, feeling, and reacting is personality in the narrow sense of the word. It is this core, this constantly reacting system, that we have particularly in mind when we talk of personality. Since, however, it is only in an abstract sense that personality can be so defined, what we are really talking about in discussing health of personality is the concrete human being and the relative success of his endeavor to play his part in relation to other human beings and to the institutions through which social life is carried on.

Present State of Knowledge About Personality

At the present time there is no one authoritative theory of personality, nor are there several consistent, fully developed theories from which to choose. There is, instead, a slowly accumulating body of factual knowledge and of observation about the course of children's development and about the behavior of children and adults that may someday provide the basis for an embracing view.

Knowledge about personality comes from no one source of information. The anthropologist's knowledge of personality differences from culture to culture, the sociologist's knowledge of the social process, the physiologist's knowledge of the growth of the nervous system, the geneticist's knowledge of heredity, the psychiatrist's knowledge of the processes of emotional illness and health, the psychologist's knowledge of changes in mental functioning with development and with all manner of physical and social circumstances—these and other kinds of knowledge are needed if we are to understand human behavior.

In none of these areas has scientific investigation gone beyond a promising beginning. Nevertheless, the facts and ideas accumulated up to this time serve several useful purposes. They are sufficient for the formulation of meaningful questions, the base from which worth-while research must start. They are sufficient to make us aware of the errors of the past and the present: the overemphases and the underemphases, the oversights and the unsupported assumptions in our thought and action in regard to children. They are sufficient to make us recognize the dangers of hasty application and to give us promising suggestions for action.

For example, it is well established that loving care is essential for the well-being of children. This principle suggests for research the questions: How can such care best be provided, and how can adults who are not spontaneously affectionate toward children be helped to develop such an attitude? It has been discovered that it is useless to exhort parents to be loving, that, moreover, such advice can be destructive to parents' self-confidence and hence harmful to children. Such knowledge makes us wary about overemphasizing a child's need for affection to the neglect of many other needs that parents can more effectively do something about. It also keeps us from attempting to apply one part of the formula for healthy personality development without regard to the whole.

Nevertheless, this principle regarding the importance of loving care for the well-being of children has already had revolutionary consequences where it has been wisely applied; for instance, in certain institutions for children. It is to be expected that the principle will have even greater usefulness when its relation to other principles is well worked out.

There is such a thing, then, as being too cautious in the use of knowledge. Part answers do not give whole solutions, it is true. There has been too much popularizing and applying of ideas that are only half developed and half understood. We cannot wait, however, for complete knowledge or wholly developed theory, if only because there is no such eventuality in science. We must make such integration of presently known facts and presently formulated theories as seems reasonably tenable, and we must apply this new knowledge with due caution and a sense of social responsibility.

Nor can we rely wholly upon science for ideas about how to help children develop in a healthy manner. The insight and intuition of wise practitioners in all professions add much to the knowledge that we may act upon. Such insight and intuition must not, of course, deny or shun scientific findings. They must not basically contradict existing theory, though they may well point to the next systematic step to be taken. Properly used, however, insight and intuition add richness and depth to scientific knowledge, which, without them, may be somewhat remote from the intricacies of the individual personality and its developmental needs.

The Course of Personality Development

Many attempts have been made to describe the attributes of healthy personality. They have been put succinctly as the ability to love and the ability to work. A recent review of the literature suggests that the individual with a healthy personality is one who actively masters his environment, shows a unity of personality, and is able to perceive the world and himself correctly! [1] Clearly, none of these criteria applies to a child. It seemed to us best, then, to present for the Conference's consideration an outline that has the merit of indicating at one and the same time the main course of personality development and the attributes of a healthy personality.

Our outline follows a developmental scheme worked out by Erik H. Erikson, a psychologist and training psychoanalyst who has made anthropological studies and has had much experience with children. It is an analysis that derives from psychological theory and from knowledge in the fields of child development and cultural anthropology. The whole is infused with the author's insight and personal philosophy. Two characteristics of this formulation should be noted. First, Erikson views healthy personality development against the background of the personality deviations that have been studied so extensively in recent decades. Second, he concentrates on those aspects of healthy personality that to him appear to be universal, not restricted to the ideals of one particular nation, culture, or faith. [2]

In each stage of child development, Erikson says, there is a central problem that has to be solved, temporarily at least, if the child is to proceed with vigor and confidence to the next stage. These problems, these conflicts of feeling and desire, are never solved in entirety. Each shift in experience and environment presents them in a new form. It is held, however, that each type of conflict appears in its purest, most unequivocal form at a particular stage in a child's development, and that if the problem is well solved at that time the basis for progress to the next stage is laid and a degree of "sturdiness" in personality secured for the future.

In a sense, personality development follows biological principles. Biologists have found that everything that grows has a ground plan that is laid out at the start. Out of this ground plan the parts arise, each part having its time of special ascendancy. Together these parts form a functioning whole. If a part does not arise at its appointed time, it will never be able to form fully, since the moment for the rapid outgrowth of some other

[1] Marie Jahoda, "Toward a Social Psychology of Mental Health," *Problems of Infancy and Childhood,* Supplement II, Josiah Macy, Jr., Foundation, New York, 1950.
[2] The following account is a condensation and, to some slight extent, a revision of Erikson's thesis, to which are added some facts and theories noted by other contributors to this report. For Erikson's own statement of his ideas, see "Growth and Crises of the 'Healthy Personality,'" *Problems of Infancy and Childhood,* Josiah Macy, Jr., Foundation, New York, 1950; also *Childhood and Society,* W. W. Norton & Co., New York, 1950.

part will have arrived. Moreover, a part that misses its time of ascendancy or is severely damaged during its formative period is apt to doom, in turn, the whole hierarchy of organs. Proper rate and normal sequence are necessary if functional harmony is to be secured.

Personality represents the most complicated functioning of the human organism and does not consist of parts in the organic sense. Instead of the development of organs, there is development of locomotor, sensory, and social capacities and development of individual modes of dealing with experience. Nevertheless, proper rate and proper sequence are as important here as in physical growth, and functional harmony is achieved only if development proceeds according to the ground plan.

In all this it is encouraging for parents and others who have children in their charge to realize that in the sequence of his most personal experiences, just as in the sequence of his growing capacities, the child can be trusted to follow inner laws of development. He needs from adults chiefly love, encouragement, and guidance.

The operation of biological laws is seen, also, in the fact that there is constant interplay between organism and environment and in the fact that problems of personality functioning are never solved once and for all. Each of the components of the healthy personality is present in some form from the beginning, and the struggle to maintain it continues throughout life.

For example, a baby may show something like "autonomy," or a will of his own, in the particular way in which he angrily tries to free his head when he is tightly held. Nevertheless, it is not until the second year of life that he begins to experience the whole conflict between being an autonomous creature and a dependent one. It is not until then that he is ready for a decisive encounter with the people around him, and it is not until then that people feel called upon to train him or otherwise curb his free-questing spirit. The struggle goes on for months; finally, under favorable circumstances, some compromise between dependence and independence is reached that gives the child a confident sense of being an individual.

The sense of autonomy thus achieved is not a permanent possession, however. There will be other challenges to that sense and other solutions more in keeping with later stages of development. Nevertheless, once established at two or three years of age, this early sense of autonomy will be a bulwark against later frustrations and will permit the emergence of the next developmental problem at a time that is most favorable for its solution.

So it is with all the personality components to be described. They appear in relative isolation early in life. The struggle to secure them against tendencies to act otherwise comes to a climax at a time determined by the emergence of the necessary physical and mental abilities. There are, throughout life, other challenges and other responses but they are seldom so basic and seldom so decisive as those of the critical years.

In all this, it must be noted in addition, there is not the strict dichotomy that the analysis given below suggests. With each of the personality components to be described, it is not all or nothing: trust *or* mistrust, autonomy *or* doubt, and so on. Instead, each individual has some of each. His health of personality is determined by the preponderance of the favorable over the unfavorable, as well as by what manner of compensations he develops to cope with his disabilities.

The Sense of Trust

The component of the healthy personality that is the first to develop is the sense of trust. The crucial time for its emergence is the first year of life. As with the other personality components to be described, the sense of trust is not something that develops independent of other manifestations of growth. It is not that the infant learns how to use his body for purposeful movement, learns to recognize people and objects around him, and also develops a sense of trust. Rather, the concept "sense of trust" is a short-cut expression intended to convey the characteristic flavor of all the child's satisfying experiences at this early age. Or, to say it another way, this psychological formulation serves to condense, summarize, and synthesize the most important underlying changes that give meaning to the infant's concrete and diversified experience.

Trust can exist only in relation to something. The primitive origin of a sense of trust probably lies in the earliest experience of finding basic needs taken care of in appropriate and consistent ways. However, a clearer sense of trust cannot develop until the infant is old enough to be aware of objects and persons and to have some feeling that he is a separate individual. At about three months of age a baby is likely to smile if somebody comes close and talks to him. This shows that he is aware of the approach of the other person, that pleasurable sensations are aroused. If, however, the person moves too quickly or speaks too sharply the baby may look apprehensive or cry. He will not "trust" the unusual situation but will have a feeling of uneasiness, of mistrust, instead.

Experiences connected with feeding are a prime source for the development of trust. At around four months of age a hungry baby will grow quiet and show signs of pleasure at the sound of an approaching footstep, anticipating (trusting) that he will be held and fed. This repeated experience of being hungry, seeing food, receiving food, and feeling relieved and comforted assures the baby that the world is a dependable place.

Later experiences, starting at around five months of age, add another dimension to the sense of trust. Through endless repetitions of attempts to grasp for and hold objects, the baby is finally successful in controlling and adapting his movements in such a way as to reach his goal. Through these and other feats of muscular coordination the baby is gradually able to trust his own body to do his bidding.

The baby's trust-mistrust problem is symbolized in the game of peekaboo. In this game, which babies begin to like at about four months of age, an object disappears and then reappears. There is a slightly tense expression on the baby's face when the object goes away; its reappearance is greeted by wriggles and smiles. Only gradually does a baby learn that things continue to exist even though he does not see them, that there is order and stability in his universe. Peekaboo proves the point by playful repetition.

Studies of mentally ill individuals and observations of infants who have been grossly deprived of affection suggest that trust is an early-formed and important element in the healthy personality. Psychiatrists find again and again that the most serious illnesses occur in patients who have been sorely neglected or abused or otherwise deprived of consistent and appropriate love in infancy. Similarly, it is a common finding of psychological and social investigators that an individual diagnosed as a "psychopathic personality" was so unloved in infancy that he has no reason to trust the human race and, therefore, has no sense of responsibility toward his fellow men.

Observations of infants brought up in emotionally unfavorable institutions or in hospitals with inadequate facilities for psychological care support these findings. A recent report says: "Infants under six months of age who have been in an institution for some time present a well-defined picture. The outstanding features are listlessness, emaciation and pallor, relative immobility, quietness, unresponsiveness to stimuli like a smile or a coo, indifferent appetite, failure to gain weight properly despite ingestion of diets which are entirely adequate, frequent stools, poor sleep, an appearance of unhappiness, proneness to febrile episodes, absence of sucking habits." [3]

[3] Harry Bakwin, "Emotional Deprivation in Infants," *Journal of Pediatrics*, 35:1949.

Another investigation of children separated from their mothers at six to twelve months and not provided with an adequate substitute comes to much the same conclusion: "The emotional tone is one of apprehension and sadness, there is withdrawal from the environment amounting to rejection of it, there is no attempt to contact a stranger and no brightening if a stranger contacts him. Activities are retarded and the child often sits or lies inert in a dazed stupor. Insomnia is common and lack of appetite universal. Weight is lost, and the child becomes prone to intercurrent infections." [4]

Most significant for our present point: these extreme reactions are most likely to occur in children who up to the time of separation at six to nine months of age had a happy relation with their mothers, while those whose relations were unhappy are not as strikingly affected. It is at about this age that the struggle between trusting and mistrusting the world comes to a climax, for it is then that the child first perceives clearly that he and his environment are things apart. That at this time formerly happy infants should react so badly to separation suggests, indeed, that they had had a faith which now was shattered. Happily, there is usually spectacular change for the better when a mothering person appears and love is restored.

It is probably unnecessary to describe the numerous ways in which stimuli from without and from within may cause an infant distress. Birth is believed by some experts to be a painful experience for the baby. Until fairly recently doctors were likely to advise that babies be fed on schedule and that little attention be paid to their cries of hunger at other times. Many infants spent many of the waking hours of the first four months doubled up with colic. All of them had to be bathed and dressed at stated times, whether they liked it or not. Add to these usual discomforts the fact that some infants are handled rather roughly by their parents, that others hear angry words and loud voices, and that a few are really mistreated, and it will not be difficult to understand why some infants may feel the world is a place that cannot be trusted.

In many primitive societies the attention accorded infants is more in line with natural processes. In such societies separation from the mother is less abrupt, in that for some time after birth the baby is kept close to the warmth and comfort of its mother's body and at its least cry the breast is produced. Throughout infancy the baby is surrounded by people who are ready to feed it, fondle it, and otherwise comfort it at a mo-

    [4] John Bowlby, M.D., *Maternal Care and Mental Health*, World Health Organization, Geneva, 1951, p. 22.

ment's notice. Moreover, these ministrations are given spontaneously, wholeheartedly, and without that element of nervous concern that may characterize the efforts of young mothers made self-conscious and insecure by our scientific age.

We must not exaggerate, however. Most infants in our society, too, find smiles and the comfort of mother's soft, warm body accompanying their intake of food, whether from breast or bottle. Coldness, wetness, pain, and boredom—for each misfortune there is prompt and comforting relief. As their own bodies come to be more dependable, there is added to the pleasures of increasing sensory response and motor control the pleasure of the mother's encouragement.

Moreover, babies are rather hardy creatures and are not to be discouraged by inexperienced mothers' mistakes. Even a mother cat has to learn, and the kittens endure gracefully her first clumsy efforts to carry them away from danger. Then, too, psychologists tell us that mothers create a sense of trust in their children not by the particular techniques they employ but by the sensitiveness with which they respond to the children's needs and by their over-all attitude, their faith in themselves and in the baby as a trust of a wider community.

For most infants, then, a sense of trust is not difficult to come by. It is the most important element in the personality. It emerges at the most vulnerable period of a child's life. Yet it is the least likely to suffer harm, perhaps because both nature and culture work toward making mothers most maternal at that time. It is good that this is so, for there are inner rages and discomforts which, though they cannot be avoided, must be compensated for, if a lasting sense of trust is to ensue.

The Sense of Autonomy

The sense of trust being firmly established, the struggle for the next component of the healthy personality begins. The child is now twelve to fifteen months old. Much of his energy for the next two years will center around asserting that he is a human being with a mind and will of his own. A list of some of the items discussed by Spock,[5] under the heading "The One Year Old," will serve to remind us of the characteristics of that age and the problems they create for parents: "Feeling his oats"; "The passion to explore"; "He gets more dependent and more independent at the same time"; "Arranging the house for the wandering baby"; "Avoiding accidents"; "How do you make him leave certain

[5] Benjamin Spock, *The Pocket Book of Baby and Child Care*, Pocket Books, Inc., New York, 1945, pp. 194–198.

things alone?"; "Dropping and throwing things"; "Biting humans"; "The small child who won't stay in bed at night."

What is at stake throughout the struggle of these years is the child's sense of autonomy, the sense that he is an independent human being and yet one who is able to use the help and guidance of others in important matters. This stage of development becomes decisive for the ratio between love and hate, between cooperation and willfulness, for freedom of self-expression and its renunciations, in the make-up of the individual. The favorable outcome is self-control without loss of self-esteem. The unfavorable outcome is a lasting sense of doubt in others and in oneself, and a sense of shyness and shame.

Before the sense of autonomy can develop, the sense of trust must be reasonably well established and must continue to pervade the child's feeling about himself and his world. Only so dare he respond with confidence to his new-felt desire to assert himself boldly, to appropriate demandingly, and to hurl away without let or hindrance.

As with the previous stage, there is a physiological basis for this characteristic behavior. This is the period of muscle-system maturation and the consequent ability (and doubly felt inability) to coordinate a number of highly conflicting action patterns, such as those of holding on and letting go, walking, talking, and manipulating objects in ever more complicated ways. With these abilities come pressing needs to use them: to handle, to explore, to seize and to drop, to withhold and to expel. And, with all, there is the dominant will, the insistent "Me do" that defies help and yet is so easily frustrated by the inabilities of the hands and feet.

For a child to develop this sense of self-reliance and adequacy that Erikson calls "autonomy," it is necessary that he experience gradually and frequently that he is a person who is permitted to make the choices that he is ready to make and yet learn to accept and tolerate restrictions where necessary. For prolonged periods he may demand the right to choose, for example, whether to sit or whether to stand, whether to approach a visitor or to lean against his mother's knee, whether to accept offered food or whether to reject it, whether to use the toilet or to wet his pants. He thus tries to learn some of the boundaries of self-determination. He inevitably finds that there are walls he cannot climb, that there are objects out of reach, that, above all, there are innumerable items of behavior that arouse approval or forceful disapproval in the adults. His experience is much too small to enable him to know what he can and cannot do with respect to the physical and social environment, and it will take him years to discover the boundaries that mark off what is approved, what is tolerated, and what is forbidden by his elders, whom he finds so hard to understand.

As problems of this period, some psychologists have concentrated particularly on bladder and bowel control. Emphasis is put upon the need for care in both timing and mode of training children in the performance of these functions. If parental control is too rigid or if training is started too early, the child is robbed of his opportunity to develop, by his own free choice, gradual control of the contradictory impulses of retention and elimination. He thus may learn to fear his own inadequacy, as well as the adult.

To others who study child development, this matter of toilet training is but a prototype of all the problems of this age range. The sphincters are only part of the whole muscle system, with its general ambiguity of rigidity and relaxation, of flexion and extension. To hold and to relinquish refer to much more than the bowels. As the child acquires the ability to stand on his feet and move around, he delineates his world as me and you. He can be astonishingly pliable once he has decided that he wants to do what he is supposed to do, but there is no reliable formula for assuring that he will relinquish when he wants to hold on.

The matter of mutual regulation between parent and child (for fathers have now entered the picture to an extent that was rare in the earlier stage) now faces its severest test. The task is indeed one to challenge the most resourceful and calm adult. Firmness is necessary, for the child must be protected against the potential anarchy of his as yet untrained sense of discrimination. Yet the adult must back him up in his wish to stand on his own feet, lest he be overcome by shame that he has exposed himself foolishly and by doubt in his self-worth. Perhaps the most constructive rule a parent can follow is to forbid only what "really matters" and, in such forbidding, to be clear and consistent.

Shame and doubt are emotions that many primitive peoples and some of the less sophisticated individuals in our own society utilize in training children. Shaming exploits the child's sense of being small. Used to excess, it misses its objective and in some cases may later result in open shamelessness, or, at least, in the child's secret determination to do as he pleases when not observed. Such defiance is a normal, even healthy response to demands that make a child feel that his body and his vital needs and wishes are evil and dirty and that he regard those who pass judgment as infallible. Young delinquents may be produced by this means, and others who are oblivious to the opinion of society.

Those who would guide the growing child wisely, then, will avoid shaming him senselessly and avoid causing him to doubt that essentially he is a person of worth. They will be firm and tolerant with him so that he can rejoice in being a person of independence and can grant independence to others. As to detailed procedure, it is impossible to prescribe, not only because we do not know enough and because every situation is different but also because the kind and degree of autonomy that parents are able to grant their young children depend on feelings about themselves that they derive from their own particular upbringing and from their particular place in our varied society. Just as the child's sense of trust is a reflection of the mother's study and realistic faith, so the child's sense of autonomy is a reflection of the parents' own sense of personal dignity. Such appears to be the teaching of the comparative study of cultures.

Personal autonomy, independence of the individual, is an especially outstanding feature of the American way of life. American parents, accordingly, are in a particularly favorable position to transmit the sense of autonomy to their children. They themselves resent being bossed, being pushed around; they maintain that everybody has the right to express his opinion and to be in control of his affairs. More easily than people who live according to an authoritarian pattern, they can appreciate a little child's vigorous desire to assert his independence, and they can give him the leeway he needs in order to grow up into the upstanding, look-you-in-the-eye kind of individual that Americans admire.

It is not only in early childhood, however, that this attitude toward children must be maintained. As was said at the outset, these components of the healthy personality cannot be established once and for all. The period of life in which they first come into being is the most crucial, it is true. But threats to their maintenance occur throughout life. Not only parents, then, but everybody who has significant contact with children and young people must respect their desire for self-assertion, help them hold it within bounds, and avoid treating them in ways that arouse a lasting sense of shame or doubt.

This attitude toward children, however, must be the same toward all people, and it must be reflected continuously in free institutions. Great differences in educational and economic opportunity and in actual equality before the law, discrimination of all kinds are threats to this ingredient of mental health. So, too, may be the overmechanization of our society, the depersonalization of human relations that is likely to accompany large-scale organization of all kinds.

Parents, as well as children, are affected by these matters. In fact, parents' ability to grant children the kind of autonomy Americans think desirable depends in part on the way they are treated as neighbors, employees, and citizens. Throughout, the relation must be such as affirms personal dignity. Much of the shame and doubt aroused in children results from the indignity and uncertainty that are an expression of their parents' frustrations in community and work life. Special attention must be paid to all these matters, then, if we are to avoid destroying the autonomy that Americans have always set store by.

The Sense of Initiative

Having become sure, for the time being, that he is a person in his own right and having enjoyed that feeling for a year or so, the child of four or five wants to find out what he can *do*. To be any particular kind of person, he sees clearly, involves being able to do particular kinds of things. So he observes with keen attention the activities of adults (his parents, the milkman, the truck driver, and so on), tries to imitate their behavior, and yearns for a share in their activities.

This is the period of enterprise and imagination, an ebullient, creative period when play and phantasy substitute for literal execution of desires and the meagerest equipment provides material for high imaginings. It is a period of intrusive, vigorous learning, learning that leads away from the child's own limitations into future possibilities. There is interference with other people by physical attack, there is intrusion into other people's ears and mind by loud and persistent questioning. There is intrusion into space by vigorous locomotion and intrusion into the unknown by consuming curiosity.

By this age, too, conscience has developed. The child is no longer guided only by outsiders; there is installed within him a voice that comments on his deeds, and warns and threatens. Close attention to the remarks of any child of this age will confirm this statement. Less obvious, however, are experts' observations that children now begin to feel guilty for mere thoughts, for deeds that have been imagined but never executed. This, they say, is the explanation for the characteristic nightmares of this age period and for the overreaction to slight punishment.

The problem to be worked out in this stage of development, accordingly, is how to experience the borderlines of excessive will without too great a sense of inhibiting guilt. The fortunate outcome of the struggle is a sense of initiative, delineated by conscience. Failure to win through to that outcome leaves the personality overburdened, and possibly overrestricted, by guilt.

It is easy to see how the child's developing sense of initiative may be discouraged. So many of the projects dreamed up at this age are of a kind which cannot be permitted that the child may come to feel he is faced by a universal "No." In addition, he finds that many of the projects are impossible of execution and that others, even if not forbidden, fail to win the approval of the adults whom he has come to love. Moreover, since he does not always distinguish clearly between actuality and phantasy, his overzealous conscience may disapprove of even imaginary deeds.

For healthy personality development it is very important, therefore, that much leeway and encouragement be given to the child's show of enterprise and imagination and that punishment, again, be kept for things that matter. Boys and girls at this stage are extraordinarily appreciative of any convincing promise that someday they will be able to do things as well, or maybe better, than father and mother. The phantasy of being and even replacing father and mother is common. They enjoy competition (especially if they can win) and insistence on goal; they get great pleasure from conquest. They need numerous examples of the kinds of roles adults assume, and they need a chance to try them out in play.

The ability that is in the making is that of selecting social goals and persevering in the attempt to reach them. If enterprise and imagination are too greatly curbed, if severe rebukes accompany the frequently necessary denial of permission to carry out desires, if no avenues are offered for making up for failure and misdeeds, a personality may result that is overconstricted. Such a personality cannot live up to its inner capacities for imagination, feeling, and performance, with the result that it may overcompensate by immense activity and find relaxation impossible.

Constriction of personality is a self-imposed constriction, an act of the child's overzealous conscience. "If I may not do this, I will not even think it," says conscience, "for even thinking it is dangerous." Resentment and bitterness and a vindictive attitude toward the world that forces the restriction may accompany this decision, however, and become an unconscious but nonetheless influential part of the personality. Such, at least, is the warning of psychiatrists who have learned to know the inmost feelings of emotionally handicapped children and adults.

This developmental stage has great assets as well as great dangers. At no time in life does the individual become more ready to learn avidly and quickly, to become big in the sense of sharing obligation and performance. If during this preschool period the child can get some anticipatory sense of the various roles and functions that he can perform as an adult, he will be ready to progress joyfully to the next stage, in which he will find pleasurable accomplishment in activities less fraught with phantasy and fear.

There is a lesson in this for later periods of personality development as well. As has been said before, those conflicts that come to a head at particular periods of a child's life are not settled once and for all. The sense of initiative, then, is one that must be continually fostered, and great care must be taken that youngsters and young people do not have to feel guilty for having dared to dream.

Just as we Americans prize autonomy, so, too, do we prize initiative: in fact, we regard it as the cornerstone of our economic system. There is much in the present industrial and political mode of life that may discourage initiative, that may make a young person think he had best pull in his horns. What these tendencies are and what they may do to youngsters and to their parents, who, too, must feel free if they are to cultivate the sense of initiative in their children, is a subject that warrants much serious discussion.

The Sense of Duty and Accomplishment

The three stages so far described probably are the most important for healthy personality development. With a sense of trust, a sense of autonomy, and a sense of initiative achieved—and, with them, caution, self-control, and conscience—progress through the later stages is fairly well assured. Whether this is because children who have a good environment in their early years are likely to continue to be so favored, or whether it is because they have attained such strength of personality that they can successfully handle later difficulties, research has not yet made clear. We do know that nearly all children who get a good start continue to develop well, and we also know that some of those who start off poorly continue to be handicapped. Observations of this sort seem to support psychological theory in the conclusion that personality is pretty well set by about six years of age. Since, however, some children develop into psychologically healthy adults in spite of a bad start, and since some who start well run into difficulties later, it is clear that much research is needed before this conclusion can be accepted as wholly correct.

To return to the developmental analysis, the fourth stage, which begins somewhere around six years of age and extends over five or six years, has as its achievement what Erikson calls the "sense of industry." Perhaps "sense of duty and accomplishment" would make the meaning clearer. At any rate, this is the period in which preoccupation with phantasy subsides and the child wants to be engaged in real tasks that he can carry through to completion. As with the other developmental stages, there are foreshadowings of this kind of interest long before six years of age. Moreover, in some societies, and in some parts of our own society, children are trained very early to perform socially useful tasks. The exact age is not the point at issue. What is to be pointed out is that children, after a period characterized by exuberant imagination, want to settle down to learning exactly how to do things and how to do them well.

In contrast to the preceding stages and to the succeeding ones, this stage does not consist of a swing from a violent inner upheaval to a new mastery. Under reasonably favorable circumstances this is a period of calm, steady growth, especially if the problems of the previous stages have been well worked through. Despite its unspectacular character, this is a very important period, for in it is laid a firm basis for responsible citizenship. It is during this period that children acquire not only knowledge and skills that make for good workmanship but also the ability to cooperate and play fair and otherwise follow the rules of the larger social game.

The chief danger of this period is the presence of conditions that may lead to the development of a sense of inadequacy and inferiority. This may be the outcome if the child has not yet achieved a sense of initiative, or if his experiences at home have not prepared him for entering school happily, or if he finds school a place where his previous accomplishments are disregarded or his latent abilities are not challenged. Even with a good start the child may later lapse into discouragement and lack of interest if at home or school his individual needs are overlooked—if too much or too little is expected of him or if he is made to feel that achievement is beyond his ability. It is most important for health of personality, therefore, that schools be conducted well, that methods and courses of instruction be such as will give every child the feeling of successful accomplishment.

Autobiographies of juvenile delinquents show time and again a boy who hated school—hated the fact that he was marked out as stupid or awkward, as one who was not as good as the rest. Some such boys find in jobs the sense of accomplishment they miss at school and consequently give up their delinquent ways. Others, however, are handicapped in job finding and keeping by the very fact that in school they did not develop the sense of industry; hence they have work failure added to their other insecurities.

Nor is delinquency the only or the most likely outcome of lack of success in school. Many children respond in a quieter way, by passive acceptance of their inferiority. Psychologically, they are perhaps even more harmed.

Our Puritan tradition maintains that children will not work except under the spur of competition, so we tend to fear the suggestion that all should succeed. To help children develop a sense of accomplishment does not mean, however, merely giving all of them good marks and passing them on to the next grade. Children need and want real achievement. How to help them secure it, despite differences in native capacity and differences in emotional development, is one of the school's most serious challenges.

School, of course, is not the only place in which children at this stage of development can secure the sense of industry. In work at home there are many opportunities for a child to get a feeling of mastery and worthwhile endeavor. Rural youth groups and their urban counterparts cater to this need, and many recreation programs put as much emphasis on work as on play. School, however, is the legally constituted arrangement for giving instruction to the young, so it is upon teachers that the professional responsibility for helping all children achieve a sense of industry and accomplishment chiefly rests.

In addition to aiding personality development in this way, teachers have many opportunities for reconfirming their pupils' sense of trust, autonomy, and initiative, or for encouraging its growth in children who have been somewhat hampered by previous life experiences. Teachers cannot work alone, of course, either in aiding a child in the development of new capacities or in strengthening old ones. Jointly with parents and others they can do much, not only for children of already healthy personality but also for many whose development has been handicapped.

The Sense of Identity

With the onset of adolescence another period of personality development begins. As is well known, adolescence is a period of storm and stress for many young people, a period in which previous certainties are questioned and previous continuities no longer relied upon. Physiological changes and rapid physical growth provide the somatic base for the turmoil and indecision. It is probable that cultural factors play a decisive part, for it has been observed that adolescence is less upsetting in some societies than in others.

The central problem of the period is the establishment of what Erikson calls a "sense of identity." The adolescent seeks to clarify who he is and what his role in society is to be. Is he a child or is he an adult? Does he have it in him to be someday a husband and father? What is he to be as a worker and an earner of money? Can he feel self-confident in spite of the fact that his race or religion or national background make him a person some people look down upon? Over all, will he be a success or a failure?

By reason of these questions adolescents are sometimes morbidly pre-occupied with how they appear in the eyes of others as compared with their own conception of themselves, and with how they can make the roles and skills learned earlier jibe with what is currently in style. Not all of this struggle for identity is conscious. What is at stake is a deep sense of continuity of individuality, reaching back into the individual's earliest experiences and forward into his expectations and opportunities.

In primitive societies, adolescents are supported by rituals in this period of doubt and indecision. Through initiation rites, often seemingly cruel in character, young people are tested out (and test themselves out) and are then welcomed into a socially recognized age category in which rights and duties and mode of living are clearly defined. In our society, there are few rituals or ceremonies that mark the change in status from child-hood to youth. For those who have religious affiliations, confirmation, joining the church, may serve this purpose in part, since young people are thereby admitted, in this one segment of their lives at least, to the com-pany of adults. Such ceremonies serve, in addition, to reaffirm to youth that the universe is trustworthy and stable and that a way of life is clearly laid out.

Graduation ceremonies might play a part in marking a new status were it not that in our present way of life adult status is so ill defined. What rules of law and custom that do exist are too diverse to be of much help. For example, legal regulations governing age of "consent," age at which marriage is permitted, age for leaving school, for driving a car, for join-ing (or being required to join) the Army or Navy mark no logical pro-gressions in rights and duties. As to custom, there is so much variation in what even families who live next door to each other expect or permit that adolescents, eager to be on their way, are practically forced into standardizing themselves and one another in their search for status. In this they are ably abetted by advertisers and entertainers who seek their patronage, as well as by well-meaning magazine writers who describe in great detail the means by which uniformity can be achieved.

In this urge to find comfort through similarity, some adolescents be-come stereotyped in behavior and ideals. They form cliques for self-protection, and they fasten on petty similarities of dress and gesture to assure themselves that they are really somebody. In these cliques they may be intolerant and even cruel toward those they label as "different." Unfortunate as such behavior is, and not to be condoned, intolerance serves the important purpose of giving the group members at least the negative assurance that there is something they are not. Such intolerance must be guided toward worthier discriminations.

The danger of this developmental period is self-diffusion. As Biff puts it in *The Death of a Salesman,* "I just can't take hold, Mom. I can't take hold of some kind of a life." A boy or girl can scarcely help feeling somewhat diffuse when the body changes in size and shape so rapidly, when genital maturity floods body and imagination with unclear or forbidden desires, when adult life lies ahead with such a diversity of conflicting possibilities and choices.

Whether this feeling of self-diffusion is fairly easily mastered or whether, in extreme, it leads to delinquency, neurosis, or outright psychosis depends to a considerable extent on what has gone before. If the course of personality development has been a healthy one, a feeling of self-esteem has accrued from the numerous experiences of succeeding in a task and sensing its cultural meaning. Along with this, the child has come to the conviction that he is moving toward an understandable future in which he will have a definite role to play. Adolescence may upset this assurance for a time or to a degree, but fairly soon a new integration is achieved and the boy or girl sees again (and with clearer vision) that he belongs and that he is on his way.

The course is not so easy for adolescents who have not had so fortunate a past or for those whose former security is broken by a sudden awareness that as members of minority groups their way of life sets them apart. The former, already unsure of themselves, find their earlier doubt and mistrust reactivated by the physiological and social changes that adolescence brings. The latter, once secure, may feel that they must disavow their past and try to develop an "American" personality.

Much has been learned and written about the adolescent problems of the boys and girls whose early personality development has been impaired. How they can be helped, if their disorders are not too severe, is also fairly well known. The full implications of these findings for parents, teachers, and others who would guide youth are still to be worked out but, even so, there is considerable information.

Less well understood are the difficulties and the ways of helping adolescents who grew up in cultures that are not as common. These boys and girls may have been privileged in having had a childhood in which there was little inhibition of sensual and active pleasures and in which development proceeded by easy, unself-conscious stages. For them, difficulties arise if their parents lose trust in themselves or if their teachers apply sudden correctives or if they themselves reject their past and try to act like the others. The new role of middle-class adolescent is often too hard to play. Delinquency or bizarre behavior marks the failure.

How to reach these boys and girls, how to help them attain their desire is a matter not well understood. It is clear, however, that they should not be typed by pat diagnoses and social judgments, for they are overly ready to become "bums," or whatever else they happen to be called. Those who would guide them must understand both the psychology of adolescence and the cultural realities of the day. There is trust to be restored and doubt and guilt and feelings of inferiority to be overcome. The science of how to do this is still pretty much lacking, though here and there teachers, clergymen, probation officers, and the like are highly successful in the task.

Hard though it be to achieve, the sense of identity is the individual's only safeguard against the lawlessness of his biological drives and the autocracy of his overweening conscience. Loss of identity, loss of the sense that there is some continuity, sameness, and meaning to life, exposes the individual to his childhood conflicts and leads to emotional upsets. This outcome was observed time and again among men hard pressed by army life, for which their upbringing had not prepared them. It is clear, then, that if health of personality is to be preserved, much attention must be given to assuring that our country makes good on her promises to youth and, in these times of changing history, redoubles her efforts to assure a strong sense of continuity and meaning to her growing citizens.

The Sense of Intimacy

After the sense of identity, to a greater or less extent, is achieved it becomes possible for the next component of the healthy personality to develop. This is the sense of intimacy, intimacy with persons of the same sex or of the opposite sex or with oneself. The youth who is not fairly sure of his identity shies away from interpersonal relations and is afraid of close communion with himself. The surer he becomes of himself, the more he seeks intimacy, in the form of friendship, love, and inspiration.

In view of the early age at which boy and girl attachments are encouraged today, it may seem strange to put the critical period for the development of the sense of intimacy late in adolescence. The explanation is that, on the one hand, sexual intimacy is only part of what is involved and, on the other, boy-girl attachments of earlier age periods are likely to be of a somewhat different order. Regarding the latter point, it has been observed by those who know young people well that high-school-age boys and girls often use each other's company for an endless verbal examination of what they think, feel, and want to do, and what they like or dislike in people and ideas. In other words, these attachments are a means by which each one seeks to define his own identity.

In contrast to this use of friendship and companionship, boys and girls late in adolescence have need for some kind of fusion with the essence of other people and for a communion with their own inner resources. If, by reason of inadequacies in previous personality development, this sense of intimacy cannot be achieved, the youth may retire into psychological isolation and keep his relations with people on a formal, stereotyped level that is lacking in spontaneity and warmth, or he may keep trying again and again to get close to others, only to meet with repeated failure. Under this compulsion he may even marry prematurely, in which case the role of mate may not be one he can sustain, for the condition of true two-ness is that each individual must first become himself.

In this area of personality development, as in the others, cultural factors play a part in sustaining or in discouraging the individual in his development. American culture is unusually successful in encouraging the development of the feelings of independence, initiative, industry, and identity. Psychiatrists feel that it is somewhat less successful in the area of intimacy, for the nation's traditional ideals have supported a certain subordination of this aspect of life to the claims of work and duty. Consequently, American adolescents are likely to get too little support from their parents for their desire to sense intimately the full flavor of the personality of others, and to find too little confirmation of this desire in story and song. In quite a few, then, the sense of intimacy does not develop highly, and they have difficulty in finding in close personal relations a true outlet for the tension that is the result of the culture's emphasis on efficiency.

There is some evidence, however, that a change in conventions and customs in this respect is in the making. Too abrupt change in any such cultural matter is not to be urged, but it is to be hoped that frank discussion can bring about gradual alteration in attitude and overcome the dangers inherent in rigidities, which may not be as traditional as they often seem.

The Parental Sense

"Parental sense" designates somewhat the same capacity as that implied in the words "creativity" or "productivity." The individual has normally come to adulthood before this sense can develop fully.

The parental sense is indicated most clearly by interest in producing and caring for children of one's own. It may also be exhibited in relation to other people's children or by a parental kind of responsibility toward the products of creative and inventive activity of other sorts. The mere desire for or possession of children does not indicate that this component of the healthy personality has developed. In fact, many parents who bring their children to child-guidance clinics are found not to have reached this stage of personality development.

The essential element is the desire to nourish and nurture in its essence what has been produced. It is the ability to regard one's children as a trust of the community rather than as extensions of one's own personality or as beings that one merely happens to live with.

Failure to develop this component of the healthy personality often results in a condition which has not been adequately categorized clinically. Although a true sense of intimacy has not developed, the individual may obsessively seek companionship. There is something of egotism in this as in his other activities, a kind of self-absorption. The individual is inclined to treat himself as a child and to be rivalrous with his children, if he has any. He indulges himself, expects to be indulged, and in general behaves in an infantile or immature manner.

There are both individual and social explanations for the failure to develop an adequate parental sense. Individually, the explanation may be found in the inadequate development of the personality components previously described. In some people this failure goes far back. Because of unfortunate experiences in childhood they did not arrive at a firm sense of trust, autonomy, and the rest. In others it is only inadequacies in later stages, especially in the development of the sense of intimacy, that are at fault.

Socially, as has been suggested throughout this analysis, healthy personality development depends upon the culture's ideals and upon the economic arrangements of the society. In order that most people may develop fully the sense of being a parent, the role of parent, both mother and father, must be a respected one in the society. Giving must rank higher than getting, and loving than being loved. The economy must be such that the future can be depended upon and each person can feel assured that he has a meaningful and respected part to play. Only so can most individuals afford to renounce selfish aims and derive much of their satisfaction from rearing children and from participating actively in the shaping of the world in which these children will live.

The Sense of Integrity

The final component of the healthy personality is the sense of integrity. In every culture the dominant ideals—honor, courage, faith, duty, purity, grace, fairness, self-discipline, whatever they may be—become at this stage the core of the healthy personality's integration. The individual, in Erikson's words, "becomes able to accept his individual life cycle and the people who have become significant to it as meaningful within the segment of history in which he lives."

To continue Erikson's description,[6] "Integrity thus means a new and different love of one's parents, free of the wish that they should have been different, and an acceptance of the fact that one's life is one's own responsibility. It is a sense of comradeship with men and women of distant times and of different pursuits, who have created orders and objects and sayings conveying human dignity and love. Although aware of the relativity of all the various life styles that have given meaning to human striving, the possessor of integrity is ready to defend the dignity of his own life style against all physical and economic threats. For he knows that, for him, all human dignity stands or falls with the one style of integrity of which he partakes."

The adult who lacks integrity in this sense is likely to wish that he could live life again. He feels that if at one time he had made a different decision he could have been a different person and his ventures would have been successful. He fears death and cannot accept his one and only life cycle as his chance to meet the ultimate of life. In the extreme, he experiences disgust and despair. Despair expresses the feeling that time is too short to try out new roads to integrity. Disgust is a means of hiding the despair, a chronic, contemptuous displeasure with the way life is run. As with the dangers and the solutions of previous periods, doubt and despair are not difficulties that are overcome once and for all, nor is integrity so achieved. Most people live through periods when they fluctuate between two extremes; as individuals, few either attain to the heights of unalloyed integrity or fall to the depths of complete disgust and despair. It is here, however, that man needs the solace and the guidance of the great systems of faith, art, and wisdom, which attest to a common integrity for humanity.

Even in adulthood a reasonably healthy personality is sometimes secured in spite of previous misfortunes in the developmental sequence. New sources of faith may be found. Fortunate associations and circumstances may aid the individual in his struggle to feel autonomous. Imagination and initiative may be spurred by new responsibilities, and feelings of inferiority be overcome by successful achievement or new orientation. Even late in life an individual may arrive at a true sense of

[6] Erik Erickson, "Growth and Crisis of the 'Healthy Personality,' " *Problems of Infancy and Childhood,* Supplement II, Josiah Macy, Jr., Foundation, New York, 1950, p. 55.

who he is and what he has to do and may be able to win through to a feeling of intimacy with others and to joy in producing and giving.

For the healthy personality development of children and youth it is necessary that a large proportion of adults attain a sense of integrity to a considerable degree. Not only parents but all who deal with children have need of this quality if they are to help children maintain the feeling that the universe is dependable and trustworthy. Integrity is more easily attained and sustained when the culture itself gives support, when a meaning to life is clearly spelled out in tradition and ceremony and roles are clearly defined. Our culture, with its rapidly changing technology and its diversity of value standards, leaves much for the individual to work out for himself. In the American dream, however, and in Judaeo-Christian tradition on which it is based, there are values and ideals aplenty. In the interest of the welfare of children and youth, in order that a generation of happy individuals and responsible citizens be reared, it is highly important that these values and ideals be ever again reasserted and that the promise of American life be kept.

Are Parents to Blame?

This, then, is a summary description of what health of personality consists of, how its various components emerge when conditions are favorable, and what some of the necessary conditions appear to be. It is clear that the healthy development of personality is the resultant of many factors, no one of which can be held chiefly accountable. We Americans, however, like to find *a* cause for each disaster, *a* cure for each difficulty. Moreover, if causes and cures are thought to be in human hands, we are inclined to blame whoever is held to be causing and not remedying the difficulty.

Currently, the popular explanation of difficulties in personality development is parental mishandling, and parents are the targets of widespread criticism. Under the onslaught, parents themselves confess to guilt, though as to what they are guilty of most are exceedingly vague.

There are several things wrong with this situation. First, under our code of fair play, blame and guilt should attach only to deliberate intent, even though measures may have to be taken to assure that ignorance is dissipated and carelessness avoided. In the theory that attributes children's maladjustments to their parents' mistakes in rearing them, however, deliberate intent, and even ignorance of the best methods, are regarded as relatively infrequent causal factors. What parents are chiefly accused of is not loving their children adequately and not being able to play the parental role as mature adults. Even if this theory were wholly correct—and it has already been suggested that it is only one part of a complicated explanation—the condition should arouse regret for misfortune rather than blame, for surely no parent would deliberately desire and seek to be incapable of caring for his children.

Second, in personal relationships, blame and guilt only make matters worse. If parents feel blameworthy regarding their feelings about their children, they will make irrational attempts to right the wrong and in so doing probably increase the already existing tension. What is really needed is, as Erikson puts it, "deeper humility before the processes that govern us, and the ability to live with greater simplicity and honesty." [7] The cultivation of such attitudes will do more to improve parent-child relations and children's health of personality than any amount of attempts to right a wrong.

Finally, it is literally not true that there is a simple, cause-and-effect relation between parents' behavior and children's development. Parents and children are people and, being people, both are influenced by all the varied factors that make or mar human happiness. As people, too, they influence each other, so that mutual regulation of their actions and feelings is called for. Mutuality rather than simple causative sequence is the rule of personality development.

Three main aspects of the developmental process may be discerned: the organic, the interpersonal, and the social. Parents play their direct part in a child's development in the second of these but, even so, their actions and feelings are both based upon and are responses to the organic aspects of their own and their children's functioning, and to their own situation in society.

In the preceding account of the course of healthy personality development, the interrelationship of these three aspects has been briefly described. In each developmental phase it is clear that organic and social factors converge to create a crisis for the maturing ego. At one time, it is rapidly emerging sensory and muscular abilities pitted against social demands for conformity and acquiescence. At another, it is the physiological and emotional changes of adolescence and the necessity for decisions regarding adult roles. In each phase, the individual organizes his experience in his own peculiar way and finds his own peculiar mode of functioning in relation to the persons who are of chief importance to him.

The development of personality, then, is a very complicated process,

[7] Erik Erikson, *Childhood and Society,* W. W. Norton & Co., New York, 1950, p. 30.

involving all aspects of the organism and its environment. It is not merely a matter of child and parents, nor is it to be conceived as the action of numerous environmental forces on a organism otherwise inert. Parents are not the whole of a child's environment, and in the part they do constitute they operate not only as individuals but also as representatives of the society to which they and their children belong. Moreover, they and other people are important to children not so much as separate entities as for what they say and do and for the material things they provide. And it is what the child does with their contributions that counts for most.

In all of this there is much mutuality of effort and effect and much interplay with other factors and conditions. In fact, so intricate is the process and so interrelated the various factors in it that it is only artificially that even individual and environment can be separated and the relation of one to the other discussed. As with biological development, so with psychological and social: there is, as Gardner Murphy puts it, "full reciprocity of inner and outer events." The life process is as much a matter of world as of organism.

In any analysis, however, there must be abstraction. In the following elaboration of the description of some of the influences affecting personality development, we shall therefore follow conventional lines and consider, as separately as possible, the effects of physical characteristics, of interpersonal relations, and of cultural and social factors. It will soon be apparent, however, that this artificial division cannot be maintained and that the influence of any one of these aspects of the life process is dependent upon the action of the others.

For example, whether congenital sensitivity of a particular kind will make the healthy development of personality more or less difficult will depend, among many other matters, not only on physiological factors but also upon the parents' feelings about having a child of this kind, upon how individuals of this sort are regarded in the part of the society to which the child belongs, upon the opportunities the environment affords for the development and utilization of the peculiar capacities, and upon the kind of aesthetic and spiritual experiences it provides.

These are matters to be kept in mind when a particular child's development is under consideration, and they are vital to general theory also. It is hoped that the following analysis along particular lines will not detract from an appreciation of the interrelatedness of the whole.

✗ II ✗

The Influence of
Congenital Characteristics

THE first set of factors to be considered is the organic. The chief questions asked are whether personality development is affected by reaction tendencies that are present at birth and whether physical and mental disabilities, congenital or acquired, influence it adversely. Do babies at birth differ from one another in ways that affect their responses to the environment? Are children who are "handicapped" in one or another way also handicapped in personality development? We can also ask in this connection whether factors operating prenatally are of importance, whether illness, acute or chronic, is likely to affect health of personality, whether diet and nutrition are influential. In short, do the character of the physical organism and the factors affecting biological functioning affect the individual's ability to develop in ways that are psychologically and emotionally sound?

The extent of influence of constitutional factors on the behavior and character of individuals is a topic on which scientific opinion has fluctuated greatly. Fifty years or so ago, constitutional factors were thought to be of prime importance, and development was regarded as largely a matter of their maturing. Children were considered miniature editions of the adults they were to become, and parents were called fortunate or unfortunate, depending on what kind of children they had happened to acquire. Within the last quarter-century an almost complete change-about of scientific thought took place. Environment became the clue to almost all differences in human functioning, and parents were held responsible for the kind of children they turned out.

At present, scientific opinion stands somewhere between the two extremes. Some prominent investigators have returned to the concept of constitutional types and corresponding psychological characteristics that cannot be altered by environmental influences. Most research and professional workers do not go so far. Many are of the opinion, however, that

29

congenital reaction tendencies, the nature of which is largely unknown, do play an important part in personality formation. What some of these congenital reaction tendencies are will be described below. First, however, note must be made of the present conception of "constitution" and "heredity" and of the part that environment plays in the formation of the organism that is the newborn babe.

The Influence of Prenatal Factors

"Constitution" is currently conceived as the sum total of the structural, functional, and psychological characters of the organism. It is, in large measure, an integral of genetic potentialities influenced in varying degrees by internal and external environmental factors. It is not a biological *given,* a structure destined to function in a predetermined manner. Rather it is a *process,* a series of operative questions that even by the time of birth have not become final declarative answers.

What is given is the genotype, the complex of genetic potentialities with which the organism is endowed. Each individual's genotype is a unique physicochemical system comprising particular kinds of potentialities that have definite limits. These inherited genetic potentialities are contained in the genes (upward of 20,000 in number) in the chromosomes transmitted from the mother and from the father. The genes, self-duplicating giant protein molecules of great complexity, are organic catalysts that accelerate essential chemical reactions, the original builders of the body, which they serve to differentiate according to the type of medium or other conditions that surround them in their interactive chemical relations. Genes do not determine characters or traits but responses of the developing organism to the environment.[1]

The manner in which the genotype functions depends in part upon the environment in which it undergoes development. Even the identical genotypes of single-egg twins do not result in identical individuals at birth, for the environment is somewhat different for each of them. Heredity, accordingly, is not constituted merely by the genotype, but by the genotype as modified by the environment in which it has developed. It is the resultant of the dynamic interaction between the two.

Since this is so, it may be possible to influence the heredity of a growing organism by influencing its prenatal environment. Numerous experiments involving plants and nonhuman animals have shown this to be true, and there is some evidence suggesting that it is true for man also.

[1] H. J. Muller, *Genetics, Medicine and Man,* Cornell University Press, Ithaca, New York, 1947, p. 16.

Whether the changes that might be induced are such as would directly affect personality development is, however, an unanswered question.

Various conditions in the mother may affect the prenatal environment and, consequently, the development of the genes' potentialities. Among them are the following: maternal nutrition, drugs, infections, maternal dysfunction and sensitization, maternal age and number of children, and maternal emotional state. The following review of a few of the findings in regard to the influence of these factors suggests their importance for children's well-being.

Nutritional Deficiencies

Little is known for certain about the effects of specific nutritional deficiencies on the development of the human fetus. If the mother is near to starvation or if she has a severe disease of the thyroid gland, the fetus may not survive but, generally speaking, the embryo is well protected against minor disturbances of nutrition. Warkany and his associates [2] report, however, that experiments on animals suggest that nutrition may be a decisive factor in the production of certain physical abnormalities. How the damage is done is not clear, but it seems likely that the lack of certain vitamins or proteins or the presence of some complex toxic disturbance occasioned by the mother's state of malnutrition are responsible.

There is some evidence also that a generally poor maternal diet is associated with various conditions unfavorable to the development of the fetus or to the birth of the child.

Comparing two groups of women of similar socioeconomic status, one having a poor diet but no sign of a deficiency disease and the other a diet that had been made good, Ebbs found that a significantly larger proportion of the first group than of the second had a "poor-bad" prenatal maternal record and condition during labor, and the average duration of the first stage of labor was longer. More of the babies of these mothers had a poor record during the first two weeks of life and more suffered from colds and from anemia during the first six months. The proportion of miscarriages and of premature births was also slightly excessive. [3]

These findings seem to be confirmed by a group of research workers at Harvard. Burke and her colleagues, reporting on the findings of a ten-

[2] J. Warkany, "Etiology of Congenital Malformations," *Advances in Pediatrics,* Vol. 2, 1947, Interscience Publishers, New York, p. 1.

[3] J. H. Ebbs, *et al.,* "The Influence of Improved Parental Nutrition upon the Infant," *Canadian Medical Association Journal,* Vol. 46 (1942), pp. 6–8. See also F. F. Tisdall, "The Role of Nutrition in Preventive Medicine," *The Milbank Memorial Fund Quarterly,* Vol. 23 (1945), pp. 1–15.

year longitudinal study of 216 mothers and their children, state that every stillborn, all except one of the infants that died during the first few days after birth, all premature, and all functionally immature infants were born to mothers who had had an inadequate diet during pregnancy.[4]

Diet and nutrition, however, may be influenced by many environmental factors, inside as well as outside the mother's body. Emotional stress, for example, may severely disturb the mother's nutritional economy,[5] and socioeconomic and cultural factors are of great importance in determining the nature and quality of a mother's diet. It is not enough, therefore, to say that a pregnant woman should eat well. What she eats and how she utilizes what she eats are probably influenced by the whole possible range of factors from the chemical to the psychological.

Drugs

Certain drugs taken by the pregnant mother may seriously affect the fetus. For example, some cases of congenital deafness have been traced to the mother's use of quinine for malaria during pregnancy, and morphinism has been reported in the infants of mothers who were morphine addicts. The obstetrical practice of dosing the pregnant mother with barbiturates and similar drugs prior to delivery may so overload the fetal blood stream as to produce asphyxiation in the fetus at birth, with either permanent brain damage or subtle effects of a kind that lead to mental impairment. Fortunately, the present trend is away from heavy sedation.

Disease in the Mother

Some virus and bacterial diseases in a pregnant mother apparently can do more or less damage to the developing organism. Among these diseases are smallpox, chickenpox, measles, mumps, scarlet fever, erysipelas, and recurrent fever. Rubella (German measles) is especially harmful. Contracted by the mother in early pregnancy, it may product cataract, deafness, and mental defect in the infant.[6]

Noninfectious, functional disease may also adversely affect the fetus. Pregnant women suffering from high blood pressure have a high rate of

[4] Burke, Beal, Kirkwood, and Stuart, "Nutritional Studies During Pregnancy," *American Journal of Obstetrics and Gynecology*, Vol. 46 (1943), pp. 38–52.

[5] B. F. Sieve, "Vitamins and Hormones in Nutrition"; "Emotional Upset and Trauma," *American Journal of Digestive Diseases*, Vol. 16 (1949), pp. 14–25.

[6] N. McA. Gregg, "Congenital Cataract Following German Measles," *Transactions of the Ophthalmology Society of Australia*, Vol. 3 (1941), p. 35; C. Swan, "Rubella in Pregnancy as an Aetiological Factor in Congenital Malformation, Stillbirth, Miscarriage, and Abortion," *Journal of Obstetrics and Gynaecology of the British Empire*, Vol. 56 (1949), pp. 341–363, 591–605.

fetal loss, and their own death rate is high.[7] Diabetes may result in still-birth or neonatal death.[8]

In instances in which the genotype of mother and fetus differ in the substances borne on the surfaces of the red blood corpuscles, the mother may become sensitized and produce antibodies inimical to fetal development. This usually results in anemia in the fetus at a relatively late fetal age. The Rh incompatibilities constitute a well-known example of this condition. Fortunately the disease (erythroblastosis) which this may produce in the fetus does not occur as frequently as the facts of heredity would suggest.

Age and Previous Pregnancies

Maternal age and number of previous pregnancies are other factors that are somewhat associated with certain developmental abnormalities in the fetus. The optimum period for childbearing is apparently from twenty-three to twenty-nine. At other ages the maternal and infant mortality rates are slightly higher, and some conditions, such as Mongolism and congenital hydrocephalus, are a bit more frequent among the offspring of women who are in their late thirties or older.[9] There is evidence, too, that first-born children and those born at the end of a long series of pregnancies are somewhat less viable than others. These, however, are statistical findings. The majority of children who are first-born or last-born or born well after the mother's thirty-eighth birthday are as healthy as their siblings.

Mother's Emotional State

The influence of the last-mentioned of the factors listed above, the emotional state of the mother during pregnancy, is far from well established. Investigations conducted by the Fels Institute suggest, however, that severe emotional disturbance in the mother may produce marked increase in the activity of the fetus. There is some evidence, too, that infants of mothers who suffer severe emotional disturbance during the latter part of pregnancy are likely to have an irritable, hyperactive autonomic nervous system. Regarding his finding on this point, Sontag says:

[7] L. C. Chesley and J. E. Arnetto, "Pregnancy in the Patient with Hypertensive Disease," *American Journal Obstetrics and Gynecology,* Vol. 53 (1947), pp. 372–381.

[8] J. L. Gaspar, "Diabetes Mellitus and Pregnancy," *Western Journal of Surgery,* Vol. 53 (1945), p. 21.

[9] L. S. Penrose, *The Biology of Mental Defect,* Sidgwick & Jackson, London, 1949; B. Malzberg, "Some Statistical Aspects of Mongolism," *Am. J. Ment. Deficiency,* Vol. 54 (1950), pp. 266–281.

Irritable or poorly balanced adrenergic-cholinergic systems probably constitute an important part of the rather poorly defined syndrome commonly labeled constitutional inadequacy or nutritional diaphysis. Early feeding difficulties based on motor and sensory abnormalities of the gastrointestinal system are in many cases of autonomic origin. The presence of feeding difficulties of a motor or secretory nature from birth must presume their etiology in basic disturbances during intrauterine life. In prenatal development of such a condition, prolonged nervous and emotional disturbance of the mother during the later months of pregnancy seems to be important.[10]

This is not to say, however, that the mother's psychological state, as such, is transmitted to the fetus, that the old myth of "maternal impressions" marking a child is true. In regard to this, Corner summarizes the facts as follows:

. . . Subject only to certain technical reservations, nothing gets through the placenta from mother to child unless it is capable of being carried in solution by the blood, and of passing through the walls of the villi and of their blood capillaries, which together constitute an exceedingly fine-meshed semipermeable membrane. There is no other means of communication between mother and child. In particular it should be emphasized in capital letters that there is no connection between their nervous systems. Not a single nerve fiber crosses the placental barrier; there is no channel for the transmission of feelings or intentions, moods, memories or ideas. The infant is in fact completely shut off from its own mother save for the exchange of simple chemical nutrients and wastes through a screen so fine that it will pass nothing but the smaller molecules of matter.[11]

It seems possible, however, that the gross chemical changes that may occur in the mother during a period of severe emotional tension are transmissible to the fetus. Mother and fetus have an endocrine pool in common, which forms a neurohumoral bond between them. Stimuli originating in the cerebral cortex of the mother may set up reflexes that pass directly into the autonomic nervous system or are mediated through the feeling-tone center, the thalamus, to the lower autonomic centers of the hypothalamus. By whatever route such reflexes travel, the autonomic nervous system acts upon the endocrine glands, and these pour their secretions into the blood. Such secretions, with the possible exception of the

[10] L. W. Sontag, "The Significance of Fetal Environmental Differences," *American Journal of Obstetrics and Gynecology,* Vol. 42, p. 1001.

[11] George W. Corner, *Ourselves Unborn,* Yale University Press, New Haven, 1945, p. 53.

hormones of the pituitary gland, are known to be capable of passing through the placenta to the fetus. Hence, stimuli originating in the central nervous system of the mother, by leading to chemical changes in the mother, may be able to produce changes in the fetus. Whether such changes affect later personality developments is, however, unknown.

All in all, then, it is clear that newborn infants differ in their potentialities both because of differences in their genetic equipment and because of differences in the prenatal environment in which the genes operate to produce fetal development. The evidence cited regarding environmental influences has been largely negative in nature, has dealt largely with inimical factors, with influences that have handicapped rather than aided. In the present state of knowledge this is all the evidence there is. Nevertheless, it seems reasonable to postulate that there are agents that may influence the fetal environment for the better rather than for the worse and that, to some extent, these are the opposites of the agents whose detrimental influence has been described above. If these agents can be discovered, it may be possible, even before birth, to increase the likelihood that the genetic potentialities of the individual will be realized.

The Influence of Congenital Characteristics

All who have had the opportunity of watching many children of like ages have been impressed with the high degree of individuality which each one shows. Even as newborn infants they differ not only in such physical characteristics as weight and height but also in the manner in which they react to events. Some, when put to the breast or given the bottle for the first time, begin to suck vigorously almost at once; they "know what to do." Others suck weakly at first, lose their hold upon the nipple, and learn gradually. Some squall at the slightest provocation; others cry only in extremity. Some squirm and thrash about energetically and move even while asleep; others show less bodily activity and of a more gentle variety. Some, while sleeping or eating, are disturbed by the slightest noise; others remain imperturbed under the same circumstances. Some seem fragile, others robust. This does not begin to exhaust the list of observable differences among infants but it will suffice to illustrate the point that the behavior of infants shows much variability.

It is a curious fact that all investigators in the child-development field have registered their awareness of such differences, yet most have directed their scientific inquiry toward what children have in common. Clinical psychiatrists, on the other hand, have tended to stress the uniqueness of each individual, practically to the exclusion of any systematic comparison among children. A few recent studies have attempted to bridge the gap between these two approaches. Psychological and medical research workers have begun to turn their attention to sources of variability in the development of children, and some clinicians, notably psychoanalytic research workers, are studying child development in a more general and more systematic manner.[12]

At present, however, factual, tested knowledge concerning individual differences among children is so scarce that there is doubt of the wisdom of including it in this report. On the other hand, the topic is of such importance and has such impressive practical implications that a speculative discussion seems better than none at all.

The material presented in this section will be confined to personality characteristics that appear to be congenital. It is important to remember, however, that there is no sure way of knowing whether or not a given trait is of this kind. The assumption that a trait is congenital is made under two kinds of conditions: (1) differences in the behavior of infants were noted so soon after birth that experience could not reasonably be held accountable for their presence; in addition, these characteristics proved stable, i.e., the personality attribute noted in earliest infancy continued to characterize the individual in later life. (2) Personality characteristics, which may not have become apparent until a later point in development, were noted in some children and not in others, quite independent of the environment and the particular experiences of the child. It is reasoned that since such traits apparently do not differ under different cultures, with different family constellations, with different interpersonal relationships, etc., they must be intrinsic to the organism.

In the following analysis we shall first describe some of the congenital differences in children and then consider whether and how the course of healthy personality development may be affected by them.

Activity and Vigor

Those who work with young infants know that some are more active than others. All babies move their bodies, and babies generally are more restless and active when they are hungry and uncomfortable than when

[12] See, for example, various studies by Rene Spitz, such as "Hospitalism: An Inquiry into the Genesis of Psychiatric Condition in Early Childhood," *Psychoanalytic Study of the Child,* Vols. I and II (1945, 1946), International Universities Press; "The Role of Ecological Factors in Emotional Development in Infancy," *Child Development,* Vol. 20 (1949). Also, R. A. Spitz and K. M. Wolf, "Environment versus Race as an Etiological Factor in Psychiatric Disturbances in Infancy," *Journal of Nervous and Mental Diseases,* May, 1946; "The Smiling Response: A Contribution to the Ontogenesis of Social Relations," *Genetic Psychology Monograph,* No. 34, 1946

they are content and satisfied. Yet some will rarely be altogether quiet; their movements are vigorous and tend to involve all or most of the body. Others move delicately and with less intensity. The former group are likely to impress one as vigorous and animated, the latter as either delicate or placid. Moreover, beyond the age of two or three weeks, the active ones are likely to register their response to stimulation from without by an increase in bodily activity. When they are spoken to or when a noise attracts their attention, they kick and wriggle with excitement. The more quiet babies often do just the opposite. If a toy is shown them or they are played with in some other way, they are likely to decrease or even cease movement; they respond to the stimulation with a still, absorbed kind of attention.

Dr. Margaret Fries, a psychoanalytic research worker, has given special attention to this kind of difference among infants.[13] In connection with her work in a large metropolitan hospital she observed infants during the first days and weeks of life and was especially impressed with the great differences she noted in regard to their activity level. She continued to observe the same children as they grew older and to assess their degree of activity. She concluded that markedly active infants are likely to be markedly active at later ages as well, and that children who are relatively quiet as newborns tend to remain relatively inactive individuals in later childhood.

More important than the mere stability of this characteristic is Dr. Fries's observation that the interests and needs of children who are from the beginning markedly active, medium active, or low in activity are different. On the basis of case studies she showed that if a relatively inactive youngster happens to be born into a family of active, outgoing individuals it is possible that personality difficulties may arise from this discrepancy. She reasoned that energetic, outgoing parents are likely to expect active behavior from a child and may require of him responses that he is not constitutionally equipped to make. Similarly, more placid and reflective families can be distressed by the enormous energy an active child displays, and consider as aggressive and "naughty" ways of behaving which are quite normal and necessary to the active child. Dr. Fries is of the opinion that healthy personality development will be advanced if parents, doctors, educators, and the like, learn to recognize the child's congenital

[13] Margaret Fries, "Factors in Character Development, Neuroses, Psychoses and Delinquency," *American Journal of Orthopsychiatry*, Vol. VII (1937); with B. Lewis, "Interrelated Factors in Development," *American Journal of Orthopsychiatry*, Vol. VIII (1938); "Psychosomatic Relations between Mother and Infant," *Psychosomatic Medicine*, Vol. VI (1945).

predisposition in this respect and adapt their ways of handling each child accordingly.

As is true of most studies, Dr. Fries's findings are tentative and not conclusive. Other investigators have questioned whether activity level remains constant and whether it is a constitutional trait.[14] All are agreed, however, that infants do differ in activity and that their needs and satisfactions vary accordingly. It is therefore also agreed—and this is of importance to our problem here—that the most beneficial way of dealing with a particular child (with the aim of helping him to develop his personality optimally) will depend in part upon whether he is very active or markedly placid.

Sensitivity: General

The processes by which an infant first becomes aware of the world in which he is to live and of his own place in it are of great importance to his development. These early experiences, like all experience to all of us, come to him through his sense organs. He hears, he feels, he sees, he smells. He feels sensations that arise from within, such as painful muscular contractions signifying hunger. And he receives innumerable sensations that come from outside himself, such as the touch of his mother's hand, vibrations as the buggy is pushed, the breeze, sunlight, and bath water on his skin. The sight of things and people alters strangely as people come close and withdraw, and as he is rolled from one position to another, lifted and put down again. Everything he learns of his environment, and everything he does in response to it, occurs through the medium of perception.

Perceptual processes are of special importance for the very earliest phases of development for an additional reason. The immature individual, especially during the first year of life, is, in general, somewhat more fragile and easily disturbed than he will be later on. Even adults can be made nervous by excessive perceptual stimulation, such as continued loud noises, overly bright illumination, violent motion, etc. Adults, however, are sturdy enough to tolerate sharp stimulation with minor discomfort or, at worst, temporary interruption of normal functioning. Moreover, they are seldom helpless; they can protect themselves by moving away from heat or cold, by turning the head or closing their eyes against intense visual stimuli. Small babies, however, cannot protect themselves in the face of unpleasant perceptual sensations; once they perceive, they cannot

[14] See, for example, Lillian E. Malcove, "Margaret E. Fries' Research in Problems of Infancy and Childhood," *The Psychoanalytic Study of the Child,* Vol. I (1945), International Universities Press.

help but respond. Consequently, continued and overly intense perceptual stimulation is not infrequently the cause of severe fatigue, tension, and distress in infants, and may possibly lead to real disturbance in development.

It is known that adults differ greatly in acuteness of perception. The hearing of some people is keener than that of others. Some detect fine nuances in the shading of colors, and others make only grosser visual distinctions. Some can judge distances and weights with greater precision than can others, and some seem generally more responsive to all sorts of sensory stimulation. Among artists, for instance, one finds a high proportion of especially sensitive persons, using "sensitive" in the physiological meaning of the word.

Scientifically minded pediatricians and psychologists have noted that even during the first few weeks of life babies differ from one to another in respect to what may be called "generalized sensitivity." Some startle at even slight sounds, others startle only when the stimulus sound is a very loud one. If a lamp is turned on or sunlight hits the face, some babies merely blink, others grimace, whimper, or even cry. Some have to be moved very gently or else will be upset; others are not bothered by being moved rapidly, swung about, bounced, or even tossed in father's arms. A little later, yet still during the first few months, some babies seem much more aware than others of nuances of color and of brightness. Similarly, some seem to react earlier and more strongly to the differences between familiar and unfamiliar persons.

Observing such behavior differences one receives the distinct impression that the world is a very different place for the less sensitive babies than for the highly sensitive ones. The imperturbable, robust baby, it would seem, faces a somewhat simpler problem in orienting himself to the outer world. He perceives and responds to only the stronger stimulations. The lesser ones—small noises, vibrations, changes in light and temperature—seem barely to be noticed or responded to. At the other extreme, the very sensitive infant is almost continuously flooded with strong sense impressions to which he must respond. For him there are fewer periods of quiescence. Perceptual stimulations of relatively great intensity may be overwhelming and temporarily quite upsetting to him, whereas the same stimulation may be well tolerated by less sensitive babies.

It has been thought that perceptual sensitivity is related to many characteristics of personality and temperament, although no conclusive studies have yet been carried out. Many students of child development have speculated as to whether sensitivities of this sort are inborn or acquired and what role they play in personality development. It is only very recently, however, that scientific inquiry has directed itself to the perceptual functioning of young children.[15] In presenting this material here we raise questions for further research. We do so in the belief that a workable theory of personality development requires knowledge of this sort, and that the factor of perceptual sensitivity is important for the care and practical management of children.

Such sensitivity, in and of itself, does not, we believe, bear a direct relationship to intelligence or even to the capacity for good adjustment. It seems probable, however, that many of the babies commonly called "nervous" are also highly sensitive. But under circumstances that provide protection from too much harsh stimulation (and most mothers protect their babies from extreme heat and cold, from too much handling, too much noise, etc.) highly sensitive babies develop in as healthy and wholesome a fashion as do other babies. Their behavior and their needs may in some respects be different from those of other babies but they are altogether normal. "Tough-skinned" babies, by the same token, may in earliest infancy seem a little less aware of things about but they, too, soon respond alertly and adequately to their world as they experience it. Throughout this discussion it should be kept in mind that the individual differences referred to are all encountered among entirely healthy, normal, well-developing children.

Sensitivity: Specific

In addition to variation in generalized sensitivity, people also differ in particular perceptual spheres. Some adults, for instance, are described as "visual-minded," by which is meant that they are keenly aware of visual impressions and that visual images play an especially large role in their memory and imagination. Similarly, some people are markedly more sensitive to smell or temperature or pain or sound than they are to the other sense impressions. Such evidence as exists strongly suggests that differences in the relative sensitivity of some perceptual spheres over others exist in earliest infancy as well. Some babies respond more strongly to sound than to sight or motion; for some, touch (which is an important sense to all babies) may be the outstandingly sensitive area of perception.

What bearing does this have on personality development? Like gen-

[15] P. Bergman and Sibylle Escalona, "Unusual Sensitivities in Very Young Children," *Psychoanalytic Study of the Child*, Vols. III, IV (1949), International Universities Press: Albrecht Peiper, *Die Eigenart der kindlichen Hirntätigkeit*, Georg Thieme, Leipzig, 1949.

eralized sensitivity, its importance lies in the way in which the outer world presents itself to the child. The degree of generalized sensitivity influences how much of the sounds and sights and motions that surround him the baby will perceive, and how intensively he will perceive it. Differential sensitivities influence the kind of sense impressions that will play the relatively largest role in the child's experience of his environment and orientation to it.

It may well be, for instance, that some babies first recognize mother as distinct from all other persons primarily by the way in which she touches, holds, and moves them. The firmness of her grasp, the tempo and rhythm of her movement may be the important clues by which the kinesthetically minded baby recognizes her. To a baby predominantly sensitive in the auditory sphere, the sound of her voice may be an outstanding clue, and to a visually sensitive baby it may be her contours, her size, and her coloring that are most important.

It follows logically (and observations seem to support the notion) that different degrees of sensitivity in various perceptual spheres are among the factors that determine the important sources of pleasure, as well as of pain and discomfort, for the young child. One child more keenly aware of sound than other perceptions, for instance, will experience the pleasures of being fed, cuddled, and played with, in association with the sounds which occur incidental to these situations. He is more likely to be influenced by music than are most children, and sudden or loud noises·will frighten him more readily.

For the sake of clarity, this description oversimplifies the real state of affairs. Except for children with severe physical handicaps, such as blindness or deafness, all kinds of perception in combination help to define the child's experience for him. At the same time, the most characteristic components and individual flavor of his experience will vary with variously distributed sensitivities. Also, a child is not either sensitive or robust; rather, there are an infinite number of gradations in sensitivity within each child and among children. And lastly, the way in which a child uses his perceptual apparatus depends to some extent on the stimulation he receives. Ours is a visually oriented culture. Especially after the first six months or so, children's toys, the manner of their teaching, and the experiences most typically provided for them have such strong visual components that visual clues will be important in the learning of all children, even those whose natural preference would be another modality. One might put it that the experiences we typically provide for children are especially well adapted to those at least moderately sensitive in the visual sphere, and that they may impose a slightly more difficult task upon those children who spontaneously emphasize other channels of perception.

Tempo and Rhythm

It is generally true of people that some are quick and others slower in everything they do. Some are "slow but sure," others fast and precise, or fast and erratic. Most people can be said to have a characteristic rhythm to their activities, which may range from staccato to largo. Common sense, with justice, associates this characteristic with personality traits. We describe one person as "sharp as lightning," and a slower harmonious pace is often associated with good nature and warmth. Great literature, which remains one of the best storehouses of psychological wisdom, offers many examples for this popular conception; for instance, one might think of Don Quixote and of Falstaff.

A number of studies have thrown some light on tempo differences among infants, especially in regard to bodily functions such as sleep, movement, eating, digestion, and elimination.[16] There have not been systematic studies of this aspect of personality in its totality. Observed facts suggest, however, that a child's pace is likely to be fairly general, i.e., infants who eat and digest rapidly are also infants who tend to move quickly. Characteristic tempo and movement are among the things which unify most or all aspects of functioning in a given child, permeating all his behavior.

More definite statements await further research. We mention this source of variability in the behavior of young children because, if further study confirms our expectation that tempo differences characterize infants at birth and tend to remain characteristic of the individual through life, then this factor will influence the child's response to the demands we make of him. Skill in adapting techniques to the child's natural mode of functioning will make a significant difference in the amount of frustration imposed on children in the course of rearing them. In this way all aspects of personality development can be seen as related to this factor of characteristic tempo.

Bodily Resilience and Vulnerability

The younger the child, the more does his whole bodily apparatus function as one closely related unit. Respiration, circulation, the nervous sys-

[16] See Nancy Bayley, "Mental Growth in Young Children," *Yearbook National Society for the Study of Education,* Vol. 39 (II), 1940; also, Nancy Bayley, "Consistency and Variability in the Growth of Intelligence from Birth to Eighteen Years," *Journal of Genetic Psychology,* No. 75, 1949.

tem, the digestive system, and the rest have so little independence of one another that a change in one of these body systems is likely to bring on a simultaneous change in the functioning of all the others. If a baby cries, for instance, he is seen to flush (circulation), his breathing becomes shallow and more rapid (respiration), his hands become fisted, the entire body tenses (muscle tonus), and other functions are also either prevented from taking place or temporarily altered. In addition, the human child is born in a state of relatively great physiological immaturity. All his bodily functions are more vulnerable, more easily upset, than they will be after he has had a year or two in which to grow and consolidate them. Many sorts of necessary protections, such as temperature regulations, which later become automatic, self-regulating physiological mechanisms, are not established in the young baby. Thus, if the responsible adults fail to feed the child and keep him warm and to protect him from noxious influences, the child will die.

Medical observation and research have shown that this is not true in quite the same way for all infants. More important for our purpose is the fact that within the same baby some body systems may be relatively more resistant and others relatively more vulnerable. All infants, of course, may contract an infection on exposure or may acquire a digestive disorder as the result of improper feeding. Over and beyond this obvious fact, however, many babies seem to have characteristic bodily reactions to a great variety of disturbing causes. In response to an inoculation, for instance, or to a common cold or to a marked and sudden change in routine, some babies characteristically develop a fever, others a digestive disorder, others a skin irritation or a feeding or sleeping disorder. It is as though one part of the physiological apparatus, in many babies at least, is a relatively weak spot. This particular body system is the one most likely to show a reaction to any disturbance that may occur in the functioning of the entire organism. It is also this particular body system that is most vulnerable to noxious influences from the environment and hence is the channel through which physiological disturbance is most easily brought on.

While the fact that such differences exist very early in life is well established, the cause and effect of these differences are just beginning to attract scientific inquiry. This aspect of the child's development has become especially important to research workers in the field of psychosomatic medicine. In brief, it has been posited that psychological experience and personality characteristics are related to physiological traits.[17] In certain

[17] See, for example, numerous articles in *Psychosomatic Medicine*.

disease categories, adults suffering from the given physical ailment, such as arthritis, gastric ulcers, and allergies, have been found to have important personality characteristics in common. Certain kinds of personality organization have even been dubbed as the "typical diabetic" or the "typical arthritic" personality. Scientists are by no means agreed in the interpretation of these findings. The gaps in knowledge are so great that it seems wise to go no further than to acknowledge the fact that psychological experience is not isolated from bodily functioning but, on the contrary, very closely linked with it. Certain unitary principles of organization, or at least corresponding modes of functioning, exist on the physiological and on the emotional level.

It is not easy to assess the significance of different strengths and weaknesses in various body systems for personality development. This source of congenitally present variability in the behavior of infants has been included in the present analysis for the promise it holds of adding to our understanding in the future. Its present applicability to the task of aiding healthy personality development is close to nil. Two points of view, which do not contradict one another, are advanced by those engaged in studying such matters. Both relate bodily functioning to personality development.

The first of these proposes that congenitally given physiological characteristics predispose simultaneously toward the development of certain somatic illnesses rather than others and to certain kinds of personality characteristics rather than others. Such an assumption implies that if an infant shows more than ordinary skin sensitivity (as well as some other bodily characteristics, and only if there is no specific external cause to bring on the skin irritability) this is likely to mean that he will be predisposed toward developing allergies and eczema rather than other ailments. Such an infant would also, according to this speculation, be more likely to show the psychological traits typically associated with allergies. In other words, one would expect him to show the "allergic personality," whether or not he had occasion actually to develop allergies. This statement is a legitimate speculation, but as yet no empirical evidence has been collected that is sufficient to attest to the validity of such a notion or to prove it false.

The second point of view, also not scientifically established as yet, is more limited in scope but better supported by established fact. Psychoanalytic investigation has shown that as the child develops, different body zones and body systems come to be of special importance at successive developmental stages. Specific biological or physiological needs characterize each phase of development, and to a considerable degree the child's well-being and developmental progress depend upon his opportunities to satisfy these needs. Since some body systems are more vulnerable than others, this vulnerability may be thought to be of especial psychological significance at that point in the child's development at which the body system in question is of special dynamic importance. For instance, in very early life, during the phase in which the chief problem is that of developing trust, pleasures derived from sucking and other mouth activities appear to be especially important to the child. Most respiratory disturbances affect mouth functions; they interfere with easy breathing and often irritate portions of the mouth and throat. One might speculate that proneness to develop respiratory difficulties is somewhat more disturbing to the well-being of a child at this early age than later, when the child has moved on to a developmental phase in which the mouth is of less importance in the total economy of the organism.

One can also consider the possible effect of such a lifelong tendency to overreact with one part of the body upon the child's total development. The mere fact of repeated skin irritations, for instance, probably makes the skin and the sense of touch more important to the child than they would otherwise be. Whether or not normal developmental sequences are affected when certain bodily sensations are especially intense remains to be learned. Some psychological case studies of children who did experience such focusing of attention and painful experience on certain parts of the body suggest that this may occur. If a disruption, or perhaps modification, of normal developmental events due to such concentration of sensation in a certain body part exists, then this may help to explain some of the seemingly unreasonable emotional reactions that children sometimes show to illness and to medical care.

Intellectual Endowment

Child psychologists have devoted more attention to the problem of "intelligence" than to any other aspect of development, and viewpoints about it have changed with scientific advance. Prior to 1930, it was generally held by psychologists concerned with the measurement of intelligence that the degree of intellectual endowment was a fixed characteristic of the organism and that, while adverse influences might prevent a child from realizing his abilities to the full, the degree of intellectual ability a child possessed could not be altered by education or other means. Since that time important discoveries have somewhat altered these ideas.

About 1930, considerable data were amassed that seemed to show that intelligence is but one function among many that make up a living, changing personality, and that environmental influences do alter the degree of intellectual capacity.[18] One of the most convincing arguments for this point of view was the following. It had long been known that feeble-minded parents produce more feeble-minded offspring than do parents of normal intelligence. Feeble-mindedness was therefore thought to be transmitted by heredity. Experiments were then conducted which so arranged things that children of feeble-minded parents were placed in foster homes at a very early age. It was found that these children, in large proportion, made good developmental progress and, well into school age, showed no signs of mental retardation. The high frequency of mental retardation among the offspring of retarded parents therefore seemed attributable to the kind of life experience that feeble-minded parents provided for their children. Other studies appeared to indicate that the I.Q. can be raised by means of nursery school and other kinds of enriching experience.[19] It was therefore concluded that the intellectual differences between high and low economic groups are explainable on the basis of the limitations or advantages in education and other important conditions of life that necessarily accompany these groups. Some investigators went so far as to believe that mental abilities are almost entirely a function of experience, provided there is no definite damage to, or abnormality in, the nervous system.

Since 1930, scientific thinking on this matter has become more sophisticated. Psychologists no longer argue in terms of either one kind of cause or the other, but in terms of complicated interrelations among many factors. There is no doubt that barren, limiting, and in other ways unfavorable early experience can stunt intellectual growth and permanently damage mental competence, just as it can stunt physical growth and cause irrevocable damage to bone and tissue. On the other hand, there is no doubt that wide differences in intellectual ability exist—ranging from feeble-mindedness to genius—among children whose environment is neither bad enough to retard normal developmental progress nor so superior as to explain the extraordinary ability of the highly gifted. Many carefully conducted studies have shown that intellectual functioning

[18] The best summary of studies suggesting that environmental influences alter intellectual ability is to be found in the Proceedings of the 1929 White House Conference. A brief summary of this same material is also given in George Stoddard and Elizabeth Wellman, *Child Psychology,* The Macmillan Company, New York, 1934.

[19] Studies tracing in detail the effect of nursery-school attendance, and the like, have in large proportion appeared as publications in the "Monograph Series" of the Iowa Child Welfare Research Station.

(which need not be identical with intellectual capacity) changes with changes in the experience and especially in the emotional state of the person. In fact many authorities feel that it is quite false to think of intellect as apart from feelings and from personality as a whole. We begin to see that such intellectual abilities as abstract thinking, memory, and even mechanical skill have a great deal to do with a person's fears and hopes, with the degree to which he is under emotional stress, and with the ways he has devised of getting along in spite of the dissatisfactions and obstacles to fulfillment that every human being must accept.[20]

Intellectual ability, accordingly, is viewed very differently now than in 1930. Psychologists have learned enough about the conditions under which adults and children make a success of living to know that intellect as such is not as all-important as it was once thought to be. They have developed a wholesome skepticism of their instruments of measurements; they recognize that intelligence tests do not capture all that should be included in the concept of intelligence and that they barely touch upon such qualities as capacity for wisdom or creative power.

When intellectual ability is regarded as but one facet of the whole personality, its importance in the context of all else that is known about development increases, just as its importance as a single element decreases. A formulation of current thinking about intellectual differences, which is compatible with the facts presently known but which may be changed as new facts come to light, might read as follows: Children probably are born with differing potentialities for intellectual development. Some are so constituted that if their experience provides nourishment and stimulation of the right sort they can exceed the great majority in intellectual achievement. The intellectual development of the others will also depend upon their opportunities for learning but no amount of encouragement will enable them to go beyond a relatively fixed level of achievement that falls below that of the most highly talented. Not only the absolute level of attainment that a person may reach but also his particular pattern of mental functioning and the way he uses and molds his intelligence are influenced to a high degree by the influences to which he is exposed during the early years of life and to some extent by the influences which affect him throughout life. Not improbably, no human being ever realizes all his potentialities for intellectual achievement.

It is self-evident that level and kind of intellectual endowment have a significant influence upon the course of personality development. Even

[20] Rapaport, Schafer, and Gill, *Diagnostic Psychological Testing,* Vol. I (1945), Chicago Year Book Publishers, Inc., Chicago; also Vol. II (1946).

with the handicap of subnormal intelligence and the hazard of genius omitted, it would still be difficult to say "the more intellect the better" from the point of view of healthy personality development. One element that makes for adequacy in personality functioning at any age is that the person feels reasonably competent to meet the demands and exigencies that confront him. The life demands that face American children are, however, widely different. A high order of abstract intelligence may present genuine obstacles to harmonious personality development to the child of an economically underprivileged rural family whose environment may not provide scope and depth for the development of his faculties and leave him restless and dissatisfied. A child of good average endowment born into a family of scholars may fall so short of meeting the exceedingly high intellectual standards of his milieu that the development of a real sense of initiative or industry or an acceptable identity is almost impossible for him.

Adult life in our society offers an almost infinite variety of ways in which different kinds and degrees of mental ability can productively be used. If we could free ourselves from ideas about the greater desirability of certain kinds of mental ability and could provide all children with the kinds of experience and teaching they need for the optimal development of their capacities, most of the variations in degree and kind of intellect could cease to be a source of discouragement and hopeless ambition to children and parents.

Pattern of Development

Development is never an even, smooth process. All children develop more rapidly during the first year of life than they ever will again, and in general there is a slowing down in the pace of growth with increasing maturity. Most children develop in spurts, so to speak, even within this general trend. There will be rapid gains for a while, to be followed by a period during which manifest change is almost at a standstill, succeeded by more intensive developmental advancement, and so on. In some children the swings from rapid progress to near plateaus are wide, in others the phases alternate more rapidly and do not last as long. Some children characteristically show a series of minor fluctuations interspersed with an occasional major spurt, and some seem even to lose ground every once in a while. The pattern of these cyclic alternations varies from child to child. Most authorities consider this pattern of growth and development an inherent characteristic of the organism and a prime source of individual differences among children.

These facts, too often disregarded, are of importance if a general concept of personality development is to be used in evaluating the status of a given child at a given time. A child who at a particular time seems advanced over his contemporaries may be heading for a period of lesser growth, at the end of which he may conform to expectations for his age. A child who seems less mature than average may be at a point in his development just in advance of disproportionately rapid gains. A true picture of a child's developmental status can therefore seldom be obtained by a single examination, no matter how thorough this may be.[21]

Another difference in the course of development that appears to be partly congenital is the relative rate and sequence of development in different functions. For instance, during the second year of life and beyond, all children gain in motor coordination, all begin to use words and phrases, all begin to comprehend and solve simple problems involving spatial relationships, and all learn to interpret and appropriately respond to gesture, facial expressions, and other means of social communication. Some children, however, may follow a pattern somewhat as follows: Between twelve and eighteen months, there may be marked advances in the control of bodily movement but next to no gain in language development and social comprehension. Between eighteen and twenty-four months, development may shift focus, and within a month or two the child may "make up" the seeming lag in areas that facilitate communication with others, yet may not progress at all in motor skills. Other children may follow a different course. For instance, during the first half of the second year they may gain most in their ability to manipulate objects and learn the relationships among sizes and forms and weights, and next may achieve muscular control in the more skillful use of the body, deferring the major spurt in language development until the third year. Apparently, few children show relatively even developmental gains in all important spheres.

Numerous attempts have been made to correlate developmental progress in particular spheres to environmental circumstances.[22] For instance,

---

[21] Actually this statement applies more to children of less than approximately two and one-half years than it does to older ones. Also, it is true within the normal intelligence range only; both retardation and very superior endowment can often be correctly assessed by a single examination.

[22] See, for instance, Wayne Dennis, "Does Culture Appreciably Affect Patterns of Infant Behavior?" *Journal of Social Psychology,* 1940; Arnold Gesell and H. Thompson, "Learning and Growth in Identical Infant Twins: An Experimental Study by the Method of Co-twin Control," *Genetic Psychology Monograph,* No. 6, 1929; Arnold Gesell, "Relation between Maturation and Acculturation," *Archives of Neurology and Psychiatry,* No. 57, 1947; Nancy Bayley and Harold Jones, "Environmental Correlates of Mental and Motor Development: A Cumulative Study from Infancy to Six Years," *Child Development,* No. 8, 1937.

motor-coordination skills have been related to such factors as how much play space and play opportunity the children had, how many toys they owned which stimulated activities of this kind (such as wagons and tricycles), and how frequent the opportunities were for the children to have contact with somewhat older playmates whom they might try to imitate. While the opportunity for practice and the direct incentive for certain kinds of play do seem to have some influence, the relationship between the age at which children first learn to perform certain skills (thereby demonstrating their developmental maturity in that respect) and the degree of encouragement and opportunity they had is surprisingly low.

The picture that emerges from the studies may tentatively be described as follows: Children appear to have not only their own speed and rhythm of growth but also something of an inherent pattern which in part determines the sequence in which development in various areas will proceed with greater and lesser intensity. It is, of course, possible to retard a child's development in certain respects by preventing or severely restricting activities which he would otherwise perform spontaneously. However, in respect to many functions it has been found that after the restrictions were removed the children soon learned the skill in question and the artificial retardation proved a very temporary one.

For instance, in some experiments, one group of children were actively taught such skills as climbing stairs or walking, and another group of children of like age were severely limited in their opportunities for moving about freely. After the children with special training had accomplished the experimental task they were, of course, superior in ability to those who had been restricted. When the restrictions were removed from the latter group, the previously retarded group, even though its members received no special training, not only rapidly learned the skill in question (this, of course, at an age when the skill would ordinarily be developed) but after some weeks or months (depending upon the particular skill) there was no longer any difference in the ability and developmental status of the two groups.

Such facts need to be evaluated cautiously and in the context of several qualifying considerations. First, by definition, inherent developmental patterns can exist only in relation to that portion of development that is primarily maturational in nature. This includes not only bodily growth but also some aspects of intelligence and perhaps special talents, such as artistic bent. Inherent patterns of this sort cannot exist in connection with developmental processes that are primarily the result of learning, in the broadest sense of the word. The effect of such inherent developmental patterns upon the accomplishment of the various phases of personality development is therefore only indirect.

Second, the concept of inherent developmental patterns is tentative and based on incomplete knowledge of the facts. It is entirely possible that more extensive and more subtle study may bring to light relationships between components of the child's experience and the pattern of the developmental process that are not yet suspected. For the time being, the acknowledgment of some individual patterning of the course of development reinforces our conviction that human nature cannot arbitrarily be shaped and formed. Our expectations in regard to children's behavior, our ways of measuring their progress, and our methods of rearing and teaching them will be the better, the more we take our cues from the inherent lawfulness of development as we observe it, and the more we respect the intrinsic individuality of each child.

Individual Differences and Personality Development

In the analysis of personality development made in Chapter I it was assumed that behavior characteristics that most children have in common reflect, to a considerable extent, the underlying processes of personality development. It was demonstrated that typical, "average" behavior can often be understood as a manifestation of personality at its various phases of maturity. Individual differences bear a different relationship to personality theory. They are among the factors that modify not the basic changes that take place as personality grows but the various specific forms this development may assume. Particular characteristics that a child possesses on a congenital basis will influence how he will solve the conflicts that each stage of development presents, and they may also influence the relative ease or difficulty with which certain of the developmental tasks are accomplished.

It would exceed the scope of this presentation to consider each of the individual differences that have been mentioned above in its possible relationship to each developmental phase. Instead, we shall illustrate the point at issue by showing the possible relation of one among the individual differences to each of the first three phases of development described above. We hope to show that a consideration of the individual characteristics of children can enrich the more general personality theory and bring the abstract concepts closer to the living reality of child behavior.

The Sense of Trust

The sense of trust is first developed as the baby becomes aware of the world about and of himself, as he finds that comfort and relief from distress can be counted upon as he needs them, that his surroundings are reliable, predictable, and stable, and that his own sensations and movements are trustworthy clues that help him to recognize objects, obtain pleasure and relief, and generally orient himself to his existence. Among the congenital individual differences that were enumerated, perceptual sensitivity may be the one of most immediate relevance to this phase of personality development.

Sensitive infants, we have supposed, are more insistently bombarded by perceptual stimulations, they are more often and more intensively excited by sounds and sights, by touch and motion, by temperature changes and by sensations of pain than are more robust ones. These excitations are painful and disturbing only when they are more intense than the organism can tolerate. In many instances the richness of sensations and the finer distinctions of which the more sensitive infant is aware afford him a greater variety of pleasurable experience than is available to the more robust baby.

It is our speculation that for children who are especially sensitive, the trust-mistrust phase of development is especially complex and imposes more than ordinary strain upon the organism. A sense of trust cannot develop, it has been said earlier, until the child is able to recognize and to anticipate some aspects of his environment. A more sensitive baby quite likely has the advantage in regard to early awareness of things about, since he presumably responds to a higher proportion of the events surrounding him. Such acts as recognition of the mother or of the bottle or of being about to be put to sleep are probably identical with a recognition of the sensations (visual, tactile, etc.) which are aroused within the baby by the corresponding situations. However, if it is true that the world of the more sensitive baby is more complex, consisting of a greater number of different sensations, then the task of orienting himself to this world is also a more difficult one. In addition to the fact that this simplest form of orientation is made more difficult for him, the markedly sensitive baby is also more vulnerable to experience that can disturb the emerging image of the world as a safe, comforting, trustworthy place. Every time the baby is in distress, every time he needs relief and cannot get it, every time he approaches something with the expectation of pleasure and is hurt instead—on each such occasion the baby momentarily loses or is weakened in his sense of trust.

All infants, of necessity, experience some distress and pain; as a matter of fact, these experiences are an impetus to growth. The very sensitive baby, however, is one who may feel as painfully intense the events that produce only moderately strong reactions in most babies. The ringing of a telephone, the noise produced as he moves his rattle at an age when he does not yet know how to let go of it on purpose, the sunlight on his face, the excitement of a visit with the grandparents, many such ordinary events may cause him discomfort and severe fatigue. This adds to the number of occasions when he feels mildly hurt and may well mean that for him it is a bit more difficult to overcome hesitation and apprehension in the face of new experience. Incidental observation of infant behavior seems to suggest, in fact, that babies who are especially sensitive in their perception are also babies who comparatively early in life, and comparatively strongly, show apprehension and acute discomfort in response to change. Approach by an unfamiliar person, being placed in a new crib, the first spoon feeding—many such "firsts" in the baby's life are likely to be greeted with crying or other signs of distress more often by the more sensitive baby.

It should probably be mentioned, in a manner as speculative as all that has gone before, that the greater complexity of the developmental task in no way implies that it will be solved less well. Once the sensitive infant is oriented to this more bewildering world of his, he has a richer environment in which to live. There is every reason to believe that highly sensitive children acquire a sense of trust as competently and as completely as do other children.

There is good reason to believe, however, that sensitive children will be helped in acquiring a sense of trust by a different set of circumstances from that which would be most helpful to more sturdy babies. For instance, markedly sensitive babies can be protected from overstimulation. It may be that the mother might let such a baby play with toys only until he shows signs of restlessness rather than stringing them across the crib for hours at a time. Or she might rarely let him be played with by the relatives until he shows by his behavior that such an experience is no longer upsetting to him. Or she might reduce household noises while the baby sleeps, even though most infants can readily sleep amid confusion. The robust baby often has intensely pleasurable experience, and hence experience likely to enhance a sense of trust, when played with actively by being jiggled, talked to, tickled, and the like. Many sensitive babies can best obtain the same kind and degree of pleasure if they are held gently, or even merely spoken to, patted, or sung to.

The fact is that most mothers recognize individual differences of this kind in their children and modify their actions with them in just such ways as have been mentioned. They thus do the very thing needed to help their babies acquire a basic sense of trust. It merely remains for us to understand this as a constructive mode of action that bears a direct relationship to a fundamental aspect of personality development.

The Sense of Autonomy

Once the first crucial developmental conflict has, in principle, been solved, the baby knows of himself as distinct from other persons and from objects. When he has thus learned a good deal about his most immediate surroundings, he will begin to feel himself as a person in his own right, someone capable of acting on his own impulse and purpose, someone capable of choosing between opposing suggestion and command and following directions, someone that can himself have an influence on what happens to him rather than being altogether dependent on the dictates of other people and of circumstance. The feelings of adequacy and of well-being in later life depend upon the development and maintenance of a sense of autonomy. Feelings of self-worth and of counting for something in this world are essential aspects of healthy personality functioning at any age.

The difficulty in developing such a sense of self lies in the great number of obstacles to freedom of action that actually exist. The child somewhere in the age range from eighteen to forty months literally does not know what he can do and what he cannot do. This is true of even simple bodily activities. He has to learn which objects are too heavy for him to lift, which fences too high to climb, which shelves too high to reach, which games too difficult for him to play. Even more important, he must learn what adults will allow him to do and what will be frowned upon, punished, or prevented. Whenever he becomes aware of the limits to his self-determination, his belief in himself is somewhat shaken, and he experiences feelings of doubt in his own strength or of shame and embarrassment at having been found at fault. It is necessary that there should be a good balance between experiences where he may have the satisfaction of independent action and experiences that teach him the necessary limits to freedom. Too few occasions to exercise independence will lead to self-doubt and to feelings of inadequacy; too few limiting experiences will make it impossible for the child to carry out the purposes of his own choosing for lack of appreciation of what can and what cannot be done.

Most of the sources of difference in reactions and behavior tendencies of children will contribute to the particular way in which a given child will work through this dilemma. The difference that consists of stronger or lesser impetus to bodily activity furnishes a good example.

It has been said above that some children experience much stronger impulses toward movement and expend much more energy of an active, outwardly directed sort. These are the youngsters who, once they have learned to walk or creep, are on the move all the time. They are the youngsters who will not stay contentedly in their high chairs or play pens, who will object to the use of sleeping bags that confine motion, and who "get into everything." One might say that these children seem to have a stronger need for autonomy, or at least for the kind of activity that leads to autonomy, than do children who are only moderately active. We speculate, therefore—supported by observations and by case-study material—that the developmental phase that involves autonomy is an especially difficult one for children who are very active, as well as for those at the other extreme, those who are less active than most. The very active child needs especially patient help in realizing and accepting the necessary limitations; the quiet child needs special encouragement and incentive to act on his own.

For very active youngsters (and their parents as well) this developmental phase makes for a great amount of frustrating experience. The child wants to run all over the room but has to stay in the high chair to finish his meal. He wants to climb up to the top shelf and get at the cookie jar but he is too small and awkward to do so; yet handing him a cookie jar may offend him all the more. He shows a great urge to do things by himself, from buttoning his coat to crossing the street, and at every turn he encounters either his own weakness or the superior strength of the adult to thwart his purpose and often to enrage him. Because his need for activity propels him into more enterprises than other children, he has more occasion to get into trouble; that is, to feel helpless anger or discouragement at failure. Thus, for such a child there is a difference in life experiences in terms of the sheer frequency of situations that cannot be other than frustrating. It requires inventiveness and humor on the parents' part to find enough scope for the child's active exploration and yet to keep him out of harm's way.

Moreover, children who are especially active tend to feel as restraint or as frustration circumstances which need not have that meaning to less active ones. Holding still while being dressed or at the table, having to wait for a promised outing—such little situations that keep the child from doing as he wants to do at that very moment can be felt by him as frustrating interference, whereas most children would feel them less intensively or not at all. It is clear that a strong need for self-initiated action is a healthy basis for acquiring a strong sense of autonomy, but it brings with it many obstacles and difficulties in establishing a secure feeling of when and how it can be exercised.

The child who enjoys playing for long periods of time in more or less the same spot, who becomes absorbed in watching things as much as in doing them, whose energy seems to be directed relatively more to quiet pursuits that may require concentration and effort but not physical motion, has his own and different way of establishing a sense of self-determination. Rather than trying his strength to the limit and straining at the bit, he is likely to exercise determination by resisting pressure that is put upon him. Such a child may stubbornly refuse the food he is given just because he is told to eat it now; he may insist on wearing his coat indoors even to his own discomfort, in order to assert his will. Such children may have fewer opportunities to experience the pleasure of self-direction, but also fewer occasions to be hurt at the limitations to their freedom. The parents' tact in interesting such children in doing things by themselves and letting them feel the glow of such accomplishment, and in understanding the stubborn willfulness so often seen in youngsters of this age, will be a significant factor in helping relatively inactive children to resolve, in their own quiet way, the task of achieving a real sense of self-determination.

The Sense of Initiative

The child, having developed a sense of confidence and of his own strength, is ready to direct his energies to the development of what has been called a "sense of initiative." With wide variation in the actual age at which this aspect of personality functioning becomes crucial, we expect it to occur approximately within the age range of three and six years.

By that time, personality has become rather complex. This is the developmental period during which the child goes beyond the sense of himself as a person in his own right to the experience of himself as someone who can initiate and execute enterprises. He changes from being primarily interested in whether or not he can do things by himself to being primarily interested in the activities themselves. It is an age when planning, imagining, purposive striving for goals, and interests that go beyond the immediate situation become important.

A firm sense of initiative may be threatened by all the experiences that prove to the child that his plans are futile, that he cannot do what he sets out to do, or, most important perhaps, that his wishes, plans, and actions are not approved by the adults who are important to him. Inevitably, a air share of the projects planned by a four-year-old violate the social customs and rules of behavior that he must learn. His comprehension is now sufficiently advanced so that he can have a guilty conscience over acts and desires, whether he has actually done them or merely contemplated them. Phantasy now plays a large role in his life. He uses his imagination to extend the range of his experience by imagining himself in situations that fascinate him, and by imaginative planning of his play. He also tends to use phantasy to make up for the shortcomings in his real experience. The things impossible to him to be and do he can imagine, and the punishment that he expects for real or thought-of activities he can mete out to himself in phantasy.

At these ages the child's experience is so diversified that every one of the individual differences that have been mentioned plays a definite role in determining just how this process of becoming an activator will take place. The activity level clearly has a bearing on how much the child will be impelled to carry out his interests in real action and, therefore, on how often he is likely to encounter the experiences of real success and of real failure. Perceptual sensitivity, there is reason to believe, is related to the readiness with which a child phantasies, and also to the vividness which his imagination has for him.

In order to bring yet another kind of individual difference into the picture, we shall speculate about the ways in which different rates and patterns of development can alter the process by which a sense of initiative is developed. In all phases of development it undoubtedly makes a difference how fast the child is growing, how "advanced" he is in comparison with his age mates. For children in the three-to-six-year age range, this factor appears to have special psychological significance. In making plans and carrying them out, an important measure of success is whether the child can accomplish as well as the next one. A four-year-old may draw an airplane to his entire satisfaction, until he sees a plan drawn by his five-year-old brother that is obviously better. No amount of praise for his effort will make him feel again that he succeeded at this task. The initiative phase is characterized by competitiveness, and children so greatly need to find some standards to define success and failure that they will develop rivalry with one another even if attempts are made to discourage this.

A child who develops rapidly, especially in bodily growth and manual dexterity, which lead to tangible superiority, is encouraged to feel capable in whatever he undertakes to do. Such a sense of adequacy is of course helpful in the development of initiative, but it may also lead to complications. For it is characteristic of children so young to develop ambitions far beyond their skills. In imagination, certainly, and to some extent in action, they try to compete not only with older children but also with adults. The youngster whose relatively accelerated developmental rate leads him to attempt more and more difficult tasks may therefore find it especially difficult to recognize and accept himself as the small child he really is.

Children whose developmental pace is on the slow side probably encounter more serious difficulties in establishing a firm sense of initiative. The four-year-old a bit smaller than his contemporaries, or less apt in his movements, or less able to express himself in words or one who has all these differences in combination, has the same need to explore and to exploit as do his friends. At every turn, however, he sees himself excelled. Discouraged from really attempting, he can easily develop an image of himself as a weak person who cannot hope to accomplish his goals or as someone who would do better not to strive too hard, since he will experience only pain.

Depending on many other circumstances, such youngsters, unless given understanding help, may react in a variety of disadvantageous ways. For instance, they may develop with such an image of themselves that they miss much of the fun and exhilaration of even the accomplishments well within their range. Or they may try to make up for the disappointments of real life by phantasy activities of more than ordinary intensity. In any case, they must probably apply more energy than the children who develop more rapidly, and they probably require more help in resolving the conflict between the desire for very great power of action and the feeling of futility and guilt. Quite frequently one sees children, at a later age, who are notably bright and able yet seem to feel and act as though they dared not meet their contemporaries on equal terms. In some cases, these are children who combine a relatively slow developmental pace with good endowment but failed to achieve a real sense of initiative at a time when they felt themselves at a disadvantage.

Fortunately, there are almost as many ways of achieving a sense of initiative as there are kinds of children. Once again, the responsible adults can help the child to find the methods that will work for him, based on an understanding of what it is the child is trying to accomplish. Almost always it is possible to find some spheres of activity in which a child can succeed, though he may be at a disadvantage in respect to other things. For instance, providing a child who cannot ride a tricycle with blocks and crayons and paint or providing the one who is not yet interested in stories or in conversations with picture puzzles and the chance for free play with other children can go a long way toward giving children a sense of initiative on the strength of activities that suit his nature.

When differences in the development of children are considered, it is easy to think of them in terms of "better" or "worse," desirable or undesirable. Such differences to which a value is attached do, of course, exist. It is better to have a strong physical constitution and to be in good health than to be physically vulnerable or handicapped. It is more desirable to have high intellectual endowment than to be limited or retarded mentally. In this chapter, however, we have discussed differences that do not carry such significance. It is every bit as normal to be active and outgoing as it is to be contemplative and quiet. It is no more desirable to develop in rapid spurts with pauses in between than to develop at a slower and relatively even pace. The world would be a very dull place if all of us had the same kinds and degrees of sensitivity.

In our society we emphasize the dignity and individuality of each human being, yet in our thinking about children we tend to expect the same of each and are easily led to believe that the same methods of training and education will bring the same results for all. However meager the knowledge of individual differences, it is sufficient to enable us to declare that children will become healthy in personality only as adults learn that children are not alike, that they differ in their needs and must be treated accordingly.

✦ III ✦

The Influence of
Physical Limitations

IN addition to varying in constitutional make-up, children also differ from one another in physical health and in the extent to which they are free from crippling or disabling conditions. Some children have few, if any, obvious disabilities, and some are so severely limited by disease or disorder or crippling condition that they are commonly labeled "handicapped." The implied dichotomy is not justified, however. There is probably no child who is up to par in every respect and few who are totally disabled. What exists in fact is a wide range of capacities and abilities. Each child, if measured at a given time, would have a different combination of ratings with respect to the various attributes. Some children, unfortunately, would rate very low in certain capacities. Nevertheless, there is no exact line separating the normal from the handicapped, and there is much variation both within and among children with respect to abilities and disabilities.

Recognition of these facts should do much to destroy the myth that children suffering from physical limitations or limitations in mental capacity are a group apart, a peculiar kind of creature with thoughts and feelings and desires that are different from those of other people. Instead of being regarded as handicapped children (that is, a special breed of children), they should be looked on as children who have handicaps or limitations of a specific kind and degree as one of their characteristics.

The question for consideration in the present analysis, however, is not whether children who suffer from more than usually severe physical or mental limitations are different from others in personality make-up but whether the presence of these limitations makes the course of healthy personality development unusually difficult. If so, to what is the difficulty to be attributed? Is it a natural concomitant of the affliction itself? Do interpersonal and social factors play a part? What may be done to make matters better?

It seems clear that to some extent the answers to these questions depend upon the degree and kind of limitation under consideration. In a few children, the brain pathology or the mental defect is so extreme as to make personality development of more than the most limited kind impossible. In some, the limitations are so slight or of such a character (tone deafness, for example, or a peculiarity of gait) that whether they affect personality development or not is almost wholly incidental. For the most part, however, it seems undeniable (though scientific demonstration is largely lacking) that, in one way or another, a deviation sufficient to be labeled a marked physical handicap is likely to be an impediment to personality development as well.

In some children, the nature of the handicap may dictate some of the ways in which health of personality will be hard to achieve. For example, a child who suffers from spastic paralysis will undoubtedly have difficulty in developing trust in the functioning of his own body, and one who is confined to bed with a chronic illness is likely to encounter especial difficulty at adolescence when the problem of determining his identity is acute. For many, however, it is not the handicap itself but the reaction to the handicap of the people who are significant to him emotionally that counts for most.

Except in a few extreme instances, no real separation between the effect of the handicap and the effect of personal and social factors on personality development can be made, for the two sets of influences are inextricably intertwined. In the following analysis we shall review briefly the general findings about the effects of physical factors and their concomitants on personality development and functioning. Next, certain specific disabilities that occur rather frequently or that have aroused public concern will be discussed, with particular reference to their bearing on health of personality. Finally, some of the variations in the psychological reactions of children to chronic illness or other disabling conditions will be described, and some suggestions will be made for helping the children deal with their disabilities.

Some General Considerations

There is a popular impression that for adequate functioning of personality good physical health is required. Sickness, it is commonly supposed, makes for irritability or discouragement or other feelings that handicap the individual in dealing with others and in conducting his affairs well. Research workers who have closely watched the course of children's physical and intellectual development say that childhood illnesses are often reflected in retardation in developmental progress. Psychiatrists say that during illness children often regress to earlier phases of development. Accordingly, although there are few studies dealing with this exact question, it seems probable that serious illness and chronic illness may handicap personality development unless special care is taken to counteract the adverse effects.

A sudden illness is probably a blow to the sense of trust that the outside world and one's own body are dependable. Frightening accidents must have a similar effect, especially on a child too young to understand clearly what has happened. This would be particularly true if the illness or accident involved much pain, or if the child were an unusually sensitive one. The care and attention an ill child receives may, however, be compensating factors. Many young children are "good" and happy during illness and convalescence, perhaps because the attention they receive assures them that they are well loved.

Illness is likely to interfere in numerous ways, too, with the emergence and the sustaining of a sense of autonomy. For a young child many of the experiences through which the sense of being a person in his own right is attained are interfered with by illness. The pleasures of exploring and mastering may have to be confined to what can be done in bed. Prohibitions are probably more numerous; there are more things that have to be done for the child. This state of affairs is particularly hard on an active child, as parents will attest.

To children who are struggling to become autonomous and to older ones who are not particularly secure in this sense, the rules and regulations of the sickroom are hard to endure. If they are too strictly and needlessly enforced, especially in an illness that lasts a long time, the young child may give up the struggle and lapse into too much dependency. The older one who is not very sure of his status may develop doubt that, as a sickly creature, he amounts to much.

So it is with the other feelings about the self. Illness strikes hardest at those components of the personality that are in the making but may have bad effects upon those that have already been fairly well achieved. For example, children from four to six are especially likely to feel guilty about being ill, to feel that they must have done something terribly wrong to be so punished. Children six to twelve are most affected by the curbs that illness may put upon their desire to learn and to achieve. Adolescents are most disturbed because illness adds to the difficulties of knowing what kind of person they are and what the future holds in store.

Less clear than the effects of illness are the effects of poor nourishment and low vitality. Research workers in the field of diet have shown that undernutrition and malnourishment result in listlessness and apathy, and that malnutrition in early life leads to lasting physical defects. More specifically, emotional disturbances have been reported in children suffering from marked deficiency of Vitamin B. A study of young men under starvation conditions revealed that undernutrition affects every organ and function and profoundly influences emotional states.

In the absence of scientific studies, we may speculate that low vitality may be handicapping to all the components of a healthy personality. Trust that "all's right with the world" is certainly to some extent a matter of physical well-being. In the extreme, for one near to starvation, it must be extremely difficult to maintain trust. The listlessness and discouraged attitudes of peoples in the postwar period have been attributed in considerable part to lack of food and to chronic ill health.

Children who are lacking in energy probably have a hard time asserting themselves, either against their parents in the autonomy period or in competition with children later. They may easily develop feelings of inferiority through not having the stamina to be successful in their studies, in sports, or on the job. Adolescence may bring to such children apathy and indecision and overwhelming doubt that they will ever amount to much. With such a start, the later problems of personality development are unlikely to be well met.

The picture is not always as gloomy as this, of course. With encouragement and sustaining affection from parents and other adults, children who are handicapped by low vitality may find ways to inner security that are not of the common run. The children whose personality development is threatened chiefly by this condition are probably those who live in areas in which most of the adults, too, are undernourished and "worn down." Though it seems doubtful that, as parents, such people can give e·notional support to their children in the later stages of development, .hey may be adequately affectionate and, through very lack of energy, may aid them in their development as young children by putting little in the way of their attempts to be independent.

Children who suffer from physical handicaps or long-continued chronic illness have other impediments to the development of a healthy personality. Some of these are specific to the defect or disorder. For example, a child with impaired hearing is often criticized for being slow, inattentive, and vague, while actually he is suffering from a disorder of communication, an important means to personality growth. Blind children and those who have severe impairment of vision are somewhat similarly deprived.

Since their disability is clear for all to see and is one for which people usually have sympathy, their chief difficulty in personality development arises out of their almost necessary overdependency on adults. Children with cerebral palsy have a very different situation, for the brain injury itself may make for emotional disorders.

There are, however, so many ways in which physical disabilities and chronic illnesses are alike in their hazards for personality growth that specialists are inclined to stress the similarities instead of the differences. Without attempting to list all the possibilities, we may note a few of the most important. And we should add, at the outset, that not all "handicapped" children are so adversely affected. In fact, many of them develop unusually well.

First, children who are disabled are likely to suffer from loss of social contacts, decrease in outlet for their pent-up emotions in physical activity, deprivation or serious decrease in opportunity to learn to live in child-life situations, and from feelings of dependency and rejection—self-rejection, rejection by their peers, by their parents, and by the wider social community.

Second, disabling conditions and chronic illnesses may have adverse effects upon parents' feelings about their children and their behavior toward them. Some parents, for instance, may be oversolicitous, adding to the children's difficulties by their babying. Others may try to force children beyond their capacities and so add to their feelings of inferiority. Some parents may feel so personally inferior at having physically disabled children that they may push them aside or treat them coldly.

Third, the disabling condition, especially if it develops after early childhood, is likely to affect the child's feeling about himself. Consciously or unconsciously, the child may feel that he is to blame for the condition, that it is a punishment for bad deeds, that it is a sign that his parents do not love him, or that it constitutes a claim upon them because it was they who were at fault. For these and other reasons, the disabling condition may contribute to all the negative aspects of personality development—to mistrust, self-doubt, feelings of inferiority, and the rest.

These latter two kinds of consequences of handicapping conditions are often related. A recent study of the social and emotional adjustment of children following upon the "blue baby" operation indicates that the youngsters who had difficulty in entering into normal activities were the ones whose parents had been (and probably still were) either oversolicitous or "unfeeling" in their attitudes. Fortunately, most of the parents had maintained a middle course. Their children made an amazingly rapid social recovery, indicating, probably, that in spite of a severe physical limitation personality development may be normal.

In all this there is need for much more research. Certainly disabling physical conditions do not make normal personality development impossible. Almost as certainly they may interfere with that development and make the full utilization of capacities difficult. An important research task is to discover the means by which parents and professional workers can help children to function well in spite of physical disabilities.

Aiding the Child Who Is Handicapped

Too often, people, in their earnest efforts to help children who have marked limitations, overlook the importance of the kind of adjustment sought. There is a vast difference between passive, hopeless, and defeated acceptance, on the one hand, and the capacity to find peace of mind and satisfaction in life, on the other. Yet passive acceptance is all too often foisted upon children who have suffered deprivations resulting from physical or mental deficiencies, and a great deal of the "lack of motivation or drive" attributed to them is due to its slow infiltration. If these young people are to live adequate lives with attendant satisfactions, the single most important "stock-in-trade" they can have is their own capacity to master their environment. Without this, they feel themselves victims and ultimately either give up the battle for satisfaction or seek to punish the world with antisocial behavior.

One of the frequent correlates of maladjustment is the state of being dependent. Dependency of this kind is a psychological limitation resulting from the feeling that one cannot control or deal with the environment and must rely upon someone else to do it for one; it is caused by a disability being superimposed upon the normal dependency of childhood. If disabled children are given an opportunity to test their own abilities, they are likely to achieve a realistic appraisal of what these abilities are, and so eventually are able to measure their efforts to master their environment in realistic terms. When this occurs they are likely to attain self-realization because they are striving for an attainable goal.

By active participation in the life of the home and in play with contemporaries the disabled child discovers how to handle himself. Parents are not infrequently inclined to overlimit such a child's active participation because they fear he will not do well and will become discouraged. While this may occasionally occur, far more often the child is able to exceed his parents' expectations and, with their encouragement and support, will try and try again.

The right to try is God-given, and no child should be discouraged from it even though he may fail. When he does fail and the adult sees that it is due to actual limitations, he can show the child that he can accomplish some particular task by going about it in another way. But first and foremost the child should have ample opportunity to try his way and learn how to cut the task to the dimensions of his capacity. Only in this way can independence and initiative develop.

Overprotection of children with limitations is also likely to engender in them the feeling that their limitations excuse them from all responsibility. This leads to the development of individuals who look upon their disability as an alibi for not even attempting to participate in life. Attitudes like this are fostered by parents and sometimes by teachers who say, "Don't bother with it, Johnny. You know you can't walk that far, and you can't carry such a load."

Still another matter that parents often forget and that is of great importance to the physically limited child is the understanding that each individual can make a contribution that is more or less unique to himself. No one can do everything he attempts. Someone may be better at one thing or another. The child with a limitation in the movement of his hands may be able to do things with his head or with his feet that someone else cannot do as well. He will be able to make his contribution in his own way.

The key to healthy development of personality is a sense of security. This is why it has been so often emphasized that parents' most important contribution is to help their children to feel that they are genuinely loved and wanted. All children need this assurance; children with physical limitations need it in an especially high degree.

An incapacitated or chronically sick child has a deep effect on any parent, and so a strain is often imposed on the parent-child relationship. Acceptance of the disability on a realistic basis can be, and often is, achieved, and then the relationship between the parents and the disabled child is as healthy as with a physically normal child.

But parents do not always respond rationally to the painful fact of having a chronically sick or markedly limited child. Frequently they feel personally injured and attacked by fate, or they feel as though the fact that they had a defective child reveals a shameful weakness in themselves. There are few mothers who do not feel at least somewhat responsible for a child's congenital defect or birth injury, or even for a chronic disease, operation, or accident leading to invalidism. Some can hardly disguise their resentment and act it out in punishing attitudes. Often they reveal their feelings through the rigidity with which they hold their children to a restricting diet or painful medical schedule. Others, in their attempt to cope with these tendencies, lean over backward, sacrificing their lives completely, to the detriment of both the patient and other members of the family.

These unfortunate attitudes on the part of parents are in part reflections of the attitudes of the community in general. To the extent that this is true, revision of parents' attitudes requires community change.

In all ages, people have been inclined to sort out and stigmatize the deviant. Even the intellectually superior or those especially talented in an art form are tagged with such labels as "genius" or "master," and not without derogation, for "geniuses" and "masters" are often assumed to be "eccentric" and so, in a sense, inferior to "us ordinary mortals." Prejudice of this kind is not just an accident, nor does it occur only in an occasional individual who lacks broad understanding of others. Rather, it is a device by which man seeks so to manipulate his social milieu as to make of himself a preferred individual; this he does in part by pointing out the real or imagined limitations of others. The blind, the lame, the halt are readily singled out for such purpose. This is a matter of much consequence, and adequate means must be found to cope with it if children who must live with limitations are to have a fair chance to develop sound personalities.

Several additional aspects of social reactions to physical and mental disabilities deserve attention. Curiosity is common and no more surprising than if it were directed toward a foreigner wearing unusual clothes. Oversolicitousness helps to appease the conscience of those who harbor deep rejection; basically, it may be an attempt to make up for unconscious hostility. Many feel "uneasy" in the presence of disabled persons— whether because they fear the different and poorly understood, or because of uncertainty as to how to behave without seeming to patronize. Some are revolted by such disfigurements as cleft palate and lip, burn scars, and extensive facial hemangiomas.

Some physically limiting conditions are specially stigmatized. Among these are epilepsy and cerebral palsy. From antiquity, convulsive seizures have been associated with possession by devils. Few people continue to believe this, but seizures still seem to be deeply repellent to many. This situation is further complicated by a general belief that the condition is evidence of a tainted family stock and that repeated convulsions inevitably lead to mental deterioration. Even though therapy is effective in about four-fifths of the cases, the general public and professional groups continue to be so skeptical that comparatively few epileptic children have been able to obtain treatment. Cerebral palsy, too, is regarded as evidence of a family taint, so much so that children suffering from this affliction may be hidden away in order that the family may avoid being shamed.

Parental and community attitudes toward children who are handicapped are thus closely related, and both children and their families react in large measure according to community expectations. Accordingly, the child, his family, and the community need reorientation and education simultaneously. Thus, services directed toward establishing healthy parental and community attitudes must accompany those directed toward the social and emotional adjustment of the disabled individual if the disabled child is to accept his limitations, make full use of his assets, and relate to society in a mature and realistic way.

Some Specific Handicapping Conditions

For the most part, we have said, handicapping physical or mental conditions, whatever their nature, impose rather similar strains on the healthy development of personality. The feelings of the parents about the disability, and the attitudes of the community toward persons who are afflicted are important elements in that most important factor, how the child feels about himself. In these respects there is much individual variation, with the result that some children develop well in personality despite serious physical or mental handicaps, while others find the achievement of emotional well-being very difficult.

Despite the similarities, there are, however, some specifics in the various diseases and defects that are useful for people who would aid these children to know about. It is obviously impossible to describe here all or even most of the handicapping conditions or to say much about any one of them. Therefore, a few of those that have aroused widespread public or scientific interest have been selected for description, comments about them having been prepared for the Conference by authorities in the field. They are presented here to illustrate the kind and amount of variation that disabling conditions involve and to emphasize that, in spite of their differences, handicaps have much in common, so far as their effect on children's lives is concerned.

Epilepsy

Epilepsy is a disorder that illustrates unusually well that the ill effects on personality development are attributable to a combination of physical, interpersonal, and social factors. Physically, the disorder handicaps by reason of the intermittent and unpredictable seizures. This in itself might make the establishment of a sense of trust in the workings of one's own body difficult and might make it more than usually hard for the individual to feel confident about himself and his abilities. These natural struggles of the developing personality are greatly accentuated, however, if the attitudes of the people whose affection and support the growing child needs are tinged with guilt and unconscious anxiety.

These people who are so important to the child are likely to share the widespread belief that epilepsy is evidence of tainted family stock and that repeated convulsions inevitably lead to mental deterioration and mental illness. Such ideas almost necessarily make parents ashamed, fearful, and guiltily protective, while they incline others to shun the afflicted one or at least to treat him as a child who is very different from others and not to be relied upon. In consequence, the child is likely to feel, in some vague way, that he is at fault, that he is atoning for some unnamed crime of his own or of his ancestors. Even if he escapes such guilt feelings, the reality situation of school and playground is likely to be such that he has less than the usual opportunity to achieve and succeed. Feelings of inferiority and inadequacy are almost inevitable consequences of the way he is treated, and the normal struggle to acquire a clear sense of identity (a sense of being on his way toward goals of his own choosing) is complicated both by these attitudes and by the handicapping condition itself.

Actually, there is little basis in fact for these adverse attitudes on the part of parents and the public. While the causes of epilepsy are still largely unknown, it seems fairly well established that it is not hereditary, and certainly not in the sense of being attributable to past misdeeds of family members. Moreover, mental deterioration is not a necessary consequence of continued seizures nor does it regularly or even very frequently accompany the disorder. As to mental deficiency, children with epilepsy run the usual gamut from idiocy to genius, and they are only a little more likely than other children to be underendowed.

Mental defect, when it is present, may compromise the patient's future more than the seizures. One of several conditions may be responsible for the lack of normal intelligence. In some children, the defect is only coincidental, the result of poor constitutional endowment or of congenital maldevelopment of the brain. It may derive from brain damage acquired at birth or may be the result of some early infection. In other children, frequently repeated and severe convulsions may cause organic brain damage, or a profound dysrhythmia of epilepsy may prevent intellectual growth. In comparison with constitutional and pathological factors, chronic convulsions are, however, relatively unimportant as causes of mental defect. In still other youngsters, a temporary and reversible mental retardation may result from the use of excessive medication or from the psychological and social deprivations that have been experienced.

The adverse attitudes and ideas about epilepsy are especially unfortunate because, realistically, epilepsy is a more hopeful disorder than most of the other handicapping conditions of childhood that involve the central nervous system. This is because the disorder in at least two-thirds of the patients is due not to structural damage but to an altered function or physiology of nerve cells. In addition, the chances of improvement or even of complete relief from seizures have greatly improved in recent years. The present drug armamentarium includes phenobarbital, dilantin, mesantoin, tridione, paradione, and phenurone, in addition to auxiliary substances. With the skilled use of medical and surgical therapy now available, the large majority of patients can be relieved of most of their seizures, and many can be permanently aided.

From the standpoint of physical health, then, epilepsy is a major problem that can be solved effectively and economically if the needed medical facilities are made available all over the country. For health of personality, however, it must be recognized that the handicap of epilepsy is social as well as physical. Medical agencies that carry on treatment programs emphasize that the beneficent results of elimination or reduction of the seizures are lost if the individual cannot return to school, is subjected to the frustrations arising out of overprotection or other adverse attitudes at home, is isolated from normal social contacts and play opportunities, and cannot return to work or be trained for a job. They find that parents are insufficiently informed about how epileptic children should be handled and that they are more prone to guilt feelings than parents of children who are handicapped in other ways. They see that these children are likely to be deprived of adequate schooling and that, as young people and adults, they are likely to be discriminated against on a job.

In view of all this, it is clear that the lack of health of personality that often accompanies epilepsy is only to a slight extent a necessary consequence of the disorder itself.

Cerebral Palsy

In contrast to epilepsy, cerebral palsy is representative of a kind of physical defect which may by its very nature produce personality deviations, since it involves specific brain injury. Even so, it is recognized by all authorities that much of the difficulty children who suffer from this disorder encounter is attributable to parents' anxieties and community attitudes of much the same kind as those that adversely affect children who suffer from epilepsy.

Cerebral palsy is a term used to designate any paralysis, weakness, incoordination, or functional aberration of the motor system resulting from brain pathology. It is thus distinguished from spinal palsy, which is a motor involvement due to degeneration or injuries to the spinal cord by traumas such as bullet wounds, by infections such as poliomyelitis, or by developmental defects such as spina bifida. It is also distinguished from peripheral palsy caused by injury to a motor nerve, for example by severance of the nerve or by certain poisonings, notably arsenic or lead.

Factors incident to labor and birth are first in importance in the production of cerebral palsy, with prenatal factors second in importance, and postnatal third. Various types of specific causes include trauma, infection, asphyxia, developmental defects, and several other anatomic and physiologic disturbances in the brain.

Since the brain is the seat not only of muscular control but also of the emotions, the sensations, intelligence, and behavior control, as well as many other functions, it is obvious that injury to this organ may result in a multiplicity of symptoms, depending on the location and degree of involvement. It is thus possible for brain injury to result in paralysis, convulsions, mental deficiency, emotional and behavior abnormalities, and sensory defects, such as loss of hearing, vision, or touch. Sometimes a child suffering from cerebral palsy has only one of these defects; more frequently he has several of them, although generally one type of symptom predominates. By definition he must have a motor defect, such as paralysis, weakness, or incoordination. Whether he has any of the other defects depends on the areas of the brain involved.

There is generally little association between the degree of physical and mental involvement in cerebral palsy. In some children the mental defect predominates; in others, the physical defect. In the latter case, a child may have excellent mentality and yet, because of his physical handicaps, may look and act like a mental defective. Actually, somewhat more than half of the individuals with cerebral palsy have an intelligence quotient of 70 or above.

As a result of the restrictive nature of their handicaps and of the way they are regarded by the rest of the community, children with any kind of motor crippling are likely to have emotional and behavior problems as secondary characteristics of the ailment. In the case of the cerebral palsied, however, there may also be primary emotional problems because of the specific brain injury. Nevertheless, even in such cases children will develop more or less well, depending on how they are handled by those who have them in charge. Since many of these children are avoided and held in derision by their age-mates and neighbors, since parents frequently feel ashamed of them and try to hide them away, putting them in institutions for the feeble-minded regardless of mental capacity, it is little wonder that many of them develop more poorly than their physical incapacity would imply. Under the best of conditions of treatment and training, few of these children can attain normality in speech, gait, and other skills. Many of them, however, can be greatly aided by careful educational measures, especially if these are conducted with due attention to children's and parents' feelings and desires. It is a hopeful development that parents of handicapped children are organizing for discussion and action, for these children's best hope lies in their needs being understood.

Visual Defects

In contrast to epilepsy and cerebral palsy, disorders of sight and hearing imply no involvement of the brain. Nevertheless, they, too, may put impediments in the way of children's healthy personality development, not only because of the natural limitations to development they impose but also because of their probable social and emotional concomitants.

Children with partial visual impairment react to their handicap with the same mechanisms as children with other types of physical disability. The visual defect does not directly affect personality development except in case of total blindness. There the factor of dependency seems to influence to some extent the child's over-all personality adjustment. Although emotional problems among children with visual defects have frequently been observed, examination usually indicates that the child is reacting to many factors in his total situation (e.g., his medical treatment, his parents' attitudes toward his handicap, the attitude of his social group, the community resources provided for his education and training) as well as to his actual visual loss.

In order really to know how visual defects influence personality development, much scientific research is needed. The following observations from clinical experience should be regarded as impressions rather than valid conclusions.

The emotional reactions to visual loss may be divided into the following categories for purpose of discussion: reactions to partial loss of vision, reactions to cosmetic defects, reactions to chronic and progressive disease, and reactions to blindness.

Partial visual loss includes myopia, hyperopia, and refractive errors that make it difficult for the child to compete with children of normal vision. Some of these children show little reaction to their loss, while others fail in school, show nervous strain through overactivity and irritability, or become passive or withdrawn. The latter are usually the children whose vision is low enough for them to be considered candidates for specialized training, such as sight-conservation classes. Some show resistance to this specialized type of education because it makes them "different." As they grow older and are ready to leave school they may express resentment at the lack of facilities for vocational guidance and suitable job training for placements within their abilities.

The cosmetic defects to be considered are chiefly strabismus and enucleations.

Children with strabismus react fairly directly to the external pressures which their defect causes. The defect sets the child apart from his peers; their attitude toward him may create problems because his feelings of security are involved. Lack of inner security may stimulate the withdrawing or the aggressive type of behavior that is also seen in children with other obvious and apparent physical defects. Personality development may also be hampered because the child blames the defect for what are really normal anxieties of emotional growth. This reaction has been particularly observed in adolescents.

The effect of an enucleation on personality development is influenced by many factors—cause, age, sex, parental attitudes, etc.—with the result that some children appear to have little or no reaction to the loss of an eye, while in others there is marked personality change. The psychological significance of the eye undoubtedly has bearing on the loss of this important organ, but there has been little study of this important topic.

In chronic and progressive diseases of the eye which accompany general systemic diseases (uveitis, retinitis pigmentosa, diabetic retinitis, for example) there may be gross decrease in vision. This may create great anxiety in the patient and serious emotional responses, some of them associated with true depression. However, the complicating factors of the accompanying illness, such as diabetes, which carries a threat to life itself, are significant in the ability of these young people to develop maturely. The quality of the will to live is centered in their attitude toward the disease, which in turn affects their response to their visual loss.

Reactions to blindness are partially dependent upon whether the blind-

ness is congenital or acquired, on its cause, on the age at onset, as well
as the social influences surrounding the child.

In children congenitally blind and in those who become blind shortly
after birth, the handicap is one that creates deep and prolonged dependency needs. Although the child has within him most of the abilities
to make a satisfactory adjustment to life, the handicap influences the rate
and method of learning, as well as the ability to learn. The most significant factor in the child's adjustment, however, is the quality of the
parent-child relationship. This factor far outweighs training and education in enabling the blind child to develop a normal personality. Because
blindness realistically creates need for great dependency, parents and
others frequently "do for" the child to a degree that keeps him from
developing strength of personality and from learning how to relate to
others in a mature manner.

Lack of knowledge regarding the emotional development of the young
blind child has been a factor in the confusion regarding the mental
abilities of the congenitally blind. Many blind children who later prove
educable are diagnosed as mentally retarded before they reach school age.
Some recent research on blind infants gives considerable evidence that
some of these children are retarded because of emotional deprivations
and insecurity rather than because of actual mental deficiency.

Regardless of the degree of the visual handicap, the attitude of the
family and other significant persons to the handicap are of extreme importance in the child's adjustment. All these people should be informed
about what can be expected of a child who is blind.

The necessary dependency of the blind child must be recognized and
yet he must not be protected to a degree that interferes with his drive to
develop from one emotional level to another. In planning for aid to the
blind, services that are directed toward establishing healthy parental and
community attitudes and toward the social and emotional adjustment of
the handicapped individual should be given equal consideration with
educational and training programs. Objective evaluation of the visually
handicapped child with respect to degree of disability, type of education
required, need for segregation or nonsegregation are all of tremendous
importance if the visually handicapped child is to accept his limitations,
make full use of his assets, and relate to normal society in a mature and
realistic way.

This approach to work with blind children is one that applies to the
adjustment of all handicapped children. Regardless of type of disability,
the basic problems of all handicapped children and their parents are

similar. The element of dependency that is created by a handicap is a major problem that affects not only the patient but his entire family. Meeting and overcoming this dependence is the great challenge around which a treatment program should center. This may call for a variety of services—medical, psychological, educational, psychiatric, and social— that may be available only in large clinic centers. The general principles underlying these efforts can frequently be applied, to a large extent, by general practitioners and public school teachers. Once parents can see possibilities for the child and are relieved of anxiety about his mental capacity and their ability to teach him, they show great resourcefulness in carrying out a constructive program. The warmth and interest of professional people in whom they have confidence is one of the major assets in their success.

Hearing Impairment

A great many children have impaired hearing. Unlike most other disabilities, a handicapping amount of hearing impairment does not show. A child with impaired hearing "limps" only socially, "fumbles" only psychologically, "stumbles" only vocationally. Such a child is frequently regarded as slow, inattentive, vague. He may be overaggressive or underassertive; in either case, he is commonly considered a "problem child," at home and at school.

The core of hearing disability lies deep in human behavior. Hearing involves much more than the comprehension of sound; it is very much a part of the dynamics of behavior. The most serious effect of hearing impairment is that it produces a communicative disorder, an interference with the back-and-forth-ness between minds that is the essence of being human. These things are well known.

Not so well known, perhaps, is the fact that a great deal can be done to reverse, to alleviate, or to compensate for a handicapping hearing impairment. Much has happened in the past ten or fifteen years to motivate changes in an approach to the problems of children with impaired hearing. There have been far-reaching advancements in electronics, specifically in the production of vacuum-tube hearing aids, and in the design and development of precision instruments for auditory diagnosis and training. Moreover, the use of antibiotics and of radium therapy in medicine has radically altered the nature and extent of handling many problems, and new surgical techniques have been brought to bear on certain types of impairment. Wartime experience in the special handling of individuals with impaired hearing has taught valuable lessons in the ideas and techniques of rehabilitative management. All these developments have stimulated efforts in case finding and in diagnosis, as well as research in both basic and applied problems of hearing and hearing impairment. The result has been the emergence of a new branch of science called "audiology." Audiology is a highly derivative, eclectic field of knowledge. It represents a synthesis of several fields—among them otology, physics, psychology, linguistics, biophysics, psychoacoustics, and pedagogy—undertaken for a specific purpose: to study and treat the problems that relate directly to hearing and hearing disorders.

Hearing is one of man's primary means of relating himself to his environment. At least three levels can be discerned in this relationship. At the most primitive level, a person is aware of sound around him; this awareness links him closely with the world of movement and change, and without this link that world is materially changed. Somewhat more refined behavior is associated with sounds as signals or warnings or directions. Certain noises and sounds characterize certain conditions or events, and we learn to respond accordingly to the horn, the clock, the doorbell, the dripping faucet, and so on. Presumably the most refined level of hearing is directly related to man's use of language symbols.

Perhaps man's most distinctive characteristic is his ability to use symbols to communicate with his fellows. Indeed, a good argument can be made that the child's developing use of language symbols constitutes in large part what is commonly considered the growth of "mind," and that our measures and comprehension of intelligence are determined, or at least controlled in large part, by the development of language habits. Speech and hearing are the two basic elements of communication and of language. Together with their derivative forms, reading and writing, they provide the foundations for much of human behavior. Communication is not a simple process, however. The learning, the perceiving, and the production of language involve a complex relationship among auditory, visual, and muscular stimuli and responses, and between peripheral and central nervous systems. Inasmuch as language is chiefly learned through the hearing mechanism by imitation, the child learns to speak not only because he hears but as he hears.

Communication begins very early in infancy, as the baby reacts to the requirements of food and creature comfort. Soon he begins to babble, a stage of development which is probably a pleasurable combination of muscular and auditory stimulation and response. Toward the end of the first year and through the second year the baby experiments freely with sounds, and his combinations begin to reflect the rhythm, form, and structure of the speech that he hears. This is the onset of language. In the third year the child usually becomes sharply aware of himself as a being different from others and takes enormous strides in relating this self to the world. His use of language takes a great spurt and moves on at an increasing rate until, by the age of eight or nine, the basic language pattern is fairly well established and is an important aspect of behavior and adjustment.

For better or worse, the direction of this development is intimately related to most other forms of the child's behavior. This is the reason we tend to judge much of childhood behavior and development in terms of language. In a way, it may be said that the eyes and ears are the antennae of the "mind." When the period of onset of speech and the development of language habits is seriously deviant, it is reasonable to check vision and hearing.

That all three of these levels of hearing—the primitive, the significative, and the symbolic—contribute to normal behavior and development in infancy and childhood, as well as in adolescence and adulthood, is an aspect of health and welfare that is not as yet generally appreciated. Unfortunately, perhaps, our habits of communication are so universal that they are apt to be taken for granted. The relations among hearing and understanding and behavior, moreover, are so diverse that they have not as yet been adequately defined and described in reasonably objective terms. These things need a great deal more study.

A fundamental idea upon which to build an understanding of the problems of impaired hearing is that its effect is always more extensive than the dysfunction of the hearing mechanism itself. However hearing may be defined functionally, it is never an end in itself, nor solely an activity of the end organ. Biologically, hearing is a means of contact between the individual and his environment; behaviorally, it is the pathway to much that is called "normal development"; socially, it constitutes, with speech, the communicative link among people at all levels of activity. The actual perception of sound, as a function of the hearing mechanism, is only part of the picture. In terms of behavior and communication, the basic disorder associated with a permanent hearing handicap is not the lack of hearing but the lack of ready means of contact with the physical world and the lack of back-and-forthness between minds. That is why, if the mechanism of the ear is put in as good repair as medical science can achieve and there still remains a hearing disability, attention must be centered on the psychologic, social, and educative aspects of communication. Impaired hearing can never be divorced from the dynamics of behavior.

Many of the problems of impaired hearing in children have to do not only with hearing but also with understanding. An amount of hearing loss that might be negligible in an adult may be a tremendous deterrent for the child. Moreover, not only the amount but the type of impairment is important. Hearing impairment is not a single, clear-cut entity; it has a wide variety of forms and extents, with equal variation of effect and amenability to treatment. When the trouble is reversible or may be materially lessened, as is often true, it is important that this be done as early as possible. Fortunately, much of this work can be undertaken with minimal medical care and with relatively little expense in time and money.

For various reasons, a great deal of what has been done about impaired hearing in children has been centered in the school-age child. There is, however, the whole group of preschool children in whom the problems of prevention and mitigation are even more important. The child from two to six is at his peak as a language-learning, developing, behaving personality. Whatever interferes with the normalcy of activities in this age range takes its greatest toll in the personality development of the child.

There is no longer any need for a child to arrive at the age of five or six with a hearing impairment that is undiagnosed, unmeasured, untreated, and uncompensated for by early guidance and training. Once the diagnostic picture has been clarified, in both physical and developmental terms, and appropriate medical treatment carried out, parents should be helped to work out a program designed to stimulate language and behavioral development. The key to audiologic work with preschool children (the age of eighteen to twenty-four months is the time to begin) is parental insight and understanding. It is no rare thing nowadays for a child aged four, with a severe hearing impairment, to be well on the way toward a good vocabulary and a happy adjustment to the family and the world around him. It should go almost without saying that special clinical work should extend only so far as to demonstrate the facts and the nature and direction of the remedial steps that are necessary. From that point on, the child may progress to regular school, with or without the need for special adjunctive education, or to a special school, depending on the extent and character of his disability and the nature of his other needs.

Rheumatic Fever

As illustrative of the influence of a severe disease, in contrast to a physical defect, on the healthy development of personality, rheumatic fever has been chosen for description. The effect of this disease, as of other potentially traumatic experiences, on emotional development is different for every child, depending on the meaning of the experience to him. Nevertheless, there are some generalizations that can be made, some of which apply to other severe disorders as well.

The meaning of rheumatic fever to a child will depend in part on the disease itself, its severity and clinical course, and on the methods used for treatment. It will depend also on the previous personality development of the child—on his constitution, his age, his other life experiences, including his relationships to parents, siblings, age-mates, and other significant figures, and his general pattern for coping with problems. And, because a child is so much influenced by his parents, the meaning of the disease to the child will depend in part on its meaning to his parents.

Among the potentially affective factors are the following: age of onset, fear of death, degree of illness and pain, need for nursing care, separation from parents and age-mates, physical restrictions, and reaction of parents. Much could be said regarding each of these points but the following must suffice here.

The disease is very rare under the age of three, so before the onset of the disease some of the fundamental emotional structure of the child has already been built. How a given child reacts to the disease will depend in part on how well his personality development has progressed. Moreover, depending on when it starts, the disease may retard or distort certain developmental stages.

With this disease there is real possibility of death, either early in the acute attack or at some future time if the disease progresses. The young child may not have a clear understanding of this, but even he may reflect the fears of his parents. Older children, more often than is recognized, are aware of the possibility of death through what they overhear and guess, and they may be very much afraid. A child may even deny the illness and refuse to cooperate in treatment because of this fear.

Any sick individual tends to regress, at least temporarily, to earlier patterns. Some of these earlier patterns, such as enuresis, thumb sucking, feeding problems, more intense dependence on the mother, may worry the parents and start a vicious circle in the child-parent relationship. If previous levels of development were more satisfactory to the child than the present one, or if they were not very well dealt with originally, it may be difficult for the child to move away from this regression. Sometimes, however, a successful encounter with a physical illness seems to precede a real spurt in emotional development.

Many medical procedures have potentially traumatic implications for a child—because he often does not or cannot understand the real purpose of the procedure and because his phantasy life is so rich and so concerned with inner problems. Venapunctures, transfusions, blood-pressure recording, rectal temperatures, oxygen tents, X rays and fluoroscopies may be interpreted in bizarre ways and may seem to confirm to the child the reality of some of his anxieties and feelings of guilt.

In the early stage of the disease, a child is almost completely dependent on his mother or a nurse for his bodily functions: he is fed, put on a bedpan, given a bed bath, lifted from one position to another. This physical dependency may be threatening to some children, welcome to others. One child may deal with it by outright rebellion; another may be overly passive.

Often a child with rheumatic fever must be taken from his home to a hospital or a convalescent home. Separation from his parents may be very traumatic for a preschool child and may seriously interfere with his later ability to form emotional relationships with people. It is usually less traumatic for a child from six to preadolescence, although it may still be serious for some such children. The implications of separation from his parents for an adolescent are different; they may reinforce emotional conflicts having to do with his attempt to become independent.

A child with rheumatic fever may, at some point in his treatment, have to be isolated from his age-mates. If this is for a long period, as it may be, a school-age child may be slowed up in developing relationships with his peers. An adolescent may suffer acutely, since his orientation is so much toward his age-mates in his struggle for independence, for recognition as an adult man or woman, and for a firm set of values for himself.

Physical restriction of a child three to six years of age interferes with his expression of aggression. For an older child it means, increasingly, interference with his moving about in the society of his playmates and friends. It may mean interference with methods of play that are important to his emotional development. It may mean interference with schooling, which is so important to him as a way of learning to understand and deal with reality. It may interfere with creative activities, such as art and music, and thus deprive the child of a constructive method of dealing with emotional problems.

The reaction of parents to the illness may be very complex. There will usually be real fear; there may also be anxiety related to the parents' own emotional reactions to illness and possible death. Parents may feel guilty for a variety of reasons. They may blame themselves for heredity or for inadequate care previous to the illness, both of which factors are often stressed in health-education literature. They may, without knowing it, blame themselves for hostile thoughts they have had about the child from time to time or for past deeds on their consciences.

Then, too, a mother will usually give herself emotionally and physically to the care of an acutely ill child at a level that cannot realistically be maintained. As the disease drags on, conflicts and inconsistent treatment will be apt to occur. The dependence of the child and the need for restricting his activity may be welcome to some parents in meeting their own emotional needs; to others, it may be almost unbearable. The care of the child and the mother's attitude toward him may create conflicts between the parents. All these reactions of the parents will be bound to affect the parent-child relationship one way or another, and thus affect the child's emotional development most profoundly, especially if the child is young.

As the effects of the disease are individual for each child, so the methods for dealing with them must also be individualized. The only thing that could help every child would be a sure fast cure of the disease. Some precautions and measures, however, are rather generally applicable.

For the child it is important that attention be given at every step to the potential emotional problems. It will usually help if he is given an opportunity to talk about his fears and his angry feelings and to tell as much as he can about what the experience means to him. Allowing him to take some active part in managing the situation is usually helpful also. A young child may be given a chance to choose, for instance, whether he gets his medicine straight or in applesauce and to make other decisions within the limits of the medical treatment that is required. An older child can be given a more decisive role. The child's regressive behavior at the onset of illness should be accepted, but he should be helped to regain his former developmental level as soon as feasible, through encouragement and through giving him increasing responsibility. The limits of his physical restrictions should be made clear to him. He should be treated consistently. He should be prepared for new experiences, in so far as possible, by understandable and realistic explanations. He should be given opportunities for play, schooling, and creative activities consistent with his physical status and his age.

For the parents much can be done. They should have a careful and realistic description of the medical picture and prognosis. They should be allowed to talk about their worries. They should be helped to see whether they are being unrealistically indulgent or restrictive. And they should be helped to understand what the experience means to their child and how they can best give him support.

Professional personnel involved in the treatment of the child can help greatly if they do their utmost to be consistent; if they accept the hostile or fearful attitudes of the child or his parents without rebuke or excessive reassurance; if they consider every procedure in the light of the emotional as well as the physical effects and minimize trauma by eliminating unnecessary procedures. They should watch the child's emotional status in relation to his age and previous level of development. They should be as definite as possible about restrictions and cut them off as soon as it is medically safe to do so. They should consider the emotional as well as the physical needs in planning for a period of separation from the family. They should discuss the emotional problems with a psychiatrist and request case consultation if it seems indicated.

Allergies

Allergies provide a final example of the interrelation of physical and emotional factors in the effects of disease and defects on personality development. They are representative of disorders that are thought by some authorities to be psychogenic in origin. If they are of this nature, it would seem that they do not so much hamper growth of personality as give evidence that difficulties in that growth have been encountered.

Not all allergists agree about the significance of emotional factors, however. Some pay no attention whatever to emotional aspects, feeling that a discovery of a specific allergy in a child and the development of appropriate medication is sufficient. Others maintain that the allergy itself accounts for disturbances in behavior, and that removal of the allergy clears up the emotional and social problems of the child. Some allergists, however, working in association with psychiatrists, take the position that, in the production of attacks, a specific emotional condition of the patient is of equal importance to the sensitivity, that psychological and allergic factors stand in a supplementary relationship to each other. In many cases, at least, it is not a question of either an allergic or a psychological etiology but of some sort of cooperation between them.

The assumption on which this latter group works is that a specific psychic conflict working together with the allergy will produce attacks. It has been observed that allergic children have a high degree of sensitivity, both physiologically and psychologically. The allergic child is said to be "touchy" in disposition, emotionally insecure, and given to anxiety, especially in relation to any change of condition in his environment. Given his constitutional sensitivity, the child is likely to react to certain emotional situations with an outbreak of physiological symptoms. To what extent the child "uses" the attack to express his emotions is a highly individual matter.

In a series of asthma cases studied at the Chicago Institute for Psychoanalysis, a characteristic early disturbance in the mother-child relationship, usually resulting in an exaggerated fear of separation from the mother, was found. Moreover, in the series of patients studied, it was observed that the asthmatic attack did not always occur when the patient was exposed to the allergens, and, conversely, attacks did occur when the patient was thrown into an emotional conflict, even when the allergens were not present. The conclusion was drawn that removal of the emotional conflicts would help the children to be less sensitive to the allergens, and such did seem to be the case when psychological treatment was carried on.

The connection between emotional conflict and other allergic disorders, such as urticaria, eczema, and hay fever, has not been studied as carefully. Some research workers are of the opinion, however, that emotional factors are of importance in these disorders also, at least in some cases.

Whether or not the combination of constitutional sensitivity and emotional conflict is of major importance in the production of allergic reactions, there would seem to be little question that the presence of an allergy may be emotionally disturbing both to the child and to the parents. Many allergists recognize, for example, that in dealing with allergic children the mother is a special problem. She herself may be a sensitive person and may have suffered from many of the feelings she sees in her child. She is, therefore, apt to be overanxious and often contributes to the child's emotional upsets. She is usually a hovering mother. At the same time, her strength and patience have often been drawn upon so much, especially if the child is asthmatic, that she is both angry with the child for not improving and angry with herself that her own ministrations have had such poor results. This produces a clinging on both sides.

Such observations, made by many allergists as well as psychiatrists, differentiate allergic children from other handicapped children in only a limited way. What seems clear from all the examples of handicaps here cited is that physical and emotional factors combine to make the lot of the disabled child more difficult than average; how much more difficult depends in large measure upon the attitudes of parents and other persons important to the child's well-being.

The Psychology of the Child Who Is Handicapped

In view of these findings regarding the close connection between emotional and physical factors in the development of personality in children who are disabled, it seems important to consider the kinds of psychological reaction these children may display. Knowledge of reactions frequently encountered may help parents and others who work with these children to understand them better and to help them more effectively.

For every child the process of growing up means an almost incessant effort to cope with self-centeredness, with competitiveness and envy, with demands for unlimited and unqualified love and admiration from his parents. Efforts to rear children well are directed toward facilitating this struggle: toward supporting them when help is needed, toward mitigating the demands life makes to the point where children can deal with them a bit at a time, and toward compensating children with love and kindness when life is hard. In all these respects the situation of the child who is seriously disabled and of the parents who would help him is more difficult than usual.

In its fundamental form, the problem of disability and defectiveness exists as an ever-present concern in all of us: as a reaction to imagined or real illness, accidents, and shortcomings in appearance and performance. Knowledge of the psychology of this condition should provide a basis for understanding the specific problems of children who are disabled.

The basic concept for such an understanding is that one's own body, just as one's personality in its integrity, is the center of one's normal interest. Usually this is a well-balanced, unobtrusive interest, but inner or outer events may sometimes diminish it and sometimes make it more intense. For instance, under certain circumstances, a normal, well-established interest in oneself can be shifted to other persons and objects so that their well-being may become more important than one's own health or life. Under other circumstances, interest may become so centered upon one's own personality and body that even the usual contact with other persons and events is excluded.

The shift to overconcern about oneself is especially likely to occur when outside dangers threaten security and integrity. Illness and accident and the emergence of any one of many disabling conditions are among such dangers. When these appear for longer or shorter periods, it is not unusual for the individual to retire within himself, as we say, to lose self-confidence, and to become prey to sometimes irrational fears. This reaction to bodily damage is particularly frequent in individuals who are troubled by emotional conflicts of a kind that they can keep under control only as long as they can think of themselves as sound in body and bodily functioning.

Children share with adults this concern about their own body and this apprehension about its malfunctioning. Whatever the reality of a disability and its cause may be, a child is inclined to link it up with his inner apprehensions. He may interpret the disability as proof of punishment for whatever he has learned to call bad about his thoughts and deeds. He may think that it resulted from his parents' lack of love for him. He may regard it as a sign that he is an outcast or, less often, a "chosen one." He may think of it as a debt owed him by his mother or the world, on which he may build never-ending claims and demands. He may have other ideas about the disability, including the scientific, but he is unlikely to be able to accept it with complete objectivity and equanimity.

According to the different meanings that disease and handicap may hold for them, children's reactions and habitual attitudes toward themselves and toward the handicapping conditions will differ. Some of these reactions and attitudes may interfere with the necessary management of the disorder. Some may lead to severe personality distortion. At best, they will be no more than minor disturbances in the course of healthy personality development, equivalent to other not-too-great obstacles in the way of happiness.

Children's reactions to disabilities will also differ according to their age and the kind of frustration the disability imposes. For example, a disability that spells interference with fulfillment of interests and realization of talents or that involves disfiguration will have a much greater effect on the feeling of security of an adolescent than of a younger child. Conversely, separation from the family, residence in a hospital, dietary restrictions, and limitations on mobility will have a much greater impact on a younger child than on an older one.

Perhaps the most important task of those who work with these children is to understand the signs and symptoms of the various emotional conflicts disablement may arouse, and to provide the children and their parents with means of coping with them and, hopefully, of eliminating their permanent psychological effects. Not all children will suffer in the ways described below, nor will many conform exactly to the types here outlined. Nevertheless, in greater or smaller measure these are the ways children may feel about, and react to, handicapping conditions. If we exaggerate for some children, it is only to make clear what the psychology of a child who is disabled may be.

A child (or adult) who is handicapped may show what is frequently referred to in the literature as the "psychology of the cripple." Such a person expresses in his bitterness, withdrawal, and aggression toward the fortunate, healthy world, a deep conviction that injustice has been done to him and that lack of devotion or care or interest must be the cause of his condition. Hostility toward others is the result.

People who are responsible for the care of such children often approach them with warmth but feel hurt and helpless when their friendliness is answered with hostility and disdain. Quiet equanimity and patience, with unobtrusive signs of friendliness and understanding, will deprive these children of the arena for their battles and of the opponents whom they want, compulsively, to punish and to hurt. At the same time, such attitudes will demonstrate to the children that true devotion does exist, and that people can be relied upon and trusted.

There is a second type of child whose emotional conflicts, although of a similar nature, lead to proud and rebellious behavior instead of a destructive campaign against the world. This patient does not ask for justice or love but for respect. He reacts to pity or overkindness with extreme rejection. Young boys are more likely than girls to react in this way.

This type of child, too, easily hurts the feelings of the persons in his environment by his aloofness and sensitivity. The only effective way to be of help to such a child is to accept him on his conditions. The necessary demands for diet, physiotherapy, adjustment to regulations, for example, must never be made in a patronizing, even though kindly, form. Instead, appreciation of the child's courage, patience, reasoning power, and strength should be emphasized, and the conviction that this child can fulfill the requirements better than anybody else should be stressed.

In contrast to these two reactions to disablement, a child may respond with excessive, though often unspoken, desire for signs of affection, care, and attention. He needs someone to stand by him through his distress; he is not ready to make any independent move toward progress. Unconsciously, such a child is demanding interest and unfailing effort on the part of others. This need often interferes with the child's desire for improvement, for being helpless assures him of the greatest amount of consideration. Very often this child is regarded as overdemanding, almost devouring, a special responsibility and burden. As a result, he frequently provokes irritability and defensiveness in those who take care of him.

A more extreme example of somewhat the same underlying feelings is seen in children (more often found from adolescence on, and more frequently in girls than in boys) who perceive suffering and restrictions as desirable gratifications and protract them to the utmost because of their emotional value. These patients, like the dependent-demanding ones, find great difficulty in getting well and react negatively to improvement, often to the point where they secretly (sometimes without being aware of it) counteract therapeutic measures. They demand sympathy and are inclined to exaggerate, but not to resist, painful experience.

The reaction of the people responsible for the care of children who act in these ways is often one of impatience and rejection. Despite this natural feeling, it is a mistake to tell the child directly that he could do better or feel better if he really wanted to. To attack such children with the suspicion that they are using their condition to gain attention only forces them deeper into this method of gaining love, and only increases their expressions of helplessness and suffering. In other words, if we say, "It's not so bad!" then the child feels that his condition must be made to appear worse.

On the other hand, people who have these children in charge must not try to fulfill their demands for attention unlimitedly, for the more they give, the more the children are encouraged to cling to their disabling attitudes. Nevertheless, some of the children's needs for attention must be met or the children will feel rejected and turn away. What is required in such cases is a greater than usual amount of attention and interest combined with a friendly but firm demand that the child make a contribution to the effort to help him recover or find a new way of life. At the same time, the child must be introduced to a new kind of personal relationship, for at base his reaction represents a defect in personality structure.

These dependent-demanding and these masochistic children usually have not discovered that striving and achievement are followed by admiration and affection. They live in the conviction that only helplessness and pitiful conditions arouse kindness in others. Work with these two types of children must be slow and cautious, for these attitudes are only with infinite patience overcome.

In contrast to these children, there is a relatively large number of children to whom disease seems like the answer to anxious expectation. These are the children who are concerned with thoughts and wishes they disapprove of or with acts that they have committed (mostly of an aggressive or sexual nature) that they consider bad. Their troubled consciences lead them to expect some kind of punishment or retaliation. For them the process of illness or the facts of disability are filled with threatening connotations beyond the objective hardships, and every phase creates devious anxieties. This often results in terrified refusal and resistance when new methods of treatment or medication are prescribed. The necessity of operation can throw them into a state of panic.

In order to cope with these deep anxieties, special efforts have to be made to reassure these children and give them the feeling of our protective strength. For any kind of patient of whatever age, an essential part of the doctor's role, for instance, is to renew in him the childhood feeling that he has nothing to fear, but for no type of patient is this conviction of greater importance than for those with anxieties and guilt feelings. Furthermore, it is especially advisable to give such patients simple and comprehensible explanations and information about pending medical procedures, in order to allay the devious and always exaggerated neurotic anxieties and to replace them with knowledge of reality, which almost never is as bad as imagination pictures.

As a final example, there are some children whose reaction to illness or disability is a feeling of helplessness for having been abandoned or deserted and not loved. Such a child begins to give himself up and develops apathy that can lead to a complete passivity and withdrawal. Food, medication, anything offered to him may be refused. This condition is most unfavorable to recovery or to coping with the disability, for a wish to cooperate, a desire and striving for improvement are necessary for adjustment and emotional well-being. A large amount of attention, stimulation, and care from the persons who have the child in charge is usually necessary to reverse this condition, for the child must again become attached to people around him so that he may come to accept himself.

The reactions described here, we have said, are extremes. Much more vividly than descriptions of milder reactions could do, however, they indicate the interrelation of physical and psychological factors and suggest some of the ways in which the presence of severe or chronic illness or other physical disability may increase the difficulties of healthy personality development. Moreover, the very variety in the reactions, as well as the fact that some handicapped children are not so affected, suggests that physical disability is not the sole cause of these children's difficulties.

We conclude this analysis of the influence of organic factors on personality development, then, with the generalization that physical handicaps do handicap personality development but that they do not, by any means, make health of personality impossible. The manner and extent of their operation depend upon various other factors, the most immediate of which appear to be the attitudes of the people who have the children in charge. It is to these other factors, then, that we turn next, and take for first consideration that subject we have already frequently referred to, the parent-child relationship.

∠ IV ∠

The Importance of
Parent-child Relations

THE preceding two chapters have made it evident that organic factors frequently exert their influence on personality development in conjunction with those of interpersonal relations. There is no biological "given," it has been shown, no static, immutable "heredity" that determines from the outset that one child shall be healthy in personality and another shall progress only with great difficulty. Some few neurological conditions may produce such instability that personality development is seriously impeded but, for the most part, the influence of even major physical handicaps and disorders may be mitigated by sensitive handling of the child by the parents and others.

The data presented also make clear that children do not start as identical physical organisms, to be made or marred depending on how wisely the parents "bring them up." Instead, there are great differences among children from the time they are born (and earlier), as well as differences that emerge or are acquired quite outside the realm of parental influence. By these differences the job of parent may be renderd more or less difficult.

Then, too, parents themselves differ, constitutionally and otherwise, probably even more than children, so that what may seem a difficult task of child rearing to one parent will seem congenial and pleasant to another. Moreover, children influence parents even as they are influenced by them, and in this, too, organic factors play a part.

In the preceding chapters, considerable attention has already been given to some of the specifics in the relations of parents and children and to some of the ways in which parents, by their attitudes and behavior, may help their children develop in a healthy manner. The present chapter, accordingly, is confined to a review of some of the scientific studies bearing on the question of the influence of parent-child relations on children's well-being. This is a subject that has received so much attention from writers and lecturers on child rearing that parents are beginning to feel that they are to blame for all inadequacies in their children. We hope to show that "blame" is not the word for it. If parents can be relieved, in some measure, of feelings of anxiety and guilt in this connection, they will probably have more energy and intelligence to give to meeting the real challenge of the job of bringing up children.

The Mutuality of Parent-child Relations

Facts already presented indicate that parents and children influence each other greatly, and that organic factors may affect that process. It has been noted, for example, that a child who is constitutionally passive may be a disappointment and a cause of worry to a mother or father who is exceptionally energetic. There will have to be accommodation both ways if there is not to be continual frustration. For another example, a newborn who is slow in learning to suck may arouse anxiety in a mother who already doubts her ability to produce healthy offspring. The resulting tension in the mother is likely to make nursing unpleasant to the child. This, in turn, will increase the mother's anxiety or cause annoyance, and so a cycle of mutually unfavorable reactions is started.

Even under the most favorable circumstances, mother and child, father and child have to learn how to get along with each other if happiness is to ensue. On both sides the learning process starts early. The parents have to learn how to approach the child so as not to startle him, and how to hold him so that he feels comfortable. Nursing calls for mutual accommodation between mother and child. At an early age children try out various tactics in order to secure their desires. What works with one mother will not succeed with another; what one child tries will not occur to another. In the various possible combinations of mothers' and fathers' and children's ways of behaving, there is room for many types of parent-child relations to develop, and for various degrees of satisfaction to ensue. Probably only parents know in detail what this statement means in everyday living.

Numerous clinical studies testify that there is a close relation between parents' attitudes toward their children and the adequacy of the children's social and emotional adjustment.[1] Child-guidance workers find that "problem children" often have "problem parents," and a recent report of a long-time study of a cross section of school boys comes to much the same conclusion.[2] All the boys who turned out well had parents whose

[1] See, for example, many reports published in *Smith College Studies in Social Work.*
[2] Edwin Powers and Helen Witmer, *An Experiment in Delinquency Prevention,* Columbia University Press, New York, 1951.

attitudes toward them were rated "favorable," and almost all who were neurotic, psychotic, or chronically delinquent had parents whose relationship with them was distinctly unfavorable.

In this, however, one must be suspicious of which came first: the children's difficult behavior or the parents' adverse feelings and behavior. Very careful observational studies from earliest infancy will have to be conducted before this question can be answered with assurance. Probably there will be no single answer. Sometimes it is the child's behavior, perhaps in early infancy, that starts the unfortunate cycle of development; sometimes it is the parents' anxiety and insecurity that start the difficulties. Child-guidance workers report that very seldom can they be of lasting assistance to a child unless his parents, particularly his mother, are able and willing to change their feelings and ways. They do find, however, that in some cases improvement in the child's behavior precedes improvement in parents' attitudes, and in some cases it is the other way about. Sometimes, in other words, the parents have to "let up" on what they are doing before the child is free to move ahead; sometimes the child has to "act nicer" before the parents can show their love. Such findings underline the psychological dictum that there is mutuality in the responses of parents and children, that the process of adjustment is not a one-way street.

If in the subsequent analysis we stress the parents' part more than the child's, it is only that we have more information about it. Parents' attitudes have been the chief subject of study, even when the topic for investigation is entitled "parent-child" relations, and activities designed to improve those relations are usually directed toward parents. In this there may be much merit, in that parents are the older and presumably wiser elements in the situation. It may be, however, that age and intelligence are not of chief importance in this endeavor in which emotions count so largely. Perhaps, for the usual family, more could be accomplished by activities directed toward modifying the children's behavior, and perhaps more research should be directed to discovering what there is about children and child rearing that so often makes the parents' job seem difficult.

Attitudes More Important Than Techniques

Studies indicate that parents' attitudes toward children and their feelings about them are more important determinants of children's health of personality than the particular techniques of child rearing they employ. Popular books and articles often imply, if they do not directly say, that such acts as breast feeding, toilet training at the "right" time, permitting children to play with water and dirt, not interfering too much with expressions of aggression are in and of themselves of great importance. Logically, such statements can be considered sound only if we suppose that most people belonging to earlier generations or to societies different from our own are unhealthy in personality. Actually, research confirms what clinicians believe: that it is the over-all emotional tone of the home that counts for most, and that the specific techniques are valuable chiefly when employed by parents who can carry them out with confidence and with genuine concern for the child's well-being.

Take breast feeding for example. Orlansky, after analyzing the pertinent studies, comes to the conclusion that whether bottle or breast feeding is preferable depends in part on the mother's psychology and on the custom of the section of society to which mother and infant belong. "We have seen no evidence," he says, "to favor the current belief among some pediatricians that breast feeding is inevitably more advantageous to the child than artificial feeding. . . . Above all, the character of the mother must be evaluated before an intelligent opinion can be ventured as to whether breast or artificial feeding will better serve to promote the healthy development of the child's personality." [3]

Length of breast feeding (that is, time of weaning) also seems not to be as definitely associated with children's emotional well-being as some authorities maintain. Hoefer and Hardy [4] and Pearson [5] report studies that appear to show that a moderate duration of breast feeding is better than one that is either longer or shorter, but an investigation conducted by Maslow and Szilagyi-Kessler [6] definitely contradicts this hypothesis. Orlansky concludes that there is no present evidence of a "linear correlation between length of breast feeding and any major aspect of personality studied."

Self-demand feeding is another technique currently recommended as favorable to healthy personality development. Orlansky states that up to the time he reviewed the literature little had been done to subject this

[3] Harold Orlansky, "Infant Care and Personality," *Psychological Bulletin*, January, 1949, pp. 4–5. See also H. K. Faber and T. L. Sutton, "A Statistical Comparison of Breast-fed and Bottle-fed Babies during the First Year," *American Journal of Diseases of Children*, Vol. 40 (1930), pp. 1163–1176; B. C. F. Rogerson and C. H. Rogerson, "Feeding in Infancy and Subsequent Psychological Difficulties," *Journal of Mental Science*, Vol. 84 (1939), pp. 1163–1182.

[4] C. Hoefer and M. Hardy, "Later Development of Breast-fed and Artificially-fed Infants," *Journal of the American Medical Association*, Vol. 92 (1929), pp. 615–619.

[5] G. Pearson, "Some Early Factors in the Formation of Personality," *American Journal of Orthopsychiatry*, Vol. 1 (1931), pp. 284–291.

[6] A. H. Maslow and Szilagyi-Kessler, "Security and Breast-feeding," *Journal of Abnormal and Social Psychology*, Vol. 41 (1946), pp. 83–85.

theory to empirical test. He himself is of the opinion that, as with other specific disciplines, self-demand feeding "does not exert a specific, invariant psychological influence upon the child. Its effects can be gauged only from the study of the parental attitudes associated with its administration, of the child's constitutional endowment, and of the entire social-historical situation in which the emergent personality is located."

In general, Orlansky concludes—and most child-guidance workers would agree with him—that particular techniques of infant care do not have a "specific, invariant psychological impact upon the child. Instead, it appears that the effect of a particular discipline can be determined only from knowledge of the parental attitudes associated with it, the value which the culture places upon that discipline, the organic constitution of the infant, and the entire socio-cultural situation in which the individual is located. In short, it is contended that personality is not the resultant of instinctual infantile libidinal drives mechanically channeled by parental disciplines, but rather that it is a dynamic product of the interaction of a unique organism undergoing maturation and a unique physical and social environment." [7]

Studies confirm, however, the dictum of modern psychology that in order to develop in a healthy manner children must have from their parents solicitous care for their well-being, care that includes love, guidance, and discipline. For their emotional security and for their intellectual development, children have to know that their parents love them and have to be clear about the rules of the game. They have to know what is allowed and what is not allowed and have to have limits set to their actions. Both theory and observation indicate that "permissiveness" can be carried too far, that children not only need but even want to be kept under reasonable and kindly control.

Effects of Deprivation of Maternal Care

A voluminous review of the studies on one aspect of the influence of maternal care—what happens to young children when they are deprived of it—has recently been published by the World Health Organization. The author, Dr. John Bowlby, opens the review with the following remarks:

Among the most significant developments in psychiatry during the past quarter century has been the steady growth of evidence that the quality of parental care which a child receives in his earliest years is of vital importance

[7] Orlansky, *op. cit.*

for his future mental health. . . . What is believed to be essential for mental health is that the infant and young child should experience a warm, intimate, and continuous relationship with his mother (or permanent mother substitute) in which both find satisfaction and enjoyment. . . . It is this complex, rich, and rewarding relationship with the mother in the early years, varied in countless ways by relations with the father and the siblings, that child psychiatrists and many others now believe to underlie the development of character and of mental health.[8]

Bowlby later elaborates upon this generalization as follows:

The child needs to feel he is an object of pleasure and pride to his mother; the mother needs to feel an expansion of her own personality in the personality of her child; each needs to feel closely identified with the other. . . . Such enjoyment and close identification of feeling is possible for either party only if the relationship is continuous. . . . Just as the baby needs to feel that he belongs to his mother, the mother needs to feel that she belongs to her child, and it is only when she has the satisfaction of this feeling that it is easy for her to devote herself to him. The provision of constant attention . . . is possible only for a woman who derives profound satisfaction from seeing her child grow from babyhood, through the many phases of childhood, to become an independent man or woman, and knows that it is her care which has made this possible.[9]

In support of these statements Bowlby cites numerous studies, conducted in various countries, that show the effects on personality development when children are separated from their mothers and are deprived of the kind of solicitous care a mother normally provides. The studies are in almost complete agreement that this deprivation leads to serious emotional and intellectual retardation, and some of them suggest that it may have adverse effects upon physical growth as well.

The extent and quality of the damage, it is shown, vary with the age at which the deprivation occurs, with the length of time it persists, and with the quality of the substitute care that is provided. The over-all generalization would seem to be strengthened by these findings.

All children under seven years of age are vulnerable, it is said, with the possible exception of infants under about three months. But the damage is greater, and also different, when the child is under thirty months when the deprivation takes place than when he is older.

[8] John Bowlby, *Maternal Care and Mental Health,* World Health Organization, Geneva, 1951, p. 11.
[9] *Ibid.,* p. 67.

The effects on infants are those that were cited in Chapter I when the development of the sense of trust was under discussion: they are listless and unlikely to smile; they sleep poorly, fail to gain weight even when fed the proper foods, and become markedly retarded in development. Such effects have been observed as early as one month of age, and all students of the subject agree that they are frequent in the second half of the first year of life.

Children one and two years old are likely to respond to separation first by "agitated despair," expressed in screaming or moaning and in refusal of food and comfort, and later by apathy and regression to infantile habits. Those three to five years old are less vulnerable. Many of them can be prepared for prolonged separation by explanations ahead of time and are relatively unaffected if handled in a loving and wise manner by the parent substitutes. Vulnerability diminishes even more after that age, but even children as old as sixteen may be adversely affected by forced removal from home, responding to it by nervous symptoms and delinquency.

The length of the stay away from home also influences the effects, although age is a factor that is of importance here. Studies of infants show that the longer the stay, the greater the deterioration in developmental progress, suggesting that the ill effects are cumulative. Apparently no strictly comparable studies of older children have been made.

The seriousness of adverse effects also varies, as would be expected, with the degree to which the children are deprived. The infants most extremely affected were those brought up in an institution in which, for hygienic reasons, each one was kept in a separate cubicle, where he saw nobody except when having his most pressing needs attended to. Better results were secured when deliberate attempts were made to compensate for the lack of "mothering." Care in foster homes appears, in general, to be less disadvantageous than care in institutions. Under whatever arrangements, the results are the better the less the children are deprived of solicitous ministrations.

Long-time follow-up studies of individuals who were deprived of maternal care early in life and retrospective studies of some who suffered from the most extreme forms of mental disorders confirm these findings and indicate that the ill effects of prolonged deprivation are seldom transitory.

Moreover, the long-time effects vary with the amount of deprivation and the age at which it occurs. Extreme deprivation in infancy and early childhood apparently leads to an inability to form close relations with

people and to give or receive affection. It is also likely to affect intellectual development, especially the ability to conceptualize, and it makes
for lack of social conformity. (These ill effects are avoided or greatly reduced if "mothering" is restored after a short period of deprivation, but
they are likely to be permanent otherwise.) Periods of deprivation interspersed with those of satisfaction are said to result not in the isolated,
asocial type of behavior but in emotional ambivalence and antisocial
actions.

On the basis of evidence of this sort, Bowlby concludes that almost any
home, even one that is emotionally disadvantageous, is better than a good
institution or perhaps even a foster home. Social workers who have had
much experience with foster care of children might consider this an exaggerated statement. They, however, operate on the same principles
Bowlby is espousing when they are careful to maintain a child's contacts
with his own family throughout foster care, to make the period away
from home as brief as conditions permit, and to provide through foster
care the affectionate relations that children so much need.

Bowlby's reasoning on this point is as follows:

The services that mothers and fathers habitually render their children are
so taken for granted that their magnitude is forgotten. In no other relationship do human beings place themselves so unreservedly and so continuously
at the disposal of others. This holds true even of bad parents—a fact far too
easily forgotten by their critics, especially critics who have never had the
care of children of their own. It must never be forgotten that even a bad
parent who neglects her child is nonetheless providing much for him. Except
in the worst cases, she is giving him food and shelter, comforting him in his
distress, teaching him simple skills, and above all providing him with that
continuity of human care on which his sense of security rests. He may be
ill-fed and ill-sheltered, he may be very dirty and suffering from disease, he
may be ill-treated, but, unless his parents have wholly rejected him, he is
secure in the knowledge that there is *someone* to whom he is of value and
who will strive, even though inadequately, to provide for him until such time
as he can fend for himself. . . .

Once a child is out of his own home he is lucky if he finds someone who
will care for him until he is grown up. Even for good foster-home agencies
the rate of replacement is deplorably high; even in good institutions the
turnover of staff is a constant problem. However devoted foster-parents or
housemothers may be, they have not the same sense of absolute obligation to
the child which all but the worst parents possess. When other interests and
duties call, the foster child takes second place. The child is therefore right to
distrust them—from his point of view there is no one like his own parents.[10]

[10] *Ibid.*, pp. 68, 69.

Some Reasons for Adverse Parental Attitudes

In this analysis of some of the components of the parents' contribution to a child's well-being, it will be noted that chief importance is attached to the continuity and dependability of parental ministrations, interest, and concern. In popular writings, the word "love" is used instead, and parents are admonished to love their children if they would have them thrive. Such a substitution of a vague word for the specific ones seems rather unfortunate, especially since "love" has many connotations and does not necessarily include behavior of the desirable kind.

These observations raise the question why some mothers have unfavorable attitudes toward their children and whether such attitudes indicate lack of love. Most parents maintain a continuity of interest and concern on which their children can rely. There are, however, qualitative differences in parents' attitudes and mode of relationship with their children. It is not so much that some parents love their children less than others do (love is scarcely a measurable quantity), it is rather that in some the "parental sense" is less fully developed, while in others various factors, internal and external, interfere with its demonstration. Whatever the reasons, it is a fact that some parents are better able than others to develop and sustain a relationship that gives children the backing they need for growth toward independence.

Of more or less unfavorable attitudes and modes of relationship there are many kinds. American child-guidance workers, following the lead of Dr. David Levy, commonly speak of overprotection, rejection, and ambivalence. Dr. Bowlby lists as the commonest an unconsciously rejecting attitude underlying a loving one, an excessive demand for love and reassurance on the part of the parent, and a parent's obtaining unconscious satisfaction from the child's behavior despite conscious condemnation of it. Despite their differences, these adverse attitudes are alike in that they involve the child in a struggle with the mother that deflects him from the normal course of personality development.

Studies of the effects of these various kinds of parental attitudes on children's personality development have been largely limited to clinical investigations. These indicate so frequent an association between parental attitudes regarded by psychiatrists as disadvantageous and behavior and personality problems in children that it is often concluded that all children who live in emotionally disadvantageous homes turn out poorly. This generalization, however, has not been subjected to rigorous scientific examination. In fact, in one of the few long-time studies of an unselected series of children it was found that some of the children from emotionally unfavorable homes developed well.[11] Nevertheless, the clinical evidence is sufficiently convincing to warrant the assertion that great efforts should be made to foster between parents and children the kind of mutual satisfaction in one another on which the child's healthy personality development apparently so much depends.

So much has been said in both popular and professional literature about the "rejecting" mother and her lack of love for her children that some special attention to this concept seems called for. To us it seems that the concept "rejecting" is unsatisfactory on at least two counts.

First, a mother's relation with her child, particularly when she and the child are involved in a cycle of hostile projections, is far too complex to be described accurately by any one word. Such a word may serve well for purposes of statistical classification—to indicate that negative feelings are dominant in the mother and that certain behavior patterns are to be expected in the child—but beyond this its value is limited, and it may even hinder the search for a deeper understanding of a particular mother's relation with her child.

Second, this concept overstresses the negative aspect of the mother-child relation, almost to the exclusion of other aspects that are present in almost all cases. It is a one-sided concept that implies that a mother's feelings are wholly those of hatred and dissatisfaction, and it leaves little room for consideration of what interacting forces in family life may be leading to the ascendancy of hostile feelings in both parent and child as they struggle to find a way of living together.

Child-guidance workers know many mothers to whom this term "rejecting" is applied. They find that most such women have positive feelings for their children disguised and buried under their anger. They find that most of them want to develop a happy, comfortable relation with their children, no matter how negative may be the struggle they are engaged in.

In all family relationships there are many different feelings: approval, affection, and love; disapproval, annoyance, and anger. Sometimes warm, loving feelings predominate; sometimes hatred and wrath. But even when one member of the family is angry at another for a considerable period of time, this does not necessarily preclude the existence of love. People often become most angry and behave most cruelly toward those they love best. This is because they are likely to be most deeply dis-

---

[11] Jean Walker MacFarlane *et al.,* "Looking Ahead in the Fields of Orthopsychiatric Research," *American Journal of Orthopsychiatry,* Vol. XX (1950), pp. 87–88.

appointed or most severely hurt if these people do not behave as they want them to or do not live up to their expectations.

Mothers are especially likely to have such reactions. Mothers usually have wishes and ideals in regard to the kind of relationship they want to have with their children, and ambitions for the children as well. When things do not work out well, they are likely to express their disappointment and anger in criticism, reproof, or punishment of the child. The child may respond either by doing as the mother desires or by himself becoming angry and resentful and behaving worse than ever. If he takes the first course, the mother's anxiety and anger are allayed and she again shows her love for him. If, however, the child meets anger with anger, the mother's anxiety and dissatisfaction may increase. Soon a situation commonly labeled "rejecting" develops, and the child feels much disliked. Yet the mother may still love the child, though the love may be so buried that she and others are scarcely aware of it.

Disappointment over unachieved desires is of course not the only basis for the development of this kind of unsatisfying parent-child relations. Another fertile source is a mother's fear that her child's development will suffer because of poor elements in his heredity. For example, a mother may fear that her child will grow up to resemble a relative who has been considered bad or a failure or a disagreeable person. Then, too, if there has been physical or mental illness or delinquency in the family a mother may fear that her child's development will not be normal. Again, a mother who is unhappy because of difficulties in her own emotional life or in her social adjustments may be anxious lest the child have similar problems.

In such situations a mother tends to watch everything her child does with an eye to these eventualities and to interpret his behavior in the light of her fears. Too often, because of excessive anxiety, she misinterprets what the child does. Thus, if the child does one or two things that remind her of a relative whom she has disliked or disapproved of or that bring to mind her own problems, the mother is greatly disturbed. She feels that she must change the child's behavior to save him from the fearful fate. Hence she may reprove and punish him more severely than his actual behavior warrants and make such exaggerated complaints about him that it seems as though she greatly dislikes him. Only when her underlying anxiety and fear are revealed is it clear that love is an element in her motivation.

Sometimes, too, a mother's expression of disapproval and apparent dislike of her child may hide her longing for a good relationship and her fear that she is incapable of achieving it. The following brief description of a child-guidance-clinic case makes clear that this and other factors may lead to behavior on a mother's part that looks like complete dislike of a child, and that may hide the basic love.

For three months after she had first sought the help of a child guidance clinic Mrs. Ainsworth's weekly interviews with the social worker were full of complaints and criticisms of her sixteen-year-old daughter, Anabel. It seems as if she completely rejected the girl and had only hostile feelings toward her. She was always comparing Anabel unfavorably with her two-year-old brother, who never caused the mother any trouble. And she was always making remarks such as the following about Anabel:

"I'm ashamed to tell you how much I dislike Anabel." "She has always been careless and irresponsible, and now she is boy crazy besides." "I try to stop nagging her, but I just bottle up all the irritation until I explode and give her a good bawling out." "Anabel was such a sickly, whiny baby. She has been a problem in one way or another ever since she was born. I simply detest the girl. If she were not too old I certainly would beat her unmercifully. She makes me so infuriated that I could die—or else kill her."

On her side, Anabel felt that her mother had never been satisfied with her and that she never would be able to please her mother. She said she really did love her mother but she didn't think her mother believed her. Her mother hated her most of the time, she said.

It took about three months for Mrs. Ainsworth to exhaust her anger at Anabel. Along with her anger at the girl, however, she frequently referred to her own childhood experiences, telling how she had both feared and hated her own mother. Finally she was able to say that from the time of Anabel's birth she had been worried about what her relationship with a daughter might be. She had not had any such anxiety about herself and her son. "When Anabel was born and I knew she was a girl, I made up my mind that she would never have any reason to resent me the way I did my mother. But she had temper tantrums and disobeyed me. So I thought that I had failed as a mother and that she must hate me the way I hated my mother."

After Mrs. Ainsworth had admitted her anxiety about her relationship to her daughter, she could see that she might have been reading into the girl's behavior more than was really there. It was then possible for her to believe that the girl was sincere when she told the psychiatrist that she loved her mother. From this time on, the relationship between mother and daughter was better, and Mrs. Ainsworth began to find things to praise in Anabel. As they ended their clinic interviews, Mrs. Ainsworth said that she felt very differently about Anabel. "Now I am proud of her and I have the same warm feelings for her that I have always had for my son."

We may ask, then, why many parents have difficulty in conveying to children the love they feel. Some of the personal reasons have already been suggested. The over-all answer is that in all emotional relations numerous kinds of feelings are involved and that numerous conditions, internal and external, are influential in determining which shall predominate at a given time.

"Neurosis" has become the pat answer to why parents cannot express their love adequately. Those who have worked most with parents and children know, however, that this is only a partial answer, and that this answer obscures the complexity of the conditions that lead to unsatisfactory parent-child relations.

It is true that parents' own unhealthy personality development can predispose them to poor relations with their children, though this is by no means a certain eventuality. Psychiatrists point out that whether or not a parent's neurosis interferes with the child-rearing process (and what part of that process it interferes with) depends largely on what the neurosis centers about. The fact that child-guidance workers find neurosis in many parents is no proof that all or most neurotic individuals encounter difficulties in child rearing.

Neurosis, however, is far from the only answer to why parents may have attitudes toward their children that are not as helpful as might be desired. The social and economic situation plays a large role also. Money worries, marital difficulties, resentment about the way they are treated at work or in other social relations, inadequate preparation for parenthood, uncertainty about one's role as a parent: these and numerous other factors may interfere with the free expression of parental love.

The whole culture, too, combines to assist or to make difficult the process of child rearing. This point is of special relevance here because parents need not only love for their children but also confidence in their ability to rear them wisely if they are to do a good job. For the latter, they need society's backing.

Genuine self-confidence is hard to come by in a society such as ours, where tradition as a source of rules for child rearing is on the decline. Because families have been small for several generations, many parents have had little opportunity as youngsters to share in the rearing of young children. As adults they are likely to live, physically and, in many cases, emotionally, apart from their parents and grandparents and cannot look to them for advice. Nor is the older generation itself always certain that its ideas are right.

Moreover, our traditional competitiveness more or less handicaps young couples in learning from each other. Admission of difficulties comes hard to us, for we fear to be rated as failures. Intimacy, too, is something we are rather afraid of. So young parents, especially those of the middle class, try to go their own way, maintaining a good front in the matter of child rearing and avoiding the seeking of counsel except in extremity.

Some Favorable Social Changes

Fortunately, various factors seem to be working toward increasing parents' self-confidence. First, within another generation the new ways of bringing up children may themselves become traditional. Rooted as they are in "naturalism," in acting upon one's best impulses, they may take hold faster than the artificial, "scientific" methods of a generation ago, which called for rigid routines and the smothering of native desire to be solicitous. If this happens, young parents' confidence should increase, since they will not feel so alone and so much in disagreement with the older generation.

Second, there is some evidence that young people are finding it easier to talk with each other frankly about the pleasures and discomforts of child raising. Shared "baby-sitting," cooperative nursery schools, parent discussion groups work to this end, as, to some extent, do the numerous magazine articles, radio programs, and the like, that assure parents that having problems is to be expected. What is most needed, however, is a general lessening of fear of emotions and a renewal of the old American conviction that in diversity there is strength.

Third, psychiatrists and social workers have learned how to take the average American's desire for self-reliance into account in their professional practice and so have made the admission of difficulties easier for their patients. Other professions are adapting to their own needs this new knowledge about how to work with people. Widespread acceptance of people as they are, with no desire to condemn or boss or reform, should be of great help to parents, many of whom are weakened in self-confidence by the implied disapproval they sense about them.

Fourth, pediatricians and parent educators are devising methods of fostering parents' self-confidence before difficulties in rearing children arise. They put much reliance on instruction about what children are like, what their differences from one another are, what kinds of behavior they are likely to be showing at stated ages. Such information, given ahead of time and with professional sanction, should ease parents' anxieties and be helpful generally in broadening the public's conception of the infinite ways in which children can vary and still be healthy in personality.

We may sum up this brief and rather discursive analysis, then, by saying that healthy personality development in children does depend in large measure on the character of the parents' attitudes and the nature of the parent-child relationship. These important factors, however, are so interrelated with numerous others that parents should be supported and should seek support in their efforts to bring up a healthy generation rather than blaming themselves or being blamed.

↗ V ↗

Income Level and
Health of Personality

HEALTH of personality, the preceding analysis suggests, is the resultant of biological, interpersonal, and social and cultural factors operating in favorable conjunction in the daily life of the human being. In the next two chapters, we want to consider what happens to the developing child or youth when economic conditions are not favorable and when prejudice and discrimination abound.

The influence of economic factors on health of personality has already been touched upon. It has been said that child-rearing efforts are greatly facilitated if parents feel that they are competent, respected persons sure of their place in society. The economic arrangements of the society play a large part in the promotion of such feelings in parents. Students of industrial psychology have discovered that worry and insecurity are detrimental to a worker's efficiency and productivity. Sociologists and psychologists are now reversing the question and are asking what effect poor job conditions have upon the home life of workers. So far, only tentative answers have been secured, but it looks as though fathers and employed mothers may carry over into home life dissatisfactions arising out of the way they are treated at work, with consequent detriment to parent-child relations.

More broadly considered, the general character of a society's economic arrangement reflects upon parents' ability to convey to children a sense of trust in the future and a feeling of dignity and worth in productive endeavor. Impersonality in work relations, jobs in which workers have no feeling of having an important part to play in bringing a task to completion, insecurity of tenure and uncertainty as to rights: these and other characteristics of some types of modern employment adversely affect workers' feelings of confidence and importance. Health of personality in adulthood requires that the person feel that he is a person who matters and that life has dignity and meaning. If economic arrangements do not sustain these beliefs, children's personality development is likely to suffer.

104

More concretely, economic arrangements affect personality development through their effect upon family income. The possible influence of low income on children has already been noted. Poor diet and poor physical health, which make personality development difficult, are attributable in part to lack of money. Poor parent-child relations may arise in part from marital disharmony that has an economic base. Children may develop feelings of inferiority and self-doubt because status in school and among age-mates depends in part upon the size of the family income and all that that implies. Parents and youth may come to think that the world is against them if hard work does not bring the promised rewards. These are but a few of the ways in which size of income may influence the adequacy of personality functioning under American conditions.

Actually, the connections between economics and psychology in the life of an individual are very complicated and have not been subjected to anything like adequate study. In fact, it seems likely that the pertinent questions regarding the connections have not even been asked.

Regarding the influence of one aspect of economics, low family income, on health of personality, there is, however, some information, and it is that which will be brought together in this chapter.

Some Evidence of the Adverse Influence of Low Income

Generally speaking, low income affects personality development functioning along the lines already described. It may handicap physical development and efficiency of biological functioning. It may create tensions in interpersonal relationships, especially within the family but also in a child's relations with peers and others. It may handicap for social and cultural reasons, both because it may put the child in a disadvantaged social class and because it may make him feel that he has been deprived of his rightful heritage of equality of opportunity.

These effects are closely interrelated. Even the biological are probably somewhat culturally defined, in that the expectation of good health and high vitality is so much an attribute of American culture that their absence is more detrimental to personality than would be the case in a society accustomed to very low standards of living. This being so, it is not possible to line up the effects of low income in neat, mutually exclusive categories nor yet to trace out all their interconnections. The following account, therefore, is merely suggestive. Much more study and analysis must be undertaken before a comprehensive picture of the effects of low income on children's well-being can be drawn.

Before the argument along these lines is presented, however, some evidence to the point that low family income and inadequacy in personality development are associated is called for. With one exception, the few studies we found on this subject agree that children whose family income is low are more likely to be emotionally maladjusted than those whose parents have more money.

Differences of this sort develop early and persist, if the evidence of the few available studies is to be believed. Gesell and Lord,[1] for example, report, on the basis of a small but carefully controlled investigation, that children from well-to-do homes excel those from homes of low income in "verbal, practical, and emotional abilities." Springer,[2] studying about eight hundred children in grades four to seven in New York City, found that those from poor neighborhoods rated significantly higher in neurotic traits than did those who lived in middle-class neighborhoods. Thom and Johnson[3] found that the majority of a series of well-adjusted high school students came from homes and neighborhoods that were rated good or excellent. Stagner,[4] from a study of a small group of college students, came to the conclusion that lack of money fosters nervousness, moodiness, and depression. Terman,[5] following into adult life a series of children of high intellectual endowment, discovered that those who rated highest in achievement were more likely to have come from good homes, in the economic and educational sense, than those whose achievement was poor.

One of the few studies that did not immediately support these findings dealt with bright children in two schools in New York City. The investigator, Helen Davidson,[6] found that the children of various income levels did not differ significantly in feelings of inferiority, introversion or extraversion, constriction or childishness, degree of social or personal adjustment, and emotional control. She points out, however, that her study was conducted in two unusually good private schools and that the disparities in income were not great. She concludes that when school and community situations are favorable, bright children from economically dis-

[1] Arnold Gesell and E. E. Lord, "A Psychological Comparison of Nursery School Children from Homes of Low and High Economic Status," *Pedagogical Seminary,* Vol. 34 (1927), pp. 339–356.

[2] N. N. Springer, "The Influence of General Social Status on the Emotional Stability of Children," *Journal of Genetic Psychology,* Vol. 53 (1938), pp. 321–328.

[3] Douglas A. Thom and F. S. Johnson, "Environmental Factors and Their Relation to Social Adjustment: A Study of a Group of Well Adjusted Children," *Mental Hygiene,* Vol. 23 (1936), pp. 379–413.

[4] Ross Stagner, "Economic Status and Personality," *School and Society,* Vol. 42 (1935), pp. 551–552.

[5] Lewis M. Terman and Melita H. Oden, *The Gifted Child Grows Up,* Stanford University Press, California, 1947.

[6] Helen H. Davidson, *Personality and Economic Background,* Kings Crown Press, New York, 1943.

advantaged homes can overcome some of the handicaps that low income imposes.

In considering the implications of Davidson's study, the question of selective factors might be raised. It seems probable that the kind of children such schools choose for admission and the kind of parents that permit their children to attend are out of the ordinary. Such families probably have traits that counteract some of the disadvantages of low income. Nevertheless, the study serves to emphasize the point that not all children are harmed by low income. If, however, the lack of disadvantage is largely limited to those who are bright, who have unusual school opportunities, and who have parents who are interested in their education, the position of the majority of children of low income is not good.

One final comment as to the influence of economic status on health of personality may be made, though it is one for which research data are lacking. This is the frequent observation of clinical workers that life in families of wealth and position also is likely to impose heavy strains on children. As one psychiatrist put it informally, and probably exaggeratedly, "The children of Park Avenue are the most emotionally disadvantaged in New York." It appears to be true that in this social class children are under especial pressure for conformity and achievement and that they are, moreover, often denied the close association with their parents and, as infants, the mother's solicitous care that are so important in personality formation.

Low Income and Physical Health

In Chapter III, dealing with the effects of physically handicapping conditions on personality development, it was noted that a sick child, a child who is seriously malnourished, a child who suffers from some crippling condition is likely to have more difficulty in developing in a psychologically healthy manner than a child who is not so disabled. It was made clear in that chapter that the physical handicap is not the only disabling factor in such a child's situation, that these children are likely to suffer because of the attitudes displayed toward them as well as the fact that they are physically limited. Nevertheless, there seems to be little doubt that ill health and low vitality, in and of themselves, are detrimental to the full flowering of a child's potentialities.

Incidence of Disease

If this rather obvious generalization is accepted as true, the most elementary connection between low income and difficulties in personality development will be established when it is shown that poverty increases the likelihood of poor physical health. Unfortunately for our argument, there are very few figures available as to the incidence of disease and disability among children in the various income classes in the United States. Nevertheless, the fact that there is a relation between economic status and incidence of disease and defect among people in general is quite well established. It seems fairly likely that the incidence of disability among children follows the same pattern as that of the general population.

Various studies confirm the common-sense observation that people are more likely to become ill if their income is very low.

The largest of these studies, one conducted by the U. S. Public Health Service in 1935–36,[7] covered two and a half million persons who lived in representative urban communities. In those days of economic depression it was found that families on relief had disabling illnesses one and a half times more frequently than well-to-do families, and that these illnesses were both more severe and of longer duration. Moreover, these families were three times as likely to be afflicted by chronic illness, and they had three times as many annual days of disability per person as did those whose income was high.

This survey, and a smaller one dealing with rural families conducted ten years later,[8] indicated that outside the lowest income groups (families with income under $1000 a year) there was not much association between income level and incidence of disabling illness. This finding may be partly attributable, however, to the fact that chronic illness is very common among older adults regardless of economic status, and that respiratory and acute communicable diseases occur very frequently in children of all economic levels. When these facts are taken into account and the comparison is made with respect to children only and with respect to a disease that is chronic—rheumatic fever in this instance—a much more marked association is revealed. The rate per 100,000 white persons five to nineteen years old who lived in cities varied in 1935–36 from 43.8 in families having an income of $3000 a year or more to 58.7 in families whose income was under $1000 and 100.1 in families on relief.[9]

One recent testimony to the adverse effects of extreme poverty on

[7] "Illness and Medical Care among 2,500,000 Persons in 83 Cities, with Special Reference to Socio-economic Factors," *National Health Survey:* 1935–36, United States Public Health Service, 1945.

[8] Charles R. Hoffer, "Medical Needs of the Rural Population in Michigan," *Rural Sociology,* Vol. 12 (1947), pp. 162–168.

[9] Selwyn D. Collins, "The Incidence of Rheumatic Fever as Recorded in General Morbidity Surveys of Families," Special Supplement to *Public Health Reports,* 1947.

health was furnished to the President's Commission on Migratory Labor in 1950. A representative of the Michigan State Department of Health reported that the tuberculosis rate among migratory workers in Saginaw County was 19 per 1000 as compared with 1 per 1000 among "normal" residents. The health officer of Cameron County, Texas—a county that has a large number of both migratory workers and "wetbacks"—said the infant mortality rate for the county was 83 per 1000, as compared with a national average of 30. Tuberculosis, infant mortality, maternal mortality, dysentery, enteritis, smallpox, typhoid: all are much more prevalent among migratory workers than among the general population, the report makes clear.[10]

There is some evidence, too, that severe physical defects may follow from the life conditions that poverty produces. Blindness is a case in point. As Rollo Britten,[11] a careful student of the subject, puts it, no categorical answer can be given to the extent that blindness appears as a cause of low economic status or as a result of it. The reaction goes both ways, and it is of most significance that, whether or not the blindness is associated in its origin with factors involving economic or environmental level, it acts as a deteriorating influence on such level. It is a fact, however, that both total blindness and blindness in one eye were found by the National Health Survey to occur about four times as frequently in families with income under $1000 as in those of $5000 or over. These unfortunate conditions were also much more prevalent among Negroes than among white people, another bit of evidence that factors associated with low income may be responsible.

Summing up a review of the relation of socioenvironmental factors and physical impairments, Britten says:

In spite of the ambiguous nature of available data . . . the following facts stand out:

1. Serious impairments result in lower economic status.
2. This relation is true even for impairments in a group of people able to be about.
3. To an important extent, the components of low economic status are causes of physical impairments, forming a vicious circle.
4. Certain elements in the environment are particularly significant in this connection, such as occupation, housing, nutrition, and insufficient medical care.[12]

[10] *Migratory Labor in American Agriculture,* Report of the President's Commission on Migratory Labor, 1951, p. 153.
[11] Rollo Britten, "Physical Impairments and Socio-economic Factors," *The Milbank Memorial Fund Quarterly,* Vol. XXVI (1948), pp. 391 f.
[12] *Ibid.*

Poor Housing and Dietary Deficiencies

The relatively poor health of children in families of low income is attributable in part to bad housing and dietary deficiencies. As evidence of how bad their housing can be, the director of a Florida county health department reported to the President's Commission on Migratory Labor:

One of our public health nurses visited a nursery maintained on a private farm and found 48—I did not say 4, I said 48—infants on two double beds. A sanitarian reported 180 people living in 60 rooms, with only one toilet stool that worked.[13]

As to diet, the following was the testimony of a physician in Texas:

A survey which I made and photographed, in the Mathis, Texas, labor camps, showed that 96 per cent of the children in that camp had not consumed any milk whatsoever in the last six months. It also showed that eight out of ten adults had not eaten any meat in that time.[14]

Malnourishment, studies have shown, is far from confined to children of lower income levels. Nevertheless, it is obvious that low-income families are likely to have less adequate diets than those who have more money. Studies show that, by and large, diet does improve when income increases.[15]

To the seemingly simple question (actually, it is not simple), how many American children have an inadequate diet, there is at present no satisfactory answer. There are data, however, on the food consumption of urban families of various income levels during specified periods in 1942 and in 1948. The figures for the latter survey, made in the spring of 1948,[16] indicated that families whose income was under $2000 consumed 25 per cent less milk, 14 per cent less meat, and nearly 30 per cent less fresh or canned fruits and vegetables than those whose income was higher. They made up in part for the loss in calories—but not for the loss in vitamins—by eating greater amounts of cereal, sweets, and dried fruits and vegetables.

More generally speaking, the degree to which dietary level was affected by income varied with the nutrients and their food sources. Families of all

[13] *Migratory Labor in American Agriculture, op. cit.,* pp. 135, 154.

[14] See H. K. Stiebling, "Are We Well-fed?" U.S. Department of Agriculture Misc. Publication 430, 1941.

[15] See *Nutritive Content of City Diets,* U.S. Department of Agriculture, Bureau of Human Nutrition and Home Economics, October, 1950.

[16] *Ibid.*

income levels had a fairly similar intake of calories and iron. Higher income, however, meant diets more nearly adequate in calcium and riboflavin (secured largely from milk products), in ascorbic acid (tomatoes and citrus fruits), in vitamin A (green and yellow vegetables), and in protein and niacin (meat, poultry, and fish), all these being nutrients very important to healthy functioning.

Diet quality has also been shown to be somewhat related to size of family, which itself is related to income to some extent. In the spring of 1948, urban families of two, three, and four persons did not differ greatly in the quality of their diets, but the diets of families of five or more persons were distinctly poorer. These larger family units constituted about one-fifth of the urban housekeeping families at that time and undoubtedly included a sizable proportion of the children.

The higher the total family income, the less difference family size made in diet quality, this survey revealed. At all income levels, however, the diets of five-person or larger families were considerably lower in calcium and ascorbic acid than those of smaller families. Apparently, an income must be high, indeed, before a large family can spend enough on milk, tomatoes, citrus fruits, and leafy vegetables to get a diet that is nutritionally the equivalent of that of small families. Further testimony to the relation between inadequate diet and low income is given by the fact that between 1942 and 1948, a period when incomes were rising, diets improved.

These statistics on the relative incidence of disease and defects and the relative quality and sufficiency of diets are only suggestive of the ways in which size of income may affect children's health through determining to a considerable degree the extent to which needs for food, shelter, medical care and the like are met. Also suggestive are figures that show that the mortality rates vary with economic status as do the size and well-being of the newborn.[17] Taken together, these and other findings make it quite clear that low income makes good physical health less likely.

Size of Disadvantageous Income

How low must income be to operate so disadvantageously? It was noted above that in terms of 1935 prices, only when urban family income was under $1000 a year was the relationship between income and incidence of illness of all types clear cut. The picture changed when chronic illness was considered, especially when it was a chronic illness, such as

[17] See, for example, H. Bakwin, *et al.*, "Body Build in Infants," *Human Biology*, Vol. 6 (1934), pp. 612–626; and *American Journal of Diseases of the Child*, Vol. 48 (1934), pp. 1030–1040.

rheumatic fever, in a child. In that instance, both the incidence of new cases and the prevalence of the disease increased consistently as income went down. The top income category in the study cited (the *National Health Survey*) was $3000 and over—the equivalent of $6000, at least, in 1950 prices. Other studies cited are not so specific on this point.

It must also be noted in this connection that economic conditions conducive to health can be produced by means other than that of raising individual family incomes. Free school meals, subsidized housing, medical care, improved recreational facilities, and the like, have somewhat the same effect.

This being so, even were the needed facts about the relation of health to economic conditions available, it would probably be impossible to specify the exact income level below which detriment to children's health is to be expected.

Low Income and Family Relations

According to current theory and observation, healthy development of personality is dependent to a large extent upon the child's receiving loving care from his parents and others who have him in charge. It follows, therefore, that any conditions that deprive children of their parents' attention and affection, that create worry, anxiety, insecurity in parents, that make them feel inadequate and of little account are hazards to personality development. Poverty and its concomitants constitute one set of such conditions, as is well known. In this respect, then, as well as in respect to physical health, low income may handicap the healthy personality development of children.

It seems unnecessary to review in detail here the various ways in which the emotional aspects of the family life of children may be adversely affected by low income. The high incidence of family "breakdown"—quarreling and abusive treatment, immorality, inadequate care of children, desertion—in families whose income is very low has often been noted by students of the subject. Recently, some investigators have been maintaining that such behavior on the part of parents is normal in slum culture. Whether it therefore has less disastrous effects on the personality development of children than would otherwise be expected is, however, a question that has not yet been answered.

The tensions that may arise when homes are overcrowded and cold, when there is not enough to eat and wear, when jobs are scarce and ill paid, when the future is a subject of constant worry: these tensions and their sources are an old story to all who are concerned with the welfare of children. Not that all the adverse conditions that develop in families of low income are economic in origin or that concern about money matters is confined to families whose income is meager. What we are maintaining is that low income may be one important factor in family disharmony and malfunctioning and that it may in this way, as well as in others, adversely affect children's development.

Less well recognized, perhaps, are the effects unemployment and inability to earn sufficient money may have on the status of the breadwinner and on his relations with his wife and children.[18] In our society a man's feelings of adequacy and self-worth are highly dependent upon successful achievement, which itself is largely indicated by money earned. Success is a relative term, of course. Not every man aspires to millionaire status, and what counts for success in one segment of society is not the same as in another. Nevertheless, within any particular social group or class there are standards to be attained. To fall far below his fellows is a blow to the pride of most American men, and a likely cause of family disharmony. A research worker who interviewed a series of unemployed fathers during the depression days reports on this point as follows:

The general impression that the interviews make is that in addition to sheer economic anxiety the man suffers from deep humiliation. He experiences a sense of deep frustration because in his own estimation he fails to fulfill what is the central duty of his life, the very touchstone of his manhood—the role of family provider. The man appears bewildered and humiliated. It is as if the ground had gone out from under his feet. He must have derived a profound sense of stability from having the family dependent on him. . . . Unemployment changed all this. It is to the relief office, or to a relative, that the family now turns. It is to an uncle or neighbor that the children now look in expectation of a dime or nickel for ice cream, or the larger beneficences, such as a bicycle or an excursion to the amusement park.

The combination of circumstances that can make the family life of children of the poor so unfavorable can be portrayed much more effectively in novels or autobiographies than in a statistical or sociological report.[19] Nevertheless, the case records of welfare agencies contain abundant evidence that low income and family tension are connected. While no com-

[18] Mirra Komarovsky, *The Unemployed Man and His Family,* The Dryden Press, Inc., New York, 1940; Ruth Cavan and Katherine Ranck, *The Family and the Depression,* 1938, Martha Gellhorn, *The Trouble I've Seen,* William Morrow and Company, Inc., New York, 1936.

[19] For an extreme example, see Ethel Waters, *His Eye Is on the Sparrow,* Doubleday & Co., Inc., New York, 1951.

prehensive study of the results of the work of these organizations has been made, all who are familiar with their day-to-day experiences know that in many families the provision of financial aid has reduced family stress and improved parent-child relations.

The adverse effects of poverty on the emotional aspects of family life are attributable in part to the value most Americans attach to achievement. Ours is a "doing" society, and people are prized not so much for what they are as for what they accomplish. In most respects, we are not born into a status nor do we grow into it "naturally"; rather, we struggle for a status—in school, in work, even in recreation—and even in the family we are not wholly certain of our place. This being so, money, the sign of accomplishment, is highly important, and scarcity of it creates strains out of proportion to the actual deprivations it imposes. This suggests that it is not always the actual amount but sometimes the relative amount of income that counts—that and the expectations and ambitions of the family members.

Reports of family life in mountain areas of the Southeast appear, by contrast, to support this observation. Family life and child rearing in the Cumberlands, a section of the country in which poverty is the rule, have been vividly and sympathetically described by Claudia Lewis:

"The child [she writes] leads an apparently compliant, happy life. His long natural babyhood of close physical proximity to his mother, his privilege of sucking at the breast at any time, even long after he is eating the solid foods others eat; the late beginning and simply managed matter of toilet training; the few prohibitions relative to "Do not touch this, Do not play there, Do not go in here"; the relatively little insistence on washing and keeping clean; the space in the yard that is his to play about in and especially the presence of both his parents and the fact that he is not shut out from their life or their emotions, not deprived of their company day or night, not told that he must stay home, go to bed, keep away—all these things make his childhood a time of ease. He does not often have to picture his parents as those "grown up people who can do everything they want to but won't let me do anything." [20]

Ambition, striving, and family friction over money matters are rare in this section of the country, and children, concludes the author, are much less likely to be tense than those who live in poverty-stricken urban areas.

[20] Claudia Lewis, *Children of the Cumberland*, Columbia University Press, New York, 1946. See also Mandel Sherman and Thomas R. Henry, *Hollow Folk*, The Thomas Y. Crowell Company, New York, 1933.

Low Income and Schooling

For the full flowering of his potentialities, which we are calling "healthy personality development," a child needs, in addition to good health and favorable family relationships, educational opportunities in line with his intellectual capacities. It is well known that under our economic system children's opportunities for education depend to a considerable extent upon the financial status of their parents, and that, moreover, the parts of the country in which most parents are poor are the ones in which the schools are the least well staffed and equipped. Not so well known is the fairly well-established fact that children from very poor families may be denied equal educational opportunities because their intelligence is underrated by most tests; hence the instruction they receive may not be fitted to their ability. Evidence in support of these points will be presented below.

Influence on Amount of Schooling

The most extreme example of denial of educational opportunities is seen among the children of migrant workers, that most poorly paid segment of the population. Their situation with respect to education was recently summed up in the report of the President's Commission on Migratory Labor:

Migratory life involving four to six months away from home is bound to cut into children's schooling, but their itinerant status is not the only obstacle to migrant children's education. School opportunities for migrant children are limited. Inadequate school facilities, community opposition to the admission of migratory children to the schools, discrimination because of color or economic status, family income too low to supply necessary clothing and food are among the handicaps they suffer. Moreover, poverty compels them to work when other children are in school. Retardation, irregular attendance in school, and emotional disturbance are logical results of their status as migrants. Moreover, nonenforcement of child-labor and compulsory attendance laws, crowded schools, lack of teachers and school facilities are all characteristic of the migrant child's educational environment.[21]

As proof of these statements and evidence that the trouble does not lie entirely with migration itself, figures were cited showing that in states where many migratory workers have their "home base" (states that are

[21] *Migratory Labor in American Agriculture,* Report of the President's Commission on Migratory Labor, 1951, p. 167.

not lacking in financial resources) as many as 60 per cent of the children of migratory workers do not attend school.[22]

Poverty is one of the chief causes of this nonattendance, poverty so extreme that in many cases migrant families can survive only if all possible members work. In these families, children as young as five or six years may work alongside the adults at "stoop" labor.

Just how large is the total number of children under sixteen who work for wages is unknown, but in October, 1950, when schools were in session, the Bureau of the Census estimated that 150,000 children ten to thirteen years of age and 165,000 who were fourteen or fifteen were employed in agriculture. Of the children under fourteen, over a fourth were not even enrolled in school.[23]

In conclusion, the Commission on Migratory Labor wrote:

Hundreds of thousands of the children of migrant workers are today getting little or no education. They face the prospect of being slightly, if any, better able to improve their earning power or to raise their level of living than have their parents before them. This is no fault of theirs, but is the inevitable result of present public policies in many parts of our Nation. These policies are creating a new generation of persons, inherently as competent as other Americans, who will be compelled to spend their lives in poverty because the communities in which they spend their childhood do not provide them with even the rudiments of an education.[24]

Along with extreme poverty may go parental disinterest in schooling. How frequently this is a factor in the grossly inadequate schooling of some American children is not known, but it is a fact that in some isolated, mountain areas in the Southeast, and in other sections where poverty abounds, a considerable number of young children do not attend school even though facilities are available. For the most part, however, school-attendance laws are well enforced, and most children do go to school, regardless of their parents' feelings about the value of education.

Amount of schooling and family income are highly correlated, however. A review of studies testifying to this point was presented to the Subcommittee on Low Income Families of the 81st Congress.[25] Among the figures cited were the following. Parents in the upper-income group in

[22] *Ibid.*, p. 169.
[23] *Ibid.*, p. 161.
[24] *Ibid.*, p. 171.
[25] *Low-income Families and Economic Stability, Materials on the Problem of Low-income Families,* Joint Committee on the Economic Report, Government Printing Office, 1949, pp. 16–19.

small cities in New England, the South, and the Middle West send nearly all their children through high school and about 90 per cent of them to college. In the middle-income group, when these surveys were made, about 60 per cent of the children finished high school but only 15 per cent went to college, while in the lower-income group only 30 per cent graduated from high school, and only one in twenty went to college.[26]

These differences in children's schooling beyond the elementary grades are far from wholly attributable to differences in intelligence. A study made in 1940 showed that in a group of students with an I.Q. of 117 and above, the income of parents was directly related to college attendance. The youths who belonged to families with an income of $5000 and over had five times as great a chance of going to college as did those from families of a lower income.[27] Other studies cited in the Subcommittee report support this finding. Regardless of intelligence, the report writers state, "Educational opportunity in the United States, at least above the grammar-school level, still depends upon economic status to a marked degree." At least a fifth of the boys and girls aged sixteen and more than a third of those aged eighteen who have sufficient intelligence to profit from further schooling drop out of school. Lack of money is an important factor in that situation.[28]

Influence on Intelligence Rating

The influence of low income on educational opportunity is not fully accounted for by figures such as these, however. In a more subtle way, low income may handicap a child educationally because along with it may go homes so intellectually impoverished, as judged by middle-class standards, that the child may be accounted dull at school even though his intelligence is as good as that of the majority.

Studies carried on by one school of anthropologists over the last twenty years have shown that American society is considerably stratified, and that each of the social-status levels (identified as upper, middle, and lower) has a way of life that differs somewhat from the others.[29] This is particularly true, they say, of the lower level, especially that subdivision of it that they call "lower-lower," or slum culture, urban and agricul-

[26] Cited in *General Education in a Free Society,* Harvard University Press, Cambridge, Mass., 1945, pp. 86–87.

[27] Helen B. Goetsch, *Parental Means and College Opportunities,* Columbia University Press, New York, 1940.

[28] Estimate cited from *General Education in a Free Society, op. cit.*

[29] See, for example, Lloyd Warner and Paul S. Lunt, *The Social Life of a Modern Community,* Yale University Press, New Haven, 1941; Lloyd Warner, Robert J. Havighurst, Martin B. Loeb, *Who Shall Be Educated?* Harper & Brothers, New York, 1944; James West, *Plainville, U.S.A.,* Columbia University Press, New York, 1945.

tural. Adults in this segment of our society fight and curse as a matter of course and consider school and matters intellectual unimportant to their future. Their children, naturally, follow the same line of behavior and opinion, for in the context of slum life it is realistic, adaptive, and socially acceptable.

When these slum children enter school they enter an environment in which middle-class standards are the rule. In that environment their behavior is likely to be considered delinquent, and their lack of interest in books a sign of inadequate mental capacity. When they are tested for intelligence they are found to rate on the average about ten points below the children of higher economic status, a difference that increases to as much as twenty-three points by the time they reach fourteen.[30] Being so rated, they are usually assigned to the "slow" sections or the "special classes," where the quality of the instruction may be less adequate than in the rest of the school system.

Studies under way at the University of Chicago throw doubt on the validity of these ratings of the intelligence of slum children.[31] According to their findings, one explanation for the poorer showing of these children from poverty-stricken homes is that the more favorably situated children have greater training and motivation. Another explanation is found in the kinds of problems set in the intelligence tests, problems that are likely to deal with words and concepts much less familiar to slum children than to those who come from homes of higher economic status.

For example, one problem set in a widely used test asks:

A symphony is to a composer as a book is to what?
( ) paper; ( ) sculptor; ( ) author; ( ) musician; ( ) man

On this problem, 81 per cent of the children from the higher economic groups being studied answered correctly, and only 51 per cent of the children rated as of low economic status. When the question was changed to the following:

A baker goes with bread like a carpenter goes with what?
( ) a saw; ( ) a house; ( ) a spoon; ( ) a nail; ( ) a man

one-half of each group gave the correct answer.

On a test newly designed to eliminate economic and social differentials

[30] Figures cited by Allison Davis in an address given at the Midcentury White House Conference on Children and Youth, Washington, D.C., December, 1950.
[31] *Ibid.*

in intelligence ratings of children six to nine years old (a test tentatively standardized by Robert D. Hess), the average score of white children from the lower socioeconomic group was slightly higher than that of the upper-class children at six years of age and equaled it at the next three age levels. Apparently, the real intellectual ability of children of all economic levels is about equal.

These findings that children in families of lower economic status have much more ability than presently thought are far from conclusive. Some psychologists doubt their correctness. If substantiated by further research, however, they challenge the ingenuity of American teachers to provide the kind of training that will develop the latent capacities of the children of the poor and so help to equalize their opportunity to participate in American life on the basis of their abilities.

Low Income and Social Standing

In the work of the anthropologists cited above there is much evidence that low income and low social status go together and that children from the lowest level of American society are looked down upon and discriminated against. To be shamed and made to feel unworthy, to be told by word or deed that one is inferior and of little account interferes seriously with the healthy development of personality, it has been made clear. It follows, then, that in addition to affecting personality development indirectly, by putting obstacles in the way of physical well-being, good family relationships, and proper education, extreme poverty is likely to act directly, by lowering the sense of self-esteem.

This kind of effect of poverty on personality is, in part, a function of the American value system. In societies in which social stratification is taken as a matter of course, this result probably does not follow. If the individual citizen expects to live and die in the social class in which he was born, he gets a sense of self-worth by performing well the duties expected of him. He does not judge his accomplishments by other classes' standards nor is he so judged by others. Moreover, in such societies there is likely to be a tradition of *noblesse oblige* and of reciprocal rights and duties among classes. In our society, however, movement upward is held to be the rule, inability to succeed in this way is a sign of incompetence, and consideration and respect are accorded only to those among the poor who by manner of living indicate that they too are striving to better their position.

The anthropologists cited above have shown that children become conscious of class lines after the first few years at school, and that cliques and other closed forms of association develop that exclude most of the children of the lower economic levels. The exclusion is not limited to children from the slums. One investigator reports that in the community she studied there was little interaction between upper-middle-class and working-class children.[32]

Hollingshead's study in this regard is frequently referred to.[33] In the town whose high school youths he investigated, the lowest economic class was concentrated "north of the tracks and below the canal." This area was referred to by many names symbolic of its undesirability: "down by the garbage dump"; "where the river rats live"; "behind the tannery"; "the bush apes' home"; "squatters' paradise where you'll find the goddamed yellow hammers"; "the tannery flats"; and "along the towpath."

Speaking of high school children from this section of the town (class V, he calls them) Hollingshead observes:

The Class V adolescent has been subjected to a family and class culture in which failure, worry, and frustration are common. He has not been trained at home to do his bit in school. His parents have not ingrained in him the idea that he must make good grades if he is to be a success in life. Moreover, the class system as it functions in the school does not help him to overcome the poor training he has received at home and in the neighborhood. We believe that such factors as these have as much influence on the differences observed as native intelligence.[34]

One girl told the investigators:

"Frankly for a lot of us there is nothing here but just going to classes, listening to the teachers, reciting, studying and going home again. We are pushed out of things. There is a group of girls here who think they are higher than us. They look down on us. We won't mention any names but they are a group of girls from the higher families. They have a club that is supposed to be outside the school but it's really in the school. They just go from one club to another and hog all the offices. They snub us and won't talk to us." [35]

That children in such communities suffer not only exclusion but active rejection is shown in the following incident recounted by Hollingshead:

On another occasion we saw a group of 5th grade girls torment another

[32] Celia Burns Stendler, *Children of Brasstown,* University of Illinois Press, Urbana, 1949.
[33] A. B. Hollingshead, *Elmtown's Youth,* John Wiley & Sons, Inc., New York, 1949.
[34] *Ibid.,* p. 174.
[35] *Ibid.,* p. 202.

5th grade girl whose father ran a hog farm. The girls had driven Mamie into a corner of Central School next to a high wire fence. There they were singing a song someone had composed about the Dill family. We caught but two lines of the doggerel in the excitement of Mamie's crying and the noise of the playground but they told the story: "Mamie Dill lives on a hill, Mamie Dill lives on swill." [36]

James West, who studied the folkways of a small town in the Midwest, reports that in these communities there is a rueful recognition of the fact that upward mobility is no longer easy and that occupational status has become closely associated with educational achievement. Our Plainville man said, "They used to say any boy could be President. A boy's got about the same chance of being President nowadays as he's got of being Charley McCarthy or as a girl's got of getting to be a movie star." [37]

West maintains, on the basis of his study, that the two main classes in Plainville are in effect "mutually exclusive systems into which people are born," and that lower-class youths can hardly improve their position without leaving town. Moreover, by the time they leave, "lower class youths are so well indoctrinated with the sense of their own social inferiority that the best they can expect or look for is a job with good wages."

Warner, in a study of another small town,[38] notes that the struggle for acceptance and place is particularly difficult for the children from the "lower-lower" class. These children live in "little houses which are sometimes tar-paper shacks, sometimes small bungalows that huddle across the canal and on the towpath down the river or on the other side of the railway tracks in Polak Town and Ixnay." To many residents of Jonesville they are the "goddamned Polaks" and "those dirty poor whites, the hillbillies, the poor and unfortunate." Not only do these children receive less by way of comforts and opportunities than children whose parents can maintain a higher level of economic living but they are less likely to participate in the group activities of the community that might conceivably supplement to some extent their education and their social knowledge. In a study of school friendships, the author found that the child from the lower-lower class "is seldom mentioned as a friend and then only by children of his own social position, but he is often mentioned as a person his classmates do not like."

[36] *Ibid.,* p. 339.
[37] James West, *Plainville U.S.A.,* Columbia University Press, New York, 1945, p. 134.
[38] W. Lloyd Warner and Associates, *Democracy in Jonesville,* Harper & Brothers, New York, 1949.

What chance do young people have for moving out of this despised class? Unfortunately, this question cannot be answered at all accurately. The studies that have been made suggest that there is less upward movement than formerly and that those who do rise out of the most deprived groups are unlikely to rise far.[39]

The Lynds, studying "Middletown" in 1924, reported that progress up the industrial ladder was slow and that those who got as far as foreman were blocked in farther advance by the entrance of college-trained technicians. When they repeated their study in 1935, still less chance for promotion from the lower-income class was found. Instead of there being one ladder to economic success, it seemed that there were really two: one a workman's ladder that was becoming shorter and harder to climb, and one for the middle-class that retained the old characteristics.

Havighurst and Taba [40] throw some light on conditions associated with upward mobility. They point out that the children from the lower classes who have a higher-than-average reputation among their age-mates have parents who are eager for them to stay in school. "Although these parents were poor, many were said to have clean, well-kept homes and neatly dressed, well-groomed children. In many instances the families were said to have strict moral and religious standards." [41]

When parents do not back their children in their ambitions, success is likely to be achieved only at the cost of emotional maladjustment. Two instances of this sort are cited by these authors. These children came from families with a low reputation in the neighborhood. Despite this fact, their school-achievement scores were above average and beyond what might be expected on the basis of the intelligence-test scores. "The girl, however, was said to be resentful of her status and jealous of those above her. She adhered to a strict moral and ethical code. The boy had strong feelings of inferiority and was quite depressed. He ignored members of his social class and used his abilities in athletics to gain recognition from young people of higher social class than his own." [42]

One other case, described as an example of successful upward mobility, seems equally dubious from a mental-health angle.

[39] See, for example, John W. McConnell, *Evolution of Social Classes*, Washington, D.C., 1942; P. E. Davidson and H. D. Anderson, *Occupational Mobility in an American Community*, Stanford University Press, California, 1937; John Unseem et al., "Stratification in Prairie Town," *American Sociological Review*, 1942, pp. 331–342.

[40] R. J. Havighurst and Hilda Taba, *Adolescent Character and Personality*, John Wiley & Sons, Inc., New York, 1949.

[41] *Ibid.*, p. 58.

[42] *Ibid.*, p. 127.

To move up from the lower class position to which he was born to the middle class position to which he aspires [David] has learned the necessary skills and attitudes. He is a hard worker, has good manners, and takes care to maintain a good reputation. Furthermore, he has no strong personal attachments to people, and he will always be able to subordinate friendships and emotional relationships to his desire to get ahead in the world. He is the type of person who may be expected to leave the small city where he grew up and search for success in a larger community.[43]

The general effect on children of having low ratings from their fellows is remarked upon by the authors.[44] The children feel disliked and inferior, conscious of personal as well as social deficiencies, and unhappy about their situation. They respond with neurotic symptoms or with self-assertive, defiant, and antisocial conduct.

The towns in which these studies were conducted were small communities that were not increasing in size or economic production. It may be, therefore, that daily life in such towns and the ideas and values held by their inhabitants are not really representative of the bulk of American communities.[45] Specifically, the social ostracism of children on the basis of social status (that is, on the basis of who they are rather than on the more "American" basis of their ability and their accomplishments) may be more marked there than would be the case in larger cities, where schools themselves may follow social class lines, where "family" counts for little in the job market, and where there are enough people within any subgroup to make the opinions and attitudes of outsiders of less importance. Regarding this, however, we can only conjecture. The situation described in the studies cited does affect many thousands of American children. Whether it affects the majority of those whose economic status is low, only studies conducted in other kinds of communities can discover.

Incidence of Low Income in the United States

In view of these findings about the various ways in which low family income may handicap a child's personality development, the question of the extent of low income among American families becomes one of prime importance. To answer that question involves defining "low income"; and that, in the context of our argument, is a very difficult thing to do.

[43] *Ibid.,* p. 128.
[44] *Ibid.,* p. 110.
[45] For an elaboration of this criticism, see Florence Kluckhohn, "Dominant and Substitute Profiles of Cultural Orientations," *Social Forces,* Vol. 28 (1950), pp. 387–393.

Many of the studies cited in the preceding sections were not specific about income figures. This was not because the investigators were careless but because, in many respects, it is not only the actual but also the relative size of family income that counts.

Nevertheless, there is an important sense in which the actual size of family income determines the American child's chance of developing in line with his potentialities. As has been indicated by the findings of studies in the health and education fields, each increase in family income level up to a certain point (studies some years ago put it at about $5000) means a decrease in incidence of chronic illness and an increase in adequacy of diet and in likelihood of schooling commensurate with intelligence.

Current American standards must form the basis for our conception of what is poverty and what is not. It is true that the food and housing enjoyed by many of our poorest families are distinctly better than that of the great majority in many countries. Judged by some foreign standards, surprisingly few families in the United States have inadequate income. The same would probably be true if standards accepted in our own country a few generations ago were used. But since the central fact of American economic life is continuous growth, continuous development, and a steady gain in the standards of living, studies of the relation between family income and child welfare in the United States are appropriately made in terms of today's American standards.[46]

According to studies made by the U.S. Bureau of Labor Statistics, in the thirty-four largest American cities, in 1947, an income of from $2,734 to $3,111 a year was needed if a family of four was to meet "prevailing standards of what is needed for health efficiency, nurture of children, social participation, and the maintenance of self-respect and the respect of others."[47] This definition, it will be noted, takes into account the various factors we have described as pertinent to the relation between low income and health of personality.

In contrast, the Subcommittee on Low-income Families (Joint Com-

---

[46] It is proper, however, to note that today's standards are related to those of earlier years, as one would expect. For example, the cost of a "minimum comfort" budget for a family of five developed by William F. Ogburn for the National War Labor Board in World War I would have amounted to about $2,606 in 1947. The Bureau of Labor Statistics City Worker's Family Budget, developed in 1947, ran between $2,734 and $3,111 for a family of four in the 34 largest cities of the country. (For the Ogburn budget, see *Standards of Living*, Bureau of Applied Economics, Inc., 1920. For the BLS budget, see *City Worker's Family Budget*, U.S. Bureau of Labor Statistics, December, 1947, p. 38.

[47] *City Worker's Family Budget*, U.S. Bureau of Labor Statistics, December, 1947, p. 9.

mittee on the Economic Report, 81st Congress) took $2000 a year as an across-the-board figure of inadequate family income, regardless of size of family or place of residence. In 1950, this was an income fairly equivalent to the $1000 level at which in 1935–36 the National Health Survey found the chance of ill health definitely increased. No such single figure can be really satisfactory, for the variation in cost of living with size of family and place of residence is too great. Nevertheless, as a reference point for some statistical comparisons that are facilitated by the use of a single figure, it has advantages. In addition, there would seem to be little doubt that in urban areas, and perhaps in any area that is within the prevailing money economy, $2000 a year in money income for a family with children is below any generally accepted minimum standard of economic welfare.

Number of Children in Low-income Families

How many American children live in families of low income according to these standards? Estimates made for the Midcentury White House Conference on Children and Youth indicate that in 1950 only about half of the children who lived in cities belonged to families with an income that met the Bureau of Labor Statistics standard.[48]

For the country as a whole, more than a fourth (27.8 per cent) of the children were in families with cash income of less than $2000, and just about half had under $3000. A little less than 10 per cent of all the children in the country had a family income of over $6000, a level some studies seem to imply is the one at which health and educational needs can comfortably be met.[49]

Who are these children whose family income is under $2000? What proportion do they constitute of the nearly 45 million children under eighteen who, in the spring of 1950, lived with their parents? For our purpose, the question can perhaps be answered best by distinguishing between families containing both parents and those in which the father is absent. First, however, the total population distribution of these children by residence and type of family should be noted. In 1950, it was as follows, in thousands:

[48] Estimate prepared by the U.S. Children's Bureau for the Midcentury White House Conference on Children and Youth. See *Children and Youth at the Midcentury: A Chart Book,* Health Publications Institute, Raleigh, N. C., 1951, Chart 23.

[49] These figures and all others cited below relating to number of children in March, 1950, according to income level and characteristics of their families, were taken from data of the Bureau of the Census compiled for the Midcentury White House Conference on Children and Youth.

All children	44,623
Living with both parents	40,523
Living with father; no mother	674
Living with mother; no father	3,426
Children in families	42,253
Living with both parents	39,252
Living with father; no mother	535
Living with mother; no father	2,466
Children in subfamilies [50]	2,370
Living with both parents	1,271
Living with father; no mother	139
Living with mother; no father	960

Nearly 10 per cent of the 40.5 million children who lived in normal homes (homes containing both a mother and a father) and about 1.6 per cent of the 2.5 million who lived in broken homes headed by a mother had an income of under $2000 a year.[51] Since these children constituted a little less than one-fourth of the children who lived with both parents and about two-thirds of those who lived with only their mothers, it is clear that the broken home is an important factor in the low-income situation.

Reasons for Low Income in Normal Families

In families containing both parents, a major factor in the low-income situation is the *father's occupation*. The odds that a child is in a family group whose income is under $2000 increase as the father's occupational status declines. For children with fathers in the professional group the odds, in 1948, were one in ten. They rose to three in ten for children of "common laborers," and to eight in ten for children of farm laborers.[52]

In round figures, the occupational situation of fathers in families with income under $2000 was as follows: [53]

[50] A subfamily is either a married couple (with or without children) or a parent and child under eighteen who live with relatives.

[51] In the count of normal homes, subfamilies are included; in the count of broken homes, they are excluded. Children in subfamilies constituted 3.1 per cent of all children in normal homes, and 4.9 per cent of those in such homes where income was under $2000.

[52] Bureau of the Census, *Income of Families and Persons in the United States: 1948*, Current Population Reports, Consumer Income, Series P. 60, Number 6, February 14, 1950, page 20.

[53] Children whose fathers were not in the labor force (about 700,000) and those whose fathers were under 25 years of age (about 700,000) are excluded from this tabulation.

> 3.0 million children had fathers who were farmers
>
> 1.9 million had fathers who were farm laborers, "common laborers," or in domestic service
>
> 1.7 million had fathers who were factory workers, craftsmen, or such
>
> 1.0 million had fathers in other occupations (including clerical, sales, professional, managerial)
>
> 1.2 million had fathers who were unemployed

These figures indicate that children of low-income families fall into two main groups. One is composed of children of farm laborers and farm operators. The second is composed, primarily, of children of nonfarm workers whose skills are low. To this latter group belong fathers who are laborers or domestic servants, and also a considerable proportion of the unemployed.[54] It also includes substantial numbers of persons who, though classified with the higher occupations, are essentially unskilled. The "operative" group, for example, includes gas-station attendants and truck drivers. The "clerical-sales" group includes grocery clerks, peddlers, and shipping clerks. Even the "professional–semiprofessional" group includes street photographers, laboratory technicians, and palmists. It seems a reasonable possibility, therefore, that a substantial number of the low-income people who are classified in higher occupational groups actually work in occupations that require little training.[55]

A second factor related to low income is *race*. In 1950, just about one-fifth of the white children belonged to families with an income under $2000, but for children who were not white (for the most part they were Negroes) the proportion was 57 per cent.

The racial difference was most marked in cities. The urban rate was 10 per 100 white children and 38 per 100 nonwhite children in "normal" families. On the other hand, it was in rural farm areas that the rates for all races were highest. In such places, 52.7 per cent of the white children and 90.3 per cent of the nonwhite children lived in families whose income was under $2000 a year.

People who are other than white are overly represented in the lower-paid occupations. For example, in 1949 such men constituted about 8 per cent of all family heads but about 20 per cent of those who were

[54] Unpublished tabulations of the U.S. Bureau of the Census' Current Population Survey for April, 1950, show that roughly one-third of the unemployed were in common labor or service work; just under a third were operatives and related workers.

[55] Data on earnings in individual occupations are available from the 1940 Census. Though of limited applicability, they tend to confirm this statement. U.S. Bureau of the Census, 16th Census of Population, *The Labor Force*, III, Table 72.

servants, 20 per cent of those who were farm laborers, and 26 per cent of those who were urban laborers.[56] Even within these various groups they tend to have lower incomes.

Age is another factor that is generally mentioned in connection with the problem of low incomes. It is, however, of relatively little importance here, since the very young have few children and the old have few under eighteen years of age. Thus, in the spring of 1950, of all children under eighteen in lower-income families, only 700,000 had fathers under twenty-five years of age while 8.8 million had fathers who were between twenty-five and sixty-four.[57] Hence neither youth nor lack of work experience on the part of their parents can explain the low family incomes for most of these children.

A fourth factor frequently discussed in connection with low income is the fact that businessmen, farmers, and professional men may sustain temporary losses in a given year, although their incomes are generally high. Less than 5 per cent of all children in low income families in 1950 would fall into any such group,[58] however; hence it is not an important consideration in studying the problems of these children.

The "normal" families, then, who have too little income are chiefly those in which the fathers are employed in occupations requiring little training. Many of these families are Negro, and many—Negro and white —are farmers or farm laborers. It is often argued that these latter families do not need as large an income as city dwellers, and to some extent this is true. Nevertheless, some of the economic factors we have shown to handicap healthy development of personality (especially lack of money for health care and education) operate even more disastrously in rural areas than in cities. Complacency about these low incomes in city or

[56] Census data for April, 1949, on occupation of head of family by color appear in U.S. Congress, Joint Committee on the Economic Report, *Low Income Families and Economic Stability*, 1949, Table A–4.

[57] The figure for the under-25 group was estimated as follows. Census data show that the number of children with parents aged under 25 and over 64 in the under $2000 family income group was 8.34 million. Data for all children under 18 living with their parents in March, 1950, indicate that 88 per cent of those with parents in the under-25 and over-64 age groups had parents under 25. This percentage, applied to children in normal families, gives 7.34 million with parents under 25 years. Because of the method of estimation, a small number of the armed forces in the 25–64 age group are included in the figure of 7.34.

[58] Less than 5 per cent of all spending units with 1949 incomes under $2000 had negative incomes from business operations. (Estimated from data appearing in the *Federal Reserve Bulletin*, August, 1950, Tables 2, 7, 9.) Moreover, less than 5 per cent of this group had incomes of more than $3000 in the previous year. (*Ibid.*, Table 7.)

country seems unwarranted, for the usual idyllic picture of the happy life of the country child is unjustified.

Sources of Income of Broken Families

In the spring of 1950, some 4.1 million children lived in broken homes. 3.4 million of these children lived with their mothers, 2.4 million of them in homes that the mother headed.[59] In perhaps 60 per cent of these fatherless families the mother was widowed; in most of the others the father was absent by reason of separation, divorce, desertion, or lack of marriage. Because of their number and importance to the child, families headed by women call for special attention in analyzing the source of the family income.

In contrast to less than a fourth in normal families, two-thirds of the children in broken homes headed by a mother had a family income of less than $2000 a year.[60] Less than two children in ten in this group lived in families with incomes above $3000. This is, then, characteristically a low-income group. With the absence of a normal family goes the absence of a normal income.

What sources did the mothers heading these families of low income draw upon to feed and clothe their children? [61]

For 172,000 children, the answer was simple—and difficult. There was no current income. The mothers drew upon savings made in earlier years. They relied on gifts from relatives. And they marked time until income could be earned or received from some other source.

For 377,000 children, the family income came chiefly from social-security sources—from old-age-and-survivors' insurance, from Federal-state aid to dependent children, and to a minor extent from rents and dividends.[62] The average payment per child under the aid-to-dependent-

[59] *Current Population Reports: Population Characteristics,* U.S. Bureau of the Census, December 4, 1950, p. 17.

[60] *Current Population Reports: Consumer Income,* U.S. Bureau of the Census, May 23, 1951, p. 2.

[61] The following data apply to the 1.6 million children living with their mothers in families. There were in addition 856,000 living with their mothers in subfamilies and 176,000 living with their fathers in families or subfamilies, where the incomes were under $2000. It is from the combined group of these 2.7 million children and an additional one million living with relatives that the 1.6 million on the ADC program in April, 1950, were drawn in considerable part. For data on status of father in ADC families, see Elizabeth Alling and Agnes Leisy, *Aid to Dependent Children in a Post-war Year,* Public Assistance Report No. 17, Federal Security Agency, 1950, p. 31.

[62] A special Census tabulation for the White House Conference shows that 377,000 children lived in families with female heads where the total income of under $2000 was nonearned income—income other than wages, salaries, or earnings from the operation of a business. The dominant importance of transfer payments—aid to dependent children, social insurance, unemployment compensation, etc.—at low income levels is

children program ran at about $350 at an annual rate.[63] It is hardly surprising, therefore, that most of these families without earners appeared in the low-income group.

Three hundred and fifty-three thousand children lived in homes in which the less than $2000 income came chiefly from the work of an older sibling, other relative, or their own labor. (In perhaps 40 per cent of these families, more than one person worked.) [64] In this group it was not unusual for a child in his late teens to support the family.

The income for the families containing the remaining 706,000 children (more than four out of every ten in this income group) came from the mother's work.

The typical income for families headed by working mothers was well under $2000 in 1949. Since these women probably received some income from sources other than their own work, the typical working mother must have earned considerably less than that amount.

Three factors are chiefly responsible for this low level of earnings. First, women's earnings are usually lower than men's. Second, many of these women are too young and too poorly educated [65] to command high wages. In the third place, nonwhites form a greater proportion of deserted and divorced women than of all married women,[66] and earning rates among nonwhites are usually below average.

---

indicated in unpublished data used by the Department of Commerce for estimating an adjusted income distribution for the U.S. in 1948. For this distribution, see *The Economic Report of the President,* January, 1950, p. 140.

[63] From data in the *Social Security Bulletin* one can estimate an average ADC payment of $73 per family in 1949. Alling and Leisy (*op. cit.,* p. 16) indicate that the average number of children per family on the program in June, 1948, was 2.54. Hence an annual per-child figure runs to $344.

[64] Data for all households in 1949 where the head was not in the labor force (except those with male head, wife present) showed 37.7 per cent with other persons working, 15.5 per cent points of which—or 41 per cent—represented families with more than one worker. (U.S. Bureau of the Census, *Marital and Family Characteristics of the Labor Force in the United States,* April, 1949, Series P–50, No. 22, Table 7. Since 72 per cent of these households had a female head (U.S. Bureau of the Census, *Marital Status and Household Characteristics,* April, 1949, Series P–20, No. 26, Table 6) and since the unpublished 1950 data show that 39.2 per cent of the children (as compared to 37.7 per cent of the heads above) were in families where the mothers did not work but others in the family did, it is reasonably safe to use these data to represent households with female heads and thence, as 1946 data indicate, to represent families with female heads.

[65] A more precise measurement of the size of these groups is impossible because of sampling-error differences among the various unpublished Census tabulations used and because no data are available to cross-classify number of women by occupations, as well as by number of children and income.

[66] U.S. Bureau of the Census, *Characteristics of Single, Married, Widowed and Divorced Persons in 1947,* Series P–20, No. 10, Table 2. Nonwhites constituted 10 per cent of all women, 12 per cent of the divorced, and 25 per cent of the separated.

The net effect of these various factors shows up in the kinds of jobs these mothers hold. More than half of them are day workers or waitresses. A fifth are factory workers. Less than 15 per cent are in white-collar jobs—clerical, sales, or professional. The widowed or separated working mother, in other words, is a handicapped person so far as earning power is concerned.

Place of Residence as a Factor in Low Income

Various statements made above suggest that one of the chief factors in low income is place of residence. Associated with that are occupation and race. A breakdown of figures to take account of all these factors at once is not available.

Some facts in regard to occupation and race have already been noted, however; and the relation of these factors to place of residence is well known.

First, the distribution of children by residence must be noted. Of the approximately 45 million children in the United States, in 1950, who lived with their parents, 25.6 million were in urban areas, 10.3 in rural nonfarm areas (to use the U.S. Census Bureau's terminology), and 8.7 in rural farm areas.

Census figures for 1950 show that, in contrast to 27.8 per cent for the country as a whole, only 17 per cent of the urban children belonged to families whose money income was under $2000. The corresponding proportion was 22 in rural nonfarm areas. In rural farm areas, however, it was 60 per cent. Obviously, residence is a factor of prime importance.

The position of the child who lives in a broken home is, however, almost as likely to be unfavorable in the city as in the country. Two-thirds of all the city children in broken homes headed by a mother had a family income of under $2000, in contrast to 11 per cent in normal families. The corresponding rural nonfarm proportions were 78 and 58 per cent, respectively.[67] Loss of the father is apparently much more likely to lower the economic status of a child in a city than on a farm.

If the rural situation in general is bad, it is even more so for those rural children who are classified as nonwhite. In 1948, about one-tenth of the 5,680,000 farm families were headed by nonwhite males. Nearly half of these families (260,000) had a cash income of under $1000, and 85 per cent of them had less than $2000. The corresponding percentages for white farm families were 18 and 41, respectively. Families headed by a

[67] The figures for families headed by a father were 19 per cent in urban areas and 78 per cent in rural farm areas.

woman, white or nonwhite, were about as badly off then, as the nonwhite families with male heads.[68]

Consideration of the relative status of city and farm children with respect to income always raises the question of how much the farm family benefits from nonmoney income. Differences such as the ones cited above are often brushed aside as unimportant, on the assumption that farm children's parents require much less cash income to provide for the children adequately.

Studies conducted by the Bureau of Agricultural Economics of the U.S. Department of Agriculture throw grave doubt on this argument. They show that, in 1948, the aggregate value of products produced on the farm for home use and the net rental value of the farm home averaged $604 per farm. Rental value of the home varied greatly, of course, from farm to farm, but value of the products used in the home [69] was much less affected by general economic level. In consequence, low-income families receive a proportionately higher share of their total income in goods and services than do other farm families, with perhaps as much as 40 per cent coming from such sources.[70]

Even such an addition does not spell prosperity or even an adequate standard of living for many farm families, however. According to a 1948 report of the U.S. Bureau of the Census, one-fourth of the farm families in the country (1.7 million out of the total 6.7 million) received under $1000 in cash income. Even if it were assumed that cash constituted only one-half of their total income, these families would have received less than $40 a week. On this income half a million of these families would have had to take care of five or more persons. All in all, the extreme poverty of large numbers of American children who live in rural areas is unquestionable.

Cumulative Effects of Low Income [71]

The immediate and separate effects of low income upon children in terms of inadequate diets, poor housing, limited health care and educa-

[68] Bureau of the Census Report, cited in *Materials on the Problem of Low-income Families, op. cit.,* p. 37.

[69] The average value of products by income groups in Illinois in 1946 varied from $304 for operators having gross cash receipts of less than $1000 to $519 for those with receipts of $40,000 or over. "Income Size Distribution for Illinois Farm-operator Families," R. F. Daly, unpublished MS. Cited in *Materials on the Problem of Low-income Families, op. cit.,* p. 40.

[70] See U.S. Department of Agriculture, *How Families Use Their Incomes,* Misc. Publications No. 653, p. 54.

[71] From an unpublished address by Eveline Burns ("Differences in Family Income and Their Effect on Family Life") to the Midcentury White House Conference on Children and Youth, Washington, D.C., December, 1950.

tional opportunities, and poor family relations have been pointed out above. What is perhaps more important is the fact that these effects are cumulative. In the first place, in the low-income groups the contribution which the family itself can make to the welfare of its own children is necessarily greatly circumscribed. The low-income mother is more likely to be an earner in order to eke out the family income. In 1950, 18 per cent of the mothers in normal homes with children under eighteen were at work. In broken homes, typically headed by a woman, half of the mothers worked, and almost the same proportion held for children living in homes where the father was disabled. Thus, in addition to the more obvious material and physical deprivations, these children in the low-income families were deprived of the normal care and support which we think of as being the most valuable foundation for healthy development.

The ability of the family to make its maximum contribution is also limited in these income groups because the exercise of economy and wise spending, so necessary to make limited dollars stretch, is particularly difficult in the circumstances in which they live. Not only are the parents usually less well educated than those who have more money; their restricted housing also precludes the possibility of buying and storing food in anything but small quantities, and they have to resort to buying on credit and cannot therefore shop around for bargains.

Low incomes have cumulative effects also in that the opportunity to rise in the income scale is the more restricted the lower the income. Educational opportunities are limited not only because of the inability to pay necessary fees and maintenance but also because of the pressure on sons and daughters to take jobs as soon as possible in order to contribute to the family income. Where economic mobility involves geographical migration, this group is again at a disadvantage—the disadvantage of ignorance of available opportunities and of necessary resources to finance the costs of migration.

The effects are cumulative, too, because there is a great geographical concentration of low-income families. Perhaps 40 per cent of the nonfarm low-income families live in the South; there are relatively few in the West. Of the agricultural low-income group, there is a great concentration throughout the Appalachian Region, Piedmont Area and into the South, and in some regions around the Lake States. We know that the well-being of children and families, while primarily dependent upon the income of the family itself, is also considerably affected by the social services and other community resources available. This concentration means that whole areas are poor, so that the available resources tend to be least adequate precisely in those areas where the need for them is greatest.

Cumulative effects are to be expected also because there is a considerable concentration of low incomes in certain groups that for other reasons are also at a disadvantage. Negroes figure more heavily in the low-income groups in proportion to their representation in the population as a whole. Migrants are another group that has not only the disadvantage of low economic status but also the social and cultural disadvantages of not being an accepted and integral part of any one community.

Our society does not have to accept this situation. There is much that we can do if we have the will. Given that we have successfully applied our minds to the analysis of the causes, there are many remedies to hand, and there is no reason to believe that we cannot invent others as we find occasion for them. Already we have done much during the past fifty years to reduce the proportions of our population who live under the conditions here described. Through institutional changes, such as the social-security system, public education, minimum-wage laws, and the like, safeguards have already been provided for all the population. Because of them even the least well-off children today are probably better off than many at the beginning of the century.

Specific attacks upon the problems of specific groups can also be made as the causes of their poverty are identified. The problems of the migrant worker are even now being studied. There is no reason why methods for dealing with the problems of total communities whose living standard is far below the average should not be developed. Again, much can be done through the dissemination among today's parents of knowledge that can be applied by the family itself. The heartening improvement in nutrition standards over the past seven years shows what can be done by the application of new knowledge.

Basic to a successful attack upon the problems of the most disadvantaged children, however, is knowledge of the causes of their situation. Much information about the causes of the low incomes of so large a proportion of our children is available, but on every hand there is evidence that more is needed. Modern research techniques, the use of budget studies, cost-of-living indexes, censuses and sample studies have not yet been exploited to their fullest. Success in dealing with the most significant problem created by differences of income (namely, the low level of living of those at the bottom of the scale) calls for vigorous support of efforts to increase our knowledge of the social and economic causes of a situation which all deplore.

The Effects of
Prejudice and Discrimination

ANOTHER source of difficulty for children and youth is found in the fact that the treatment accorded individuals in the United States depends, in part, upon the racial, ethnic, or religious groups to which they belong. The nature and extent of discrimination and prejudice are unknown in any exact sort of way, and there are many subtleties in the situation and many crosscurrents that have not been adequately explored. Nevertheless, it is unquestionable that, in many respects and to a greater or less degree, Negroes, Jews, Latin Americans, Orientals, Southern and Eastern Europeans, Indians, migrants, and, as has been indicated in the preceding chapter, all whose economic status is very low are likely to be regarded as socially inferior and to be discriminated against.

Without going into any detail as to why this is so or what the nature of the prejudice and discrimination is, we want to review here briefly what effects this may have on the health of personality of both those who discriminate and those who are discriminated against.

Definitions and Limitations

The kind of prejudice we are talking about has been defined as a negative attitude toward ethnic, racial, or religious groups that violates important norms or values nominally accepted by the culture. Such a definition, it will be noted, puts prejudice in the context of the society in which it is exercised. Discrimination is similarly defined. It consists of differential treatment of individuals considered to belong to a particular social group, especially that differential treatment that violates important institutional standards.[1]

In spite of a wealth of material on the existence of prejudice and discrimination, on its origins, and on means of reducing these un-American

---

[1] Definitions paraphrased from Robin Williams, *Reduction of Inter-group Tensions,* Social Science Research Council, 1947.

attitudes, there is little in the scientific literature on the precise effects of prejudice and discrimination on health of personality. This is due in part to the difficulties inherent in answering the question and in part, probably, to the fact that most of the effort of research workers has gone into finding ways of eliminating the obviously bad situation rather than in demonstrating that it is bad.

What research of a scientific nature there is appears to confirm the deductions that logically follow from the description of the course of healthy personality development given above. In connection with what follows it must be remembered, however, that the various minority groups that are affected by prejudice and discrimination differ greatly in their situation, and that the impact of adverse circumstances varies considerably from individual to individual. There are great differences between the situations of, say, Jews and Negroes, and within each group there are further differentiations. Such matters as the emotional balance and good sense of the individual's parents, the character of his physical and intellectual make-up, the part of the country he lives in, the opportunities of his neighborhood and community will determine to some extent whether, in what way, and to what degree he is affected by prejudicial and discriminatory practices.

In spite of these many considerations, it seems highly probable that prejudice and discrimination work very much to the disadvantage of the personality development of most minority-group members in one way or another.

How Personality Development Is Affected

The way in which prejudice and discrimination affect personality probably depends considerably on whether the individual lives within a self-contained group of his own kind or whether he is daily exposed to the contrast between himself and others. Complete isolation is rare and is probably getting rarer. Nevertheless, there are rural areas and sections of large cities in which Negroes and Mexicans, for example, rear their children considerably apart from others, and in which tradition gives stability to life. For children brought up in such circumstances the early stages of personality development are probably passed through with relative equanimity, so far, at least, as the influence of prejudice and discrimination is concerned.

Difficulties for children so reared come when they leave home or when they move out of the close family circle to mingle with other youths in small towns and cities. Such a change is likely to take place at adolescence, the time at which a sense of identity should be in the making. Sudden exposure to the fact that they are not considered as good as other people is very disrupting to personality development. It is a shock to the sense of trust, an incitement to feelings of doubt and shame. To determine who one is and what one can do is doubly difficult under such circumstances. Some youngsters will break from their old standards and try to form a synthetic equivalent of the "American" personality pattern. Others will rebel against being stigmatized and find in zoot suits and other symbols the guarantee of their self-worth.

For children who grow up in the perhaps more common situation of being daily exposed to the fact of their difference the consequences may be more serious, since their early personality development is likely to be disturbed. Trust, for example, may be difficult for them to achieve, since their parents' own sense of trust may be fragile. If achieved, it may be difficult to maintain in a world that is hostile in so many ways. The development of a sense of autonomy may also be interfered with, sometimes because parents fear that independence of action will expose little children to harm, sometimes because they want them to retain the advantages of babyhood as long as possible.

Children of minority groups who live in close proximity to the majority group are likely to find their initiative curbed by many external circumstances. Negroes probably suffer especially in this respect, for Negro mothers must early warn their children to avoid offending white people. It has been noted by research workers that urban Negroes of the middle class are likely to be strict and even harsh in their punishments, testifying perhaps to the urgency of children's behaving in ways that will not bring censure.

Initiative too much curbed arouses shame and doubt, it has been said. Such feelings are further induced in children of minority groups by the aspersions they are likely to encounter in school and community. Even if some individuals are spared such treatment and are praised for their endeavors, it is not long before they learn that they belong to a looked-down-upon or despised group and that they should be wary in what they attempt.

Feelings of inferiority growing out of an inability to achieve success in the kind of tasks that are commonly set in school are likely to characterize children whose homes do not prepare them for intellectual efforts. Some minority-group children are especially handicapped in this way. Others, who are favored by high intellectual endowment and a tradition in which scholarship is prized, may find success at this level so satisfying that they do not push on sufficiently to deal with the problems of later developmental periods.

For children who have frequently been confronted with prejudice and discrimination, adolescence is a particularly trying period. In addition to their own inner confusion, they must bear with the dominant group's own insecurities, which so often take the form of a cliquish antagonism. Some of the minority groups have no solid tradition on which to rely, and many individuals have no basic security in family life on which to depend. Nor until recently has there been much in magazines, movies, radio, and other sources of information to suggest to these youths that they and their group are persons of worth.

Almost inevitably, then, the minority-group child is thrown into a crucial conflict in his feelings about himself and in the way he estimates himself. Is he the person he feels himself to be? Or is he a person worthy of no more respect than he gets? It is clear that he must find some way to cope with this basic conflict and with the threats to his self-esteem that he meets on every side.

The particular way in which any one child deals with this problem depends, in a rather complex and intricate fashion, upon many interrelated factors, such as the amount of affection and support he feels within his family unit, the stability and quality of his family relations, the social and economic group to which he belongs, his own personal characteristics, intelligence, and personality structure. Social-class factors also play a part. The middle-class child, for example, may withdraw by exhibiting a generally defeatist attitude and by limiting his personal aspirations, or he may attempt to compensate by a rigid adherence to middle-class values and standards and an aggressive determination to succeed in these terms. The lower-class child is more likely to defy middle-class standards and expectations and to compensate by overly aggressive behavior that may take any number of forms.

In any case, an individual who is surrounded by pervasive hostility and rejection and has become ambivalent in his feelings about himself is likely to react to both the ambiguous and the objectively nonthreatening aspects of his experience with defensiveness and hypersensitivity. Minority-group children are characteristically hypersensitive and anxious about their minority status, hostile toward the members of the dominant group, their own group, and other minority groups. They exhibit a generalized pattern of personality difficulties that seems to be associated with the humiliation to which they are subjected. Not that all of them are obviously emotionally maladjusted. The majority pulls through somehow or other, but with what burden of resentment and bitterness few know.

Some Research Findings

There has not been much scientific research on the effects of prejudice and discrimination on personality formation. What research there is, however, appears to support the gloomy observations made above.

First, the current opinions of social scientists may be cited. In 1947, Deutscher and Chein [2] questioned over five hundred anthropologists, social psychologists, and sociologists regarding "the psychological effects of enforced segregation, both on the group that enforces the segregation and on the group segregated." Nearly all these social scientists stated that, in their opinion, segregation has detrimental psychological effects on members of the segregated groups even if equal facilities are provided. Almost as many said that it is also psychologically detrimental to members of the group that segregate. Professional experience and scientific research were claimed as the basis of these opinions.

The typical comments of the social scientists regarding the detrimental effects of segregation on minority-group members may be summarized as follows:

1. Special stresses are created for individuals by the discrepancy between democratic teachings with respect to equality and the practice of enforced segregation.
2. Segregation is a special source of frustration.
3. Feelings of inferiority and of not being wanted are induced by segregation.
4. Submissiveness, martyrdom, feelings of persecution, withdrawal tendencies, self-ambivalence, and aggression are likely to develop.
5. Distortion in the sense of reality may occur as a consequence of enforced segregation.
6. A few individuals gain psychologically from being members of segregated groups, but most are harmed thereby.

The opinions of the social scientists about the effects of segregation on the dominant group will be cited below.

In addition to these statements of opinion, the findings of a series of studies may be cited. Unfortunately for scientific accuracy and adequacy, thoroughly satisfactory methods of determining the effects of prejudice and discrimination on health of personality have not yet been devised,

[2] Max Deutscher and Isidor Chein, "The Psychological Effects of Enforced Segregation: A Survey of Social Science Opinion," *Journal of Psychology*, Vol. 26 (1948), pp. 259–287.

nor has a sufficient number of studies dealing with the various minority groups been made.

With respect to the first point, Otto Klineberg, summarizing the findings of experimental studies in the field of Negro personality, has the following to say:

The questionnaire studies are important mainly as raising the question of the validity of particular items, and of the variations in their meaning for different cultural groups. . . .

Conclusions obtained through the use of tests cannot be more valid than the test used. . . . Completely satisfactory research in this field will have to wait until psychologists have devised more adequate measures for the study of personality.[3]

As to the inadequate coverage, most of the studies so far conducted have dealt with Negroes and most of the rest have been concerned with Jews. Whether prejudice and discrimination operate in the same way and produce the same effects on children and youth of other minority groups, especially those who do not share the dominant American culture pattern, has not been definitely determined. The findings of the few studies that have been made suggest that the differences may be considerable but that in respect to feelings of inferiority the effects are much the same.

For example, J. W. Tait [4] studied two thousand eleven- to fifteen-year-old children of Italian-born parents living in New York City, using both personality tests and personal interviews. His problem was to determine "whether prejudice and rejection produced in children of Italian-born parents maladjustment and character traits which are ordinarily considered unfavorable." His conclusion was that "when the question is approached from the standpoint of averages, prejudice against and rejection of these children are accompanied by broad trends toward such character defects as inferiority feelings, awareness of rejection, poor social adjustment, introversion, and emotional instability."

In spite of these limitations, considerable is known about the adverse effects of prejudice and discrimination. In the following review, some of the outstanding studies are cited.

Age of Onset

First, how early in life are the effects of prejudice and discrimination

---

[3] See Otto Klineberg, ed., *Characteristics of the American Negro,* Harper & Brothers, New York, 1944, pp. 99–138.

[4] J. W. Tait, "Race Prejudice and Personality," *School: Secondary Edition,* Vol. 34 (1946), pp. 795–798.

made manifest? Various studies of Negro and Jewish children's racial concepts indicate that at an early age these children are aware of ideas and values about races, of their own place in relation to them, and that these ideas have affected the children's feelings about themselves.

For instance, among minority-group children in kindergarten, first, and second grades, Radke, Trager and Davis found evidence of negative self-feelings and of emotional conflict concerning group membership. They state:

Many children experience serious ego-threats as a result of group prejudices. Negro children reveal most vividly and often the feelings of insecurity resulting from anticipated rejection or insult from white children. The same phenomenon appears among Jewish children.[5]

These investigators add that the reactions of Negro children involve opposing forces and are indicative of ambivalent feelings toward their own race. There are "forces toward increasing rejection of the Negro, which are in line with the mores of the dominant culture; forces which arise out of a need for self-acceptance; and forces toward aggressive retaliation against whites."

These, it would seem, are rather strong statements to use in reference to children five to seven years old. Independent evidence from other investigators, however, confirms these findings and establishes the existence of these or similar processes at even earlier ages.

Goodman,[6] working with Northern children between the ages of 2:9 to 4:4, found that her Negro subjects, when required to make racial self-identifications, generally reacted "with behavior indicative of uneasiness, tension or evasion, while there was no similar tendency among the whites." She suggests: "It is possible that the psychological insecurity and the uncertainty concerning status which characterize most adult Negroes are reflected in these examples of Negro child behavior."

Horowitz, studying twenty-two nursery-school children between the ages of two and five years, came to the conclusion that "the concept of group consciousness and group identification is an intrinsic aspect of ego-development. . . . Before the ego has been completely formed, in the very process of becoming, we find it subtly approximating a visible symbol that has been socially institutionalized to aid it in its work of marking

[5] M. Radke, H. Trager, and H. Davis, "Social Perceptions and Attitudes of Children," *Genetic Psychology Monographs,* Vol. 40 (1949), pp. 327–447.

[6] M. E. Goodman, "Evidence Concerning the Genesis of Inter-racial Attitudes," *American Anthropologist.* Vol. 48 (1946), pp. 624–630.

itself off from all the not-self. . . . The individual's attitudes toward his group evidently is an integral part of himself, in terms of which he is fashioned, under some circumstances of life."

Clark and Clark [7] made a report on experiments dealing with the emotional and personal factors involved in the racial identification of Negro children three to seven years old. They found that Negro children, when required to indicate their racial preference and then to identify themselves with a brown doll which they had previously negated or rejected, showed many signs of emotional conflict and personality disturbance. Some of these children resorted to phantasy responses and rationalizations, some to escapist responses, and some even with an ironic humorous use of a racial epithet. The escapist responses were most frequent in children living in the North but occurred in some children in the South. The epithet responses were made only by children in the South. These authors conclude:

It appears from the data that coincident with the awareness of racial differences and racial identity there is also the awareness and acceptance of the existing cultural attitudes and values attached to race. . . . The negation of the color "brown" exists in the same complexity of attitudes in which there also exists knowledge of the fact that the child himself must be identified with that which he rejects. This apparently introduces a fundamental conflict at the very foundations of the ego structure. Many of these children attempt to resolve this profound conflict either through wishful thinking or a phantasy—expressing itself in a desire to escape a situation which focuses the conflict for them. By the seven-year level the Negro child seems to be developing some stabilizing ideas which might help to resolve the basic conflicts between his racial self-image and the negative social evaluation of his skin color.

Kinds of Reactions

Second, what do the investigations indicate as to the kinds of personality reactions that develop in Negroes, the group that is probably the most disadvantaged by prejudice and discrimination and by actual segregation?

The studies already cited indicate that even very young Negro children are likely to manifest emotional conflict in regard to their racial identity. They are ambivalent in their feelings about themselves and the group to which they belong, on the one hand accepting derogatory stereotypes of

[7] Clark and Clark, "Emotional Factors in Racial Identification and Preference in Negro Children," *Journal of Negro Education,* Summer, 1950.

the Negro and, on the other, feeling inferior and resentful about being so classified.

Studies of color preferences and feelings about color in the case of older Negro children, of college youths, and of mental patients come to much the same conclusion.[8] These studies suggest, however, that the feelings and reactions become more complicated as the Negro child grows older. The individual is likely to continue the pattern of rating himself lighter than he really is, but he substitutes for his frank preference of "whiteness" a preference for light shades of brown and rejects white or extremely light individuals.

Studies of the racial stereotypes of Negroes also support the generalization about ambivalence and group self-hatred. J. A. Bayton,[9] for example, compared a hundred students at a Southern Negro college with one hundred white students at Princeton with respect to racial stereotypes. He found that Negro and white college students "exhibit a high degree of similarity in the stereotypes they possess of the various racial and national groups" and that "Negro college students assign characteristics to themselves which are different from those assigned to the 'typical Negro.'"

In a subsequent study of the same sort made in the Deep South, Bayton and a collaborator confirmed these findings and concluded:

(1) The stereotype of the typical Negro as held by Negroes is not indicative of a high degree of intra-group morale.

(2) The "deep South" Negroes' stereotype of the white American reveals a sub-pattern of distrust and suspicion.

Another kind of reaction to prejudice and discrimination is open hostility. Reactions of this kind are portrayed most graphically in Richard Wright's novel *Native Son*. This fictional case history purports to describe the extent and consequences of random antiwhite hostility which is generated by the pervasive frustrations inherent in the conditions of life of the masses of American Negroes. The same writer, in his autobiographical *Black Boy*, describes some of the life history factors which seem consistent

[8] See, for example, N. N. Seeman, "Skin Color Values in Three All-negro School Classes," *American Sociological Review*, Vol. 11 (1946), pp. 315–321; Henry J. Myers and Leon Yachelson, "Color Denial in the Negro," *Psychiatry*, Vol. 11 (1948), pp. 39–46; E. S. Marks, "Factors Affecting Skin Color Judgments of Negro College Students," *Psychological Bulletin*, Vol. 39 (1942), p. 577; also "Skin Color Judgments of Negro College Students," *Journal of Abnormal Social Psychology*, Vol. 38 (1945), pp. 370–376.

[9] J. A. Bayton, "The Racial Stereotypes of Negro College Students," *Journal of Abnormal and Social Psychology*, Vol. 36 (1941), pp. 97–102.

with the blind and nonadaptive hostility displayed by his fictional character Bigger Thomas.

Whether the kind of reaction Wright describes can be attributed
wholly to Negro status may be doubted. One psychoanalyst, commenting
on the books, maintained that Bigger Thomas is fundamentally a neurotic
whose neurosis is accentuated, though by no means produced, by the fact
of his being a Negro.[10] This boy's extremely unfavorable home and neighborhood situation, emotionally and economically, probably played an
important part in the production of his extreme behavior. For many
Negro children, stable family life and adequate parental love and control
probably cushion the shock of the hostile treatment they receive from the
larger community. For others, the mores of lower-class life may dictate
behavior more or less like Bigger Thomas', regardless of parental affection and also regardless of race.

Aggressive reactions more specifically related to racial frustration are
described by Powdermaker,[11] in an analysis of changing patterns of aggression among Negroes. She maintains that direct aggression by Negroes
against whites, except in times of crisis, is rare, "since the whites have
superior power and since Negroes are highly realistic. . . ." In view of
this, Negroes are apt to channel their aggression into culturally approved
forms, such as that of substituting a colored object for the white object
of aggression, by retreating to an ivory tower, by identifying with the
white employer, particularly if he has great prestige, by diverting aggression into wit, by playing the part of the meek, humble, and unaggressive
Negro who is always deferential to whites no matter what the provocation may be. There are indications, however, that a psychological revolution is taking place and that young Negroes are refusing to assume the
unaggressive role of meekness and subservience.

The intricate complex of psychological defenses which many Negroes,
often unconsciously, have been forced to evolve in order to cope with the
disadvantaged situation in which they live has been most recently described by two sociologically minded psychiatrists, Kardiner and Oversey.[12] The typical pattern, they say, is one of aggression repressed because

[10] C. V. Charles, "Optimism and Frustration in the American Negro," *Psychoanalytic Review,* Vol. 29 (1942), pp. 270–299.

[11] Hortense Powdermaker, "The Channeling of Negro Aggression by the Cultural
Process," *American Journal of Sociology,* Vol. 48 (1943), pp. 750–758.

[12] Abram Kardiner and Lionel Oversey, *The Mark of Oppression,* W. W. Norton
Company, New York, 1951. See also, John Dollard, *Caste and Class in a Southern
Town;* also various studies conducted by the Youth Commission of the American
Council on Education, such as Warner, Junker, and Adams, *Color and Human Nature,*
Washington, D.C., 1941.

of fear of retaliation, resulting in anxiety and lowered self-esteem. These feelings induce preoccupation with self and emotional matters. Consequently, even in seemingly well-adjusted Negroes, much energy is wasted in the anticipation of hostile reactions, and numerous expedients are resorted to in order to bolster the needed sense of self-worth.

Summing up the evidence in regard to the effects of prejudice, discrimination, and segregation on the personality of Negro children in the United States, we may conclude, then, as follows:

1. There is a pattern of personality disabilities which seems to be associated with the inferior and rejected minority status of the Negro.
2. This pattern includes not only subjective feelings of inferiority, low self-esteem, ambivalent attitudes toward his own group, but also either overt or indirect hostility against both whites and Negroes.
3. The particular structure of this pattern does not appear to be the same for, nor is it found to the same degree in, all Negroes.
4. Factors such as degree of stability of family and security of the individual within the family setting, individual differences of a constitutional nature, and social and economic level appear to be relevant to the particular kind of personal adjustment made to minority status.

Effects of Anti-Semitism

Third: What is known about the effect of anti-Semitism on the personality pattern of Jewish children and youth? .

Studies of the question are noticeably few compared to the number that deal with the effects of minority status on the personality make-up of Negro children and adolescents. Practically all the studies of the personality of Jewish children compare Jewish and non-Jewish children in terms of some isolated aspect of personality rather than in regard to emotional health.

The studies of Radke and collaborators [13] and Hartley and collaborators [14] are among the few touching upon the health of personality among Jewish children. These studies show that young Jewish children are more sensitive to their religious identity than are Catholic or Protestant white

[13] M. Radke, H. Trager, and H. Davis, op. cit.
[14] E. L. Hartley, M. Rosenbaum, M. and S. Schwartz, "Children's Use of Ethnic Frames of Reference: An Exploratory Study of Children's Conceptualizations of Multiple Ethnic Group Membership," and "Children's Perceptions of Ethnic Group Membership," Journal of Psychology, Vol. 26 (1948), pp. 367–398.

and Negro children. Radke, Trager, and Davis maintain that this "intensified group consciousness of Jewish children is in part an outcome of anti-Semitism." In an unpublished paper, Radke states:

For virtually all of our groups, particularly for the adolescents, the non-Jewish world is seen as essentially hostile territory, an area so hedged about with barriers that there is considerable confusion concerning ultimate goals with respect to it.[15]

In discussing this problem from the point of view of Jewish college students, Radke concludes:

There was great variation in the attitudes of the subjects, ranging from virtual rejection of the Jewish group to a desire to submerge themselves completely with the Jewish group and as far as possible cut themselves off from the non-Jewish world.[16]

Sperling [17] compared eighty randomly selected Jewish college students with eighty non-Jewish students on the basis of questionnaires and personality tests. He found no significant problems of adjustment or any of its subsections, such as "social acceptability," "emotional stability," "objectivity," and "family relationships." The Jewish group scored themselves higher on extroversion, ascendance, and liberalism than the non-Jewish group.

In judging these findings, however, one must recall Klineberg's statement about the inadequacy of the research method employed. The problems which anti-Semitism in America presents to Jews may well produce effects on personality that are not detected by tests and questionnaires. Since skin color plays so large a part in prejudice in the United States, Jews are faced with an unstructured and ambiguous situation when forced to recognize that anti-Semitic attitudes relegate them, also, to the status of a rejected minority even though their skin is white. The quality and pattern of the personality consequences of their minority status, therefore, may be more complex and obscure than is the case with Negroes. As Lewin [18] points out, "The strength of the conflict situation increases with the weakness of the boundary between the groups concerned." In

[15] M. Radke, H. Davis, J. Hurwitz, and P. Pollack, "Group-belonging among Various Sub-groups of Jewish Children," unpublished.

[16] M. Radke, "The Meaning of Minority Group Membership to Jewish College Students," unpublished.

[17] A. P. Sperling, "A Comparison between Jews and Non-Jews with Respect to Several Traits of Personality," *Journal of Applied Psychology*, Vol. 26 (1942), pp. 828–840.

[18] Kurt Lewin, "Psycho-sociological Problems of a Minority Group," *Character and Personality*, Vol. 3 (1935), pp. 175–187.

the light of this situation, one would expect among American Jews a complexity of anxiety and conflicts that are not directly and easily expressed.

The Personality of the Prejudiced Person

Some of the social scientists whose opinions were cited above [19] stated that prejudice and discrimination are even more detrimental to the emotional well-being of the prejudiced person than to those who are the objects of discrimination. Others thought that this might possibly be the case. The comments of these social scientists may be summarized as follows:

1. Segegation is a symptom of some maladaptive psychological process.
2. It has pervasive and elusive harmful effects; e.g., increased hostility, deterioration of moral values, the coarsening of interpersonal sensitivity, conflict between ideology and practices, rationalizing, etc.
3. Inner conflicts and guilt feelings may result from membership in groups enforcing segregation.
4. There may be disturbances in the individual's sense of reality and the relation of the individual to the work around him.[20]

For the most part, however, investigators have paid more attention to the personality make-up of the person who is prejudiced than to the question of whether the presence of prejudice as a characteristic attitude in the society produces the traits that distinguish these people from others.

The most important studies along this line are those that were sponsored by the Department of Scientific Research of the American Jewish Committee.[21] In one of these, *The Authoritarian Personality,* the writers present data suggesting that there is a close correlation between overt prejudice and a number of deep-rooted personality traits. In another, *Anti-Semitism and Emotional Disorder,* the case histories of a number of individuals who had received psychotherapy were analyzed, and the conclusion is drawn that emotional predispositions are necessary but not sufficient determinants of anti-Semitism.

---

[19] P. 139.

[20] For detailed descriptions of some of these effects, see Lillian Smith, *Killers of the Dream,* W. W. Norton and Company, New York, 1949.

[21] Adorno, Frenkel-Brunswik, Levinson, and Sanford, *The Authoritarian Personality,* Harper & Brothers, New York, 1950; Bettelheim and Janowitz, *Dynamics of Prejudice,* Harper & Brothers, New York, 1949; Ackerman and Jahoda, *Anti-Semitism and Emotional Disorder,* Harper & Brothers, New York, 1950; Massing, *Rehearsal for Destruction,* Harper & Brothers, New York, 1949; and Lowenthal and Guterman, *Prophets of Deceit,* Harper & Brothers, New York, 1949.

The authors of these volumes do not claim that the personality patterns found in prejudiced individuals are the result of their attitudes, or that prejudice is the inevitable consequence or even accompaniment of these personality patterns.[22] At minimum, however, their studies do show that prejudice and discrimination are more or less accepted ways of behavior in our society, and that they provide certain individuals with an outlet for hostile feelings and other personality needs that would find other expression under other conditions. The chief contribution of the studies would seem to lie in their demonstration of the kinds of personality make-up extremely prejudiced persons have, and the environmental conditions, particularly those of family life, that produced them.

In all considerations of the findings of these investigators and others to be described below, two points must be kept in mind. First, for the most part, these investigations deal not with the "conventionally" prejudiced person but with the one who has what these writers call an "authoritarian" personality. Second and closely related, these studies deal largely with extremes, with people who rank either very high or very low on the prejudice scale.

Adorno differentiates between the "conventional" and the "authoritarian" type of prejudiced person and describes the typical personality make-up of each of them.[23] The conventionally prejudiced person, he says, is likely to be a conformist in manner, dress, and ways of thought. As women, they put much emphasis on neatness and femininity; the men want to be "regular he-men." They accept prevailing standards, and they talk in terms of "us" and "others." Their prejudice is largely a matter of their own group identification; they take for granted the correctness of the views their group expresses and do not examine matters closely. They are not violent in their expression of prejudice, for they regard violence of emotion as not "civilized" or "decent."

In contrast, the prejudiced person of the "authoritarian" type is an emotionally maladjusted individual who has achieved social adjustment by taking pleasure in obedience and subordination. He has a blind belief in authority. He admires strength and is ever-ready to attack those he regards as weak and of little account. His inability to see people as individuals, his need to stereotype them, results not from a conventional

[22] Sanford says: "Given a relationship between a personality variable and an ideological trend, it was usually assumed that the causal sequence was from the former to the latter—on the grounds that the formation of personality was genetically earlier, the most important structures going back to childhood"; see Adorno, Frenkel-Brunswik, Levinson, and Sanford, *op. cit.*, p. 56.

[23] The following is a rough paraphrase of statements made by Adorno in *ibid.*, Chap. XIX.

way of identifying in-groups and out-groups but from deep emotional need He must have somebody to punish, for his own overstrict conscience holds him to such severe account.

Else Frenkel-Brunswick [24] states that the presence of extreme prejudice in some Americans and the absence of prejudice in others derives in part from a complex network of attitudes within and related to the family.

Individuals who were found to rate very high on psychological tests for prejudice tended to have had as children a home life in which discipline was relatively harsh and threatening. In consequence, they became very subservient to their parents and fearful of displeasing them. There was little exchange of free-flowing affection in these homes. Instead, both parents and children held tightly to faithful execution of prescribed roles and duties. The values and goals the parents held before the children were highly conventional ones; the socially accepted and that regarded as useful in climbing the social ladder were labeled good, and the bad was all that was unconventional and socially inferior.

In contrast, the individuals who rated low in prejudice had parents who were less concerned about social status, less fearful of lack of conformity, and less condemning of socially unaccepted behavior. There was more richness of emotional life in these homes, more affection and less criticism. As children, these individuals could more easily express disagreement with their parents and more comfortably rebel against them. Not that all these unprejudiced people had ideal mental health as children. Frenkel-Brunswik's research seems to indicate, however, that if they had anxieties they could be more open about them and did not have to resort to the inappropriate, destructive methods of dealing with them that the greatly prejudiced used.[25]

To have very little prejudice is to be something of a maverick in our society. One may speculate that the group of individuals who rated low in prejudice may have consisted of two types: those who benefited from unusually favorable parent-child relations and were healthy in personality, and those unusually sensitive individuals whose home situation was less satisfactory and who reacted by identification with the oppressed. These latter may be the people who are most disturbed by the contradiction between democratic ideals and the treatment of minority groups. If so, it may be said that some of their personality difficulties are occasioned by the presence of prejudice and discrimination, perhaps even caused by it.

[24] *Ibid.*, Chap. X, and "A Study of Prejudice in Children," *Human Relations*, Vol. 1 (1948), pp. 295–306.
[25] Else Frenkel-Brunswik, *Human Relations, op. cit.*, pp. 295–306.

Other Studies

There are several general and theoretical discussions of the dynamics of prejudice and the nature of the personality of the prejudiced individual that are more or less in agreement with the empirical findings of the writers cited above. The contributions of Eric Fromm [26] seem to have provided the conceptual foundations upon which the hypotheses of some of these investigations are based.

Maslow, for example, speculates about the authoritarian personality and the psychological and cultural factors involved. He maintains that the unifying principle necessary for understanding the authoritarian personality is the understanding of his basic philosophy or his "world view."

Like other psychologically insecure people, the authoritarian person lives in a world which may be conceived to be pictured by him as a sort of jungle. . . . The authoritarian never loves or respects other human beings any more than the animals in the jungle can be said to love or respect each other. In the last analysis, the alternatives are to fear or be feared. . . . If the world is not a jungle, if people are not completely cruel, selfish, and egocentric, then and only then is the authoritarian wrong.[27]

Rokeach [28] regards the problem as one of the relation between ethnocentric racial and religious attitudes and general mental rigidity. He started a series of well-controlled experiments with the assumption that one of the characteristics of ethnocentric thinking is a rigidity and inflexibility of the thinking process and that this reflects a general rigidity factor. Rigidity was defined as the "inability to change one's set when the objective conditions demand it, as the inability to restructure a field in which there are alternative solutions to a problem in order to solve that problem more efficiently." Rokeach found that "children who were high in prejudice are (1) more rigid and (2) more concrete in solving arithmetic problems than children low in prejudice."

Reichard [29] took another approach and, by means of the Rorschach

[26] Eric Fromm, *Escape from Freedom*, Rinehart & Company, New York, 1941; *Man for Himself*, Rinehart & Company, New York, 1947.

[27] A. H. Maslow, "The Authoritarian Character Structure," *Journal of Social Psychology*, Vol. 18 (1943), pp. 401–411.

[28] Milton Rokeach, "Generalized Mental Rigidity as a Factor in Ethnocentrism," *Journal of Abnormal and Social Psychology*, Vol. 43 (1948), pp. 259–278; "The Effect of Perception Time upon Rigidity and Concreteness of Thinking," *Journal of Experimental Psychology*, Vol. 40 (1950), pp. 206–216.

[29] Suzanne Reichard, "Rorschach Study of Prejudiced Personality," *American Journal of Orthopsychiatry*, Vol. 18 (1948), pp. 280–286.

test, examined the personality structure of people with strong prejudices (especially against Jews and Negroes) and contrasted them with people who have little prejudice.

This study, and another that came to much the same conclusions,[30] appear to confirm the evidence obtained by other techniques, that the typical prejudiced person is a "constricted and inhibited personality suffering from the limitations imposed by a narrow ego."

Still other explanations of the extremely prejudiced person's actions and motivations are offered by several psychoanalysts. Sterba,[31] for example, from studies of individuals injured during the anti-Negro riots in Detroit in 1943, concludes that extreme prejudice against Negroes may be a continuation of infantile sibling-rivalry reaction patterns, or it may represent unconscious hatred of the father, a regression to primitive group psychology. To Zilboorg,[32] on the other hand, the explanation lies in "repressed herd aggression, with its concomitant sense of guilt," while to Bovell [33] it is to "the revelation of an inherent constitutional or somatic weakness" that prejudice (against Negroes, at least) is to be attributed.

J. F. Brown [34] combines a psychoanalytic interpretation of the motivation of the anti-Semitic with an emphasis on the role of socioeconomic determinants. He insists that in our culture anti-Semitism is always latent. "It is, therefore, available as a socially acceptable way of expending repressed and pent-up energy. Viewed psychologically," he says, "anti-Semitism represents a displacement of aggression with a projection of guilt and a rationalization of motives. . . . It is a sort of sociopathology and is overdetermined by deep psychobiological and socioeconomic causal factors."

Conclusions

Summing up the evidence and the theories, then, we may conclude as follows. There appears to be some complex relationship between the total personality structure of an individual and the amount and quality of his prejudices. This relationship cannot be stated in simple causal or specific

[30] Jane Hamilton Gullberg, unpublished study, Institute of Child Welfare, University of California.

[31] Richard Sterba, "Some Psychological Factors in Negro Race Hatred and in Anti-Negro Riots," in G. Roheim, *Psychoanalysis and the Social Sciences,* Vol. 1 (1947), International Universities Press, New York, pp. 411–427.

[32] Gregory Zilboorg, "Psychopathology of Social Prejudice," *Psychoanalytic Quarterly,* Vol. 16 (1947), pp. 303–324.

[33] G. B. Bovell, "Psychological Considerations of Color Conflicts Among Negroes," *Psychoanalytic Review,* Vol. 30 (1943), pp. 447–459.

[34] J. F. Brown, "Social and Psychological Factors in the Anti-Semitic Attitude," *Journal of Educational Sociology,* Vol. 16 (1943), pp. 351–354.

terms. The individual personality is a complex totality, and it would be expected that any aspect of an individual's feelings, values, ideas, or behavior would be in some way a reflection of his total personality pattern.

There are some individuals who are extremely prejudiced and who at the same time give evidences of serious personality aberration. This would suggest that there is some relationship between extreme and virulent expressions of prejudice and personality disturbances. There are individuals, however, who show signs of extreme personality disturbances and who do not express extreme or virulent forms of racial and religious prejudices.

In the studies conducted so far, there are no indications of a relationship between "average" amounts of prejudice and personality disturbances. There is some evidence that certain neurotic mechanisms may be used by a prejudiced individual to support or express his prejudices. There is no evidence, however, that the causes of neurotic personality are also the causes of racial and religious prejudices. Some neurotic individuals may express their neuroticism through racial prejudice; others may express it through social nonconformity and the rejection of racial prejudice.

Extreme prejudice in an individual may reflect many factors, either acting in aggregate or in different constellations. It may indicate displaced hostility from some nonrelevant source of frustration (e.g., deflected hostility from frustrating parents), or it may be an expression of unresolved guilt, anxiety, and emotional conflicts which arise from sources related or unrelated to the actual objects of the prejudice. On the other hand, prejudice may spring from basic, universal needs that differ in degree, quality, and method of satisfaction among human beings depending on whether they are stable or unstable in basic personality structure. These basic needs may be:

1. Status needs
2. Hostility needs—and the need for a socially approved hostility object
3. In-group identity needs. Ambiguity in the definition of self may be obviated by strong in-group identity feelings reinforced by the existence of a concrete out-group; feelings of belongingness may be reinforced by identification and rejection of nonbelongers.
4. Conformity needs. The acceptance of prevailing norms, values, and attitudes may be a necessary price for maintenance and strengthening of in-group status.

It is probable that these needs can be satisfied by prejudice only if the individual finds some way of protecting himself from the realization of what he is doing; otherwise he would not be able to reconcile racial and religious prejudice with American moral ideas.[35] Even so, it is possible that the basic conflict between moral ideology and the existence of racial and religious prejudice may have one or the other of the following results for the individual: It may mean that he becomes generally confused about what is right and wrong and may adopt the opportunistic, "jungle" philosophy that characterizes the "authoritarian" personality; it may result in his doubting the integrity of his parents and, with that, the honesty of any source of authority, though he may hide these doubts and rigidly follow their dictates; or it may mean that he solves the conflict by becoming a fighter in the cause of social justice.

In spite of these possibilities, and the findings of scientific workers, it seems doubtful that objections to racial and religious prejudice can be based to any large extent on the grounds of demonstrated detrimental effect on the feelings, values, ideas, or behavior of those who practice discrimination. It may be true that the majority of those who are unusually prejudiced are emotionally maladjusted. Such maladjustment, however, has sources other than prejudice. The attitudes of these individuals toward members of minority groups are only an exaggerated reflection of attitudes that are prevalent in the society. If we are to combat prejudice, then, we must take our stand on moral and realistic grounds. These prejudices inhibit social progress, defined in humanistic terms; they are a manifestation of men's more primitive propensities to debase and harm his fellow human beings; they seem in a complex way to be related to the maintenance of destructive social tensions and conflicts and drain energy away from the task of constructive solution to many and vast social problems; and they distort, constrict, humiliate, and, in extreme cases, destroy the personalities of the victims.

Some Methods of Reducing Prejudice and Discrimination

The 1948–49 *Directory of Agencies in Intergroup Relations* lists 385 agencies with 749 branches that are attempting to promote better rela-

[35] The apparent conflict in values and ideology may be made possible through the use of the following supporting mechanisms:

a. Intensification of hostility and negative stereotyping as an attempted justification of the original prejudice

b. Compartmentalization or partial and temporal expedient expression of one or more aspects of mutually contradictory ideas or values

c. Rationalizations of unacceptable ideas and of the basic contradiction

d. Phantasy—the assumption of ideas and of the role of being a member of a "favored" or "superior" race

tions among racial and ethnic groups in the United States. In addition, work of this kind is being carried on by some public schools and colleges, by some churches and synagogues, by some labor unions, and by some social-welfare organizations. An examination of the field leaves one impressed with the great amount of work that is being done to reduce prejudice and discrimination, to break down barriers of segregation, and to promote equal rights for all citizens.

Williams [36] has recently made a rather comprehensive survey of the chief methods used by the various organizations in the field of intergroup relations, and of the assumptions underlying their work. He lists the assumptions as follows:

1. Give people the facts and prejudice will disappear. A subsidiary assumption is: prejudice is unrealistic, a function of ignorance or of "distorted stertotypes," of "warped social perception."
2. Action should be directed toward (a) a direct change in values or attitudes, or (b) a change in those aspects of the situation which are regarded as productive of existing attitudes and behavior.
3. Contact brings friendliness.
4. There is some relationship (positive or negative) between the effectiveness of a program and the amount or nature of attention called to the specific problem of intergroup relations.
5. Experience in intergroup relations changes behavior and there is some transfer from this changed to other more usual situations.

On the basis of these assumptions, work is carried on, says Williams, by means of:

1. Information, education, propaganda
2. Political and legal pressure
3. Organization of intergroup contacts in industrial or other work situations
4. Organization of intergroup contacts in nonvocational settings
5. Organization of individuals and groups for adjusting intergroup differences
6. Public commendations and awards
7. Psychotherapy with individuals or small groups
8. Organization of activities of groups considered likely sources of conflict
9. Fact finding

[36] Robin M. Williams, Jr., *The Reduction of Intergroup Tensions: A Survey of Research on Problems of Ethnic, Racial, and Religious Group Relations*, Social Science Research Council Bulletin No. 57, 1947.

Effectiveness of Various Methods

Since so many methods have been tried and so much time and effort expended in the attempt to improve intergroup relations, it would seem most important to know how effective the measures have been. Attempts to answer this question have been made but without much success.

Arnold Rose, for example, summarizes the net results of relevant research over the last twenty years as follows:

There is a certain amount of conflict between the findings of the various studies. Some school and college courses dealing with ethnic problems have effected significant changes in attitude on the part of the students; others have not. Some direct contacts between members of antagonistic ethnic groups have promoted friendlier attitudes; others have not. . . . Some studies have shown a correlation between favorable attitudes toward other ethnic groups and knowledge about those ethnic groups; others have shown little correlation.

The contradictions in the findings do not mean that our knowledge about how to reduce race prejudice by planned propaganda is nil. Race attitudes are known to be so deep and tenacious that any careful study which has given us evidence that a change of attitudes has been effected is a distinct contribution to knowledge.[37]

In another place, Rose states his belief that various types of propaganda may be effective in reducing prejudice.[38] This viewpoint is criticized by Flowerman [39] as follows:

The advocates of mass propaganda for the reduction of prejudice have for years used Rose's arguments in one form or another. And their activities have often continued at the expense of more valid means of reducing prejudice and in the face of accumulating evidence against the effectiveness of unsupported pre-tolerance symbols. That mass propaganda may have an important role in the campaign against bigotry should not be denied; but it can achieve this role only with some people under certain conditions as an adjunct to campaigns that rely more heavily upon personal contacts, and in fairly specific spheres of social action. . . . Since Rose has accepted the irrationality of such prejudice, it is difficult to accept his advocacy of the rational approach inherent in mass propaganda techniques.

[37] Arnold Rose, *Studies in the Reduction of Prejudice,* American Council on Race Relations, Chicago, 1948.

[38] Arnold Rose, "The Use of Propaganda to Reduce Prejudice," *International Journal of Opinion and Attitude Research,* Vol. 2 (1948), pp. 220–229.

[39] Samuel H. Flowerman, "The Use of Propaganda to Reduce Prejudice: A Refutation," *International Journal of Opinion and Attitude Research,* Vol. 3 (1949), pp. 99–108.

Flowerman offers the following suggestions:

We must first thoroughly understand group structure relationships between leaders and followers, etc., as well as group needs before we can hope to profit from a study of techniques for change. Techniques must derive from group needs and not from armchairs or the advertising office. . . . Because he [Rose] doubts the validity of the propaganda approach to prejudice, it follows that he should likewise doubt the wisdom of studying the circumstances under which propaganda can be effective. . . . This last approach is what has been referred to as "evaluation"; it is sterile and short-sighted because it frequently ends in a blind alley with a verdict of "effective or ineffective," usually the latter. When the verdict is "ineffective," the practitioner is at a loss as to what to do next, for he is left with no alternatives.

A more fruitful approach . . . would be to inaugurate a series of related researches as part of a process of program research and development through teams of research and program specialists. Let the group and its problems be studied first, and let techniques for change emanate democratically from the needs of the group.

Objections on another basis—and a different approach to the problem of prejudice—are offered by Bettelheim and Janowitz.[40] They maintain that "ethnic hostility and prejudices have anxiety and insecurity as their roots; therefore, the effort to dispel stereotyped thinking or feeling of ethnic hostility by rational propaganda is at best a half-measure." It is their belief that the task of reducing prejudice must be carried on both individually and socially. Individuals must be aided in the attainment of greater personal integration in a context of social and economic security. A change in social climate may be necessary to bring this about. They conclude:

It is our conviction that better ethnic relations are possible within our society, and that modern education, particularly the education of the small child, could be so improved that fewer of them would need to be matured into intolerant adults. If we bring our children up wisely they will not only be happier, but also will be able to live more successfully with one another. That it seems possible to raise a generation which will be relatively free of ethnic intolerance is not only a hope but a real possibility, and hence a great challenge.

It is probably only through this type of inquiry that it will be possible

[40] Bettelheim and Janowitz, "Dynamics of Prejudice," *Scientific American,* Vol. 183 (1950), pp. 11–13.

for scientific research to contribute to the understanding of the nature of the problems involved in intergroup relations and to the determination of the effectiveness of practical programs designed to reduce prejudice and discrimination.

Obstacles to Maximum Effectiveness

This analysis of the programs and of the effectiveness of various organizations in the field of intergroup relations suggests that no program, no matter what its basic assumptions concerning the nature or cause of prejudice or its methods of work, is completely ineffectual. The real question, however, is: Are these programs having significant enough effects to warrant the amount of energy and time devoted to them? While that question cannot be answered definitely, it seems likely that the following major deficiencies interfere with the attainment of optimum effectiveness.

1. There is a startling lack of an over-all coordinating program or systematic integrating policy governing the activities of the nearly four hundred agencies working on essentially the same problem. Related agencies and, at times, the various branches of a given agency appear to be working largely in isolation from each other. This lack of integration of activities often leads to duplication of effort, wasteful and deflecting competition among agencies, and consequently a piecemeal approach to the common problem.

2. Many of the agencies tend to select the more dramatic areas for operation, at times at the expense of more fundamental problems. This tendency to veer toward the dramatic or more popular areas of activity can be understood in the light of the fact that all these agencies depend to a large extent either upon solicited funds or politically controlled public funds for their financial support.

3. The ideological preconceptions and the needs of vested interests and special privileges of the policy makers of agencies tend to determine the particular perspective on prejudice in accordance with which the specific program is developed and limited. There is also evidence that for most agencies the action program exists with little regard for the best available and relevant knowledge. Even in those agencies with a research division, the research program is frequently isolated from the main stream of practical-action programs. It is rare that an agency has its research program as an integral part of all its practical activities.

4. It is usual for specific-action programs and agencies to view the problem of prejudice in too simple terms, often in terms convenient for the continuation of their particular program. The complexity of the prob-

lem (the fact that prejudice is a multidimensional phenomenon with multiple, patterned causation and therefore requires a coordinated attack of many different approaches) seems generally to be overlooked.

Negative attitudes toward people of other races, nationalities, and religions can be changed, but the process of change is not simple. It may well be that basic psychological problems are involved and that research in areas such as the following is required: status and its determinants; the nature of hostility; problems of empathy and altruism; conformity behavior and its determinants.

It would be a mistake, however, to think that fundamental research would in itself solve the problems of how to obtain a more genuinely democratic society and how to free children from prejudice. In a basic and inescapable sense, the problem of prejudices is not only a problem of individuals but also of society. The problem of reducing prejudice and eliminating discrimination must be approached on a societal basis if it is to be dealt with successfully.

↗ VII ↙

Religion as an Aid to
Healthy Personality Development

IT is clear, in the light of the preceding analysis, that all aspects of social life play into the social and emotional development of children. Relations within the family are of prime importance, but these relations are dependent, in considerable part, on factors in economic and social life outside the confines of the home. Under these various aspects of life, binding them together and giving them meaning, are the ethical and spiritual values of the whole culture. Socially, these values play a part in determining the character of each social institution and thus affect personality in ways described above. For the individual, they become a part of personality itself.

As a final part of the explanation of how personality develops and how health of personality is affected for good or ill, we must consider, then, the question of ethical and spiritual values. To many people these values are summed up in the term "religion." In most of the following analysis we shall, accordingly, talk about the contributions of religion to healthy personality development. Depending on how religion is defined, the question may or may not be broader than that. In either case, the following analysis may serve to indicate that the possibility of healthy personality development depends at base on moral and spiritual values.

For the development of a sense of integrity, the culminating component of the healthy personality, it has been said that the individual must have some conception of the universe as meaningful and benevolent, and of his place in it. He must integrate his life around some ethical or religious concepts. Honor, grace, faith, courage: some integrating idea or ideal must replace his parents as the objects of dependency and trust. Having such a core of security in his inner being, the mature adult can transmit a sense of trust to his children and thus start them on the way to emotional well-being.

Organized religion is the social institution that has as its specific func-

159

tion the transmission of ideas and ideals regarding the moral nature of the universe and man's place in it. Many in modern society derive their basis for integration from other sources, but the church remains the one institutionalized means to this end. Anthropologists tell us that religion is pragmatically necessary to the individual if he is to overcome his shattering anticipation of death, disaster, and destiny. Socially, they say, religion is the core of civilization and the mainspring of moral values, one of the prime integrative forces in society.

The part that religion plays in the healthy personality development of American children is suggested in a statement drawn up by a committee of the American Council on Education that was representative of the three main faiths:

For us, the democratic faith means that the worth of persons and the increasing perfectibility of human institutions rests on a religious conception of human destiny. . . . We contend insistently . . . that in the effort to build a democratic society, a failure to capitalize the ideals of ethical monotheism . . . is sheer cultural madness. . . . Underneath the cleavage between Catholic and Protestant, between Christian and Jew, is the stream of Judaeo-Christian tradition with its concept of the common source and the spiritual quality of all men as children of God; the obligation to respect the supreme worth of persons and the wickedness of exploiting them; the golden quality of mercy; the meaning of redemptive love; the inexorableness of the law that he that soweth the wind shall reap the whirlwind. These are great cohesive social forces.[1]

Through these concepts and through the elaboration of their implications, children are, directly and indirectly, supported in their struggle to solve the problems and resolve the conflicts that life presents. It has been shown throughout our analysis that children's well-being is dependent in large part upon their parents' sense of self-worth and that that sense is intimately related to the values and workings of the society in which they live. The ethical and moral affirmations of religion constitute the base on which all this rests and from which social malfunctioning can be criticized. In this widest sense, then, religion is basic to healthy personality. There are, in addition, specific ways in which the teachings of religion aid the individual in dealing with his emotional conflicts, some of which are the following.

The literature of psychotherapy provides abundant evidence that the rejection of any aspect of the self interferes with the ability to live life to

---

[1] *The Relation of Religion to Public Education*, American Council on Education, Washington, D.C., 1947, pp. 46–47.

the full. It is the view of religion that man need not reject any part, aspect, or facet of himself but should accept the self in its totality as part of the plan of God for his creation. Thus, the sexual impulses, which are central in so many personality disorders, are to be recognized as a fact in human life. They are to be brought into the over-all functioning of the self and not allowed to go unrestrained. They are to be lifted up, not degraded; devoted to the purposes of God, not used wantonly. So it is with all drives and impulses. Religion provides standards and directions for their use and frowns upon their denial.

Healthy self-acceptance requires also a realistic view of oneself. Every individual has some sort of picture of what he is and what he would like to be. As he strives to fulfill his self-ideal, defeat shows him that there are lines of development that for him are impossible. If he cannot accept this fact, he is likely to develop unrealistic and self-defeating compensations or, failing that, to have a mental breakdown. Religion helps here by urging humility and by stressing the universality of God's love. It is one of the main tenets of religion that God has regard for each of his children, that he knows the abilities of each, and that he does not expect the impossible.

A realistic view of oneself involves also a recognition that one is often at fault. A religious view that does not hesitate to acknowledge the evil that is in man can be of help to the individual through its assurance that he is not alone in his wickedness nor hopelessly condemned by it. "I will heal their backslidings; I will love them freely," God told the people of Israel through the prophet Moses. In the Parable of the Lost Sheep, so lovingly sought, and in the Parable of the Prodigal Son, Christ made vivid this truth.

Unfortunately, in interpreting these ideas, religious leaders and parents often fail in their purpose. There is evidence in the case records of psychotherapists that injury may be done to personality by overemphasis on wrongdoing and underemphasis on faith in the individual's potentialities for goodness. By condemning and rejecting instead of understanding and helping, adults can make religious teachings a source of harm to children.

High ideals are a characteristic of youth. Longing for a sense of identity and trying to avoid the feeling of self-diffusion, adolescents seek examples of courage and devotion on which to model themselves, and they identify easily with the sorrowful, the brave, and the righteous. Religion, properly interpreted, is the oldest and most challenging source of such inspiration. Adolescents want to strive and want to suffer. The call to live life according to God's high purposes can be a means of integration to them.

In our rapidly changing culture, with its shifting standards of value, there is much uncertainty for youth and adults. Religion has always affirmed that amid the flux and change of human institutions and customs certain basic principles stand immutable. To those who believe, this affirmation provides the stability and certainty that are so important for emotional well-being. In the fellowship of the church, there is refuge from the world of change, relief from loneliness, and support and companionship in the quest for higher things.

In calling people to be "children of God in the midst of a crooked and perverse generation," to love their neighbors without regard to race or creed or accidental circumstance, to do the will of God in a society that ignores or denies that will, religion provides integrating ideals of the highest order. For the mature adult, as well as for the adolescent, those ideals are an inspiration and a challenge. With them as guides and with help and renewal available through religious institutions, human life, for all its struggle, may become significant, joyous, and rewarding.

In ending the first part of our report with this conclusion we do not mean to minimize the other factors that have been shown to have bearing on the healthy development of personality, nor do we insist that religion, in the narrow sense of the word, is the only source of integrating and inspiring concepts. What we mean to say is that, for the society as for the individual, maintenance of ideals is central to the purpose of individual happiness and responsible citizenship.

It is ideals, operating as guiding principles for home and society, that constitute the base from which healthy personality development can proceed. To help children grow to maturity of personality, parents, teachers, all who are significant to children must be genuine persons in a genuine society. If such a society is a truly democratic one, it will assure that all children have the goods and services and the equality of opportunity that their physical and emotional well-being requires. It is, however, only as the responsible adult members of the society maintain its basic ideals that these results will follow and a generation of children of healthy personality be reared.

PART II

IMPLICATIONS FOR THE CONDUCT

OF SOCIAL INSTITUTIONS

✦ VIII ✦

Some Cultural Considerations

OF great pertinence to promotion of health of personality is a body of facts and ideas from the field of cultural anthropology that has so far not been touched upon. This material has to do with the great variety of cultures that coexist in the United States and with the part that culture plays in making one child different from another. These are facts of great importance for the work of teachers, clergymen, doctors, social workers, and the like, so we review them briefly here in order to enrich the analysis of the work of the social institutions.

Varied Cultural Behavior

There is no such thing as *the* environment of *the* American child. We all know that, broadly speaking, a Southerner has a pattern of family relationships, an attitude toward a settled existence, toward the land, toward the stranger, toward efficiency that is different from the patterns of a person from the North or the Midwest. Again, the functioning farm provides a different background of experience from that of the suburb or the city street. Within the city, there is difference occasioned by the income bracket of the family; and within the income bracket, there is the pattern that is affected by the occupation of the father. Miners and sanitation workers and college instructors have approximately the same income but, as a rule, they provide different designs of living for their children.

Then there are differences that have little to do with geographic factors or with income bracket or occupation. There are groups in this country that have strongly patterned ways of life that run counter to the general "American" culture but that they regard as highly desirable. There are such groups in the southern Highlands, among the descendants of the first white settlers of New Mexico, and elsewhere throughout the country. Such, too, are the many Indian tribes, who value their own culture above the culture of the white people who are their neighbors, and the peoples of Hawaii and other islands. In addition, there are many groups of people in the United States who recently arrived from abroad. While admiring

165

American technology and progress, these people often cling, deliberately or unconsciously, to the attitudes and ways of their parents, rearing their children according to their own upbringing, instilling in them the values of their own culture.

When children from such different backgrounds go to school together, they bring to the classroom their different backgrounds of experience, different tools for understanding, and different techniques in human relations, even though, superficially, they appear much alike. The acts and precepts of the teacher may have different meanings for them, meanings that are often different from what the teacher intended. For example, a white teacher, thinking to encourage and reward a Hopi Indian girl for her lice-free hair, praised her publicly as the girl with the most careful mother; but the girl wept in distress, because for a Hopi to be singled out is a terrible ordeal.[1]

Then, too, although he speaks English, the words a child hears and reads may fit into no frame of reference and may, therefore, have no meaning. A study of American-born children of Chinese parents shows, for example, that to them the word "fair" means something that applies to the weather, or to a face, or to a circus; never to interpersonal behavior. Yet these were children who, in school, on the radio, in their reading, must have daily encountered this word in its application to fair dealings. What did they think when a teacher or another child said, "It isn't fair"? Specific cultural backgrounds give rise to specific interpretations of experience, specific conceptions of what constitutes good housing, a good mother, health, good food, or a dream come true.[2]

Accordingly, we cannot treat children as if they all felt and evaluated and interpreted and reacted to experience in the same way. Neither can we treat great differences in reaction and attitude as if they were always due to individual peculiarity. When a Navajo boy calls a robin's egg "green," he is not color blind or ignorant; he is classifying colors as his culture classifies them. When a Mexican boy said he had an angel whispering in one ear and a devil in another, he was neither peculiar nor emotionally disturbed nor even poetic; he was voicing his culture's expression of inner conflict.

Within a cultural group there are individual differences, of course. Not all Navajo and Mexican boys and girls are alike, any more alike than children of any other background. But there are certain basic regularities

[1] See Laura Thompson, *Culture in Crisis,* Harper & Brothers, New York, 1950.
[2] Cited by Margaret Mead, "Research in Contemporary Cultures," in *Groups, Leadership, and Men,* H. S. Guetzkow, ed., Rutgers University Press, New Jersey, 1951.

that are peculiar to each culture. They are the way in which that culture structures the universe and envisions the individual's place within it. The same basic realities, the same nature, the same biological drives are apprehended and channeled differently by the people of different cultures.

Tests of intelligence or perception or emotion or proficiency or personality have not yet been devised that can tell us what human nature is like, unaffected by culture. In some cultures, time limits cannot be used, since children have no experience of them or are blocked by them. In others, children refuse to answer the questions asked, since it would be disrespectful to show a knowledge superior to that of the investigator, who would surely not be asking questions to which he knew the answer. In Samoa, for example, children's responses tended to take the form of the most artistic solution rather than of the most "efficient."

Neither can we observe human nature before it has been affected by culture, since the infant at birth has already been so affected. His surroundings at birth are culturally patterned. Even the birth process, itself, has been affected by the culturally derived attitude of the mother toward children, toward labor, toward childbirth, as well as by the kind of assistance and companionship she has at this time. The child's first experience of the world outside the womb is affected by culture. Is he weighed and measured by competent but unloving hands, wrapped in cloth, and bedded alone in a labeled box? Is he cuddled naked against bare skin, touched lovingly, and given the breast at the slightest sign of discomfort? Even a day-old infant does not present a picture of unadulterated human nature.

Culture is powerful and pervasive, changing the character of our biological drives, affecting our thinking, our emotions, and our perceptions. For example, there are distinct patterns of aggression, sibling rivalry, privacy, jealousy, loving, frustration, play, participation in the different cultures. What was there before culture entered the picture? Are human beings jealous by nature? There are societies where there is no evidence of jealousy. There are some polygynous societies where cowives exhibit so much jealousy that the man has to apportion himself with care and tact. There are other polygynous societies where an only wife will taunt and nag her husband until he brings her a cowife, with whom she then lives amicably. Is jealousy an inborn trait, which some cultures suppress effectively? Or is it a potentiality, fostered by some, atrophied by other cultures?

Again, there are cultures, such as our own, that take sibling rivalry for granted and proceed to make it into a constructive force, using it as a base for competitive fair play or for competitive achievement. There are other cultures that present the arrival of the new infant in such a way that it is not a situation where one mother is shared by two infants but is rather the sharing of an exciting experience by mother and "knee baby." Such cultures do not accept sibling rivalry as a matter of course. To what extent this rivalry is a product of, or is fostered by, the particular culture is still an unanswered question.

Love, too, is affected by culture. In our own culture, we believe in channeling and concentrating love into an intense emotion. The Hopi, on the other hand, do not encourage intensive attachment to parents and identification with them. They say that a child must learn to love more diffusely, since there are so many clan "mothers" and "fathers" for a child to love.[3]

Even biological realities, such as hunger and the drive to eat, are channeled and transformed by culture; how else could we explain the tremendous variety of their appearance? In some societies people feel hungry twice a day; in others, three or four or five times. In some societies, people are hungry at breakfast time; in others, they are not. What I will feel like eating depends on my culture. I find it is natural to be hungry for bacon at 7:30 A.M., but unnatural to be hungry for beef stew at that time. I like clam chowder, but I would find it monstrous to eat it at the end of a dinner; strawberry shortcake may lie more heavily on a full stomach, yet I find it appropriate to end a heavy meal with it.

There is only culture behind convictions and tastes of this sort; not reason or science or biology or human nature. The drive is merely for the satisfaction of hunger. Culture tells me when to be hungry and how to still my hunger. It may also keep me from eating when I am hungry, so as not to spoil my appetite or so as to preserve my figure. It will prepare me to enjoy my food as one of the pleasures of life, or it may present the meal to me as a balance of nutrients. According to my culture, I will be eating because the food is good, or because it is good for me, or because it represents to me my mother's love and care for me, or because it is a family ritual, or because one must eat to live.

With this great variety of motivation, sensation, behavior, it is never safe to predict how an individual will react unless his cultural background is known. For example, pearl traders assumed that it was a human trait to be motivated by the hope of reward. But when they went to the Trobriand Islands, they could not persuade the natives to dive, either for pay or for desirable articles. The natives were industrious and they

[3] Laura Thompson, op. cit., p. 5.

would dive for their own purposes. They would give their children pearls to play with but they would not sell them. It appears, then, that reward as motive is a cultural phenomenon. Actually, the pearl traders managed to teach this motive to the Trobrianders, though not with unqualified success.

People not only bring a different background of experience to bear in interpreting and reacting to a new situation; more than this, the same experience affects people of different cultures differently. To a member of one group within the American scene, to share a bed with a sister into adulthood is a continual violation of privacy. And, in fact, it is a generally accepted American idea that this is an inadequate sleeping arrangement. There are groups, however, that think this is an arrangement to be preferred. Again, adequacy of housing means for us the ability of a family of parents and children to live alone. In fact, we plan our public housing in such a way that three generations cannot live together. Families of Mexican Americans, however, moved out of a Midwest housing project because, for them, such housing was inadequate. To them, adequacy meant a three-generation household.

The particular structuring of the experience, again, has a specific effect on the individual. In our own culture, we tend to see ourselves in opposition to circumstances. We pit ourselves against nature; we fight the elements and try to control them. Each experience is a problem to solve, a difficulty to overcome, an obstacle to surmount, a conflict to resolve, a fight to win, a situation to master. To the Hopi Indian, the same situations are occasions for cooperation. He conceives of himself as working cooperatively with the entire universe. He helps nature. He does not set out to subjugate and tame a wilderness; he "helps" it reach the point where it can grow corn. He works with time, not against it. He may be doing exactly the same thing as a white person does, but the experience is actually different and has a different formative effect on his personality.[4]

Culture has coherence and pervasiveness. By this we mean that culture is not a hodgepodge of customs but something rather like a system or a design. Its various parts, queer and incomprehensible when set against another background, make sense within the culture of which they are a part. Conversely, the basic assumptions and formulations of a culture are present in, and expressed through, a variety of behaviors and attitudes. For example, the children of the Hopi farmers, who "help" nature grow the corn, took to basketball enthusiastically but could not be taught to

[4] Laura Thompson and Alice Joseph, *The Hopi Way*, University of Chicago Press, Chicago, 1945.

keep score. Competition did not interest them, but they loved the team-work. Our own children, trained to value fair conflict, need the com-petitive score to give incentive and spice to the game. They can be taught cooperation, teamwork, only incidentally and in a framework of com-petition.

Knowledge of the over-all culture enables us to see acts and attitudes as valid and understandable. It can help us to modify our own dealings so that they can be effective and meaningful. We can be good neighbors, accepting and respecting other ways of life. We can distinguish between personal peculiarities and a culturally patterned behavior. Further, with an awareness of the cultural factor in thought and policy making and evaluation, we can have insight into our own motivations and assump-tions. When we see that our own is not the only possible or valid way, we can learn to view other ways of life not as deviant but as of equal dignity and validity.

Implications for Work with Persons of Variant Culture

How will the "American" teacher, doctor, nurse, social worker, etc., react to the people he works with? "Americans," like others, have learned to consider certain personality traits admirable, others despicable. How will they react to, say, Chinese children, who have learned to be submis-sive and silent? How will they treat Chinese mothers, who are self-deprecating and apologetic, following the dictates of courtesy in their cul-ture? Can they understand the actions of children of Eastern European Jewish immigrants who are, at one and the same time, accepting of per-sonal authority (for to "talk back" is a terrible act) and yet are trained to question all intellectual authority with minute critical analysis?

These children are reacting in ways based on the structuring of inter-personal relations in the cultural groups from which they come. The "American" must be aware of this background for behavior, for then he will know that the apologetic attitude of the Chinese child is not a sign of personal insecurity, and that the Jewish child who is so good at debat-ing may be indulging in an arduous feat of virtuosity rather than in crea-tive, cooperative thinking.

The place the culture accords to suffering provides another basis for possible misunderstanding. "Americans" believe that it is admirable to carry one's own burden of grief and self-doubt, to smile bravely when ill and to be a "good," self-sufficient patient. But people of some cultures find our behavior under misfortune insane, or they find it exclu-sive, depriving others of their right to help us. The "American" assumption in this case reflects the cultural stress on self-sufficiency and on individualism. It makes sense against the background of a culture of which it is a part, just as much as the belief that grief and pain must be shared makes sense within a different cultural context.

It is difficult for an "American" nurse not to be annoyed at the patient who wants constant attention, not to prefer the patient who bears her discomfort silently; it is hard for an "American" teacher to respect the child who runs to her with an account of all his ills. Yet patterns of suffering are as much a part of culture as the Italian's liking for spaghetti, and this is neither admirable nor reprehensible. A self-respecting Pole *must* answer a "How are you?" with a long list of his ills. He has a strong pattern for making himself valuable to the world, as Ruth Benedict says, "through suffering." It is wrong of him to say, for example, that he likes his job, that everything is going well with him—as wrong as it is for us to answer a casual greeting with a list of complaints. To us, against our own frame of reference, the Pole is complaining. We do not respect his behavior. But the Pole is not complaining. He is acting with pride and dignity, as a self-respecting man should act.

Workers with children and their families should also know something about the meaning of the group for the people with whom they have dealings. "Americans" use the term "group" very often. We speak of "group spirit" and "group unity," of the formation and dissolution of "groups." We teach our children to join groups of various kinds, and we expect them to go through an age when they form "clubs" of their own. We therefore find it difficult to imagine that there are people who almost never use the term "group" in their conversation, whose members do not ordinarily form groups but, like the Greeks, are born into them. When the "American" speaks of a group leader, he does not mean a father or a grandmother; but in these variant cultures, the significant grouping is the family or the extended family, and its "leader" is the head of the family.

For people of these cultures, the community of people from their native village or country of birth also forms a recognized unit. This may be a physical grouping, as when Italians from one village move to New York and settle on one side of a street. Or it may be a construct as with the Greeks who, having for centuries gone out singly to settle in distant parts of the globe, have a pattern for maintaining a close tie and participation with a community which is not physically present. In either case, the unit recognized is not the larger "American" community. Such people may fail to become responsible members of the community for the simple reason that they have failed to recognize it as a valid grouping for belonging; or, if they have so recognized it, they may have lacked completely the techniques for entering the unit and making themselves a part of it. Imaginative community workers, who have enabled people from such cultures to become incorporated in the community, have found them highly capable of extending their loyalty and sense of responsibility to the new unit of identification.

In respect to the child, there are more issues involved here. The groupings which the "American" child is taught to recognize and enter are mainly age groupings. The age grouping, strongly aided by the law of universal education, is firmly entrenched in "American" culture and is supported by our psychological tenets of child development and our family pattern which separates adult activities from child activities.

On the other hand, Chinese and Greek children, to cite only two examples, have learned to enjoy a group of assorted people of all ages, to feel at home in it, to find a significant place in it and share fully in its activity. They are born into such a unit and, by virtue of this fact, they inherit their contacts with other units. Children with this background have a basically different experience in school from their "American" classmates, though this is not evident on the surface. Not only do they find it difficult to recognize the class as a group, they also fail to profit fully from the training in group experience and participation which the school offers.

Material about other cultures contains certain implications regarding the placing of children through adoption and in foster homes. In many groups, we find a strong sense of responsibility toward relatives, so that a family will take in and rear and educate the child of a dead brother or a more distant relative. But not in all these groups is love given freely to a child who is not one's offspring. For example, the Greeks will comment to a child about the generosity and responsible behavior of his foster parents. In such cases, with physiological parenthood paramount in engendering parental love, the foster parents can never forget that a child is not actually their own. And the child himself behaves as an "orphan."

There are indications that the Eastern European Jews also, strongly as they feel the responsibility for indigent relatives, do not accept foster children completely. Full physiological relationship is so important that, according to Joffe, even half-siblings are called by step-sibling terms, not by blood-relationship terms; and when a widow marries a widower, each with children, reference is made to *my* children, *your* children, and *our* children.

These few illustrations of the ways in which people of various cultures differ in ideas and customs and values may be sufficient to make the point that culture is something the professions should take into account in their work with children and their families. The aim of all professional workers is to provide constructive experiences for the people they serve. The findings of anthropologists make it clear that this aim cannot be fully accomplished unless the cultural meaning of these experiences to particular individuals is understood and utilized.

IX

The Family

THE chief purpose of the chapters in this second section of the fact-finding report to the Midcentury White House Conference on Children and Youth is to stimulate discussion about two questions. First, what part do various social institutions play in personality development? Second, in view of the findings set forth in the preceding chapters, what changes are needed in order that the institutions may more effectively promote the welfare of children and youth? The first question is more or less factual. The second is a matter of judgment. To neither question can anything like scientifically grounded answers be given. Consequently, the present and succeeding chapters are to be regarded largely as tentative statements based on such facts and theories as could be ascertained.

Role of the Family in Personality Development

The first social institution to be considered is the basic one, the family. Regarding its role in personality development, much has already been said or implied in Part I of this report. It has been shown that the most important components of personality, those on which later progress depend, come into being in the give-and-take of family life, and that many of the customs, ideas, beliefs, and values of the society are transmitted to children by their parents. The function of the family in the economic sphere has also been commented on, and the variation in families' ability to provide adequately for the physical welfare of their children has been noted. The findings on these points may be summarized as follows.

It is in and through the family that the main components of a child's personality develop. The struggle between feelings of trust and mistrust is first worked out in relation to the parents, and it is by family members that the autonomy and initiative characteristic of our society are encouraged or denied. The family members play an important part in relation to later personality components also. The close emotional ties fostered by the dependencies of childhood make the parents' and siblings' attitudes of praise or blame highly important to the child struggling toward a sense

174

of achievement. The sense of identity, often so hard-won in adolescence, is referable in part to family status and to family feelings about it. The extent and quality of the ability to relate intimately to other persons and to oneself derives in large measure from the kind of relations that obtain within the family, and the ability to become a parent in the full sense of the word depends largely on the individual's experiences with the parental role as enacted by his own parents. Finally, the integrity displayed by parents, in manifold deeds and attitudes, sets an ideal for their children that later experiences may modify but can seldom eradicate, and this often forms the kernel of the new generation's sense of integrity.

It is through the family, too, that the child gets his first sense of what is allowed and what is forbidden, what is valued and what is despised in the society, and in the section of the society, of which he is a part. It is his family's version of these rules and values that he learns or senses, and also the emotional overtones they add to it. The way the culture's requirements are transmitted to the child determines to a considerable extent what use he will make of them and what their meaning to him will be. Consequently, family behavior and feeling in this regard are very important in personality development.

In its economic function, too, the family affects the personality development of children. Economically, it has been pointed out, the family is the great unequalizer. To a considerable extent it is family income that opens doors or limits opportunities for children. The fact that children are reared in homes varying widely in socioeconomic resources means that they have varying social inheritances as well, and this is reflected in their intelligence, their emotional well-being, their physical health, their occupational opportunities—in short, in almost all aspects of their lives.

Perhaps enough has already been said, then, to demonstrate that the family has the basic role to play in promoting the well-being of children and youth. It is this fact that makes many of us, in characteristic American fashion, blame the family for what we think is wrong with the behavior and attitudes of children and young people, and also makes us fear that the family is losing its functions and going out of existence. Blame and fear, in fact, characterize so much of current discussion about the family, and anxiety about child rearing characterizes so many parents, that a consideration of what might be done to improve the situation must start by asking whether things are really as bad as they seem.

Is the Family Disappearing?

First, a few figures. The popularity of marriage is not declining. More marriages take place when jobs are numerous and in time of war, but over the years, and particularly since 1940, an increasing proportion of the adult population of the United States has married or remarried. There were about 17,400,000 marriages between 1940 and 1949, as compared with 8,300,000 in the first decade of the century. The marriage rate was about 9 per 1000 population in 1900 and about 11 in 1949.[1] Apparently, then, the family is not declining, so far as willingness of individuals to enter into marriage is concerned.

On the average, marriage is being entered into at an ever earlier age. In 1890, half of the men who married for the first time were 26 or younger, and half of the women were under 22. This seems fairly young. But by 1949, the median age for men had moved down to 22.7, while for women it was 20.3.[2]

Apparently, in spite of all the talk about its difficulties, marriage is not something that young people seek to avoid.

Once married, interest in having children appears to be on the increase. While over the years the long-time trend in the birth rate has been down, nearly 4,000,000 babies were born in 1947, the largest "crop" in United States history. Since then, the number has declined a bit, but even so, the drop in the birth rate has been smaller than was expected. Some further decline is anticipated, if only because the decline in births during the depression years means that during the 1950s and 1960s there will be fewer than in, say, the 1920s.

More evidence to this point is furnished by the fact that during the 1940s there was a considerable increase in the number of preschool children per 1000 women of childbearing age. In 1940, there were 281 such children; in 1947, the high point, there were 367. The increase was especially great in cities, where it amounted to almost 50 per cent; and it was much larger among college graduates (77 per cent) than among women who had not completed grade school (25 per cent).[3, 4]

These various figures, then, demonstrate that the family is not disappearing. On the contrary, interest in family life, in undertaking its responsibilities, is as strong or stronger than ever. This is true despite the mounting divorce figures. For years, the divorce rate climbed, and it took a big spurt upward during the war years. Two hundred and sixty-four thousand divorces were granted in 1940; 610,000 in 1946. By 1949, how-

[1] National Office of Vital Statistics.

[2] U.S. Census Bureau, "Current Population Surveys."

[3] Figures from U.S. Bureau of the Census.

[4] In spite of these changes, however, it is still true that the birth rate is highest and the ratio of children to adults greatest in farm areas and among Negroes and others whose economic status, on the average, is low.

ever, the number was down to 386,000—a rate per 1000 population that was about in line with the long-time trend.[5]

The decline of the family as a social institution is not proved by the high divorce rate, however. Most people, apparently, do not get divorced to escape family responsibilities. More than half of the divorces are granted to couples who do not have children, and three-fourths of the persons obtaining a divorce remarry within five years. Many divorced persons, formerly childless, have children by the second marriage, and many who already have children continue to produce.

Is the Family Losing Its Function?

Even when it is recognized that families are not declining in number or size, there are still many who maintain that the family is losing its function and that its demise is thereby imminent. In evidence they cite the fact that families no longer produce the major portion of their food and clothing; that the education of children is increasingly being entrusted to the schools; that recreation is less and less a family matter; that doctors and nurses taken an ever larger part in the care of health; and so on. All this is true to a considerable extent. Nevertheless, anthropologists insist that the essential functions of the family are not being taken over by any other social institutions.

Three such essential functions have been identified: (1) to produce children and provide them with a setting of supporting affection; (2) to induct them, from infancy on, into the ways and values of the society; (3) to give them their initial identity within the community. In the United States today, there is no evidence that other social institutions are supplanting the family in these respects, nor is any society known in which this has been done. So long as the family retains these functions, it cannot be said to be passing away.

Children can, of course, be produced without benefit of family, and it is true that unmarried motherhood is on the increase. Nearly half again as many babies were known to be born out of wedlock in 1948 as in 1938, and the rate per thousand unmarried women of childbearing age was 80 per cent higher in 1948 than in 1940.[6] Nevertheless, the total was relatively very small—129,700 in 1948 out of approximately three and a half million registered births.

Few unmarried mothers, however, bring up their children wholly by themselves. Some turn to relatives; some marry very soon. Many place

[5] National Office of Vital Statistics.
[6] National Office of Vital Statistics.

their children in institutions or foster homes or give them over for adoption. Aside from the child-care institutions (and they have fewer children in their care than in the past [7]), no substitute for the family has been invented. In short, even though children may be produced outside of the family institution, very few are reared under any other social arrangement.

The value of the family in providing a setting of supporting affection is increasingly evident as knowledge about child development grows. To foster and sustain a developing sense of individuality and worth, children require not only physical care but also love, response, and personalized attention. For this task the family has advantages over any other social institution. The small number of family members and the continuity of their relation to the child ensure that his day-to-day care will be given by the same persons over and over again. This makes possible in the child the development of deep emotional attachments, to parents and to other people, and this, in turn, makes emotional growth possible. There is reason to believe that children who have been nursed and reared by too wide a circle of individuals find it difficult to care deeply for others.

In our competitive society this affectional function of the family is of especial importance. On the job, achievement rather than affectional relationships are prized, and the same is true to some extent at school and in education and recreation. Home is one of the few places in our society in which an individual can count on being valued for himself rather than for his ability. Such valuation is essential for health of personality. This is one explanation of the especial importance Americans attach to family life. The desire to continue in adulthood this source of emotional security, and yet obtain the freedom from ties to the parental home that occupational progress requires, may be one of the chief reasons for our early marriages and high marriage rate.

The second universal function of the family, the educational, is also of importance for healthy personality development. The educational function is one the American family shares with other social institutions, notably the school but also the church and recreational organizations. Education within the family differs, however, from education through these other sources in ways that are of importance to mental health.

The small size, the flexibility, and the emotional attachments of the family permit more expression of individual difference than is possible in

[7] In 1933 there were about 15,000 children in institutions for dependent or neglected children; in 1946 and 1947 only a few over 10,000. Most of these children had started life in a family and still had family connections. (U.S. Children's Bureau reports from 33 states.)

larger, more formal social institutions. Large numbers and formality of procedures have their place in the socialization process. Before they can be effective, however, a child must have the experience of freedom to express himself in his own way, and such an experience only family life, with its biological and affectional base, can adequately provide.

These characteristics of the family also facilitate training in the exercise of choice, that prime American value, in a way that takes into account the rights and roles of others. The schools continue this training, to be sure, but it is in the close relations of the family that the lessons are given in the spontaneous, unself-conscious manner that adds to their value. Family life is a mass of decisions; to decide and to act are of its essence. Even in a family in which children are given only a small share in the decision-making process, they are aware of, and intimately related to, the choices made. No other social group could provide this kind of experience for a growing child—as witness the deficiencies in this regard in children who have been reared en masse in foster-care institutions.

Then, too, the composition of the family is a great help in a child's socialization process. In the family, the child has countless experiences with persons who differ from him in age and sex and who stand in varying relationships to him. From them he learns most clearly both his difference from others and the extent and variety of his dependence upon them. He learns that he cannot expect the same response from every person, or from the same person every time, and he learns that he must approach different persons differently. He may learn, for example, to whom he may offer affection without risk of too great involvement, and whom he must avoid. He may learn that true emotion elicits warm response and that pretended emotion leads to withdrawal.

Within the family, too, he tests out the extent of his control over others and of their control over him. Can he make his brother or sister play with him if they do not want to? Can he persuade other members of his family to accede to his wishes? What are the limits of his power over them? He discovers the answers through endless experiments. If he encounters firm and consistent behavior in others, he has discovered one aspect of himself as a person. He has learned the extent of his own strength, learned that it is really his, but he has also learned that in exercising that strength he can go just so far. Beyond this, the rights of other members of the family must be acknowledged and accepted.

He also learns in the family whether people can be relied upon to support his efforts to explore and choose for himself, yet hold firm in setting limits which he must not exceed. Both warm support and holding firm are necessary for his safety and security and for his growing ability to trust himself and others. Through such support and limitation he comes to know that there are persons warmly and closely related to him who are strong enough to protect him both from the dangers from without and from his own inner impulses and anxieties.

It is lessons of this kind that the family teaches, through countless small but emotionally vivid experiences. By no other social arrangement could this kind of instruction be provided in so meaningful a way (for at base it depends upon close affectional ties), and it seems doubtful that health of personality can be secured without it.

The third universal function of the family—that of providing the child with an initial identity—is also one that cannot be performed by other social institutions and one that is of great importance in determining the individual's sense of worth. At the start, the child's social identity is of necessity based on his relationship to his family. Important as he is in his own right within his family, he does not have identity in relation to the larger community except as it is derived from his identity with his family—"the Smith youngster," "the Townsends' baby girl." Later, through other social institutions, the child enlarges upon that initial identity and becomes not only the "Jones boy" but also the "P School basketball player," the "St. Francis Church altar boy," the *"Post's* delivery boy," and so on. Even so, throughout his life, his basic identity is "Bill Jones."

The sociologists call this an "ascribed status" and point out that in our society ascribed statuses are few, most of our sense of identity and self-worth being dependent upon the status—in school, on the job, in the community—we achieve. Regardless of the advantages of this system, which makes it possible for people to receive recognition in accordance with their ability and performance, it is not one conducive to a feeling of security; hence in our society the protection of the ascribed status of family is unusually important.

An ascribed status, however, is not always beneficial to an individual. Whether the child's sense of identity with his family contributes to or threatens his personality development is largely determined by the feelings and attitudes of his parents toward themselves and toward him. This, in turn, depends in part upon the family's position in the community and upon the child's own competitive striving for positions that carry prestige. Whether he achieves a deep inner sense of self as an independent entity regardless of his "success" elsewhere appears to be closely related to the extent to which he has gained a feeling of his own worth in the family group.

There may be times, especially in adolescence, when an individual thinks he does not want to belong to his family, when he wants to dissociate himself from his family and deny all relationship to them. He may attribute his feelings of rejection to the fact that his family is "foreign," or "conservative," or "too religious," or "shiftless." And it may be true that identification with his family is a handicap, denying him access to some of the resources of the community or keeping him from desired vocational and social positions. If so, the identification with the family may be hazardous to the individual's development.

Basically, however, even the adolescent wants and needs his family. It is in the family that he can most fully test his new sense of adulthood, through a changed and different relationship to the family members. He was a child and is changing into an adult. It is through the family's acceptance of this difference in him, expressed by changes in themselves and in their attitudes and emotional response to him, that his sense of adulthood is most readily confirmed. The family structure offers him the opportunity of affirming his difference from his earlier self, yet remaining still related, still belonging. His need to separate from the family does not in any way negate the function served by the family in giving him a sense of belonging through his identity with them. For the child, and especially for the older child and youth, the danger is not that he be identified with his family but that others will reject or disparage the difference his family represents in the community. What is most needed is not greater acceptance and greater opportunities for youngsters in spite of their families but greater acceptance and wider opportunities for families themselves.

The family, we see then, has functions that are of great importance to the well-being of children and young people. Much is lost in health of personality when the operation of the family function is interfered with: when affectional relationships are disturbed, the educational process disrupted, the base for the sense of identity disturbed. No other social institution can assume these functions in their totality (which is another way of saying that these are the family's peculiar province), nor does it seem possible that they could be parceled out among several institutions with benefit to children. This being so, there seems little doubt that the family will continue to exist and will continue to discharge these basic duties.

Does the Family Prepare Children for American Life?

The ability of the family to prepare children for participation in the work and pleasures of the society—to start them on their career as happy and responsible citizens and to support them in it—depends not only upon the satisfactory performance by the parents of the functions described above but also upon the degree to which the work of the family is coordinated with that of other social institutions. The possibility of lack of coordination arises from the fact that there is no such thing as *the* American family. Consequently, there is much variation in the ways the functions of the family are performed, in the customs and values transmitted to children, and in the personality traits that are admired and cultivated.

Urban middle-class families differ somewhat from those that are rural. The family in the South differs in some ways from the family in other parts of the country. Indian, Mexican, Southern rural Negro families have their peculiar characteristics, as do those of other ethnic and racial groups. The differences along class and sectional and ethnic lines almost negate, in their extreme, the generalizations that are frequently made about the American family.

In other social institutions there is less cultural variation. Moreover, so far as a given child is concerned, there may not be a one-to-one relationship between family and, say, school and occupational system. Both of the latter institutions undoubtedly differ from one part of the country to another and within sections of society, depending upon what social class they serve or draw their members from. Nevertheless, American society is not composed of tight little congeries of cultural groups. For example, Greek-American children, who at home learn Greek-American values and customs, are unlikely to attend Greek-American schools, to find their recreation wholly among Greek Americans, and, as adults, to engage solely in Greek-American economic activities. Though there may be more of this than is commonly assumed by sociologists, the American ideal and the American social structure call for much social mobility and for considerable uniformity in customs and values.

In consequence of this possible lack of parallelism between family and other social institutions, children may be prepared by their parents and other family members for a life based on one set of values and beliefs and may find themselves in school and on the job being called upon to operate along very different lines. Not that this cultural diversity in American life is wholly to be deplored. What we are considering here, however, are not its advantages but some of the problems it may create for those children whose parents are not in the mainstream of the American way of life.

It is not sufficient to our main purpose, then, to show, as we have done above, that because the family has certain functions that are very important to personality development and that cannot be well performed by any other social institution, the family is in no danger of extinction. We must also ask whether the prevailing type of American family operates in a way that is consistent with the requirements of other social institutions and thus prepares its children for participation in later social life. And we must also demonstrate that variation from this type of family does exist and does produce individuals whose cultural expectations are different from those usually regarded as American.

The Prevailing Type of Family

The kind of family that is peculiarly American is a two-generation family composed of husband, wife, and minor children. Marriage originates these families, rather than occasioning an accretion to a family that is already formed. By marriage, husband and wife are more or less drastically separated from "their own" families, and by it they assume new loyalties and responsibilities—to each other and to their children until maturity.[8] Little contact with relatives is required. The relatives exercise little or no control over the new couple's actions. The couple and their children are free to choose their place of residence and to follow their line of best interest (largely economic) as they see fit. "Tied to his parents" is a derogatory characterization of a husband or wife in this kind of family, and deference to parents' wishes or furtherance of their interests over those of the new family can be a reason for the spouse's seeking divorce.

Since these are the structure and operating rules of the predominant American family, young people can be left free to choose their marital partners with little or no counsel from their parents and relatives. There is no "great family" to be harmed by indiscretion in this respect, no loss of anticipated income, no family honor at stake. Romantic love can therefore be the basis for marriage, and personal relationships the keystone of family life. Each generation makes its own decisions, and tradition in regard to rights and duties and prescribed roles does not count for much, since the control of an interlocking kinship system is lacking.

The development of this sort of family system in the United States is not the result of chance. The family system is closely integrated with the occupational system, and the values and requirements of the latter apparently determine the family's rules and structure. As Talcott Parsons

[8] The fact that dependent relatives are rather broadly defined in income-tax law and in the policy of public-assistance agencies suggests, however, that, with regard to economic maintenance at least, the American family is not quite so small a unit as some sociologists would maintain.

points out, occupational roles are organized around standards of accomplishment, and upward movement economically or in terms of power and prestige requires freedom from ties of all sorts—geographical, sentimental, what-you-will. It is only by being regarded as a unit, and by being a small unit with children too young to compete or otherwise interfere, that the family is saved from destruction by the occupational system. To maintain this unity, however, the family must be free to follow the husband-father in his job quest; it must not make demands on him that are inconsistent with his performance in the occupational sphere; its values and ambitions must be those that promote his advance. In addition, it must be a buffer between him and the impersonal, emotionally neutral world of work, where he is valued not so much for what he is as for what he can accomplish. Hence the high value put on personal relationships within this little family, the emphasis on being "in love," the insistence on the right to dissolve the marriage if emotional needs are not met.[9]

This kind of family, then, would seem to be the kind that the American system, with its emphasis on individual achievement and success, requires.[10] It is a family that has only slight ties to former generations, that imposes few lineal responsibilities on its children, that sets the children free to leave home, choose their marital partners, and follow job opportunities as they see fit.

Apparently, a family of this sort can provide children with the basis for reasonably good performance in adulthood, as citizens, workers, and parents. If it could not, our society would either disintegrate or change radically. For all our talk of delinquency, neurosis, marital disharmony, civic indifference, the fact remains that the majority of American youths, particularly from this middle-class type of home, are law abiding. Most of them become efficient workers, turning out goods and services of unprecedented quality and quantity; most of them marry and have pride and joy in their children; most of them take as much interest in civic affairs as the American tradition dictates. There is much that could be improved, of course (the very belief in improvement is an American characteristic), and the potentialities for the good life within our way of

[9] In this connection it is significant that most divorces are for the purpose of remarriage. It is apparently not the emotional ties of marriage that most people seeking divorce object to but the lack of emotional satisfaction with the particular spouse.

[10] The requirements of the nonindustrialized farm economy, for example, are somewhat different. There more mutual assistance and mutual responsibility among family members and between generations is called for, and with it more control over marital choice and parental behavior.

life could be better realized. We must not be misled by that belief, however, into ignoring facts and imagining the worst.

More specifically, the very structure and guiding ideas of the predominant type of American family lay the base for the cultivation in children of values that are culturally prized. Freedom of choice, freedom from emotional ties, limited responsibility for family members but much self-responsibility, pride in initiative and achievement, ability to cooperate with one's peers: all these are exemplified in the make-up and functioning of the typical American family, and are demonstrated in its child-rearing customs.

From the time he can talk—and even earlier—the child in this sort of family is urged to express preferences: for food, for toys, for activities, for people. Autonomy is early encouraged, perhaps even ahead of emotional and physical readiness. Parents, once cautionad against being overprotective, now have to be urged to cater to children's "dependency feelings" and not to arouse "separation anxiety." Compared with family life in other societies and in earlier times, little is asked of children in participation in household tasks, care of siblings, regard for parents' feelings or the family pocketbook. Instead, children are expected to take joy in their own accomplishments and to become self-reliant as soon as possible. Cooperation among siblings, while considered desirable for family harmony, is not really expected ("sibling rivalry," when not extreme, is taken as a matter of course), and more stress is put upon a child's ability to get along with his friends than with his brothers and sisters. In short, the predominant type of American family uses the affectional relationships developed between parents and children to produce traits that are peculiarly American. In this way it fulfills its functions of preparing children for participation in the work and pleasures of the society.

Other Family Types

The variations from this predominant American pattern of family life are of two main kinds. One, the historical precursor of this type, is the kind found among such otherwise dissimilar groups as the Northern urban "upper-upper" class, the Southern "aristocracy," urban or rural, and some groups of urban European background. This type accepts many of the economic tenets of American life (the importance of work, achievement, freedom of choice, etc.) but tries to combine with them "great-family" values, such as pride in kinship, responsibility to relatives, right of the older generation to considerable control, and so on.

The other variety of family is a kind that is culturally outside the mainstream—the family of the Mexicans, the Spanish Americans, the Indians, the rural Southern Negro and the mountain white, of the Chinese and other Orientals who maintain their old values and customs, of certain Southern and East European nationalities. This type—in spite of great differences within it—has in common the fact that the whole orientation of the culture of which it is a part is different from the predominant American.[11]

An exact description of the structure and functioning of the family in these two main types and in their subtypes is not necessary for our present purpose. It is sufficient to note that the divergencies exist, for it is their presence and their lack of articulation with other American institutions—school and occupational system in particular—that may create difficulties for the children who grow up in them.

Whether the family types that diverge from this predominant one also start children off well, depends, it seems, on what kind of life their children are headed for. If it is life within the parents' cultural orbit, then the answer is probably in the affirmative. The values and customs of Mexican-American family life, for example, are probably in keeping with the standards and requirements of life within the present Mexican-American community, and similarly with those of upper-class Boston.

The difficulty is that life does not stay the same. Americans are given to roving (the economic system encourages and requires it), and the family is not the only social institution that influences children's development. These facts do not greatly interfere with the efficacy of functioning of the predominant type of family, for that type is geared to change and is articulated with school, job, and other institutions' requirements. They may, however, create problems for youngsters whose attitudes and values were learned in other types of families. In so far as this happens, it may be that these types—through no fault of their own—may not fulfill the functions of the family well, so far as fitting children for participation in "American" life is concerned.

The Greek-American Family: An Illustration of a Divergent Type [12]

As an illustration of a way of life that diverges from the predominant American, and of the role of the family in fitting children for that way,

[11] For an abstract analysis of possible differences in orientations see Florence Rockwood Kluckhohn, "Dominant and Substitute Profiles of Cultural Orientation," *Social Forces*, Vol. 28 (1950), pp. 376–393.

[12] For further information about the Greeks in Greece see Peter Gray, *People of Poros*, McGraw-Hill Book Company, Inc., New York, 1942; for Greeks in the United States, Rosamonde R. Boyd, *The Social Adjustment of the Greeks in Spartanburg*, Spartanburg, South Carolina, 1950.

the following description of Greek-American customs and values is presented. It will be noted that, as with the "American" family, Greek-American family life is designed to induct children, through loving care, into beliefs and values and behavior modes that are highly regarded and to prepare them for the kind of performance of adult roles that Greek-American culture deems admirable.

Americans of Greek origin maintain their Greek culture to a great extent. The Orthodox Church, which they take with them wherever they go, has been an important factor in their integrity, as has the Greek language, the Greek newspapers, and the community gatherings with folk songs which, in many sections of the country, are frequented even by the children and grandchildren of immigrants. Greeks find it easy to adapt superficially to the ways around them, to assume a new role like a cloak, but their Greek culture, its basic motivations and satisfactions, they retain with great tenacity. Even when there is a true change in the lives of the second or third generation, there is still the Greek background, instilled at an early age at home, of values, principles, and structurings. It is this background that the American child of Greek parentage denies or is in conflict with or reconciles with his "American" culture. For this reason, it is the Greek culture in its conservative form, not in its varieties of adaptation, that will be described here.

Some Greek Values and Attributes. The core of Greek integrity is the *philotimo*—honor or love. This is protected by *entrope*—shame, bashfulness, shyness, embarrassment, self-consciousness, decency and indecency, modesty, propriety. Children are continuously admonished to have *entrope*. Through proper *entrope,* a Greek avoids any conduct which brings dishonor, and keeps from exposing to view those private feelings and experiences which to him mean weakness (or failure to fulfill his ascribed role).

Personal freedom is of the essence of the *philotimo*. The Greek regards personal freedom as the highest good. He identifies it with his country, he pictures it graphically, he sings songs to it, he personifies it. Freedom represents Greekness to him, for a Greek cannot maintain his sense of honor when in submission to the domination of others. Since the Greek child is brought up to obey his father strictly and to assume delineated roles, this statement seems paradoxical. But the Greek is so thoroughly identified with his family and his role within it that the father's authority is usually not felt as external, and family ends, with the obligations they impose, are to its members personal ends.

Self-discipline and fortitude are demanded of the *philotimo*. This means that the Greek must suffer pain and hardship without complaint, or even without paying heed. Sorrow, disappointment, failure, desperation must be borne silently, with fortitude, and not exposed to view. To suffer publicly might suggest, on the one hand, that you have no relative to help you; on the other hand, it would be a bid for pity. Only the grief of bereavement may be open and vociferous—not as abandonment but as tribute to the value of the deceased.

Greeks prize self-dependence, but the self is the family, not the individual human being. It goes against the *philotimo* to accept aid from outsiders. Only a misfortune due to an act of God does not touch the *philotimo* and has nothing to do with loss of personal worth. A Greek, however, can accept help from a family member in the appropriate order; that is, younger from elder, female from male. This is regarded as in the nature of things. Girls will depend on their father or brother or even on an uncle for a dowry, and boys will accept help from an older brother; a man will allow his father or his brothers to set him up in business without losing *philotimo*. In general, however, any need because of personal failure is kept hidden even from near relatives; one must not admit defeat.

Work is life for the Greek. Sports and leisure, weekends and vacations are the recent introductions of foreigners. There are holy days where certain kinds of work, such as sewing, are forbidden, but the common work goes on.

Diligence is a personal quality, warmly admired. To call a girl *procommene*, diligent, is to say something about her attractiveness; the terms has a pleasing emotive connotation. School children used to learn a poem about the joyous little "housewife," the diligent girl who knew no laziness, who got up early and put the house to rights. The picture evokes to the "American" an unattractive goody-goody; but for the Greek, the picture carries charm and gaiety. The Greek folk songs, sung as accompaniment at the round dances, often picture work situations—a woman singing at the loom, a group of girls laundering by the beach, spreading the clothes and playing in the sand. Folk tales make cruel fun of the lazy wife, who eventually comes to grief in her attempts to play the leisured lady.

Diligence is an internal attitude, involving self-discipline, enjoyment, interest, free incentive. It does not mean a valuation of work for its own sake. To work compulsively is to be a slave to work; and what can be worse than slavery? To work under pressure of any kind, such as a time limit or the dictates of an employer, and even to work under the compulsion of work as virtue is to deny oneself prized freedom.

It is distasteful to the Greek to organize his activities according to external limits; he is therefore either early or late—promptitude is not a virtue in his eyes. For a Greek, to work against time, to hurry, is to forfeit freedom. His term for "hurry" meant, originally, to coerce oneself. No one admonishes another to coerce himself, and a mother does not ask her child to hurry up. But a Greek has other ways to express expeditiousness. If he needs help in a hurry, he calls, "Arrive!" instead of "Come!" If he wants to reassure you about the progress he is making, he says, "Now I have finished," meaning, "I am hurrying through it."

The Greek does not budget his expenditures. He spends not according to what he has but according to the order of what he wants, and, on principle, he should want little. Simplicity and frugality are expressions of fortitude and self-discipline, and they are also actually enjoyed as dimensions of living. The Greek, though motivated by the future, does not regard the present as a means to future enjoyment; he does not live by the future. He does, however, save for the family, so that there will be the means for the education of the son or for the dowry of the daughter. He has no faith in the future and knows that it will not take care of itself. He will buy, as a rule, only what he can pay for now, and will not expand his business or his standard of living on the basis of future profits.

Unless he is indigent, then, the Greek lives well within his income. Any rise in income is sheer surplus. It does not have to go toward relieving the strain on the budget or to pay a dreaded installment. It does not raise the standard of living. The Greek likes his life; he does not see why he should give up his lunch of cheese and bread, or his delicious stews, just because now he can afford steak every day. He will not leave his roomy house in a socially undesirable district because he can afford to move to a fashionable neighborhood; that is, not unless he succumbs to the pressure of his "American" children. The surplus will be put back into the business, or saved intact for the family, or given in beneficence.

Family and Child Rearing. These, then, in broad outline, are the guiding values of the Greek American. In large part they are family centered. Even the central core, the *philotimo,* has a family orientation; it is one's honor as a member of the family that is at stake. In the Greek-American way of life, accordingly, the family is not only the unit that produces and rears children, it is also the unit that determines behavior and sentiments throughout life. Marriage only widens the circle of relatedness, with the result that in a Greek village almost everybody is kin to all the others. Since this is so, Greek-American marriage customs and child-rearing customs are necessarily different from those that are characteristically

"American," for, in some ways, they have different tasks to take into account.

Ideally, in Greece, marriages were "arranged"; that is, the families rather than the young people made the choice, for they had much to gain or lose by the transaction. In the United States, many Greek families still follow this custom. Friends and relatives are always concerned about the unmarried and are constantly suggesting "brides" and "grooms." Many marriages involving men and women from distant parts of the country are initiated in this way. Even a man who has been educated wholly in the United States may ask his mother to find a bride.

Through marriage the family is doubly extended, for entering into the network of family rights and obligations are not only the new couple but also the wedding sponsors, the "best man" or "bridesmaid" of "American" custom. With these people very close relationships are maintained throughout life. The man is likely to be chosen as the godparent of the couple's first child, a position of great responsibility, for a godparent concerns himself with the child's development and character, with his education and marriage, and may even assume his financial support. By this arrangement, nonfamilial relationships within the community are bridged in part, for children who have the same godparent are tantamount to being siblings, so much so that marriage between them is forbidden.

Thus extended, the family becomes the center of a Greek's loyalty; it and his country define society for the Greek. Hence, when a Greek speaks of valuing honesty, he means not abstract honesty—a term that has no meaning for him—but honesty in his dealings within these units; and when he speaks of his social responsibilities, he means not humanity at large but his own specific responsibilities toward the members of these units. He will follow the regulations implicit in his roles in these units, recognizing their validity and acting through personal choice. Outside of these recognized groups, to which he renders unquestioning loyalty, his rules of ethics do not apply.

How, then, does the family operate to perform its basic functions and to instill these Greek virtues in the children of each successive generation?

That the Greek-American family provides a setting of supporting affection is clear both from the child-rearing customs and from the way orphans are treated. Regarding the latter, it is taken for granted that relatives will be loved in different ways. The love that a Greek feels for children of his own body is something for these alone and cannot be extended to anybody else, not even to children he adopts or otherwise assumes responsibility for. To be an orphan in Greece is therefore a tragedy, something that all children know and dread. Not that the child will not be cared for. As long as there is an uncle or an aunt he will not be in need, he will be reared and educated, established in a trade or a business, provided with a dowry if a girl. In this way, family responsibility will be carried out. But he will never be loved as his mother loved him, freely and with complete acceptance. In the Greek view, only physiological parenthood breeds parental love; for nonphysiological parenthood there is scarcely any cultural pattern.

Greek child-rearing practices have changed in specific detail in this country, but the attitudes of the family to the young child are still largely determined by the example of earlier generations. The Greek baby is given a special place as a baby. He is expected to remain weak, in need of protection and constant, individualized attention. He is petted and cuddled. No one treats him offhandedly as a "toughie"; no one calls him "Butch." He is not expected to mature rapidly or gain independence quickly. Everyone speaks gently to him. At most, they call him "little devil," with indulgence and admiration, when he has been particularly naughty.

At an early age, however, he is taught the lesson of family unity and family cooperation. The early occasion for this is the arrival of a new brother or sister. The parents and older siblings expect that the displaced youngster may be jealous for a time, but they do not attempt to forestall it by "fairness" or to overcome it by demonstrations that he too is loved. Instead, by their very attitudes of interest in the newcomer and by their invitation to the youngster to share in the excitement and in the concern for the baby, they show him the proper conduct and feelings, and invite him to identify himself with them in this respect. Gradually, and without rebuke, the "knee baby" imbibes these attitudes, and rivalry is changed into the cherishing, solicitous pattern of older toward younger that marks the relationship of Greek siblings.

Identification with the family is encouraged in the children by the very mode of family living. After early infancy, the child is not the focus of the group and his interests are not given a special place. There are no separate mealtimes for him, no shifts in the time of the family meal in his interest. He shares in the daily affairs of the family, and in its social and ceremonial life. His very idea of living comes to be that of something shared. Sisters like to share a bedroom; a mother likes to cook with her daughters and does not regard them as being "under foot." The family is together as much as possible; it is deemed uncomfortable to be alone.

Recreation, too, emphasizes family unity. In the evening or on the weekend, families will visit other families as units, or they may go to a dance or a picnic together. For great religious ceremonials the whole family goes to church, with young children asleep in their mothers' arms or running happily between the aisles. Birthdays are celebrated not by a children's party but by a family celebration, to which whole families or single adults come and in which the greeting is not "Happy Birthday and a long life to you," but congratulations and good wishes to the family that it may enjoy the child long.

In consequence of the Greek manner of recreation, even the making of friends is family centered. A child's friends are his parents' friends and their children. Contacts with these people "happen" to a child. He does not go out from the family and make friends; friends come to him via family channels. A child, accordingly, learns no techniques for joining groups or for achieving status within groups by his own efforts. People come visiting or he is taken visiting; in either case, he is accepted as a family member, and thus he comes to regard his family as the basis for his value as a person.

The mutuality of family life is emphasized to the child, also, by the clear-cut roles of father and mother, with their evident dedication to the advancement of the welfare of the family as a whole and by the way family resources are used to that end.

The father is the head of the family, the center of authority, commanding respect and obedience from both children and wife. The mother shows utmost loyalty to her husband, waiting upon him and subscribing to his opinion. Nevertheless, she is a strong figure of fortitude and honor and may quietly be the real center of power in the home. It is she who undeviatingly upholds the *philotimo,* at whatever cost to her private feelings. Her importance is so well recognized that a young man may as likely be referred to as the son of Stavrina, the son of Stavros, with no disrespect to his father intended by the designation.

Within the family, among the siblings, there is a line of responsibility from older to younger and from male to female. Nevertheless, in the apportionment of resources, this line is not necessarily followed. Children learn from an early age and from numerous small examples that it is neither age nor sex nor individual need but family well-being that determines who shall get or do what. It may be the eldest son—next to the father, the head of the family, to whom even the mother owes obedience—who is chosen as the one to be educated or set up in business; or, again, it may be that the oldest children will stay at home and increase the family income so that a younger one may have the professional education that will reflect upon the honor of the whole group. Later, this chosen one will provide opportunities for nieces and nephews and will thus make his own advantage a family affair.

These, then, are some of the ways in which the Greek-American family operates to produce the kind of individual who is fitted for life in the Greek-American community. The fact that the character traits thus encouraged are considerably different from those that are "American" may create few difficulties for the children and youth so long as they live largely within that community, in worship, work, and play. This is made additionally possible by the fact that each new generation imbibes a bit of the alien viewpoint at school, with the result that family life itself is slowly altered.

What happens to children from Greek-American families—or from other families that diverge greatly from the "American" model—who move out of their cultural orbit and try to follow "American" patterns is not clear. Presumably, they do so with considerable emotional struggle. The part that "culture conflict" plays in the difficulties of some young people is well known. Less certain, however, is how much flexibility there is in the predominant "American" pattern itself. It may be that there is more variation in modes of living and in possible combinations of family and occupational functioning than has so far been described by sociological investigators. Much detailed study on this point is called for, for plans for improving family functioning, for making family life more conducive to children's well-being, future as well as present, depend in part upon such knowledge.

Obstacles to Effective Family Life

Our analysis up to this point leads to several conclusions about the family in the United States. First, the family is not on the decline so far as numbers are concerned. Rather, families are becoming more numerous, even when the increase in population is taken into account. Second, the family is not losing its essential functions, is not giving them over to other social institutions. Third, the values and customs of family life are such as are likely to produce in children the personality traits they will need for participation in the economic and social life of the cultural group to which the parents belong.

What, then, is wrong with the family? In what ways might its functioning be improved in order to contribute more effectively to the healthy personality development of children and youth?

There appear to be two questions at issue here. The first has to do with the institution itself, the other with individual and social factors of a different nature. First, are there certain features of the family that put especial strain upon the members? If this is so, improvement can be expected only from cultural changes. Second, do social and psychological factors make some individuals more effective than others as parents? If this is so, improvement in family life can be looked for when those conditions are altered. Close analysis may show that these two questions are considerably interrelated. In most current discussion and current research, however, they are not combined, with the result that research workers, starting from different orientations, arrive at such diverse explanations of family difficulty as emotional immaturity or maladjustment of the parents, sexual incompatibility, economic pressures, and culture conflict, and only a few take into consideration the institutional aspects of the matter.

The first question, the one concerning the family as a social institution, is difficult to discuss because, as has been said before, there is no such thing as *the* American family. The only thing that can be said in general is that the family, like any social institution, may impose strains on its members, and that the character of the strains varies from one cultural group to another. In addition, each cultural group bears its own peculiar relation to the larger American society, and this, too, makes the effectiveness of family life vary from group to group.

For example, Greek-American family life—to continue the example cited above—calls for much self-abnegation on the part of its members and much suppression of selfish aims in the interest of the collective good. These requirements probably create difficulties for some individuals and families even in Greece and thus affect personality development. It seems likely, however, that these difficulties are more frequent and perhaps more intense under American conditions, where school and other social institutions, rather than supporting the Greek-American family's values, operate in accordance with other ideals and, for instance, picture a life of individual achievement as the greatest good.

It may be sufficient for our purpose, however, to indicate some of the ways in which cultural factors may handicap the prevailing type of American family in contributing to children's healthy development, for this type is not only most numerous in the population but also most pervasive in its influence. Evidence that all is not well with families of this type is abundant. The most frequently cited indications are the high divorce rate, the (assumed) frequency of sexual incompatibility, worry and discontent over money matters, concern over child rearing and children's behavior, unsatisfactory parent-child relations. Wives and mothers are commonly regarded as most at fault, though men, too, come in for a certain amount of blame.

Low Prestige of Feminine Role

Magazine articles, reports of college professors, the records of family welfare agencies and psychiatric clinics all bear testimony to the fact that many middle-class American women are dissatisfied with marriage and family life. Many of these women say they have little fondness for the job they are called on to do—though few of them try to avoid it by avoiding marriage. What these women complain of is the "boredom" and uselessness of household tasks, the perplexities of child rearing, the lack of appreciation on the part of husbands, the sexual dissatisfaction, the ingratitude of children. Psychiatrists are apt to call these women immature, if not more seriously maladjusted. Without disputing these diagnoses, one may ask whether the complaints may not also have a cultural basis, whether they do not indicate some deficiencies in social values and social institutions.

A possible explanation of this unsatisfactory situation is found in the vagueness of the current American definition of the feminine role and, particularly, in the lack of prestige attached to the job of wife and mother.

The wife-and-mother role in the American middle-class family has been partly described above. It is to carry the major share in rearing children; to give affection and backing to the husband, whose occupational life is largely impersonal and competitive; to manage the household and perform numerous domestic tasks; and, in an emergency, to earn money and otherwise do the work expected of men. These are important duties, and many American women perform them extremely well. But they have few rewards of a prestige nature. The one duty that is most prestige giving, the rearing of children, is soon accomplished, for successful child rearing, according to the American pattern, calls for early independence of the child from the home and for the cultivation in him of ties that are nonfamilial. The result is that beyond the first few years of a child's life the mother receives little credit for her part in child rearing. Most of the praise goes to the child himself or to his teachers, though the mother may be blamed if the child does not make the most of his opportunities. There is no counterpart in American usage of the proud Greek phrase, "the son of Stavrina." "His mother's boy" has quite another meaning.

Now prestige is an important ingredient of the feeling of self-worth in almost any society. In middle-class U.S.A., it results, for the most part, from accomplishment on a job, signified in part by money earned but even more by success in a game that many are playing. It is a resultant of doing, not of being, and it is the possession of the individual, not of the family group to which he belongs. Young mothers, sensing that it is not sufficient that they merely "be," try to emulate the world of accomplishment by competing in child rearing, by vying with one another in producing children who are outstanding in all respects. In this they are almost inevitably defeated, for the children rebel, openly or subtly, at being used in this way. Moreover, what little glory does accrue from such accomplishment is of short duration, for the children are soon on their own, and what prestige they secure is theirs and only slightly the mother's. By reason of this situation, middle-class American married women are likely to feel more or less dissatisfied and unsure of themselves, not certain that what they are doing is of real worth, fearful of failure in a job that is ill defined.

The situation was somewhat different years ago, and probably still is somewhat different in rural areas and in towns dominated by rural ideas. When the wife had a clear economic role to perform within the home and when children were economic assets to the family as a whole, domestic duties and the rearing of children were accomplishments worthy of respect in the American scheme of values. At that time and in those places, careful attention was given to training girls for their domestic duties; "homemaking" was truly a career. Nowadays, this has largely changed. Girls, like their brothers, are urged to independence at an early age. Their ability to make their way among their peers and to achieve success in school and on the playground is more highly regarded than their ability to look after their younger brothers and sisters or to perform household tasks. Throughout their school years they look forward to a job, and their higher education is planned accordingly. They want to be married, to be sure, and they want to have children. But many of them, apparently, want these things much as young men are apt to want them, as a sign of their own adequacy, and not with full understanding and acceptance of the fact that what is involved is usually a way of life considerably different from that for which they have been prepared.

It was pointed out in an early section of this report that the "parental sense" is not likely to develop fully in most people unless the roles of mother and father are highly respected in the society at large. In modern, middle-class America these roles are not looked down on, but it seems doubtful that they are esteemed as much as is desirable. In consequence, it is perhaps only the most "secure" among the young women (and men) of that class, the most flexible and adaptable, who develop the parental sense to the fullest, for in doing so they are going more or less against rather than with the dominant cultural values.

Two remedies for this state of affairs have frequently been proposed. It has been urged that girls' education, both at home and at school, be so altered as to give more attention to the cultivation of the domestic abilities that will be needed later in life. It has also been recommended that part-time jobs be provided for married women, so that, among other benefits, they may share in the prestigeful activities of men.

Neither of these proposals seems really satisfactory. Change in education, if it is to help, should follow rather than precede a change of values. What is wrong at base is not so much that women do not perform their domestic duties well but that those duties are not highly regarded in the society at large. As to jobs for women, they are greatly on the increase without any planning. Necessary as they are for other reasons, in many instances they only complicate family problems. In some cases, husbands and wives become competitive; in many, adequate substitutes for maternal care being lacking, children suffer from the mother's absence from home. Actually, what may be needed is a thoughtful reconsideration of the wife's role in family life and the instituting of various measures to bring it dignity and relevance. If this is accomplished, girls will seek the kind of education they need, and mothers will take jobs, if necessary, out of pleasure and not out of frustration.

Overemphasis on Independence and Self-sufficiency

Another cultural explanation of the prevalent difficulties of middle-class American family life is to be found in the emphasis the society places on independence and self-sufficiency. It has been noted that the significant family unit is one consisting of husband, wife, and minor children. Husband and wife are expected to have severed most of their ties with the older generation and with their siblings, and it is their duty to bring up their children to do likewise within a relatively few years. In preparation for this break, children are early urged toward independence, so much so that psychiatrists are now calling attention to the prevalence of "separation anxiety" among children of about the age of two.

Independence and self-sufficiency are important personal attributes in the American scheme of things; their utility in the operation of the occupational system, for example, is clear. Nevertheless, they are not unmitigated blessings in family life.

First, it seems likely that the requirement that husband and wife break their ties with their parents imposes undue strain on individuals who, for one or another reason, enter marriage before they are emotionally mature. Students of marital disharmony report that excessive emotional dependence and too close ties to parents characterize many unhappy married couples.[13] Though a good case can be made for the proposition that psychologically immature individuals are not ready for marriage, it is also true that a marriage system that requires high standards of emotional competence is one in which frequent divorce and other evidence of family breakdown are to be expected, with consequent ill effect on the children. Under a family system in which several generations live together or in close proximity, emotional immaturity on the part of the young couple is perhaps less handicapping to the marriage and to the children's welfare. Children are probably less harmed by marital friction when other relatives are near at hand, and marital friction itself is perhaps less frequent and less extreme when "going home to mother" is not an admission of failure but an expected act in time of stress.

Again, the stress put upon independence and self-sufficiency operates to make many young married couples reluctant to seek help with problems of family relations and child rearing. Not only do these people feel that they must be independent of their parents and capable of managing their own affairs without their parents' assistance but they also deem any recourse to outsiders somewhat humiliating. (That this is the usual situation is so well recognized by psychiatrists and social case workers that some of the chief therapeutic principles concern ways of countering these attitudes.) The result is that young parents are cut off from such an easy means of diluting anxiety as frank discussion with their elders or their peers. Then tensions mount, to the detriment of their own and the children's well-being.

A third hazard of the independence theme of middle-class American culture is that parent-child relations are likely to be less close and warm than may be desirable for the healthy development of personality. An extreme of this is seen in "Momism," about which semipopular psychiatric literature has had much to say lately. This term refers to a "rejecting" attitude on the part of mothers that creates psychopathology in the children, particularly in the sons. The kind of mother there described undoubtedly does exist—one who is, as Erikson puts it, "the unquestioned

---

[13] See, for instance, Florence Hollis, *Women in Marital Conflict,* Family Service Association of America, New York, 1949; Edmund Bergler, *Unhappy Marriage and Divorce,* International Universities Press, New York, 1946.

authority on mores and manners in the home," who "shows a determined hostility to any free expression of the most naive forms of sensual and sexual pleasure on the part of the children and makes clear that the father, when sexually demanding, is a bore," who teaches self-restraint and self-control and expects children to be hard on themselves, and yet "permits herself to remain, in her own way, vain in her appearance, egotistical in her demands, and infantile in her emotions." [14]

In this picture, it will be noted, the personality traits last listed are added to certain cultural attributes that are explainable in terms of Puritanism and historical conditions. In other words, what is pictured in "Momism" is a neurotic distortion of a cultural pattern.

The cultural mode, from which "Mom" is a deviation, prescribes a "determined lack of maternalism" in the interest of independence and self-reliance. It aims at producing people who look to the future rather than to the past, who are not tied to their childhood homes but are free to follow their own best chance, who can tolerate some loneliness and deprivation of affection in the interest of freedom and economic success, who prefer tentativeness and free choice to a life that is predetermined for either good or ill. The training of individuals for such attitudes must begin early; it does—or, at least, it did—begin early in the typical American home.

American middle-class mothers are instructed by some child-development experts to see to it that even babies have considerable time to themselves. Infants should not be held and cuddled too much, some of these experts still say; a certain amount of crying may be a good thing. When children begin to creep and walk they should be taught to stay happily alone in a play pen and look to the sun rather than to the mother for warmth and light. Mothers are cautioned against being overprotective. A three- or four-year-old should be seeking out his own peers for company and exercising choice in many matters of importance to him. From that age on, independence from the home is increasingly fostered, until by adolescence it is the parents who are respectfully and interestedly listening to the child's opinions and letting him set his own goals. The wisdom of one or another of these child-rearing items may be questioned in some circles and by some professional workers nowadays, but many children are still being reared according to this pattern.

Along with this goes, almost of necessity, a playing down of emotions,

[14] For a detailed description of this kind of woman, as well as for elaboration of the general topic under discussion, see Erik H. Erikson, *Childhood and Society,* W. W. Norton & Co., New York, 1950, pp. 247–283.

an understimulation of sexual drives and of feelings generally. Overt loving and hating are kept on a lower key than among, say, Italians or other so-called "volatile" people. The ideal relationships within the family, as on the outside, are those of fairness, consideration for the interests of others, equality, and compromise. For discipline, inner self-restriction is looked to; it is not expected that even with young children much exercise of authority will be needed. The mother in this kind of family functions chiefly as an arbiter, one whose job is to see that no family member is dominated, that each is free to act as outside groups and interests demand. This being so, the mother must necessarily be somewhat aloof emotionally, must not be too closely involved with either husband or child.

Like all child-training arrangements, this scheme produces its best results when parents are healthy in personality. Parents who are not healthy will overplay certain requirements and underplay others. In extreme, the "Mom" of the psychiatrists' characterization will emerge.

A good case for the American emphasis on independence and self-sufficiency can be made by reference to America's past. There was a continent to be opened up and cultivated; freedom from home ties was necessary if men and women were to be capable of meeting the challenge. Perhaps these men and women were somewhat lonely and nostalgic; perhaps they did feel somewhat abandoned by their mothers, and somewhat guilty over abandoning in turn. Nevertheless, at best, they had great strength of purpose and great integrity, for all that they were somewhat restricted in their interests and in their emotions.

One may question, however, whether the scheme works as well now as it did formerly, whether the kind of people the country most needs are the kind this system produces. On this point no one can be certain. There are, however, some changes in American life that suggest that independence and self-reliance are somewhat less needed than formerly, and that the ability to value other people, to join in collective activities, and to stay put may be among the especially highly regarded virtues of the future.

For example, climbing the economic ladder through individual effort seems to be on the decline (valid statistics on this point, however, have not been collected), and improvement in the economic position of whole groups through collective bargaining may have taken its place. In-service training schemes, pension arrangements, jobs for married women make it advantageous that workers reduce their moving about. An increasing number of social and economic activities calls for team play rather than individual competition. There is a trend toward managing people rather than managing things—a management that at its worst means a manipulation of human emotions in the manager's interest but at best means genuine concern and consideration for the viewpoints and feelings of others.

Some Current Concerns

Changes such as these in the conduct of adult life both call for changes in child-rearing customs and may themselves be partly caused by such changes. An accurate analysis of what is taking place would require much more careful study than has so far been attempted, but there is evidence that the needed alternations are in the making. There seems little doubt that many present-day parents of young children, in the social class under consideration, are deliberately trying to bring up their children in a way that is different from that in which they were reared. They are still stressing independence and self-reliance, it is true; but they are beginning to recognize "dependency feelings" as natural and somewhat to be encouraged, and they emphasize cooperation and mutual respect. They seem to be less fearful of expressing emotion than were their parents, and of permitting expression of emotion on the part of the children. It is coming to be in style not only to have as many children as one can afford but to express love for them freely and openly and without fear of the consequences.

Such changes in the ways of handling children and of regarding them should benefit both the children and the family as an institution. The children should benefit not so much because any one set of rules and customs is better than another as because the old set no longer meets today's conditions and cannot be followed with conviction by most parents. For a generation or more, parents have stumbled along, dissatisfied with the old ways and somewhat guilty and dubious about the new. If today there is more conviction behind their actions, that in itself is a reason for expectation of improvement in their children's functioning.

Children should benefit also because these new attitudes toward and about children and the new ways of rearing them make the mother's job a more rewarding one, a task in which she can take pride, both because it is a challenge to her ingenuity and because it is one in which she and her husband join as equals.

The rules of the new child-rearing scheme are few and not very explicit; each child must be handled differently, it is said. The keynote is mutuality in accommodation—which calls for kindness and consideration and a clear sense of what may and what may not be permitted. It is a scheme that both requires flexibility on the part of the parents and creates it in the children. The prime administrator of the scheme is still the mother. The father, however, is no longer either the rather remote source of funds and wielder of final authority or a big brother to the children, almost one of them in relation to the mother. Instead, he, too, is a parent, in Erikson's sense of the word, one who takes pride and pleasure in nourishing and cherishing what he has helped to create. In thus accepting his adulthood and his father role, he becomes a better husband also— with the result that the wife finds her domestic tasks more satisfying, since she can feel that her accomplishment "rates" in the American way of life.

Changes such as these should contribute to the stability of family life in that section of our society that tends to set the pattern for the whole. With husband-wife relations and parent-child relations improved, divorce among couples with children should decline and intrafamily friction be reduced. The question of mothers working outside the home should lose its emotional overtones and become one of simple necessity or inclination. The danger of "Momism" should be restricted to the few families in which the wife is neurotically possessive rather than being rather widespread because wives are culturally dissatisfied.

All in all, then, what the predominant type of American family seems most to need in order to promote the well-being of children (and seems to be in the process of securing) is a revised conception of American values, a conception that is in line with current social realities rather than with past American history. This new conception would stress cooperation and mutual appreciation, consideration for the emotional as well as the rational aspects of life, respect for weakness as well as for strength. Translated into action in child rearing and general family relationships, it would provide a firmer basis for trust, would make of American autonomy and initiative a less selfish thing, and would introduce into American life that sense of intimacy which is at present so rare a personal possession.

One of the Ways Out: Education for Family Life and Parenthood

Changes of the sort described above come about largely from the interplay of various forces that, creating change in one social institution, bring corresponding changes in others. Improved economic conditions, reduction in tensions among ethnic groups, a revival of interest in religion and in aesthetics: these and many other kinds of change may reflect upon and improve the quality of family life.

Improvement in family functioning, however, does not have to be left solely to chance or have to depend entirely upon the repercussions of change in other social institutions. Improvement can be deliberately cultivated within families themselves, both by parents and children and by those who seek to guide them. Guidance carried on under religious, social-service, medical, psychiatric auspices is usually directed toward the alleviation of the difficulties of individual families, but that classified as parent education or family-life education is particularly aimed at effecting change in the over-all mode of family living.

Education in the Schools

Family-life education is predominantly an activity of the public schools. As schools, in general, have moved in the direction of a life-centered curriculum, education for family living has come increasingly to be recognized as one of their major responsibilities. It has been defined as "that part of a total education which equips individuals for effective membership in the family so that each, according to his capacity, contributes to home and community life." [15] Comprehensive programs offer appropriate learning experiences to family members of both sexes and all ages, beginning in the preschool and carrying on through elementary school, high school, and college, into adult education.

At the preschool level, games in which children play "family" clarify developing feelings and ideas about fathers and mothers and other family members. At the elementary level, family-life education is still largely experimental. Almost everywhere it is agreed that the teaching of human relations must be an integral part of the school program, not an adjunct to it.

In a few schools, parents, teachers, and children together study and try to improve the interrelationships that exist among them. Special attention is given to children's feelings about their own family experiences, as these are disclosed through the use of a variety of sociometric and projective techniques, films, stories, group discussions, and casual conversations. Teachers try to create a classroom atmosphere in which children may safely express their feelings, and to plan learning experiences on the basis of problems often indirectly revealed. This is probably family-life education at its best for this age group; unfortunately, it is exemplified in all too few schools. There is, however, a variety of promising experimentation under way in a number of places.

Nearly every high school in the United States is now offering a course or unit which deals with aspects of personal development and family

[15] *Vocational Education in the Years Ahead,* Division of Vocational Education, Office of Education, Federal Security Agency.

relationships, and colleges and universities are unable to meet the student demand for courses in marriage and family living. During the past twenty years or more the high-school teaching of home economics has steadily broadened until most programs are now family centered. Food, clothing, housing, family economics, and home management are more and more often taught in relation to values, purposes, and principles of good family living as currently conceived, and the teaching of child development is becoming an integral part of the homemaking curriculum. Moreover, there is a slow but definite trend toward instruction in homemaking for boys as well as for girls. High-school courses in the social studies also include units on the American family. These have tended, however, to emphasize institutional aspects of family living to the neglect of the study of interpersonal relations within the family and their influence on mental health. Teachers of biology and general science have long done their best to provide information on the biological foundations of family life.

Despite the fact that education for family living in the broad sense is a relatively new field, there seems to be increasing agreement that it is an essential part of education for life; that adequate programs cut across many subject-matter fields and do not belong to any one discipline; and that good programs are closely related to the life experiences of real children and real families in real communities, which means, in effect, that curricula must be developed cooperatively by parents, pupils, and teachers. There remains, still, widespread disagreement about who shall teach what, a prevailing lack of experience in curriculum building and integration, and the problem of inadequate provision for boys and young men.

No less widely recognized but perhaps even more important are such questions as these: How far does subject matter, however well integrated or focused on family relations, affect underlying feelings? Which are the most promising lines of experimentation by which schools may learn to use classroom situations—both human relations and the content of the curriculum—most effectively to develop understandings, foster outgoing feelings, and bring feelings and understandings into accord? How can we create in school and community the conditions propitious for healthy personality development?

"In-service" Education for Parents

Despite the fact that parental feelings derive from the whole life experience of a parent from childhood on, the advent of parenthood frequently brings with it new emotional growth and so offers fresh opportunity for building positive feelings. It also often calls for new learnings, for the mother and father may have had little experience with babies and children. Moreover, a constantly changing society and a constantly changing science are creating both new resources and new problems for parents. Many parents are in the uncomfortable position of having gained a little but not enough insight into human behavior. Unsure of themselves, of what to do, and how to do it, they appeal to the experts for help, only to find that the experts are always learning anew. The absolute answers and sure directives that parents seek are nowhere available.

One challenge to workers with parents is to provide the best available information in such fashion as to allay rather than heighten anxiety, and to lend the assurance that children's sound development does not require specific formulas and sure directives. In this, those who work with parents are sustained by an accruing body of reliable evidence that healthy personality development is not dependent upon any particular know-how but rather, and to a far greater extent, upon parental love. It is their difficult problem to preserve spontaneous love where it exists, to support it when it is threatened, and to help parents retrieve it when it is lost.

Today, all over the country, through a multitude of different channels, under more than one hundred different auspices, "parent education" (that sector of family-life education designed for those who are already or who are about to become parents) continues to deepen and widen its influence. By now it has enlisted the help of trained experts in many professions and has become a professional field in itself.

Despite the fact that this movement has undoubtedly grown up in response to parents' search for help in dealing with their children, it is at some points difficult at first glance to link up the questions parents ask with the objectives of parent education as defined by the experts. Parents ask for help on sex education, feeding problems, sleeping problems, discipline, and the like. In 1934, Witmer [16] surveyed the field of parent education and listed five general types of objectives: (1) to interpret to parents the findings of specialists in regard to various aspects of child and family life; (2) to modify or change the attitudes of parents toward their children and their behavior; (3) to act as a therapeutic device for relieving parental maladjustments; (4) to arouse in parents an interest in civic affairs, with a view to developing an alert, informed, participating democracy; (5) to provide a forum in which parents may verbalize their

[16] Helen Leland Witmer, *The Field of Parent Education,* National Council of Parent Education, Inc., New York, 1934.

conceptions of the mores and attempt to adapt them to present conditions and trends.

In tracing the history of this movement, in 1935, Brown [17] identified six stages in its development, each representing a forward thrust or shift in emphasis: (1) experts tell parents what to do and how to do it; (2) experts teach parents the principles of child development; (3) experts attempt to "teach" parent-child relationships; (4) parents and specialists together study the nature of parent-child relationships; (5) parents and specialists together study interrelationships within the family; (6) parents and specialists together study family and family-community relationships. Since 1935, still another goal for parent education has emerged: the creation, through cooperative endeavor, of neighborhood and community conditions favorable to wholesome family living and to the healthy development of children.

Both of these analyses reflect a gradual but definite withdrawal from telling, instructing, imparting to parents, textbook fashion, the findings and tenets of experts. Youngsters balky about their food often continued to be contrary after tested facts about eating habits had been imparted to their parents. The balkiness was found to derive more from interpersonal tensions and parental anxieties than from parental ignorance; facts, in most instances, proved a doubtful means for the assuaging of tense and anxious feelings.

Attention turned then quite naturally toward efforts to help parents resolve the feelings reflected in their problems, rather than merely to answer their questions. Ways for changing attitude are hard to come by, but mutual study began to replace authoritative "telling," and in some places certain kinds of parent-education activities began to develop as means for relieving parental anxiety. Few people confuse education as such with therapy for maladjusted parents, but it is becoming clear that therapeutic help has a place among services to parents.

The turn to broader concerns generally social in nature—study and adaptation of the mores, improvement in community conditions, and participation in community affairs—reflects a widening view of the forces that impinge on family life, on the feelings of family members, and so on their interrelationships and on the healthy development of children. To what extent participation in activities of this kind directly affects parental attitudes and feelings is still an open question.

Determining outcomes in parent education is difficult; fully satisfactory

[17] Muriel W. Brown, "Trends in Parent Education," *Annals of the American Academy of Political and Social Science,* November, 1935.

methods of evaluating changes in feelings and attitudes are not easy to contrive. A recent analysis [18] of child-development materials appearing in newspapers and magazines shows that although these materials are increasingly sound, they are apt to be general and to give parents little help in understanding the causes of behavior in their own children. What parents actually do with what they get from such sources no one knows.

There is evidence that verifiable changes in parent behavior do often take place when mothers and fathers have opportunity to learn by doing, as in the programs where they participate in planning, carrying on, and evaluating activities with and for children.

Obviously, there is great need for research on adult capacities for changing attitudes and on the conditions under which such changes may be expected to occur.

The Family and the Experts

Education for parenthood and family life may provide a possible way out of some of the difficulties that families currently encounter in rearing children who will be happy individuals and responsible citizens, but it is far from a panacea. Nor is large-scale change to be expected from the efforts of the various professions that help families one by one. What is at issue here is the relation of the family to the expert. Are the experts about to take over? Are parents to do nothing but carry out child-rearing schemes devised by scientists and technicians? If not, how are parents to conduct themselves in relation to these new sources of knowledge?

The prestige of the specialist is a well-recognized aspect of present-day society. It is little wonder, then, that parents sometimes feel threatened when they perceive that, although they have the responsibility for maintaining good family relationships, scientific knowledge about these matters is the possession of experts. A little reflection on the situation will indicate, however, that what has occurred is only a shift in the sources of knowledge. American parents have always used experts when in doubt about how to proceed, and they have always been the ones to determine when they should seek help and what they should do with the advice given to them.

As has been said before, throughout most of the United States the young family, established through marriage, tends to separate from other relatives and establish its own home. Historically, such separations were

---

[18] Ralph H. Ojemann, and Associates, "A Functional Analysis of Child Development Material in Current Newspapers and Magazines," *Child Development*, Vol. 19, March–June, 1948.

a necessary part of the settlement of new colonies and the later expansion to the Pacific coast. Then, as now, young couples found the courage to establish homes of their own far from their parents and relatives. In so doing they discovered that, faced with the need for being responsible for themselves and their children, they had within themselves the capacity for making endless small and large decisions required of them as home-makers and parents. They found that they were able, out of their own relationship to each other, to furnish the stability and continuity of tradi-tion that could give their children a sense of belonging.

This belief in both the possibility and the desirability of each young couple's starting a home of their own has resulted in the American tradi-tion that parents—not grandparents or family elders—know what is best for children. This tradition, however, never precluded the asking of help and advice from relatives, friends, ministers, doctors, lawyers, and others. It did imply that the decision to ask for and to use the advice rested with the parents. Even these sources of knowledge about family life and the rearing of children were not felt to lie entirely outside the family but rather to be lodged in individuals who, by the parents' choice, had been brought within the family circle through an extension of the family to include them; hence the "family friend," the "family doctor," the "family lawyer," and so on.

It is probably true that these are the sources of help still used by large numbers of young couples. But there are new sources of help that lie beyond the extended family horizon. References to these new specialists come to parents through all the media of mass communication. Through these sources many parents have become aware that somewhere there are specialists who claim to possess knowledge of the ways in which family members can change to meet more fully their responsibilities as wives, husbands, and parents. Some find the specialist in the writer of a daily column in the newspaper or in a radio spokesman for families in trouble; others look to a psychiatrist, a nurse, a teacher or a social worker for guidance.

Parents may learn to choose and to use these new resources and new knowledge, but their ability to carry their responsibility will still stem in large part from their day-to-day living experience within the family. This sometimes difficult, sometimes joyous, but always vivid and emotionally charged experience is a constant challenge to decide, to act, and, in doing so, to learn. The new knowledge gained through scientific investigations can influence and aid but cannot replace this intuitive, nonverbal knowl-edge gained through life itself.

The various professions providing services to families should take this fact into account. In striving to use all available knowledge concerning children in planning and carrying out their programs, they must not neglect the fact that, important as their contributions may be, they cannot take full responsibility for children throughout the entire period of their growth. This over-all responsibility rests only with the community as a whole and with the family. Some social institutions, such as the church and health services, participate in the child's care from infancy to adulthood; still others, such as the school, have substantial responsibility only during certain years of the child's life. But the responsibility of each of these institutions is directed toward aiding the child in specific aspects of his life. Only the family is related to him continuously and totally. Only the family, within the limits set by the wider community, can accept full responsibility for the child.

All the evidence points to the infinite capacity of the family to change —to change its composition, to redefine the way it shares the care of children with other social institutions—and yet to retain its over-all responsibility for them. Each institution has its contribution to make to children's development, but there is a fundamental distinction between taking over-all responsibility and contributing to children's welfare through providing limited services and performing limited, though essential, functions. Members of the community at large can make sure that the necessary facilities are available. Parents can endeavor to use them for maximum benefit of children, to supplement what they themselves can do for them. Those who render services to children and to families can be of greatest usefulness if they keep always in mind that the family must accept final responsibility for children's welfare. Recognition of this fact by the community as a whole, by the family, and by other institutions is the basis on which all can perform their functions and work harmoniously together for the child's maximum benefit.

X

The Church and the Synagogue

THE institutions of religion, by their origin, nature, and mission, are unique. Yet they function, in some aspects of their program, as social institutions in a community. In these areas they utilize the resources of science and, in common with other agencies of society, seek constantly to check and evaluate their work in the light of all available knowledge, experience, and research. At the same time, they seek to permeate these other agencies and all phases of personal, community, national, and international relations with the religious view of human life.

Some of the possible contributions of religion to the healthy development of personality have been described in Chapter VII of this report. Here we would consider those contributions in more detail as background for the rest of this chapter, which constitutes an analysis of the ways in which the church as a social institution may promote the well-being of children and youth.

Summarily categorized, the church's activities on behalf of children and youth are of two main kinds. First, individual churches and synagogues are a prime source of spiritual nurture. To children and youth who join in their services they endeavor to make real the basic affirmations of religion, while to their parents they offer individual help and over-all guidance in family living. Second, under religious auspices, provision is made for the whole range of children's needs—education, medical care, recreation, and so on—and efforts are put forth to influence personal and civic affairs in the interest of the children's welfare, from personal and family responsibility, through local community decency and righteousness, to interracial good will and world peace. For both of these categories of activities the affirmations of religion provide a common base, while the activities themselves constitute an opportunity to convey or demonstrate to children and youth the religious view of life.

By religion most Americans mean the relationship between God and man that expresses itself in the service and adoration of God, in forms of worship, in commitment of the whole self to the will of God, and in the pursuit of a way of life regarded as incumbent upon men as creatures and children of God. It is in this sense that the term "religion" is used in this report.

Because the major religious bodies in the United States agree generally on certain great affirmations concerning the nature of God and man, it is possible to discuss in a common document the ways in which the church may influence the personality development of children and youth. To say this is not to deny that there are important differences among the religious bodies in the United States—differences that relate to the specific interpretations of the basic affirmations, distinctive emphases, teachings, and procedures used in working toward their goals. Each of the religious bodies in the United States has its distinctive doctrine, ceremonials, and programs. To accept differences in the expression of religious aspiration is a part of the democratic way of life.

Since the institutions of religion are administered by men, their achievements reflect differences in the ability, insight, and devotion of men. In addition, because these men work among persons of differing ability, cultural background, and capacity for religious insight and devotion, and within communities of differing educational attainment and moral status, they are not always equally successful in their undertaking. It follows, therefore, that not all children and youth will have the experiences with the institutions of religion here set forth as their contribution to healthy personality development. The emphasis of this report, however, is upon the influence of religion when it is experienced under favorable conditions.

Some Contributions of Religion to Health of Personality

Religion, in its finest expression, is not just one among the interests and experiences of life. Rather, it permeates all interests and experiences and determines basic attitudes, relationships, motivations, standards of value, goals, and conduct in all phases of living. The religious individual's faith regarding the nature of God and his response thereto determines in large measure both his view of the meaning of life and his daily purposes and conduct.

It is an affirmation of religion that persons have supreme value under God. Religion affirms, too, that it is the will of God that each of His children shall live life to the full. Thus, in the religious view, each child has significance, not because of what he may produce, not because of what he may do, but because of what he is, a child of God.

Education in religion is regarded as important to understanding and responding to the reality of God. Children and youth, it is maintained, should be taught this faith by the most effective means that can be devised. This is not to deny that God may "break through" directly into human life and institutions. In the normal processes of growth, however, children and youth have the capacity to learn and should be taught a way of responding to God and, consequently, a more effective way of responding to their fellow men.

There is general agreement that each child should be taught in such a way that he may develop to the utmost his capacity for understanding and experiencing God. The human limitations of one generation must not be imposed upon the next, but each generation is under obligation to share its deepest insights with its immature members.

Religious education is concerned primarily with bringing to fruition the spiritual potentialities of the individual and in raising him to his full stature through his proper relationship to God and to man. Nevertheless, the human personality is a unit that cannot be dissected and divided into completely independent parts. The physical development of the growing child is intimately bound up with his intellectual, emotional, and spiritual progress. Whatever contributes to one aspect of growth contributes to all of them. Whatever adversely affects any one of them may operate to the detriment of all. Consequently, all the major faiths are concerned with the relation of religion to the healthy development of the total personality.

Scientists studying human beings today quite generally reject the Cartesian dualism of body and mind and consider man in his totality, trying, as Gregory Zilboorg has said, "not to overlook the spirit in the animal that he is, or the animal in the spirit that he has." They regard the self as a necessary psychological concept and ascribe to it many of the attributes that religion has ascribed to the soul. As a recent analysis puts it, the self can "judge truth, appreciate beauty, distinguish between right and wrong, and leap across the barriers of time and space through memory and imagination. Above all, it can make free decisions, and, by virtue of this, it is responsible to its Creator." [1]

It is this self with which religion deals, this self that is active both in the expansion of its own powers and controls and in its harmonious integration into the reality beyond itself.[2] Its basic drives for action, superi-

[1] Denison Allen, "Is Psychology Rediscovering the Soul?" *Religious Education,* May–June, 1950, p. 136.
[2] See, for example, Gordon W. Allport, *Personality,* Henry Holt and Company, Inc., New York, 1937; Andras Angyal, *Foundations for a Science of Personality,* Commonwealth Fund, New York, 1941; William H. Burnham, *The Wholesome Personality,*

ority, acquisition, love and acceptance, sexual expression, and so on, must be recognized for what they are, an essential part of the self, without which the self would not be whole. These drives must not be frustrated, rather they are to be integrated into the whole self, which is more than these drives and cravings.

The literature of psychotherapy provides abundant evidence that the rejection of any aspect of the self interferes with the development of the wholesome personality, the ability to live life to the full. It is well known that children who find the demands of the culture or of their own conscience in conflict with their basic drives, antagonisms, and jealousies may deny that these are part of themselves. But the part so denied does not die. Instead the unrecognized and unresolved conflict may break out in strange and sometimes terrifying ways. Such persons, instead of living life to the full, find themselves crippled in body, mind, or spirit.

It is the view of religion that man need not reject any part, aspect, or facet of himself but should accept the self in its totality, as part of the plan of God for his creation. This does not mean that an individual person should feel smugly satisfied with the total functioning of his self at a given point in time. On the contrary. But the view that man's organism was planned by an all-wise and all-loving Creator leads to an attitude of self-acceptance, which regards all aspects of the self as utilizable if properly understood and related. Such an attitude, it has been implied in previous chapters, is an important attribute of a healthy personality.

The difficulty of understanding and relating all aspects of the self is not minimized by religion. That man has a tendency to sin—or, as psychologists may put it, "a fundamental egocentricity involving the whole personality"—is one of the basic tenets of most expressions of ethical monotheism. Successful psychotherapy, it seems generally agreed,[3] involves an awareness of the unlovely elements and desires of the self. A religious view that does not hesitate to acknowledge the evil tendencies that are in man may, therefore, be helpful in bringing an individual to accept himself as a whole.

Religion, though recognizing tendencies in man toward sin, does not leave man "sunk in sin." It offers him not only hope that he may be forgiven and saved but also positive help in directing all his tendencies toward their higher expression. "I will heal their backslidings; I will love

Appleton-Century-Crofts, Inc., New York, 1932; Frances Lelands Harmon, *Understanding Personality*, The Bruce Publishing Company, Milwaukee, 1947; "Areas of Agreement in Psychotherapy," *American Journal of Orthopsychiatry*, Vol. X (1940), p. 698.

[3] *American Journal of Orthopsychiatry, op. cit.*

them freely," God told the people of Israel through the prophet Hosea. And in the Parable of the Lost Sheep, so lovingly sought, and in the Parable of the Prodigal Son, so lovingly received by his father, Jesus makes vivid this great truth of religion.

Healthy self-acceptance also means rejoicing in one's special abilities and recognizing without resentment one's special limitations. Abilities are recognized as gifts of God, to be enjoyed and used for the joy of others. Religion helps the individual to view these limitations within the framework of a lively sense of God's love; thus they can be accepted without devastating emotional turmoil.

Every individual makes for himself a picture of what he is and what he would like to be and sets up ideals for his strivings. Ideals are necessary for healthy personality development. As Karen Horney says, "Ideals have a dynamic quality; they arouse an incentive to approximate them; they are an indispensable and invaluable force for growth and development." [4] The great religions aid in personality development by offering ideals that are not cold abstractions but warm and living realities. In the Jewish religion, the "imitation of God" is regarded as the highest human ideal. "Ye shall be holy, for I, the Lord, your God, am holy," declares Leviticus. And the Talmud advises men, "Be like God; as He is merciful and gracious, so be thou merciful and gracious. . . . He heals the sick, frees the captive, does good even to his enemies, and is merciful to all." To Christians, Jesus Christ is the Divine Example upon which human beings are called to pattern their lives.

These ideals must be integrated into life in ways that are useful and that promote the growth and health of the individual. To the extent that they are related to the on-going experience of the individual will they be likely to influence that experience. A child's hereditary equipment, his age, his previous experience, his environment, all will be important in determining the helpfulness of any standard and the extent to which he attains it.

Contributions of Religion at Various Developmental Stages

The self, all psychologists agree, develops; it is not ready formed at the start. Some aspects of the stages in that development have been described in Chapter I of this report. Here we would indicate some of the contributions of religion to the child at various stages of development.

The infant, it has been said, develops a sense of trust if he is loved and treated as one who has significance. Religion affirms that such an attitude of trust is rooted in reality because God is trustworthy. The adult who in-

---

[4] Karen Horney, *Our Inner Conflicts*, W. W. Norton, New York, 1945, p. 98.

spires in a child trust that his needs can be met is teaching him the truth about the nature of ultimate reality. Parents who themselves have profound trust in the worth-whileness of life and confidence in God naturally transmit their attitudes to their children.

As the child grows, he becomes aware of himself in relation to bodily functions and things about him. He reaches out for things, takes them, lets them go. During this period he needs to develop the sense of self and to engage in self-expression. Such self-expression is not sin; it is self-affirmation. If with each discovery of new power and skills there can come joyous acceptance of a gift of God, growth will be healthy. On the other hand, if the early manifestations of selfhood are surrounded by disapproval, this rejection of the child's selfhood by those upon whom he depends may sow the seeds of self-rejection.

Thus, if the child's pleasure in recognizing "this is my own" is frowned upon and sharing is promoted too early or under compulsion, repressed hatreds instead of generous purposes may be generated. The child must be a self before he can be unselfish. He has to feel secure in the possession of something before he is asked to share it, indeed, before he can really share it. Otherwise, he gives it up under pressure from some outside force. There can come no "fullness of life" for the individual unless he is encouraged to develop his capacities.

Eternal wisdom is expressed in the ancient formulation of religion, "Thou shalt love thy neighbor as thyself." An individual who has no love or respect for himself is not likely to feel that any other human being merits love and respect. "Do unto others as you would that they should do unto you" can be realized only when one has some sense of self, some respect for oneself, some appreciation of what is good for oneself.

When the child has respect for himself, he is ready to develop the independence and initiative that are essential for wholesomeness of personality, to feel concern for others, to identify himself with others, and, as he matures, to live for others or to die for them. Consequently, the trend toward self-assertion must be balanced with the trend toward harmony with other individuals, the universe, and God.

A psychotherapist has said: "Human behavior cannot adequately be understood as a manifestation toward increased autonomy. There is a second trend, a trend toward homonomy, in which the person seeks to share and to participate, and to fit into or conform with super-individual units, such as the family, social groups, meaningful world order." [5] Preserving and cultivating this trend toward homonomy in each indi-

[5] Andras Angyal, *Foundations for a Science of Personality*, The Commonwealth Fund, New York, 1941, p. 174.

vidual so that it flowers into unselfish generosity is a major goal of religious education. Religious training would fail in its purpose were it to confine itself exclusively to preparing children to meet the demands of their relationship with God and fail to make them aware of their duties to their fellow men. An empty pietism would result that would render religion unreal and without value for the betterment of society.

If the first conflicts of adjusting self-assertive tendencies to relationships with others are properly handled in the home, the young child learns from experience a positive attitude toward beautiful things and desirable relationships, toward the great religious festivals, moral conduct, worship, and God. Where there is an atmosphere of love and affection, he comes to appreciate the advantages of solidarity and he becomes progressively social minded. Home life reveals to him the fundamental truth that we cannot get along without one another and that peace and contentment are born of subordinating personal whim and caprice to the welfare of the group.

As the child matures and becomes aware of his own self, as he comes to understand this self and to accept it, he must also come to accept responsibility for this self. He has to make decisions, to choose among possible alternatives to satisfy his needs and desires. He may have to make a choice between demands of his self-assertive drives, demands made by society, and demands made by his own conscience. This choice will be influenced by his goals or ideals.

The importance for the realization of wholesome personality of the clarification of life goals is stressed by psychotherapists.[6] But how shall the individual come to choose his goal? Is it to be a wholly individual matter? Is right merely what the individual considers to be right, and wrong merely what the individual considers to be wrong? This view can hardly be accepted on practical grounds, for the individual does not live alone. If his individual goals are wholly out of harmony with those which are acceptable to the others among whom he lives, he is likely to be rejected. Hence, his goals are influenced to a very large extent by the culture in which he lives.

The small, intimate group to which a child belongs, especially the family, may promote this selective process. But the family itself is not as dependable a source of values and goals as it once was. We are living in a period of rapid change characterized by shifting of standards and values in some areas and the breakdown of standards and values in other areas.

    [6] Oskar Pfister, "What Transformation Does Psychoanalysis Require in Ethics and Moral Education?" *The Psychoanalytic Quarterly,* Vol. V (1931), p. 410.

The period of change is so rapid that no child will grow to adulthood in the same culture of which his father was a representative in his early years.

More than ever, then, youth needs values that will give inner security and wholesome satisfaction, ideals that can be employed in public and private conduct, and concepts that interpret life and render it worth while. These religion supplies; and it identifies, interprets, and applies them to everyday living.

Human nature and human relations and human aspirations have been the concern of religion through thousands of years. Its institutions have afforded vast laboratories for dealing with human experience. The growing child may therefore find in religion a guide to the selection of life goals that will be deeply satisfying, goals that are summarized as loving God with all one's heart and mind and strength, and one's neighbor as oneself.

These goals, however, no matter how well expressed, will not be significant unless they become the child's own goals and are related to the proximate goals that he also requires in order that strain and tension may be reduced, hope and fresh endeavor stimulated. In this process of determining goals and making them his own, the growing child needs guidance. This guidance religion may supply, through the fellowship of an adult who does not dictate but helps the child to understand.

With adolescence, new needs arise and are added to those the child has sensed previously. The shelter of childhood is gone, yet the youth has not yet attained the measure of equanimity and assurance that will enable him to face life with maturity. Thus loneliness ensues—not the social loneliness usually complained of but something that lies deeper and can be abolished only to the extent that the individual shares, through spiritual life and experiences, the love and fellowship of God.

In that period there occurs the discovery of a new development in the self and a consequent deepening of awareness of, and interest in, one's identity. The problem of "self-discovery" is the central fact of adolescence, a problem that is manifested first and foremost in the relation of the self to others. It also involves many ethical and spiritual conflicts. The youth is in transition from autonomic control, in which his values and limits are largely determined by parents and teachers, to autonomous control, in which he becomes the arbiter of his behavior, guided only by his own conscience.

Religion can function as a reassuring influence to adolescents, creating a sentiment of belonging and an avoidance of guilt feeling. Through it youth may come to see that intellectual and moral conflicts are a natural part of growth and that acceptable solutions are available. Through religion the different pictures of himself that a young person has may be brought together to make one true portrait. In the struggle for integration, the absolute ideal has, in Bonthius' words, an indispensable and a therapeutic function. It is the "decisive basis for discrimination" upon which alternative or competing interests are considered. It is the "standard by which the acts and attitudes of larger wholes . . . are evaluated." [7] Individuals have many impulses and many desires. Only when these are subordinated to some one purpose that makes life really worth while can the unavoidable trials and frustrations be accepted without despair.

As Vieth puts it:

In his quest for a rich and abundant life man is frustrated by the conditions which conscribe his earthly existence. One of these is the brevity of his span of life and the inevitability of his death: Does life on this planet mark the bounds of man's existence, or does his being have ampler dimensions? A second is his dependence upon nature: Does it contain powers to be appeased, is it a sphere for mastery, or is it a ground of existence which is friendly to those who approach it with a humble spirit of understanding? A third is his relation to the culture of which he is a part: Is he merely to seek adjustment to the pattern of human culture, or is there a more ultimate frame-work of existence? [8]

Religion views this predicament of man without dismay. For it holds that, as Vieth says, "the solution goes deeper than the integration of individuals and their proper adjustment to human society and the present world. God is the ultimate reality in man's environment, and the kingdom of God is the order to which he must find adjustment." Religion thus provides a vista that enables man to view time and eternity with peace and contentment. The man who is truly successful in dealing with the conflicts of life has many wholesome interests, all of which he coordinates for some one worthy end. If this end is religious, his happiness has a stability that neither death nor calamity has the power to shake. The man who is overcome in the conflict fails because he does not find anything that makes life worth while.[9]

All in all, then, religion holds before the growing person the concept

[7] Robert H. Bonthius, *Christian Paths to Self-acceptance,* Kings Crown Press, New York, 1948, p. 191.

[8] Paul H. Vieth, *The Church and Christian Education,* The Bethany Press, St. Louis, 1947, p. 56.

[9] *Cf.* Thomas Verner Moore, *The Driving Forces of Human Nature and Their Adjustment,* Grune and Stratton, New York, 1948.

of God, all-wise and all-loving, Who knows altogether the strengths and the weaknesses of His human child, and in the doing of Whose will there may be achieved the only truly satisfying integration of the personality. "Thou knoweth us altogether, our down-sittings and our up-risings," the sin "in the inward part," and longing to "be one with Thee," proclaim the Hebrew seers. "It is He who makes us will what is good," says Saint Augustine. "We are God's," Calvin declares. "Religion is the love of God and our neighbor," Wesley tells his followers, "this love ruling the whole life, animating all our tempers and passions, directing all our thoughts, words, action." All these great religious seers bear witness to the peace that comes to the man who commits his way, all his way, unto God.

The Church and Synagogue as a Source of Spiritual Nurture

This review of some of the chief ways in which, through its basic affirmations, religion contributes to the healthy development of personality makes it clear that the church and synagogue—the social institutions that have as one of their main functions the promulgation of these truths—have a great opportunity in this regard. We must consider next, then, some of the means by which individual churches and synagogues make real these benefits to children and youth. Briefly listed, the means would seem to be the following: cooperation with parents, cultivation in the child of faith in God, promotion of his sense of "belonging," development in him of responsible participation in the activities of the religious organization, provision of a "benevolent other" in whom he may confide, and support for him in aspiration and endeavor.

Home Cooperation

Churches and synagogues are keenly aware of the primary influence of the family upon human personality. The attitudes and practices of the members of the family in regard to prayer, reverence toward God, participation in the ceremonies of religion—all such matters are of first importance in determining the child's early attitude toward and experience of religion.

All available data point to the conclusion that the influence of the parents in forming a child's ideas of right and wrong completely overshadows that of his teacher, club leader, Sunday-school teacher, and that the work of these agencies can be thoroughly nullified by the counteracting influences of a poor home. Parents have the task of serving not only as the exemplars of their religious heritage but also as its interpreters. Parents, however, have limitations and problems in the unification of their own lives around the ideals they cherish. They themselves need continual renewal, support, and encouragement, and they may require specific help in facing problems in family living and in carrying out their responsibilities toward their children.

Almost without exception, churches and synagogues evidence a deep concern for wholesome and happy family life. Both in service to parents as individuals and in affording guidance for happy family living, there is a great deal of activity on the part of most local churches and a large amount of printed material made available by most national religious bodies.

The mutual support and loyalty which the church and the home bring to each other increase the opportunity of each to minister to the wholesome development of the child. The early sense of "belonging" which the family gives the child is expanded to include the larger fellowship of the household of faith; the child's first group loyalty is enlarged to embrace "my church." At the same time, the larger fellowship of the church lifts up and makes more meaningful the family fellowship, provides larger areas of common interest and experience and ceremonials, and so strengthens family loyalty. If the home and the church support the same values, teach the same "goods," hold the same beliefs and practices, and communicate all these through similar methods, the child will have a powerful incentive toward the integration of his self.

In Chapter IX of this report there is an extended treatment of the family as a primary institution, and of its influence in wholesome personality development. Church and synagogue assert without surcease the high calling of the home under God. Children are a "heritage of the Lord," entrusted to human parents for nurture. Parents thus become coworkers with God in the highest phase of creation, the development of human beings. Churches, individually and collectively, accept their responsibility for supporting parents in this unique opportunity.

Faith, a Realistic View of Life

Faith in the potentialities within oneself, faith in the potentialities of others, faith in God, it has already been said, are necessary for the development of "mental, emotional, and spiritual qualities essential to individual happiness and to responsible citizenship." Irrational fear and doubt are of the essence of unhealthy personality.

The institutions of religion are rooted in the faith that human potentialities are real because God is real; that there is ground for hope concerning man's ultimate destiny because man is a child of God; that the mysteries of the universe may be faced without dismay because God is all-wise; that wickedness and institutional injustice need not overwhelm men because God is all-good and all-powerful; that misery and suffering may be borne without despair because God is love.

The Judaeo-Christian tradition does not teach man that faith in God means that man will be spared all the ills of life; that God's love and care mean that no struggle or suffering will come to his children. In neither the Prophets nor the Gospels is there promised immunity from effort or rebuffs or suffering to those who do the will of God. Nor does faith in God mean that man will comprehend fully all mysteries.

There are many conditions of suffering in the world, however, that are clearly not in accordance with the benevolent will of God for man as it has been revealed to man. One may say with confidence, for instance, that it is not the will of God that little children should starve while there is plenty of food available on the earth to feed them, or die from diseases that the resources of science are able to prevent. One may say with confidence that it is not the will of God that men should devote the energies of their minds and the skill of their hands to devise ever more devastating means of mass destruction of human beings. It is man's rebellion against God and his failure to live according to God's will that cause such human misery.

Children and youth, through observation, experience, instruction, and interpretation, come to understand more clearly the awful price man pays for flouting or ignoring the moral law of God. And so they may come to firmer determination to cooperate with the purposes of God for a world of goodness, love, truth, and justice. They may come to see the high price the human family pays for the freedom granted individuals to choose life goals, and so recognize the responsibility involved in the exercise of that freedom. But there is promised support and comfort to those who commit their way unto the Lord, and the ultimate triumph of righteousness through redeeming love.

Churches and synagogues call upon children and youth to have faith in God, to venture out on that faith and build upon it a life in conformity with the will of God, one that affirms goodness and joy, beauty and fruitfulness. This is not a blind faith nor a faith of unwholesome dependence. It is a faith of understanding that makes high demands on man and faces up to all that life presents to him. That man does not live the good life without putting forth effort is clearly taught by the experience of the race. The wise man of the Proverbs went by the field of the sluggard and found it all grown over with weeds, and so will it be—the institutions of religion teach their children and youth—with present-day sluggards. Man plants and cultivates and God gives the increase, but God does not promise the increase to the man who does not plant and cultivate. Without vision to lead him beyond where he is, without effort to follow the vision, and without the grace of God to make steady his steps, man does not reach real and lasting happiness.

To be able to look squarely at the life that is before them without blinders or rosy glasses and to deal with it without either false stimulation or an opiate, children and youth need faith in God. Wise teachers will not anticipate experience and overwhelm children with problems which they are not prepared to face. But they will help them face whatever needs to be faced.

Faith in God should be taught not as blind submission to whatever is but as a challenge and incentive to high endeavor. Faith should be taught not as a denial of human reason, intelligence, and freedom but as the opportunity for the full development of all potentialities so that one may freely and fully cooperate with the purposes of God.

Faith in God that is real, warm, and vital will find expression in strength and courage to face disappointment and suffering, in acts of love and mercy, in the appreciation of the precious worth of human life, in wonder and awe and reverence as one experiences the beauty and grandeur in nature, in corporate and private worship, and in virtue, ceremonial, and sacrament.

A Sense of Belonging

It has been pointed out by social psychologists that "whatever a person does or wishes to do he must have some 'ground' to stand upon." One of the most important constituents of the ground on which the individual stands is the social group to which he belongs.

Churches and synagogues vary greatly in the extent to which they are successful in giving a child this sense of belonging. In some local churches, both the clergymen and the lay adult members are more concerned about the upkeep of the church property than they are about the wholesome personality development of the children and youth in their neighborhoods; others are so concerned about decorum, dignity, aesthetic values in the services that they resist the participation of children lest they bring imperfection into the situation; others feel for one reason or another that it is more "important" to minister to adults than to minister to children; and so on.

In spite of these shortcomings, however, it seems to be true that among social institutions, churches and synagogues rank high in promoting a sense of "belonging" through their efforts to bring children and young people into the fellowship and to surround them with a sense of real community.

The occasions upon which children are received into a more responsible relationship with the total church fellowship and assume more mature obligations as growing children of God are, in most churches, considered high moments in the life of the congregation. When children in Catholic churches receive their First Communion or Confirmation, when boys in Jewish synagogues become *bar mizvah,* when children in Protestant churches assume the vows of full membership in the church, these occasions are duly signalized by the churches, surrounded with all the beauty, impressiveness, and sense of high solemnity and meaning which the tradition of the religious body affords, thus enhancing the sense of belonging.

Various types of special worship in which children and youth participate, each related specifically to the tradition of the religious body of which it is a part, are being emphasized by local churches and synagogues. Opportunities are being sought, even by busy, large-church pastors, to know personally the boys and girls in the church. Procedures are being set up which make it possible for children or young people who are lonely, insecure, unhappy, or emotionally disturbed to be related to families or mature individuals within the fellowship for more specific support and the cultivation of a more intimate sense of "belonging."

Increasingly, churches and synagogues are helping children and youth to feel that they belong by providing special places for them within the church buildings and special services and activities planned to meet their needs. There are nurseries equipped with good physical facilities and trained personnel, kindergarten rooms where programs, personnel, and materials chosen with special understanding of little children are provided. Workshops, playrooms, study rooms, and libraries are provided for young boys and girls, and extensive programs of study, recreation, group work, hobby activities, dramatics, counseling, summer conferences and camps are offered to those who are older.

In communities with limited financial resources, where facilities and equipment and competent personnel are meager, there is often an unusually large number of children to be served. Churches and synagogues in these settings are hindered by conditions beyond their control in doing all that needs to be done. But for the most part, these churches, too, are using a large proportion of their resources for children and youth.

Through all such provisions, churches and synagogues seek to give the immature members of their fellowship a feeling that, in the eyes of the mature members of the congregation, they are important.

Beyond this, in an increasing number of churches and synagogues there are being provided clergymen, especially selected and trained, to study the needs of young members, to keep in touch with them in their every-day experiences so that more and more adequately these institutions may offer to them specific teaching, services, and encouragement that will meet their current needs.

Important, too, in helping to develop the sense of belonging is the growing recognition of the necessity for active fellowship among the mature and the immature members of a church in worship, recreation, and study. There are more and more "mother-daughter," "father-son" programs. More and more "family nights" and "all-church" social events are being held under church auspices.

Since all this activity on the part of the institutions of religion is rooted in the affirmation that all the persons participating in it are children of God, the church and synagogue can minister to the deep human need for belonging, in a manner more satisfying and more abiding in its influence than can any other institution except the family.

Responsible Participation

In previous sections of this study, reference has been made to the importance for wholesome personal development of actual participation in work, of the feeling on the part of the growing young person that he is doing something which has significance, that he is responsible and to be depended upon.

Again it must be stated that there are many churches and synagogues in which it is considered good for children and youth to be seen and not heard; to be content with what their elders provide for them and to make no contribution of their own; to accept without question and without opportunity for discussion the opinion and point of view of the adult lay-men in their fellowship on all matters of social and civic affairs; and to regard ministers exclusively as lawgivers and law enforcers rather than primarily as pastors, counsellors, and teachers. Yet within the fellowship of churches and synagogues the need of young people for responsible participation in the actual life and work of the institution is being increasingly recognized, and in more and more local organizations it is being actually met.

For generations, the participation of children in the ceremonials and the music of the services has been encouraged in many communions. The services of the altar boys and acolytes, of choirboys and crucifers have been depended upon as a real contribution to the worship in many congregations. In the nonliturgical churches, participation is being encouraged through children's choirs, the use of young people as ushers and as collectors of the offerings, as leaders in Scripture readings and responsive prayers. More attention is being given to this type of participation, and it is being lifted up so that it is recognized by the adult membership as something of deep significance, both to the growing persons taking part and to the institution. Children and young people are being taught to regard their participation as a real, not a pseudo, contribution. They are being encouraged to hold themselves to the high level of performance called for by the significance of their responsibilities in the life and worship of the church or synagogue.

In the practical details of the work of the church and synagogue, too, children and youth are being given a large number of actual jobs-to-be-done, ranging all the way from distributing announcements of special meetings to the members of the parish or cleaning up the church grounds or washing the windows to working under supervision in redecorating the sanctuary or, in a few instances, working with adults for months to erect a church building.

Less widely accepted among churches and synagogues is the importance of enlisting the participation of youth in the policy and program making of the local church. There continues to be reluctance to permit young people to share in the decisions regarding the expenditures of funds administered by the congregation and in the making of programs for local church social and educational and service enterprises. Yet there are many local churches and some national religious bodies that have adopted the definite policy of youth representation on the policy-making boards and committees. It seems to be true that churches and synagogues exceed business or industry or government or the institutions of higher education in the recognition of the need for responsible participation on the part of young persons.

Within the fellowship of the church or synagogue, the fact that children and youth are a "heritage of the Lord," that they belong to the Kingdom of God, is continually being brought sharply to attention. Consequently, the officials responsible for the administrative work of these institutions are not allowed to drift so easily into disregard of the need for participation on the part of the immature members in the interest of efficiency. Synagogues and churches have wider freedom to "risk" enlisting actual participation of youth in their affairs, and hence a larger opportunity to contribute to wholesome personality development through meeting this need of children and youth.

The "Benevolent Other"

Human beings need some person or persons to whom they can talk freely about their aspirations, frustrations, joys, and sorrows. This source of relief from strain and tensions is most important for wholesome personality development.

It is here that the institutions of religion face one of their greatest opportunities. The very concept of the brotherhood of man under the fatherhood of God, which is basic to the major religious faiths in the United States, implies the sharing of one another's experiences: the weeping with those who weep, the rejoicing with those who rejoice, the admonishing in love of those who go astray, and the bearing of the burdens of the weak on the part of the strong.

There have been serious failures in actual practice in many of the institutions of religion to realize their opportunities in this area. In some situations there has been much legalism: the holding of an individual to strict account for what he did without due consideration of why he did it. Thus it might happen that a child in the church kindergarten who was destructive and belligerently aggressive would be judged solely on the basis of his outward acts and isolated from the group, rejected by the teacher, in spite of the fact that the cause of his unacceptable behavior was isolation and rejection experienced at home. Or a young person, burdened by a sense of guilt, might have been told only to atone for his sin rather than be helped also to achieve faith in his own potentialities for goodness because of the love of God.

Again, the actual program of the churches and synagogues often has been too largely dependent upon admonition and instruction to meet the needs of persons who are really distressed. Being told to "buck up," to "do what you know is right" is not helpful to a child or youth whose difficulties arise out of conditions that render it impossible for him to take charge of his life and to make wise decisions.

Yet the institutions of religion have through the ages ministered to sick souls in ways that have brought support, succor, and salvation to millions of persons. Present-day churches and synagogues are rapidly appreciating and applying the results of research in the field of mental health, psychiatry, and cultural dynamics. Thus, improved technical knowledge and skills are joined with the age-old resources in helping distressed persons to fullness of life. In increasing numbers, clergymen are being given courses in personal counseling in their regular seminary programs, and some of them, in addition, are taking professional work and degrees in psychiatry, psychology, social work, etc.

There is evidence from all sides that churches and synagogues are acutely aware of their responsibility to afford children and youth, as well as adults, fellowship with wise and trusted persons, not only in formal interviews but also in friendly informality, the opportunity to "talk over" their problems and feelings of inadequacy and guilt with someone upon whom they can depend for understanding and help rather than condemnation. Where sacramental confession is characteristic of a religious body, in addition to sacramental effects, opportunity is provided for personal counseling.

Pastoral counseling is coming to be recognized as an essential service to the mental health of children and youth. This service will, almost necessarily, be limited to children and youth who give evidence of serious disturbance. Much more than this is needed if the churches and synagogues are to grasp their opportunity and help all children and youth to realize their potentialities as children of God, liberated from nagging doubts and limiting frustrations.

Lay teachers and parents are being offered courses in understanding children and in techniques of guidance. Books and periodicals are being provided to meet the needs both of the meagerly educated and of the more highly educated.[10] These training programs for parents and lay workers with children and youth are emphasizing the fundamentals of establishing interpersonal relationships characterized by understanding and benevolence, the "affirmation of life, growth, joy, freedom." This does not mean pampering. Quite the contrary. Because of the good will of the "other," the child may talk freely and acknowledge the worst that is in him. And since he has acknowledged it himself, the child can begin to assume responsibility for it. The very freedom which the sympathetic understanding of the friendly person gives the child or youth helps greatly in enabling him to do something about his difficulty. The wise helper will give the child the sense that he is always standing by but never taking over.

In facing their responsibilities, children and youth need help also in accepting their limitations. Few human beings ever bring completely

---

[10] The national offices of most of the religious bodies in the United States provide detailed information about services, courses, and publications which they recommend in this field.

under control all their egocentric drives and hungers. If children and youth know that the "benevolent other" also recognizes these problems in his own life, they may be able to accept these limitations and face their failures without despair. One of the great sources of comfort and of courage that can come to children and youth who are trying to unify themselves around high ideals is to know that few human beings achieve perfection altogether and that fewer still achieve it all at once. Ultimate goals must be mediated to growing persons as they are able to receive them, and this can be done more successfully through warm, shared personal experience than through cold precept.

Support in Aspiration and Endeavor

Provision of the "benevolent other" is more than help in facing and overcoming personal sins, weaknesses, limitations, and failures. It is also offering the immature members of the fellowship support in their highest aspirations and their noblest endeavors. To call upon children and youth to do the will of God is to call upon them to accept the fact that they will often find themselves out of harmony with their social group, the mores of their community, the accepted practices and standards and goals of the society of which they are a part. As they become committed to judging all persons solely upon their worth as persons and not at all upon the circumstance of birth, they are likely to run into serious disapproval in their school or community. As they seek to put into practice their faith in the brotherhood of man under the Fatherhood of God through actually ministering to all forms of human need and loneliness, through promoting the causes and relationships which lead to reconciliation and peace rather than those which lead to strife and war, they are likely to find that they are supporting values that the community does not support. They need sustaining help to be able to "stand firm under the pressures of life," a sense of renewal and resource which comes from worship and religious fellowship. Fellowship provides a channel for the transmission of strength and confirming aid which are from God.

There are some churches and synagogues that fail to offer support to their children in seeking to know and to do the will of God in areas of human relationships where it is fashionable to disregard it as irrelevant or inapplicable. There are many churches and synagogues, too, in which influential individuals or groups of individuals oppose any activity that looks toward the reexamination of social customs and standards as being outside the proper sphere of interest of the institutions of religion.

Because of their nature and mission, institutions of religion should not completely identify themselves with any current social system or theory of progress. However, in dealing with the allegations that organized religion does not meet the challenge of social progress, it should be frankly admitted that there is a good deal of conservation in organized religion, just as there is in organized society and government. There is perforce conservatism in organized religion in its very conservation of religious truths, traditions, precepts, and heritages.

The principle of religious organization, however, should not be abandoned because some adherents of religion have sometimes supported political and economic reaction. Rather we must exert ourselves to encourage members of religious organizations to fulfill their ideals and to realize the potentials of their organizations. Religion has increasingly become the champion of the oppressed and the mouthpiece of social justice. In this country, Protestants, Catholics, and Jews have been crusading cooperatively for the promotion of equitable social relations between employers and employees and for understanding between the members of various religious and racial groups. In the stable institutions of religion there is to be found the basic undergirding of efforts looking toward individual and social righteousness that is essential to real human progress.

⚹ XI ⚹

The School

THE schools of the United States have been concerned with the healthy development of the whole person in more ways and for more years than those not intimately acquainted with their recent history may know. Thinking about the obligations of the school to the whole child, its responsibilities in connection with his wholesome growth as a functioning personality, has been moving ahead steadily and with wide strides. Practice has followed—experimentally, feeling its way, faster in some places than in others, hampered not only by some of the traditional forms of schooling but also, and perhaps more importantly, by the stringent difficulty of translating novel ideas and fresh dedications into corresponding lines of action.

Changing Conceptions of the School's Task

At the turn of the century, schooling was largely dedicated to imparting certain specified knowledge and skills. Almost universally, that was conceived to be the school's prime task, its sole duty. True, there was already a rich background of discussion as to the ends this knowledge and these skills were to serve. This arose largely in the course of the struggle to assure free public instruction for all.

Without the skills of reading and writing there could be no informed citizenry, and without an informed citizenry democracy could not long survive—an undisputed tenet dating back to Thomas Jefferson. Without equal access to knowledge and skills there could be no equal opportunity to move up in the world. Vocational adjustment, economic advancement, and, to a certain extent, social recognition were thought to rest almost exclusively upon effective instruction in given bodies of subject matter. Stress upon such reasons for universal schooling arose at a time that can be roughly designated as the Jacksonian era.

Earlier in national history, moral and religious objectives were the major note struck by those who wanted to make sure that every child should go to school. In colonial New England, Bible reading was held essential to salvation; consequently, each child must be schooled to read. Moreover, moral instruction by the written word was thought highly effective, and the schools were a place in which such instruction could be—and was—unremitting.

So, by the turn of the century, the schools were already, in a way, concerned with the functioning of the individual as a citizen, as a worker and member of society, as a moral character in all his doings and dealings. There was even a dawning recognition that the child sick in body could not "do so well in his studies," and his physical health began to be given some attention.

These historical factors are important to bear in mind because they continue even now to influence thinking and practice, though in different forms and in different ways. But, most significant, from the point of view of the present discussion, is the fact that all these objectives were sought through the imparting of knowledge and skills rote fashion, under threat. The child—the person—was conceived as having a "mind" and a "will" separate from his body, from his feelings, and even to a degree from his activities and his relationships with people. Such was the psychology of the day, and so the school proceeded. Its business was with the "mind" and, to a certain extent, with the "will."

For the most part, the child's "will" was thought to be fractious, if not evil, and consequently to be "broken"—more or less as a wild colt is "broken"—by restriction and discipline. The inference for instruction was that learning must be arduous, if not distasteful, else the "will" would either be left undisciplined, or perhaps turn "soft." Subject matter consisted of a traditional body of fact and precept, to be learned by rote and to affect conduct by some alchemy undefined. No one seriously asked how the ability to repeat moralistic precepts would affect morality. The "mind" was a blank until inscribed, and after that all-powerful, except, perhaps, for the rebellious will.

Another function this prescribed subject matter was supposed to perform was "the training of the mind," or "mental discipline," and for this it was assumed that some subject matter (such as mathematics, Latin, and Greek) were more effective than others. The science of a later day was to prove this assumption false. There is no general "transfer of training" from learning Latin to learning anything else; all that transfers from one situation to the next is the common elements, such as habits of work and methods of study. But the conviction was deep and strong that the mind was something like a razor, in that it could be honed up to a fine cutting edge, the more difficult subject matter serving as a whetting stone, and that the edge thus acquired would serve in all situations and last throughout life.

If the child's "will" was taken to differ from the man's in being still "unbroken," the child's "mind" was taken to differ from the man's only by being untrained and uninformed. Very few in this country studied the child's nature, his capacities, his view of the world, because he was thought to be in no essential respect other than a small adult. The days and years of his childhood were held to be without value in and of themselves; their sole value lay in the opportunity they offered to form the man. Whether this stemmed from preoccupation with the soul's salvation, from the child's economic dependence, or from the sheer arrogance of adult generations, it is difficult to say. But the fact remains.

A New View in a New Century

During the first quarter of the new century, much of this earlier thinking was either reversed or put into so revised a context as to carry novel implications for the functions of schooling, the processes of education, the range and depth of the school's concern with the child. The human being, child and man, began to be conceived no longer as a self-contained entity or even as the clean slate of an earlier day, upon which the knowledge and skills acquired by humanity in the course of its history might be inscribed by rote, but rather as a social being, the product of interchange between himself and his environment.

That the child does not survive without people to minister to him is easy to see. That he becomes what he is as a person—indeed, that he becomes what we know as a human being—solely as the result of what happens between himself and others around him—was at first difficult to accept but has with the years become a commonplace in thinking about the making of men and the various manners in which different kinds of men are made. Even the (to our eyes) odd aborigines, with distorted bodies and weird customs, who make their occasional bow in the illustrations of the *National Geographic,* can and do grow up to look and act like people of the Western world if they are raised in the Western world from babyhood.

But, by the line of thinking here examined, what the man becomes, given his native endowment, is not dependent merely upon what befalls him but also upon what he does. An experience is an interchange between a person and a situation, in the course of which both the person and the situation undergo change. By his very nature as an organism, even the infant is active and not a mere blob upon which the environment impresses itself. He yells, and his mother picks him up. He responds with bodily movements and continues to yell. She changes his position and offers him the breast. He leaves off yelling and starts to suck.

In the course of these events, both he and his mother have learned, and they are, to a greater or less degree, changed. She has learned the pleasure of nursing and a new sense of fulfillment that comes with tending the young, the dependent, the helpless. The next time he cries, she does differently, has different feelings. The infant's activity has brought about a change in his environment. Not only is his mother changed but she in turn brings the rest of his environment to bear on him in different ways.

The infant meanwhile has learned that yelling brings surcease of his distress. Gradually, as again and again he cries and is fed, he learns to identify the feelings within him and begins to identify himself as distinguished from the outer world. He begins to learn that there is an outer world and that it can bring him comfort, solace, relief, release. In these circumstances he begins to trust it. He also begins to learn that it can thwart and anger him, and, if it does so too often and arbitrarily, he begins to mistrust it.

Meaning and Purpose

Basically, the child learns to seek his ends, the fulfillment of his desires, in the outer world, through doing things in it and to it, manipulating it in ways that he discovers to be appropriate, in ways that work to bring him satisfaction. He is not merely active at random. His activity has meaning. It is directed toward ends. He has purpose, at least in rudimentary form.

What he seeks in the outer world is also to a high degree learned. His very desires take on their shape and content through his interaction with this outer world, which thus becomes an integral part of himself. The Hopi child and the child of the prevalent American culture not only seek their ends in different ways; they actually seek different things. At the period when the latter wants to become a cowboy or a locomotive engineer, the former may be making deliberate arrangements to maintain the good and happy thoughts which are part of the Hopi ideal. In the course of seeking and doing, succeeding and failing, enjoying and suffering the result of doing, both American child and Hopi child—all children—acquire a set of meanings. To the Hopi, thunderheads are a favorable omen; they portend rain for the corn, around which Hopi life, in an arid land, revolves. To the American, thunderheads are more likely to mean electricity, weather forecasts, danger to the stock, protecting finery.

The meanings are different, because each child has been interacting with a different cultural environment. In response to the meaning the thunderhead has for him, each of those two children act differently—the Hopi child does not turn from what he has been doing but is buoyed up with a flooding elation; the child of the prevalent American culture rushes to get the young chickens under shelter or runs to the window to watch the lightning.

But here another distinction makes itself apparent. For the roll of the thunder, the Hopi culture offers just one interpretation; all Hopi children learn the one meaning offered them. But the American culture is diverse and complex. Certain common meanings all may share but, whereas one child may respond to the aesthetics of the storm, another may attend to the livestock, a third seek shelter to protect his finery, and so on, with many paying no special attention whatsoever. One child may have several reactions, because he has acquired several meanings that are satisfying to him. Just which meaning or meanings he acquires depends upon his individual experience with storms and with the particular people who have been with him during storms, or have told him about storms, or have offered him alternative explanations in the written word, fact or fiction, or in pictorial or musical form.

But this experience is in part determined by his purposes. Following his purposes, he builds meanings into his life, and these meanings become a selective influence shaping his further purposes and the new meanings he acquires in the course of his further experience. For example, if his purposes are of a certain order, he is likely to seek out scientific explanations of a thunderstorm, and the persons who can give them to him, and to make weather charts and rainfall estimates, and eventually to propose to become a scientist. If his inclinations are more in the direction of artistic expression, both his human associations and his activities and plans are likely to be guided by these.

Thwarted Purpose

If, however, his purposes are thwarted—and very early in life he learned that his human environment could be frustrating and infuriating as well as comforting, supporting, and satisfying—the results are different. He does not stop experiencing, learning, acquiring new meanings and new ways of reacting to situations because of the new meanings, but what he learns, the meanings he acquires, are quite different. And they are likely to be very different, too, from what the person who thwarts him thinks they should be, or intends.

Suppose, for example, when he is quite young, it is his impulse and purpose to run outdoors and prance and yell and outshout the storm. This purpose may lead one day to the development of more and more aesthetic meanings and to artistic creativity in dance or music. Or possibly one day this child may start to seek other means to dominate the storm and make it serve his purposes, and so acquire an eventual set of meanings that would be called primarily scientific, though empowered still and imbued by his rich early aesthetic-emotional reactions.

But suppose that while he is still at the stage of jumping and yelling or running out to build streams and dikes and waterways, some importunate grown person comes to him and says, "No, that is not what you are to do when there is a thunderstorm. You must read this book about the watershed. You must make a graph of precipitation. You must take this Leyden jar in the laboratory and do as the book says and watch what happens and write it down as I tell you. Because you must learn about science. Science is essential for modern man; it is important that you understand about it. Science is written down in the book. You study the book, and then you can say what is in the book. You will understand science and be equipped for living in the modern world."

What happens? In all likelihood the child's intent and purpose is thwarted, and he is angry. He learns that this grown person is not his helpmeet and friend but his opponent who must be given in to. This adult, all adults, perhaps all persons, become to him hostile and unmanageable rather than friendly and cooperative. "Human being" becomes a phrase with a pattern of emotional meanings that are not good. He reacts to those meanings and becomes himself less cooperative, more hostile, in his further dealings with men.

What else happens? Does he learn science? Under compulsion he may learn the words in the book. This does not mean that he learns what the words mean, that he could make any use of the words if need should arise. He reads and repeats what he reads. Essentially what he learns— aside from his negative feelings toward the compelling person and all his counterparts—is essentially what he does: to read and to repeat, under compulsion and with resentment. It may even turn out that he feels resentful about reading and will do as little of that as possible as time moves on. But if, for some reason, the words in the book take on meaning for him, he may be able to use what he has read should occasion arise, but he may avoid all such occasion and be loath to do what he can do when occasion thrusts itself upon him.

Nor will he even learn that which would make it possible for it to be said of him that he knows science and is equipped to live in a scientific age. He may hate science and attempt to wangle his way out of any possible further contact with it. Hating and shunning science, he is not likely to learn very much about it. More important, unless he finds it elsewhere, he will have lost all opportunity for learning the very essence of the scientific age and of science as it is now understood—the freely inquiring mind, purposefully delving for knowledge, prediction, and control. He will not have acquired equipment for the scientific age, but more likely for an age in which all learning inhered in books was handed down by authority and used in verbal situations only.

The view of the child and of education that developed after the turn of the century said, in effect, that one must work in accordance with the child's intent and purpose and not against them—a far cry from the "breaking of the will." For the sake of achieving their purposes, man and child expend effort and energy, overcome hindrances and obstacles, undergo peril, hardship, and suffering.

The Whole Child in the Whole Environment

But if will inheres in purposes, and purposes are learned, then learning (previously identified with intellect) and motive (previously identified with will, if not with willfulness) are not so far apart; they are, in fact, one. And, indeed, this whole line of thinking led to a conception of a human being as a whole—thinking, feeling, purposing, and doing.

Furthermore, this conception of learning led directly away from treating the child as a diminutive man, without right to respect as a child, because it made clear that, with his lesser experience, he was different from the adult. As a result of his accruing experience, his doing and undergoing, his responses, meanings, and purposes change. As today shapes him for tomorrow, tomorrow again shapes him for all future tomorrows. As he lives richly today and acquires manifold meanings, he lives more richly tomorrow and so grows always closer to his fullest capacities. This day, whatever day, is therefore the foundation for all other days, and one would no more deprive the child of his day's fulfillment of purpose for the sake of something in the future than deprive him of his day's physical nourishment for the sake of all the gustatory pleasures he might enjoy in some far future adulthood. So it began to be seen that each day must be treated as an end in itself, and the child respected as a child.

There were other ways, too, in which, by this way of thinking, the child came to be respected in his own right. One was that the new view of learning was developed in close relation to scientific method and the scientific approach to life. One no longer took what was said for truth because it was said, no matter by whom. And so one looked at the child and saw that he differed from the man. One looked more carefully and saw how he differed at birth, and at each week and month after birth, and after each accruing year of growth and experience. And it came to be seen that if he was treated appropriately at each successive stage, he was always at the next stage better able to respond, to think, to perform, to create. So each stage took on its own value.

Possibly the most potent factor of all in giving the child a stature and respect of his own came from the recognition that the child did not learn by rote alone but that experience was the great teacher after all, and experience could not be confined to the book. The child as a whole lived in a whole environment and responded to everything that was in it. This fact used to be expressed by saying that learnings are not single but multiple—the child does not learn only what is set out for him to learn, but he learns ways of learning it, and habits of work, and attitudes toward the task in hand, and feelings toward the people who set it out for him to learn and others for whom they stand.

The child who is not treated with respect as a child learns from not being treated with respect—learns that he is not worthy of respect (or learns so to feel in his inner heart, perhaps even without acknowledging it to himself), and that therefore others like him are not worthy of respect. Simultaneously he learns impotent hatred of those who treat him with disrespect, for it is his basic nature to want to be loved and respected for what he is; and this hatred may also carry over to others who are in some way like those who disrespect him, even if their likeness inheres only in their being other adults or even other human beings.

So it came about that, through inquiry into the social nature of the individual and the meaning of this for education, the forefront of education moved away from traditional preconceptions about the nature of the child and the mode of his learning in the direction of a concern for the healthy development of the whole personality.

Along with this came a number of inferences for the practices of education that agree strikingly with the principles derived from another line of thought altogether—a line concerned with the health of the emotions. For education, however, they stemmed instead from concern with the individual as a social being and a social participant, and they may be summarized, at least in part, as follows:

That the child is not a small man but different in his responses and capacities from the man, and different at different levels of his development.

That one should not thwart, crush, disregard the child and his purposes but must instead treat them with respect, go along with them, cherish and honor them, for each day of life has its own value, and it is out of the fulfillment of childish purposes in always larger terms that he will conceive and ultimately achieve ever greater purposes.

That learning is complex and not simple, that purposes, feelings, attitudes, ways of life, and personal dedications are learned as well as arithmetic, geography, history, and spelling, and that these latter are not and cannot be learned without learning some of the former simultaneously.

That all learnings are social in nature, and are to be valued only in as far as they help make a kind of person who contributes richly, at best creatively, in his social milieu, and finds his basic satisfactions—and so happiness—in so doing.

A Deeper Perspective on Motive

As such conceptions as these were being studied, clarified, evaluated, carefully translated into more and more aspects of the total school program, and gaining ever wider acceptance, educational thinking was stimulated to delve still further into conditions conducive to the development of healthy, happy, and socially effective personalities. This new thought stream derived from the study and treatment of the emotionally or mentally ill, and can be roughly designated as "the mental-hygiene approach." It began to filter into books for teachers in a thin thickle about 1930, has been slowly but steadily gaining force ever since, and has by now become in some quarters a serious educational preoccupation. At first, individuals made modest tentative proposals; by now a major movement may be under way.

In many ways the "mental-hygiene approach" enlarged and deepened understandings of what had already been laid down in the advance that preceded; in no basic way has it yet proved contradictory. All there is to know about the development of a human being cannot be conjectured, even in broadest outlines, at one stroke, nor is full knowledge yet within hailing distance. But on all sides it is granted that every valid significant gain requires careful study and considered incorporation into practice. With great clarity, the new line of thought recognized that thinking, feeling, doing, relating oneself to others cannot be separated, any one from all the others; but it put greater emphasis on those facets of the personality called "feeling" than on those called "thinking," and so studied the emotional life and had much to contribute from the study.

But how could explanations of factors in personality development and functioning that came from the clinic and the hospital find their way into thinking about education and the school? How did these two streams meet? How was one in any way applicable to the other?

Some of the larger reasons are immediately apparent. Under the influence of earlier innovations, the purview of most educators had come to include the development of the whole person—his emotional life as well as other aspects of his development. Furthermore, the school had long been concerned with the functioning of the individual in his social milieu. And it had become increasingly concerned with purpose and motive. At all three points, the fields of education and mental hygiene impinge. Many who were dealing with the problems of the emotionally disturbed felt they had something to contribute. A few of those who were versed in both fields began to explore and identify interrelationships.

First, both educators and mental hygienists count among their goals the personal well-being of those with whom they deal. Since mental hygiene took its departure from medicine, the prevention and relief of personal suffering are by inference implicit in it, and a sense of personal well-being is but a more positive, and at the present time more accurate, statement of its major aim. Educators, too, have by now accepted a prevailing sense of personal adequacy, satisfaction, and validity as one of their key considerations. They are convinced that the individual's experience—whether at three, six, or thirty—must give him a feeling of self-respect, of effective impact upon his environment, of personal fulfillment. Increasingly they recognize that the "mental-hygiene approach" has identified certain impediments to the achievement of such feelings and is gradually defining some, though not necessarily all, of the conditions conducive to them.

Moreover, health and nonhealth in the area of the emotions are no more sharply distinguished than bodily illness and health. One may count oneself physically ill or well, but how many who are not ill still contend with minor ailments, discomforts, deficiencies? Similarly, there is a "psychopathology of everyday life," and it does not consist only of slips of the tongue, minor forgettings, nail-biting, and other trivial "bad habits"; it accounts also for the number of "characters" and "types" that turn up whenever a group of any size is gathered together: the perpetual gripe, the goldbrick, the keeper of the peace at all costs, the show-off, the silent one. These may not be seriously sick, emotionally in a bad way, yet they cannot be said to be as emotionally well as they might be. The mental hygienist has some helpful explanations to propose to the educator, perplexed by their behavior and puzzled about ways to assure their more wholesome growth.

Second, both educator and mental hygienist are concerned with the social functioning of the individual. At his worst, the emotionally sick person may not function socially at all; he withdraws entirely from the world or exhibits a preternatural apathy. More often he functions partially—halfheartedly as it were, without gusto, often without affection, with decisiveness, unable to take a chance, to "stick his neck out," to take responsibility, to say yea or nay. Almost always he functions misguidedly, because things, persons, and events have "special" meanings for him: he sees slights everywhere, or senses great danger where no danger is, or perceives hindrances and obstacles in exaggerated proportions. Such "special" meanings leave him disoriented, without appropriate response, unable to react to his environment in ways that are effective, either for himself or for the direction of events.

Surely all this has relevance for the educator who wants school children to grow up socially sensitive and responsible, knowing where they stand and able to take effective action. These are among his goals. The ways to seek and achieve them are not entirely clear. He does not always succeed to the degree that his earnest labors would seem to warrant. Small wonder, then, that the factors that precipitate gross failure, the failure represented in the neurotic personality, should be of interest to him.

In addition, there are those who see the troubles of the world only through the projection of their own difficulties—inability to act, apathy, the attribution of false motive, exaggeration of difficulty, purblind vision. The preamble to the charter of UNESCO begins: "Since wars are made in the minds of men, it is in the minds of men that peace will be established." And the Constitution of the World Health Organization first defines health as "a state of complete physical, mental, and social well-being" and then proceeds to affirm that "the health of all peoples is fundamental to the attainment of peace and security."

It is easy to believe that economic, social, national, and international life are disturbed by the difficulties that beset any group—by the psychological difficulties of individuals and the repercussions these always have in any group situation. The relations between individuals and their society are reciprocal, and if so many individuals are in some way warped by their experience in their social world, it seems reasonable to suppose that this warping is woven back into the institutions of which they are an inherent part. Whatever the qualifying factors, the logic of the case seems irrefutable, though it remains still to be proved.

This again, in as far as it holds, can scarcely be counted unimportant for education, which has of recent years been increasingly concerned with the social good, improved social relations, more equitable economic conditions, and a better world order.

Third, both educator and mental hygienist hold that behavior is based on purposes and can be explained in terms of purposes. In fact, the definitive link between the two lines of thought may be said to lie in stress on purposiveness. The earlier innovation, taking departure from social philosophy, cut straight to the crucial importance of purpose and purposiveness in man's experience, and consequently in what he learns in its course.

The other line of thought, originating in therapy, again arrived at purpose as essential in interpreting the development of man, his capacity for easy interaction with his fellows, for creative activity, and for personal happiness—or at least freedom from those forms of unhappiness that stem from incapacity to act, or to act with self-confidence and spontaneity. Furthermore, it saw the origin of those meanings that lead either to social effectiveness and personal happiness or to personal frustrations and qualified social contribution in the individual's social experience, though it focused attention for the most part on social experience in the early years of life, and on emotional rather than intellectual meanings.

But it is precisely here, in the concept of motivation, that the two lines of thought in a sense diverge. It is not so much that they view purpose differently or have different conceptions of it as that they see it in different perspective and context.

In the view of the education that derived from social philosophy, all motivation was subsumed under conscious purpose and intent: an identifiable and reportable wish, desire, goal, resolve. A person finds himself alone and lonesome, wants company, formulates a plan to get it, achieves his purpose, and is satisfied. Or a young man wants to be a doctor and pursues his goal through studies that last through seven or eight years. Or a mathematician sets out to solve a problem, or a novelist to write a novel. Or a poor man to make a lot of money, or a rich one to make still more money. This is purpose as it is ordinarily known: of each and all these it can be said that at least in some measure "they knew what they wanted."

To the mental hygienist's eye, behavior that is far less readily understandable is also purposive, satisfying some inner need: the person who suddenly feels lonely in the midst of company, the novelist who one day finds he can write no more, the person who always spends more than he makes, the depressed, the accident-prone. The behavior of all these, the mental hygienist says, is purposive.

Take the person who is accident-prone: somewhere in himself he feels guilty, and his accident brings him pain and punishment; somewhere in himself he feels unloved, and his accident brings him solicitous attention; somewhere in himself he is loath to do something or afraid to face it, and he has an accident that makes it impossible for him to be expected to meet and deal with it. The accident serves his purposes. He comes to rely on it again and again when the going gets rough.

He does not have the accident "on purpose," in the ordinary sense of the word—that is, with conscious intent. But the slip, the misjudgment, the failure to look, the misapprehension "happens," and the resulting injury brings something that he sorely craves at some inner core of himself. If he were aware even of what he craves, he would be in a position to find some more constructive means for achieving it. But he is unaware, and helpless.

There is much clinical evidence to the effect that an uneasy life of motive and purposiveness, of drive and yearning, is acted out, so to speak, without formulation in words or conscious intent. And this uneasy life accounts for the behavior of people who are needlessly tense, fearful, gloomy, out of tune wherever they go, unhappy and ineffective. There is some yearning they are trying to satisfy, some wish they want fulfilled, of which they are not aware. Their behavior speaks for them; they are unable to speak for themselves, for they do not know what it is they are lacking, what they seek by conduct that is odd, repetitive, not nicely adjusted either to bring them satisfaction or to cope with what confronts them.

To describe and encompass the kind of purpose which is conscious, intentional, properly gauged, and adaptive to the changing circumstances through which it must be achieved, the mental hygienists posit a part of the personality—and just a part—which they call the *ego,* which has been defined as "the organization of individual experience." To the extent that favorable conditions have made it strong, the ego exercises control over experience.

But by this theory, the personality includes more than the ego. It includes also the tumultuous demands of the unsocialized organism and the incorporated prohibitions of the parents in the early years of life. If all goes well with development, the organic energies and impulses, whether of seeking or of avoiding, of love or of hate, find constructive outlet in socialized activity, in what the person does, thinks, imagines, creates. The prohibitions of the parents are formulated into a conscience that checks on the moral quality of acts and events—with feeling but not without responsible personal judgment. The ego is in control. Experience is organized fruitfully. Learning proceeds unimpeded. There is emotional health.

When all does not go well, organic energies and impulses find no sufficient channel into socialized activity. They are embattled with overweening feelings of the forbidden that impede the process by which they would under more propitious conditions find acceptable expression in the outer world of people, things, events. But since they are, or are by this theory assumed to be, true energies, they cannot be denied. They must and do find outlet, not in socially phrased and personally meaningful behavior, but in unusual manifestations, from tics to "temperaments," and occasionally in serious emotional disturbances and mental disorders. The individual is pushed hither and yon by wayward impulses. He feels a gulf between what he should and can do. Learning is impeded. He is unable to take hold of his world and deal with it realistically to bring it closer to his ideals and his heart's desire.

Now it is strange, or perhaps not strange at all, that the definition of the ego used in this line of thought coincides with definitions of the self explicit or implicit throughout the most influential educational writing of this century. Which means only that educators in general have concerned themselves exclusively with the aspects of the total behavior of man that are accessible to ready identification and report, the ones in which socialization has progressed fairly and well, so that all is available for direct observation and examination. The odd, the inexplicable, the obscure they passed over—whether as irrelevant or as mystic it is impossible to say, but certainly as not important in describing the social nature of man or in studying its development. Now that means have been found for bringing the previously obscure to light, it becomes apparent that many of the factors back of unusual behavior are not only amenable to control but also furnish clues that are important in understanding all human behavior.

It is worth pausing to note, in this connection, that in the development of any science there is a period at which general laws apply to most instances, or to major trends, but fail to take account of exceptional phenomena. So it is not surprising that, in the study of human development, the "exceptional" should long have been considered just that, a sort of excrescence on the normative. But every scientist knows that his law is increasingly adequate, provides more accurate understanding of what takes place, as it is revised to cover more and more of the phenomena to which it is supposed to apply, when there are fewer and fewer exceptions to challenge the rule. When a law is revised, it turns out that the explanation that served for the narrower range was a partial explanation only, comparatively speaking a rough-and-ready rule of thumb that not only failed to explain the exception but also provided less accurate control over the phenomena it did in a way explain. And so it would appear to be in this instance.

This may be counted the fundamental importance of taking into consideration all the elements in behavior, even pathological behavior, when attempting to give an ever more useful account of the factors in human development. It is not so much a matter of learning about the well from the sick—though much has been learned about keeping physically well from study of the physically sick—as it is that behavior shows a wide range of manifestations, from what anyone would agree is healthy and well ordered to the slightly off base and the clearly pathological. Any explanation of behavior that covers a wider range is more likely to be a better explanation of all, including behavior that is patently sound.

Implications for Educational Theory

But what, then, does this deeper perspective on motive, this view that there are purposes of which the organized self can give no account—what does it have to offer? In what ways does it enrich the educational thinking that preceded?

For those who have come to recognize that one must not crush the child and thwart his purposes, it offers an alternative view of what these purposes are, a more useful interpretation of developmental levels, and a more comprehensive conception of the child's readiness for any kind of learning.

Purposes

The earlier educational way of thinking saw man as by nature active and purposeful, but took it that all purposes were specific and learned in the course of social experience. The corresponding assumption underlying the work of the mental hygienists is that the human organism is endowed with two basic motives or drives—the drive to secure affection and the drive to achieve a sense of competence and assurance.

These drives are perhaps related to the race-preservative and self-preservative "instincts" posited by biologists of an earlier day, and it must be remembered that mental hygiene derives largely from the work of medical men, who would be likely to choose biological terms for phrasing principles descriptive of the phenomena they observe. Many disclaim that there is sufficient evidence for biological explanation, but still find nothing in their work to controvert the conviction that all man's more specific purposes and activities, infinitely varied, are but ultimate expressions and proliferations of his drives for affection and security.

In order to lead eventually into fully socialized behavior these drives must, by this way of thinking, find certain relatively specific forms of expression and gratification at different stages—in infancy, babyhood, early childhood, later childhood, and so on. This does not necessarily mean that the drives exhibit a certain developmental sequence no matter what the environment (a "maturation theory"), even though changes in the forms through which they express themselves are to a certain extent correlated with stages in progress toward physical maturity. But it does mean, at a minimum, that in our culture, in interaction with the social medium as it is found in the Western world, these drives find characteristic forms of expression at different levels of development, and so require certain characteristic elements in the environment at each stage.

Developmental Levels

The stages identified by the mental hygienists can be roughly equated with the periods of growth described by the students of child development who worked at first without the mental-hygiene point of view. But to descriptive accounts of characteristic behavior mental hygienists added a rationale concerning the orderly development of the basic drives. The students of child development told how the child reacts at various stages of growth; the mental-hygiene approach attempts an account of why he so reacts, and this provides at least a tentative basis for more insightful and intelligent adaptation of the environment.

The two-year-old, for example, tends to say "No" an inordinate number of times, in season and out, apparently actuated only by a wanton desire to say "No," an impish delight in refusal. This the descriptive accounts of child development clearly identified. The mental-hygiene approach introduced as a rationale the child's motive to gain security by achieving autonomy, establishing his capacity to act on his own. If he is not given opportunity to do this, he may fail to develop an adequate sense of himself as an operating force in his world and so continue throughout life to assert himself with a persistent and relatively incorrigible negativism, or in some other ways equally inappropriate and unfortunate. Or he may remain always ineffective and unassertive, full of doubt.

When all that is known is that the two-year-old almost always does what seems an unconscionable amount of no-saying and in general "grows out of it," one can afford him his opportunity to say "No" without worrying about it and await the perhaps happier day on which he will leave off. When, on the other hand, one understands the purpose his many no-sayings serve, the period becomes something more than a prolonged incident to be endured with patience. The person who cares for the child can have a more sympathetic feeling toward him as he comes up with his repeated refusals. Also, these refusals can be seen in relation to the rest of what he does, all of which likewise reflects the struggle to assert himself, to stand on his own two feet, as it were, both literally and figuratively. And he may be not only permitted but actually helped to achieve the autonomy for which he strives so valiantly. Then later, should anything prove amiss with his capacity to act on his own, those who have him in charge have some index of where to look for what in his experience accounts for it, and of what new experiences are now likely to help him overcome it.

In all these ways the mental hygienists' explanations of behavior at different developmental levels may prove of inestimable value to educators and all others who are an intimate part of the growing child's experience: more sympathetic feeling toward child behavior, more complete understanding of it, greater direct helpfulness, and more astute ability to correct what may already have taken a wrong turn. For it is not only when the child is two but also when he is at various levels during the years of schooling that one is purblind if one sees, and so takes into account, only what the child now characteristically does. It is essential also to understand from this what he now characteristically seeks. And, incidentally, for those who have come to recognize that childhood is not just adulthood in miniature, this account of the strivings characteristic of each successive level of development contributes toward a more concrete conception of what children are like and of how they differ from adults who have, to some greater extent, brought these strivings closer to resolution, for better or for worse.

Readiness

On careful consideration of this conception of drives and developmental stages, it becomes clear that the mental-hygiene approach also adds a new proportion to the *concept of readiness*. Educators have accepted the idea that one does not impose reading, say, upon a child until he exhibits a certain readiness to read or to begin to learn to read. To do so would be to thwart his purposes and so to court evil consequences. But now there are also to be taken into account the child's strivings for trust and autonomy, and, by this age, for a sense of initiative (getting things started on his own) and for a sense of industry (sharing with others in bringing defined undertakings to completion). What role may learning to read play in relation to these?

Quite clearly the capacity to "read for himself" can fortify such sense of autonomy as he has already established, adding the amazing ability to gather meaning from the written word to the other things he can now manage on his own. In similar fashion, it can buttress his sense of initiative, since it unlocks the doors to so much new (though vicarious) experience that he can select and get under way in terms of "individual enterprise," so to speak. And bringing the task of learning to read to completion can contribute mightily to his sense of industry.

The child is not only ready to read but straining at the leash to make progress in these other ways as well—in ways that refer to his feelings toward himself as a person and in relation to other persons. When this is borne in mind, the process of learning to read can be phrased to serve all these purposes, and so contribute largely to his sense of worth in life and to his sound growth as a personality.

The "phrasing" may consist of many things—the teacher's approach to the learner, the interplay between reading and the rest of his activities, timing in relation to his developmental strivings. Should ability to learn be immediately capitalized upon, perhaps even hurrying interest a bit, because the task of learning to read will be strategic in assuring him that he is capable of the sense of industry he seeks? Or should reading perhaps be for a while postponed, so as not to crowd him before he is ready in his underlying search for security through shared purposeful activity? Similar questions are pertinent not only to the child's acquisition of other knowledge and skills but also to his participation in the different forms of group life appropriate to various stages of development, and to all other aspects of his learning experience.

A perhaps more crucial question arises where he fails to exhibit the readiness that might be anticipated of him. What does this indicate about the course of his progress in the definable steps on the way to maturity, and what can be done to help him? Its meaning may be little or much, but without understanding of its relatedness to the rest of what he does and of what his basic strivings at this period of his life are likely to be, there is no way of telling.

In this connection it is perhaps important to point out that the scope of individual differences is vastly increased when underlying emotional development is considered as well as constitutional factors, such as native endowment and the differing opportunities individuals may have had for primarily intellectual learning. For the experiences that may have affected emotional development may have been of quite a different order from those that offered opportunity for intellectual development. Even if propitious, they may have led to highly individualized styles and modes of expression.

The "Whole Child"

To the possible distinction between experimental factors influencing intellectual and emotional development some stringent qualifications must, however, be made. Because, *for those who have recognized that learning is complex, that attitudes and ways of life are learned along with knowledge and skills, the mental-hygiene approach has provided a firmer grasp on the wholeness of the person—physical, emotional, social, intellectual, spiritual—and a new conception of the integration of the personality.*

The "whole person" has seldom been conceived as a true whole. Far more frequently he has been conceived as the sum of a number of parts or aspects: the physical, plus the emotional, plus the social, plus the intellectual, plus the spiritual. Sometimes intellectual status has been seen as a resultant of the forces exerted by other "parts" of the personality: it was observed that the child's capacity to learn was crippled if he was physically under par, emotionally disturbed, short on the kind of social experience that would provide intellectual stimulation. The parts remained, though to a degree mutually interdependent.

This fractionated wholeness is probably to be attributed in some degree to the fact that the child is studied by a number of disciplines—medicine, psychology, sociology, and the like—each one of which sectors out a cluster of phenomena that are amenable to analysis by its particular measures and methods of study. Then the various findings have to be fitted together again to make the whole child, and so the whole has come to mean the sum of the parts, frequently in interaction. The parts are thus abstractions rather than realities, more the creations of available tools of study than meaningfully separate parts.

But the mental hygienists have found that the baby that is not properly loved fails to respond socially, does not develop intellectually, and is appallingly subject to all the ills that baby flesh is heir to. They have also found that how and when a baby is suckled can mean something akin to supporting love or its lack to him, so that he suffers many of the consequences of insufficient love if this part of what would ordinarily be called his physical care is infelicitous. And it would seem that with the young child it can also happen that if the intellectual environment is not stimulating in terms of his strivings, he becomes physically and socially apathetic.

Impressive studies have been made of bodily changes under strong emotional stress, and other studies are now under way on the relationship between certain bodily diseases and the prevailing "frames of mind" frequently associated with them. How accident-proneness may derive from emotional cravings has already been noted. And it is by now clinically established that no emotional disturbance is without some associated physical distress, some trouble in social relationships, some effect upon what a person thinks about, how he feels about it, what he does in consequence.

None of this is as unintelligible as it may at first seem. Almost everyone knows at first hand what happens to thought, feelings, body, and social responsiveness under the impact of some psychological shock, and that almost exactly the same symptoms follow on sudden and severe bodily injury. Almost everyone knows, too, that when he is ill it is not only in his body that he suffers, and how generally ill he can feel, and what his friends must endure, when he is "only blue." "He sipped no sup and he craved no crumb as he sighed for the love of a lady" was not phrased entirely from the lyricist's imagination.

Ego and Intellect

These are intimations only of the organic wholeness of the personality, and they offer more on the effects of the "physical," the "social," and the "emotional" upon the "intellectual" than on the integral functioning of the "intellectual" in the whole. A beginning, if only a small one, has been made at analyzing the relations between physical and emotional states. There is evidence, if only clinical, of how interests and intellectual preoccupations change with physical and emotional conditions or appropriateness of social relations. But the bearing of intellectual nurture on sound total development beyond the stage of babyhood has still to be carefully investigated.

Yet there is good reason to believe that the "mind" is not merely the pawn of other "parts" of the person, functioning less well when they are somehow out of repair, nor strategic only because information and intelligence are requisite (though not sufficient) to keeping these other "parts" in trim—by choosing foods wisely, finding and following expert medical advice, building rewarding social relations, and the like. More striking, perhaps, is the fact that certain kinds of psychotherapy, conducted through emotionally charged ideas, free the patient of both his emotional distress and its physical and social concomitants. In such instances, the "mind," with expert help versed in special techniques, is used to reconstruct emotions, and the person feels not only less troubled but physically better and easier in his dealings with his fellows as a consequence.

To previously available conceptions of the wholeness of the person—physical, emotional, social, and intellectual—the mental hygienists have thus added not only considerable evidence but, as it were, a new dimension to be plumbed. How gauge any activity in this fourfold organic way? How study it? How come to know more accurately the role of the "intellectual" in relation to all the rest?

This is one aspect of wholeness on which the mental hygienists are beginning to provide a firmer grasp. But by the notion of the ego and other parts of the personality they provide still another facet to the concept of integration. Everyone is acquainted with the person who knows something is "all right" but cannot do it, or the one who judges it a moral obligation to take some action which he either knows at once he cannot take or keeps postponing until the time for action has passed and he finds himself involved in yet another dilemma. Clearly there is lack of integration here. The mind sees, the heart falters, and the hand fails. There are all too many instances in everyday life when this happens, when judgment leads one way and inclination rides off in another. "The spirit is willing," we say "but the flesh is weak." Or we say that a person does not know what he wants. Or that his judgment is paralyzed. Or that he has no moral fiber.

Educators have attributed this to faulty integration in past learning situations. The person has learned to judge without having opportunity to carry through into action and to gain the accruing satisfactions. If judgment and inclination fail to jibe, it is probably because judgment has not been brought to bear on inclination often enough and with enough success to assure its taking precedence, postponing inclination, or denying it for the sake of foreseen desirable outcomes.

Mental hygienists offer another explanation. When a person sees what is right and wise and just to do but cannot do it, they assume that the ego—organized individual experience—is not yet strong enough to carry the day against a sense of the forbidden. Somewhere in the personality there dwells an overweening "thou shalt not" over which judgment, born of having tried this and tried that, having found success and failure, cannot prevail. Or the impulse life remains so comparatively strong that the lid must always be kept on tight. When the desired and the desirable fail to coincide, again they assume that the ego is weak, that basic drives and organic impulses have found too little opportunity for frank expression, and so have not become integrated with the organized experience of the controlling self.

They agree with the educators that the difficulty is attributable to past experience but the effective factors in this experience are somewhat differently identified. It is not merely a matter of providing opportunities for judging on one's own, coming to one's own conclusions, carrying these conclusions out, estimating the results, and reformulating judgment and action in accordance. This process is involved surely, but only to the extent that the ego is adequate to it. Otherwise the submerged "thou shalt nots" of the early years give rise to a sense of guilt when independent judgment is exercised and action fails to follow. Or, if it follows, there is too little basic satisfaction in it, too little exhilarating sense of adventure in accepting consequences and dealing with them, too much feeling of fear and doubt, no matter how "irrational." And the same holds when basic drives and impulses have not found adequate expression through socially acceptable channels.

For the baby or very young child in the home this means careful handling of necessary prohibitions, making them as far as possible reinforcements of his own dawning sense of self-governance as a socially responsible person. And it means also consistent and continuing efforts to help him find acceptable ways to give outward expression to the drives and impulses that may at first seem to him frighteningly ungovernable and "wrong." For the child in school it means at least that the teacher understand the forces in a child that bring about confusion and conflict, make good intellectual judgment unavailing, and either paralyze action or make it apparently capricious.

Should the difficulty be too great, past experiences having been too destructive to the developing ego, special therapeutic help may be required. But should the difficulty be not so great, it may be possible to reinforce the child's ego by standing behind him in his judgment; helping him to deal with the consequences; lending him assurance that consequences can be remade; letting him voice his feelings of incapacity and guilt until they, too, become elements that he can deal with; giving him confidence that his wayward, impulsive desires derive from his sound nature as a human being and can find their way into action and eventual fulfillment.

None of this is possible without the basic reliance of the modern educator—plenty of opportunity for deciding, acting, and judgment. But mere opportunity and exercise are not necessarily enough. For if satisfaction and increasing control are to result, integration in terms of ego strength must be always augmenting. And this entails emotional supports in relationship with others—for the child and young person, primarily with adults who may stand as counterparts for the once all-powerful and all-enveloping parents.

Some teachers have always been able to lend some such support through their acute, sympathetic sensitivity to people and to what children, in particular, are feeling and contending with. Now they and others less sensitive are offered a clearer comprehension of what is involved, and so a more adequate conception of their own role in furthering the kind of integration of the personality required for robust living and social effectiveness.

Social Experience and Emotional Life

The proposal that the integration of the personality is ultimately dependent upon relationships with people who may either support the developing ego or undermine it leads to another enlargement that mental hygienists may have to make to the established thinking of educators. *For those who have come to recognize that all learnings are social in nature, it stresses the effects of social experience on the emotional life:* not only ideas, concepts, knowledge, and skills derive from social experience, nor even just the insights and outlooks, attitudes and ideals that are related to these, but the very stuff of all feeling toward self, others, situations, and events. *In addition, it emphasizes the predominance of feelings toward persons in the child's experience, and the extent to which these feelings pervade his response to all new situations, whether primarily social in nature or not.* And it holds, furthermore, that the feeling life is prior and basic, playing such a fundamental role in experience that all other learnings are acquired in its terms.

It is widely granted that if the child's environment is propitious at the various stages of his development, both his feelings and his behavior will be sound, resilient, responsive. He feels good. He behaves in socially adapted ways. He sees things reasonably well as they are and has no blur of irrelevant meanings between himself and his world. The elements of propitiousness in healthy development need no recapitulation here, but it is to be carefully noted that they do not consist exclusively, or even primarily, of what the child responds to "intellectually," but rather in his relationships to other human beings—mother to begin with, and then mother and father, the rest of the immediate family, and gradually a widening circle for whom these first are for a long time (and in some instances forever) the prototypes. These relationships, which one would characterize in one context as social, are so heavily fraught with love and fear, attraction and repulsion, confidence and mistrust, freedom and dependence that in another context they may be said to be essentially emotional in quality.

To the infant, these feelings, as inchoate as they may be, together with the bodily comforts and discomforts to which they relate, probably compose all of experience, the whole of life as he knows it. The baby and very young child learn that their feelings change with the comings and goings, doings and responses of the persons who tend and succor, and these persons, together with the feelings that they engender, become the be-all and end-all of existence. They constitute the base from which all other persons and all the myriad things and events in the child's expanding world are explored. This is the self that interacts with on-coming events in experience and that endows these events with their meaning. Consequently this meaning must be largely emotional in nature, at least at the first, until other relationships and bearings are investigated and recognized. But always some of the original feeling elements remain, for, no matter how much subsequent experience remakes and builds the self, it is a primarily feeling self that is remade and into which all else is eventually incorporated and patterned.

This does not render the teacher impotent but rather imposes upon him a far more consequential role. For, with other adults in a position of guidance and authority, he is likely to be aggregated to the parental prototype. And the child, responding to the teacher's feelings, doings, helpings, prohibitions, general support, and responsiveness, remakes his prototype, or reenforces it and all his world that takes its color from it. This in itself lays upon the teacher an impressive, almost solemn, responsibility. In addition, when the teacher recognizes that all things and events are in experience colored by feelings toward persons—dear persons, close persons, loved and feared persons, parents and their counterparts—his role in choosing what shall enter the child's experience, and in contriving how it shall enter, becomes far more sensitive than he has in general hitherto recognized.

When the fact that all aspects of experience are colored by feelings toward persons is taken seriously into account, the educator's now basic principle that one "learns to do by doing," taken boldly, requires modification. That one does not learn to do by reading about or memorizing about or reciting about still stands, and that one cannot learn to do without doing. But it would still appear that, in certain circumstances, one may do and still not learn to do, or not learn with full effectiveness, and that this may, more frequently than one might think, be due to the color of feelings for and against persons that tend to permeate all things, events, and undertakings.

This has, in certain large ways, already been recognized. It has been noted, for example, that one may learn to read by reading, and still have no great love of reading, and read as little as possible. And it is an observation of everyday life that many people learn to cook by being called upon to cook, but they seldom learn to cook well and are likely to leave off cooking as soon as demanding occasion relents. The accountable factors may not always inhere in the manifest learning situation. Reading and cooking may have been learned in response to real life-situations, situations that called for cooking or for reading in a way that was comprehensible to the learner and to which he wanted to respond. Even the immediate social relationships surrounding the learning situation may have been friendly and helpful. And still the person may not have learned to read or to cook in any way that could be called fully effective.

The reasons are very likely complex. The bearing of readiness, more subtly conceived, has already been discussed. But here it is to be specially noted that for some children reading may be associated with persons outside the immediate learning situation but closely bound in the ties of emotion. In a simple instance, the parents may not be great readers or may think that reading is a waste of time or may read with great difficulty and strain. If the child's sense of autonomy is insufficient for him to take on reading on his own, for his independent purposes, and in his own way, it may remain for him always a little-prized accomplishment, a bothersome and seldom-used tool. Conversely, some beloved person may be a great reader, and in these circumstances the ability to read may be acquired under adverse conditions and still become much-cherished equipment, among the most warming and delightful of personal resources.

In brief, the child's purposes in regard to reading, as well as in regard to other things, may be far more closely related to persons strategic in his emotional life than to any more intellectual intent. He may love and want the love of a parent, and so find the parent's interests, and ennuis, the things he says and does and does not do, in all ways wonderful and to be emulated. Reading takes on emotional tone and meaning accordingly. Or his purpose may be to buttress an independence of which he does not feel too sure; he may want to "tell off" a parent who to him looms too large and dominant. Then he may seek opportunity to do precisely as the parent does not do, and reading either avidly or indifferently may offer him a means to distinguish himself from this parent, sometimes in no uncertain terms.

Toward Integration of the New Concepts

This is a brief and therefore in some respects perfunctory account of the deeper perspectives emerging in educational thought as a result of the infiltration of the mental-hygiene approach, and it provides no analysis of the reciprocal ways in which advanced educational thinking may contribute to the insights of those who are primarily versed in mental hygiene. As clearly as basic concerns in the two fields of education and mental hygiene converge, however, and much as it can be demonstrated that mutual enrichment is to be derived from joint thinking and endeavor, the resulting advances in the schools, though sure, have been largely sporadic to date, and more in the nature of adding one idea to another or superimposing one upon another than truly integrative.

There has been considerable advance, for example, in teaching teachers about child development in a way designed to assure a more understanding and therefore, presumably, more sympathetic approach to the characteristic behaviors of childhood. And in some still far too rare places an effort is being made to select teachers on the basis of personality characteristics that bode well for emotionally healthy relationships with children. These steps, though obviously partial, are also heartening, since teachers' feelings and understandings are so much the crux of the matter.

Programs, too, are undergoing change. In some schools, periods of time are set apart for freer expression—in art, play, or some like medium—of the motives that are more rigidly controlled at other times, and there are instances in which materials on the emotions, human motivation and relationships, have been introduced as a part of curriculum content. Far more widespread, and perhaps more significant, are the numerous attempts to phrase all curricular experiences in terms of the characteristic strivings of children and adolescents at the various stages of development. And perhaps most widely dispersed have been efforts to improve human relationships—pupil-teacher relations and the general group life of the school—and to provide expert services for children in need of special help with their emotional problems.

On due consideration, there need be no great surprise that advances should have been in general only tentative and fractional. The mental-hygiene approach gives rise only to a new perspective and calls for no radical departure from previous concerns and dedications; yet a new perspective is exceedingly difficult to perceive and, without long practice, almost impossible to keep constantly in focus. In addition, mental hygienists and educators tend to speak in different tongues and so find fruitful communication difficult and sometimes even painful to come by. The educator poses problems in terms that bewilder the mental hygienist, unversed in educational thought and objectives. And the mental hygienist, raised in the individual-to-individual relationships of therapy, offers explanations of behavior without being able to suggest how to act upon them in the group situations of the schools. The route to a new integration of thought is always beset with heavy weather.

It can still be said, however, that a number of schools at the growing edge are rapidly gaining momentum in incorporating what comes from this relatively new field into their own. There is acceleration in the way successful experience is capitalized upon, and educational literature reflects more and more searching analysis of all that is involved. There is every indication of the school's increasing concern to use to the fullest every available lead to providing for the healthy development of the whole person.

The School's Role in Personality Development

In 1948, there were 27,134,126 children in the elementary and secondary schools, 24,036,505 of them in public schools, 309,984 in private schools, 2,787,637 in parochial schools. What are the school's potentialities for furthering the healthy personality development of all these children, and what its limitations? What is its role in relation to other influences in the life of the child? What is its special function?

If it were true, for example, that the personality is set in the very early years of life, the school would be powerless in relation to it. But whereas there is much evidence to the effect that the very early years are of major importance, there is also evidence that crucial phases of development occur during the years that follow.

At about the beginning of his school life the child either develops a sense of competence to bring defined tasks to completion or falls into a prevailing mood of incompetence and inferiority in relation to what confronts him. Later, he either identifies himself as a person, a prospective husband or wife, a worker in one or another line of endeavor, or remains always uncertain as to his place in the scheme of things and confused a to his role. In the latter years of his schooling he is at an age when h learns to give and share love in a characteristically adult way, or els remains an isolate, in a world unpopulated by other warm human beings

In this development sequence the school surely has opportunity to in fluence personality in vastly significant ways, and there are many wh believe that in contemporary society these steps in growth can be successfully negotiated only through propitious school experience. It is perhaps needless to point out that school experience can also either enhance or undermine whatever basic sense of trust, of independence, and of initiative the child brings with him from his earlier life at home.

Moreover, if the school's major function, in contradistinction to that of other institutions, is taken to be that of enabling the young to understand their world and to come creatively to grips with it, then the school has a role which is not only strategic but indispensable in the development of the healthy personality. For without some such capacity, growing appropriately through the years, both child and man are the butts of whatever befalls them rather than always more surely the masters of their experience. Without sound personality, mere intellectual understanding is of small avail, but when increasing understanding and skill are part and parcel of well-rounded growth they contribute mightily to robust feelings about self, others, and the manageability of oncoming events.

All this does not mean that the school operates either without limitations in relation to healthy personality development or in a vacuum. By the time the child comes to school he may already be so emotionally crippled that, without special therapeutic help, he is unable to grow through even the best-contrived of educational experience. Moreover, along with other institutions and agencies striving to contribute ever more effectively to the child's healthy, happy, and responsible living, the school is hampered by still inadequate information about the processes of human development. The field is new, and much remains to be fathomed. Theories of learning so far laid down are difficult to bring into harmony with emerging theories of dynamic psychology.

But it is not only other agencies with consonant aims in relation to healthy personality development that influence the growing child; school, other agencies, and child function in a society and a culture that profoundly affect them all in haphazard ways. For example, much attention has been called to the conflict between the democratic tradition to which the school is dedicated and certain antidemocratic practices and attitudes to which it is often prone; e.g., authoritarianism in human relations, competitiveness rather than cooperation in the classroom and on the playground, racial segregation, and other less tangible forms of intergroup discrimination. This last includes an apparently widespread rejection, so taken for granted as to have been overlooked until recently highlighted, of children of low socioeconomic status, and an almost wholesale oblivion to what the school may mean to them and to what they may require of it.

In all this the school only reflects contradictions in the culture. Whether or not such contradictions, purely in and of themselves, are deleterious to healthy personality development is difficult to say, in view of the fact that apparently all cultures are similarly confused and conflicted. There is some evidence that such damage as there may be to the personality varies with the age at which the conflict is encountered and the circumstances of the encounter.

Far more certain is the fact that the antidemocratic end of each conflict is harmful to personality; in this culture, democracy and healthy personality development go hand in hand, democracy providing by definition the most favorable conditions for wholesome living, and in turn requiring well-developed personalities for its proper functioning. In as far as the school can select and choose among the cultural influences it brings to bear upon the child, it therefore filters out, as far as possible, those contradictory to the democratic tradition, just as it attempts to filter out all other influences deleterious to health and wholesomeness.

Some Pertinent Curriculum Considerations

Traditionally the curriculum has been identified with the "course of study," and has consisted of an enumeration of the topics to be covered in the various conventional subject-matter fields. More recently, it has come to be conceived as the sum total of the pupil's experience in the school. This change has resulted from increasing concern with the whole personality and from a new view of learning, by which purposes, feelings, attitudes, ways of life, and personal dedications are seen to be learned as well as subject matter, and by which it is recognized that subject matter is not and cannot be learned without at the same time learning attitudes and ways of life.

Curriculum Planning

Wise selection of experiences appropriate to developing personalities is seemingly less difficult at the early-childhood level than in the succeeding years of schooling. The younger child reveals himself more readily, the range of his abilities is narrower, it is comparatively easy to set a stage richly for his growth. By the time he reaches the intermediate grades he retreats from ready self-revelation to adults, and from this time till the end of his schooling the whole world of experience and knowledge, almost infinitely varied, is in some form accessible to him. How to select, arrange, and contrive successive experiences of optimum educational value remains a problem widely studied but still unsolved.

Concern with the pupil's purposes and interests was at one time interpreted to mean a kind of *laissez faire* of pupil inclination, with a minimum of adult direction. As the idea took hold that desires and inclinations are also learned in response to social situations, adult responsibility for shaping learning experiences came again to the fore, and curriculum makers looked to social demands upon the individual as a source from which to draw curriculum content. More recently there have been repeated attempts to see pupil responsiveness and social demands bifocally, as it were, since in the deepest view human inclination and its social organization cannot be so totally disparate.

From the standpoint of healthy personality development, the question of who selects and regulates the child's experience—the child himself or the controlling adult—is phrased in terms of requirements for freedom and self-regulation, on the one hand, and for outwardly imposed limits on the other. On closer scrutiny, it would appear that the educators' approach to this question and the mental hygienists' refer to different aspects of the same thing, for the culture always poses limits and provides molds through which inchoate primitive inclination must express itself. Nevertheless, the teacher concerned with healthy development is not likely to fare well on the sociological phrasing alone. His impact in his relationships with his pupils is psychological in nature, and his shrewd estimate of required freedoms and limits in each particular situation would seem to be indispensable.

Practically speaking, experimental curriculum work is now based on pupil-teacher planning, the teacher keeping his eye on the so-called "functional areas of living" and on phrasing experiences in terms of the characteristic strivings of pupils at their various stages of development. These "functional areas" have been variously defined ordinarily, they include family living and other personal relationships, civic responsibility, vocational participation, leisure-time activities, maintenance of health—and a philosophy of life pertinent to all these.

In part because the "functional areas" are indeed life areas and so not reducible to facile schematization, and in part because curriculum planning outside the conventional grooves beyond the elementary grades is still problematical, there remain many unresolved issues in each of these areas. As things now stand, these are not usually stated in terms of alternative effects on personality development, but this does not mean that such considerations are not inherent in them or are not being increasingly taken into account.

To this there is perhaps one major exception: in the area of family living and personal relationships (sometimes extended to include intergroup relations and even all human relations) recent innovations propose the inclusion of material on the dynamics of behavior in curriculum content—the amount, nature, and relationship to other curricular experiences varying from one experimental situation to another. Such innovations pose a peculiar dilemma to educators concerned with sound social and emotional growth. On the one hand, the schools are dedicated to progressive intellectualization of all facets of pupils' experience, and surely emotions and relationships with people loom large among these. On the other, there is profound and probably well-based skepticism about the degree to which intellectual understanding about emotions leads to better emotional adjustment, and considerable concern that here a little learning may prove indeed a dangerous thing. The answer is thought by some to lie in how closely "learning about" is related to "living through," and in the deftness and insightfulness of teachers.

The Question of Religious Instruction

Another curriculum issue is now becoming a matter of some public controversy. There is universal agreement that an emerging philosophy of life is both a sign of and a requisite for healthy personality development, and that help in building this philosophy and giving it intellectual formulation is a responsibility of the schools. Until recently, the Constitutional principle of separation of Church and State has been taken as a definitive bar to stating a philosophy of life in religious terms in the public schools. Now there is a considerable body of thought demanding a reinterpretation of this principle to permit either religious instruction in the schools or what has come to be called "released" or "dismissed" time from school for religious instruction.

Proponents of this idea stress widely held convictions concerning the role of religion in life and in healthy personality development, and consequently regard the making of some provision for religious instruction as a responsibility of the public schools.

Opponents counter with one or another of two main types of objections. First, regarding "released" time and even "dismissed" time, some opponents call attention to the fact that these measures are all too likely to give rise to divisive distinctions among children of different religious groups, and between these and children from families without religious affiliation—distinctions which, though deplorable, are unfortunately real, and are thought by many to affect some of the very values sought in religious instruction. Second, regarding religious instruction in public schools, an opposing point of view holds that the free play of the intelligence is the school's major contribution both to the maintenance of democracy and to the development of healthy personality, and that the time is still far in the distance when, in the school situation, the free play of intelligence can be brought to bear on matters of faith without seriously harmful effects.

Many other considerations are stated both in favor of and against involving the schools in religious instruction, but these are the main lines of thought that relate specifically to healthy personality development.

The Expressive Arts

Before turning from curriculum content to methods of evaluating curricular experience, the role of the expressive arts in education and healthy personality development is perhaps worthy of some special consideration. This is because the expressive arts have been heavily leaned upon in some places to provide outlet for emotions quite rigidly controlled in all other parts of school life. But even in those places where it is recognized that emotions can at no time be strained out of ongoing experience, the arts are used for the expression, objectification, and clarification of emotions, sometimes angry and destructive, that can find no other ready and socially acceptable outlet, and which, left unexpressed, are known to lead to some greater or less degree of emotional ill health. They are used also for the intensification and deepening of the whole emotional life. Sometimes art products serve the insightful as a means of learning about pupils' otherwise unrevealed feelings and even about the progress of their development.

But whereas it is generally recognized that drawing, painting, rhythms, and the like are a spontaneous and fruitful part of all healthy young children's activity, occasionally educators are now asking whether some older children, in accordance with their individual differences, may not find better media for artistry and creative expression in scientific experimentation, or in cooking, or in relationships with people than in any of the more conventional art forms. This leads directly to another line of thought which holds that all growth-producing learning is creative in nature, and this to still another to the effect that true adult creativity in all spheres of life can derive only from having negotiated successfully all the several developmental stages.

Evaluation

Many of the moot questions in curriculum construction would long since have been resolved were available methods of evaluation equal to determining outcomes in the total personality. Then it would have been possible to put any given proposal for achieving favorable goals in child development to the test. But the growth process is not easily amenable to statistical measurement because it is inherently irreducible to discrete units. Even the observation of isolated behaviors has its limitations because, in the sense of dynamic psychology, it is impossible to interpret any given bit of behavior except in the context of the whole.

In recognition of such difficulties, new methods of appraisal—like anecdotal records and behavior journals, a wide variety of projective techniques, and some sociometric devices—are finding increasing favor. Here the objection has often been raised that the subjective factor is so great as to render such methods no better than clinical observation in evaluating the relative success or failure of any given educational means for effecting change in feeling or in orientation toward self and others. Countering this, there is widespread opinion to the effect that to scorn the clinical is to reject the one appropriate methodology of appraisal now available in this area.

Recently a question has been raised concerning the effects upon children of constant and intensive use of evaluation in relation to all phases and aspects of school experience. Whereas the intention is to evaluate what is done in the school, the outcomes appraised lie in the behavior of the pupil. According to this point of view, he is therefore likely to feel himself under constant scrutiny, which to him may seem more unrelenting and critical than enlightening and helpful. Even when, as is ever more usual, he participates in the appraisal, he asks himself how he is doing, so to say, more frequently and persistently than is perhaps healthy. In addition, his teacher may sometimes unintentionally make him feel more threatened than guided, with inevitable repercussions on the child. This may all be particularly bad for the child who comes from a home where parents are preoccupied with the significance of his every move.

Human Relations in the School

In school as at home and elsewhere, the quality of human relations is preponderant among all factors in furthering healthy personality development, and this quality is directly related to emotional stability and warm feelings toward others. Without stability and warmth on the part of teachers, supervisors, and administrators, knowledge about, and machinery for, improving human relations rest on a shaky foundation.

While emphasizing the importance of warmth, outgoingness, and spontaneity in the teacher's relationship with his pupils, it is perhaps pertinent to call attention to what, from the mental-hygiene point of view, is conceived to be his essential role. His is not primarily the role of mothering the child in an intimate, dependent relationship that gives large play to immediate gratification of impulse. Rather, he strengthens the child in his efforts to meet the social demands properly made upon him and helps him find socially acceptable outlets for his feelings. Important among these demands and outlets are his relationships with other children and adults. The teacher properly helps him to cope with others, their feelings toward him, and his toward them. Among the teacher's chief means toward this end are his own basic acceptance of the child and the help he extends to him in attaining status in his group.

Sociometric techniques are a recently developed device intended to reveal the position of each child in a group in terms of the individuals he either seeks out or expresses a desire to be with, and the individuals who either tacitly or explicitly seek him. The teacher uses this information to surround each pupil as far as possible with others who accept him. There are those who doubt that such contrived experience of acceptance does in fact build basic confidence, or that status so acquired is felt in succeeding group situations. Evidence is still being sought. Still others question the advisability of so manipulating group situations, or even the necessity for it, when the group is small enough and fluid enough for the child to find his own way to status within it.

Concern with the contribution of group life to personality has also given rise to a movement for the study of group dynamics. Thus far, this movement has contributed a variety of techniques designed to provide greater opportunity for the play of each individual's personality in the group situation. In addition, it has focused attention on an important area of investigation in social psychology closely relevant to the school's concerns.

The pupil's opportunity to find and feel status is perhaps most profoundly affected by the size of his class, the basis on which he has been assigned to it, and the number and intensity of invidious group distinctions reflected in the school. Classes are often so large that pupils can seldom even be perceived as individuals, still less helped to achieve a sense of self-worth in their midst. In addition, overlarge classes tempt to mass methods and much ordering about. Homogeneous grouping, originally designed to protect children from unfair competition, has created at least as many problems as it has solved, largely by giving rise to a kind of invidious distinction. The sense of discouragement, failure, and unworthiness which so frequently befalls children who find themselves in groups designated "opportunity," who are counseled to take vocational rather than academic courses, or who discover that they are in the "slow" reading group in first grade has been well established. Invidious distinctions that haunt the child outside of school as well as within—discrimination on the basis of color, religious affiliation, national background, socioeconomic status—are probably even more destructive, and all too frequently the one kind of "setting aside" reenforces the other.

In effect, the whole of school organization is involved in providing the kind of atmosphere in which good human relations flourish. Teachers subject to the indignities of authoritarian administration and the harassments of unrealistic levels of attainment to which every child must be pushed, inadequate materials and equipment, too many petty clerical details, and the like, are scarcely in an appropriate frame of mind for sensitive responsiveness. In such circumstances as these, pupils inevitably suffer from mounting irritabilities. Fortunately, more and more administrators over the country are devoting their best thought and the largest part of their energies to making their schools happy places in which to live.

Guidance

The preceding discussion of the curriculum and of human relations in the school should make clear how deeply and widely the notion of guidance pervades all aspects of planning in the school concerned with providing optimum conditions for healthy personality development.

But if the younger child ordinarily finds with his teacher the individual relationship he requires, the older child, confronted with an increasing number of adults, a widening world of experience, and more and more important decisions to make, normally seeks and finds some grown person with whom he establishes a relationship of special confidence. At adolescence, too, the boy and girl turn more to people beyond the family for affection, sympathetic interests, and models of what they would like to become.

Partly in response to this, partly because so many schools cannot provide individual attention in the midst of their regular activities, and partly because the conduct of individual relationships with some youngsters on some of their problems requires special training and equipment, expert guidance workers with varying specialties are being added to the staffs of more and more schools.

The vocational counselor has at his fingertips the information required for making a vocational choice, is expert in the use of vocational interest and aptitude tests, knows about the role of work and work experience in developing healthy personality, and about where in the community such experience can be gained. The educational counselor is also expert in tests and measures, usually of the kind designed to identify academic capacities and talents, and is equipped to help youngsters plan and find the schooling that will be most productive for them. The school social worker brings special insights into human relations to bear on many kinds of problems and is, in addition, well informed on community resources.

From the standpoint of healthy personality development, the prime requisites for every guidance worker are that he be adept at using individual relationships with youngsters in ways that free rather than bind, that he be sufficiently perspicacious about the dynamics of personality to identify the problems brought to him in their fullness, and that he be equipped to help youngsters deal with their individual problems with maximum effectiveness.

But neither guidance workers themselves nor the requirements for healthy personality development would have what has come to be known as "the guidance point of view" confined to individual relationships in some sequestered corner of the school. Case conferences in which guidance counselor, social worker, doctor, nurse, and all those who know a pupil pool their insight with his teachers have been one device by which the insights of each have been shared with all, and children have come to be known not only as individual personalities but as functioning wholes.

Programs for Children with Physical and Mental Limitations

The fact that schools in general are becoming increasingly sensitive to the individuality of pupils and to the wholeness of their functioning is evidenced in part by the great expansion, during the past decade, of programs of "special education" for "exceptional children"—all those whose physical, mental, or emotional characteristics are so deviant as to make it impossible for them to profit to the full from the regular school program unadapted to their special requirements. Despite this development, the

Office of Education, Federal Security Agency, estimates that not more than 15 or 20 per cent of the children so handicapped are getting the special help they need in schools.

Children with physical and mental limitations are not a breed apart; they develop as all children do, and they respond similarly to conditions favorable and unfavorable to healthy growth. Yet their education in some cases calls for something in addition to regular schoolwork (e.g., speech or lip reading for the deaf, or Braille and opportunity to learn to care for themselves and to become acquainted with common objects by touch for the blind), and in other cases for something different, such as the adaptation of the curriculum, for the mentally retarded. Without a specially adapted curriculum, children with I.Q.s below 70 or 75 are subjected to constant failure and humiliation, which are as destructive for them as for any child, and without special learnings the blind and the deaf are cut off from communication with their fellows, and so from the association on which all healthy social and emotional growth depends. Provision for the crippled child is different in nature but it, too, looks toward facilitating his normal association with others in the group life of the school.

These adaptations and others are in essence applications of the principle that good education always takes full account of individual differences and helps each individual to understand his world and to come effectively to cope with it. In the case of children with severe physical or mental limitations, this calls for special facilities, special learning materials, special flexibility in the school program and routine. Perhaps most particularly, it calls for teachers who have not only acquired ability in imparting the particular skills needed by the deaf and the blind, or in applying procedures found most helpful with cerebral palsied or epileptic children, or in using any other technology specially devised for dealing with one or another handicap, but who have, in addition, sympathetic and insightful understanding of the social and emotional problems confronting the child who is for any reason impeded in associating freely in all types of activities with his peers. The impediment may be primarily in the nature of the child's disability or primarily in the unreasonable rejection he meets because of it. In either case, the teacher, who comes into the child's orbit strategically at the time he is ready to bring defined cooperative tasks to completion and remains an important figure while he identifies his role in life and finds his adult emotional orientations in it, deals always with the child's feelings about himself in relation to others. On the way he helps the child to feel in his group, and on the feelings he helps the group develop toward the child may well depend the child's ultimate capacity to achieve healthy and abundant living despite the limitations his disability imposes upon him.

School, Community, and Home

The school is sometimes seen as the best place for rendering services known to be needed by all children for the simple and expedient reason that all the children are there. When services are introduced for this reason alone, without effort to integrate the service with the ongoing educational program, it is somewhat as though the pupils were seen as a kind of "captive audience" and the school as a mere building to enclose them. Fortunately, however, always greater efforts are now characteristic of both schools and the personnel of special services to make the whole of the child's life in school an integrated experience.

School health examinations, for example, are less and less often isolated experiences, sometimes a little frightening, without relationship to anything that comes before or after in the school milieu. More often they are incidents in the whole functional area of health education to which not only many subject matters but the whole design of school living contribute. The school doctor or nurse, if only part time, and no matter by whom employed, functions as a regular member of the school staff, participating in case conferences and contributing the insights derived from his or her particular training. In circumstances like these, the advantages of having health services as an integral part of the school are clear.

There are those who point out, however, that, in their view at least, it is fallacious to interpret the conception of the school community to mean that at best the school reproduces in miniature all the services and activities of the community outside. The community of the school has its own function. Through it pupils learn to use all social institutions effectively and to participate in them creatively. And, in fact, this is what most schools attempt to do in the case of most social institutions and community agencies. The practice of introducing pupils to the community as a regular part of schoolwork is increasing the community's economic life; its health, welfare, and cultural institutions, and the religious, social, and cultural groups that make it up.

By later adolescence, young people feel that they can move toward adult status only if they are taken seriously in the community and are allowed after some fashion to participate responsibly in its affairs. The educational problem then becomes one of finding real opportunities for this group to do real community work where their services will be regarded neither with condescension nor sentimentality and they may grow in the spirit of community service. Youth of low socioeconomic status are thrust into adulthood by the necessity to work, but usually find themselves in the kind of job that offers little or no life enrichment and so confront school and community with another kind of problem.

All this would seem to call for strengthening the means by which school and other community agencies—such as museums, libraries, churches, health and welfare services—interested in children and youth now plan together and learn from one another, and for some special attention focusing on how the pattern of community services provides for healthy personality development.

Since the young child looks both to parent and to teacher for help in coping with the problems of expressing himself and relating himself to others characteristic of his particular stage of development, it is clear that communication between home and school should be frequent, easy, and gauged to assure a certain consistency in the demands made upon him. As the child grows older, no longer needs so much consistency in his experience, and begins to take satisfaction in managing his own affairs independently, some schools have found it advisable to discontinue taking his parents in on what he does at school.

To the kind of communication between home and school required for healthy personality development there are a number of obstacles, perhaps chief among which is lack of understanding of the fact that parents and teachers properly play different roles in the lives of children, both of them essential. This leads to occasional usurping of roles, and may even contribute to certain mutual jealousies and hostilities that all too frequently grow up in any case.

There are many open questions as to how this communication should take place and exactly what it should be about. Group conferences, individual parent-teacher interviews, home visits, letters, and various new-form report cards all are being used; obviously some of these must be supplemented by others for two-way communication. The content of communication for the purposes here proposed is never confined to a report of progress in the acquisition of knowledge and skills, and at its best varies with the parent, the teacher, and the prevailing relationship between them.

The home visit and individual parent-teacher conference also provide means by which the school may learn about the child's family and its cultural patterns. This knowledge may save the school from making a number of mistakes, both in interpreting the child's behavior and in guiding him.

In as far as home-school communication proves helpful to the parent in understanding his child and his own parental relationships, there is a certain amount of parent education implicit in it, whether called by this name or not. Because the fully trained teacher has a certain professional understanding of child development and human relations, there seems every reason for him to share with other professional people similarly equipped in helping the parents who turn to them. It has been found, however, that not every good teacher is good at parent education, and that frequently some special training for such work is advisable.

When Schooling Begins and Ends

Most children enter school at the conventional age of six, which approximates the time at which most of them are ready to gain a sense of competence in bringing shared tasks to completion and to assume some responsibility for their behavior. Considerably before this, however, the exuberant imagination and bursting curiosity of many youngsters have exhausted the resources their homes offer them for manipulation of the physical environment and exploration of relationships with people. In many of these instances, depending on home and family conditions, nursery school or kindergarten seem to be indicated as soon as the child is able to communicate his wishes and has developed a sufficiently deep sense of security and individuality. This means as early as about three years for some and later than five for others. All this points to the necessity for making nursery schools and kindergartens far more widely available, as well as for considerable flexibility in policies on age of admission.

The fact that the school contributes richly to the healthy personality development of younger children is widely accepted; there is every reason to believe that it can make a similar contribution at least throughout adolescence. Gradually, the statutory school-leaving age has been rising from fourteen to sixteen, and in some states it is now eighteen. Yet half of the students who enter high school drop out before graduation.

Many reasons and causes have been identified. Fewer than one might anticipate leave school because their earnings are urgently needed, but for many families the costs of even free public education are high—additional clothing, transportation, books, fees for student activities, and the like. The impossibility of going to college and the unlikelihood, in some communities, of finding a better job on the basis of longer schooling lessen incentive; moreover, 60 per cent of the jobs in the United States do not require either college education or long vocational training. The reasons most frequently given by the dropouts themselves reflect school failure and school misery and seem to point in the main to the fact that the school does not provide experience of value to them.

From other sources comes evidence to indicate that, as one student of the problem has put it, the term "squeeze-out's" is more apt. A large percentage come from backgrounds which leave them without the experience in abstract thought required for good showing on intelligence tests; they are not academically minded; their speech, clothing, and habits deviate from those of the middle income groups conventionally accepted as standard by the school. Early in their school careers they are segregated in large numbers into "opportunity groups," they fail, they "don't fit," and they feel it.

In as far as causes are sheerly economic, various ways out are being sought and some are being found. From the viewpoint of the school's responsibility, there is also clearly much need for seeking of ways by which children of one background may be equally valued with those of another; of curricular experiences designed less for college or vocation and more to give adolescents like these a sense of worth-while activity, interest, and achievement; of far more individual attention than has been the lot of those many who have dropped out entirely without consultation and advice. Ways are being sought, too, to provide overlapping of school and job. Supervised work experience as a part of the school program, periods of work alternating with periods of schooling, and continuation school for fully employed young workers are some of the directions in which various school programs are experimenting.

Training Teachers and Providing Schools

The school can contribute fully to the healthy personality development of its pupils only if teachers genuinely like and accept children, like the teaching relationship, and are equipped to guide and support the young as they grow and learn. All this calls for many new facets in the conventional forms of teacher selection and training.

For too long the achievement of certain academic standards has been the main, if not the sole, criterion for admission to most teacher-training institutions, with little or no assessment of the candidate's reasons for wanting to teach, emotional orientations toward children, or general stability of personality. "Character," another common criterion for admission, refers in general to dependability, freedom from "bad habits," and good repute among certain members of the community, rather than to any more specific qualifications for teaching.

But already there is some experimentation looking toward emphasis upon the special qualities and characteristics of personality that bode well for future pupils. The means by which the likely are sorted from the unlikely are still in the experimental stage; sometimes they consist of a series of interviews skillfully conducted, sometimes interviews are based on a biography or personal case history, sometimes a variety of projective techniques are used. Occasionally a candidate is admitted on condition of securing some therapeutic help in the course of training.

Training itself is again still largely experimental, with much effort devoted to finding ways by which knowledge of child development, the processes of learning and growing, dynamic psychology, and the factors that influence personality development may become something far more vital than intellectual understandings alone. Participation in nursery schools and in work with older children and young people, keeping behavior journals, making case histories, participation in interdisciplinary case conferences are on a par with courses and study, complementing rather than supplementing them.

In some places it is also thought advisable to help students cultivate adult interests beyond those they have in children, growth, learning, and, for secondary teachers, a particular "subject-matter area"—this for the sake of the linkages that are thought to develop between children's interests and the heartfelt pursuits of adults around them, the student himself, and his own further growth as a person. Generally speaking, work in the creative arts is highly esteemed for these purposes.

In some quarters it is thought that such selection and training will contribute to the solution of the problem of recruitment of teachers for the elementary grades. Poor salaries, limited community status, work under difficult conditions and often rigid supervision are among the major factors usually identified. But the argument runs that if teachers are selected because of their feeling for children and the teaching relationship, and are so educated as to become interesting people in their own right as well as more fully expert in guiding the growth and learning of children, their status will begin to rise, and a break will have been made in an erstwhile vicious circle.

No report on the schools at this time can fail to call attention, however briefly, to the inadequacy with which they are supported and the inequality in educational opportunity in different parts of the country. Larger numbers of children than ever to be schooled, lag in school building programs, higher salaries, and rising costs combine with a degree of public indifference to make money short everywhere for what the schools might do for children.

But while the average per-pupil expenditure is over $200 in fifteen states, it is less than $100 in four. One reason for this is the disproportionately large number of children to be schooled in some states—states which tend to have less than average per capita income. The results of inequality of educational opportunity show up in such statistics as those on the percentage of dropouts and the number of young men classified as educationally deficient when called up for military duty.

From the point of view of what the schools can contribute to soundness of personality, personal happiness, and responsible citizenship, the number of other ways in which inadequate support and inadequate opportunity show up in the lives of individuals and the life of the nation must be numerous and pervasive, though incalculable. Every consideration points in the direction of providing not only adequate but equal educational opportunity for all children of school age.

✧ XII ✧

Leisure-time Services

WHAT shall we do? What can we do that's fun? These often-repeated questions of children and youth have been answered by a great outpouring of goods and services by the entertainment industry (nearly the largest industry in the United States), by private philanthropy, and by various public bodies: books and magazines (comics included), music, and art; radio, television, movies, and the theater; dance halls and dance concerts and here and there some square dancing; places to swim and places to picnic; playgrounds and stadiums and all that's athletic; clubs and Y's and settlement houses; and so on and on, seemingly without end. The size of the enterprise testifies to the vastness of our economic resources and the number of our leisure-time hours.

In view of the variety of the endeavors, this brief review of the contribution that leisure-time facilities and services may make to the healthy development of personality is of necessity highly selective and gives scant attention to the great opportunities for promoting health and happiness that libraries, children's museums, art centers, and so on, afford. It can only mention parks and bathing beaches and other facilities in which children can play in their own way, unsupervised by professional adults. It deals not at all with commercial entertainment, or with those instances of it that are thought or known to be detrimental to children and young people. Nor must it be forgotten that organized recreation constitutes only a small segment of children's play, and no segment at all of the play of many children. The values to be derived from play are not to be come by solely through the activities with which organized recreation is chiefly concerned.

Leisure, Recreation, and Play

Leisure time is ordinarily bracketed in the mind with recreation, and recreation with play. Yet the babe who plays can scarcely be said to be doing so in his leisure, or even for the sake of recreation, and the same holds for the "play" of the major-league ball team on the diamond. Food

273

preparation is work for the cook and recreation for the gourmet; it is play for neither. The hobbyist "labors" far into the night.

The marking off of all the waking time of life into the two categories of labor and leisure would seem to derive, at least in part, from the cultural tradition and from the minute division of labor that has progressed with civilization. Primitive peoples engage in a variety of activities, most of them devoted to meeting survival needs, others to ceremonial, artistry, the embellishment and enhancement of the routine and everyday. But these are felt as kinds of things men do and children learn to do; they are not classified as breadwinning, on the one hand, or refreshing and regenerating, on the other. There is nothing to indicate that the happy hunting grounds would be less happy if the game were needed by the tribe for food.

The tradition in which the young now grow up distinguishes sharply between work and not-work. Work, in general, is that which one is required to do to earn one's livelihood (or to make that contribution which entitles one to consume a share of the world's goods). It is a requirement, and in most instances it is supposed to be arduous and distasteful. In the Garden of Eden, it was meted out as punishment. In a modern, mechanized, industrialized civilization, much of it is deadeningly monotonous, in itself meaningless, performed for the sake of livelihood. Some of it is performed under conditions and for wages that exploit and demean.

To compensate, there is leisure, when one may do as one wills—highly prized but to a degree suspect, for not-work may also be defined as idleness, and the devil, it is said, makes work for idle hands. The founders of an eighteenth-century American college directed: "The students shall be indulged with nothing which the world calls play. Let this rule be observed with the strictest nicety, for those who play when they are young will play when they are old." Nowadays, in the schools and elsewhere, there is "education for the *worthy* use of leisure time."

Thus the young grow up in an atmosphere in which work is equated with drudgery, but honorific; and leisure is equated with release, but suspect. And the situation is still worse confused by the fact that, until very recently, the high dignity of labor notwithstanding, leisure pursuits were considered truly worthy only if they simulated those of the erstwhile "gentleman of leisure," usually an interest in art or the humanities.

These observations on pervasive attitudes toward labor and leisure in the workaday life of adults would be of little relevance did they not condition and to a degree confuse thinking about the play and leisure-time activities of the young.

Play has, for the most part, come into its own and is almost universally recognized as a necessity for the good life for children and grown people alike. Indeed, there is reason to believe that knowledge of the value of play for children has long been a part of the wisdom of the people: "All work and no play makes Jack a dull boy." And now, to be worthy, the pursuits of leisure may take many forms and need not necessarily ape the activities of the gentleman of leisure, who lived upon the labor of others.

Yet, as work is here conceived—the bringing of defined tasks to completion, alone or in cooperation with others, with a sense of the tasks' bearing and relevance—not all the pursuits of leisure can be classified as play. Many of them could, and some of them do, classify as labor if and when they or their performance is conditioned by compulsions or restraints analogous to those found on the job. They become leisure-time pursuits solely by dint of being carried on outside of job time, by choice, solely for the joy there is in them—whether this be the joy of variety in experience, of release, of creativity, or achievement. Play, by contrast, is without defined ends in view; it may provide variety, release, even opportunity for creativity, but he who plays is not concerned with achievement. This is an important distinction in a culture such as ours, in which the pressures of achievement are so strong. It serves also to reduce the confusion about the play of the babe, for whom "leisure" is meaningless; the "play" which is part of "work" in schools; the "work" and achievement which characterize so many of the chosen leisure-time activities of both school children and grown people.

Provision for the pursuits of leisure, both achievement-oriented and play-oriented, becomes necessary in an urban-centered, industrial society where opportunities for spontaneous activity on the part of children and young people are limited, the environment in and of itself does not prove stimulating, and there are dangers of exploitation to be avoided in leisure as well as in labor. Schools, health-education programs, church-sponsored enterprises of many kinds, and a sector of the social-work field are all concerned, as well as a growing professional field devoted to recreational activities exclusively.

The wider latitude of choice inherent in leisure-time activities and the opportunity this choice provides for the more direct expression of drives and purposes endow these activities with a variety of potentials for contributing to healthy personality development. The free selection of goals and of means to their achievement, participation in spontaneous activities with no conscious ends in view, time in which to draw together the meaning of experience and "invite the soul" all represent facets of life necessary to a sense of well-being and the development of a personal philosophy, however ill articulated, without which the individual is rudderless and feels himself at sea. In this sense, they are creative. They are recreative as well when the work life is routine, imposes many restraints, offers too few opportunities for choice. And always they provide for the spontaneous, the unplanned, which, by definition, is precluded by work.

Some Psychological Considerations

Psychologists have found that play is a very different thing for children from what is commonly supposed, and that it is not the same thing for children as for adults. In play, the adult, as Erikson puts it, "steps sideward into another reality. The playing child advances forward to new stages of mastery." [1] In this conception of the role of play there are profound implications for recreation workers and for all who would provide for children and youth constructive activities for leisure time.

A child's play begins with, and centers on, his own body. It consists first of exploring, by repetition, sensual perceptions, kinesthetic sensations, and vocalizations. The child next moves on to available things and persons, touching, tasting, again exploring his narrow world.

Manageable toys become his next play objects. Through them he learns the hard lesson that the world of things has laws. They may resist management. They may break. Or they may be confiscated by adults or stronger children. These may be emotionally disastrous events if too often repeated. For then the child is deprived of the pleasure of mastery and of the prestige that accompanies it, of an opportunity to conquer, through imagined repetitions, his past injuries.

By the nursery-school years, playfulness reaches into the world shared with others. Here the child learns what kind of activities must be reserved for phantasy or solitary indulgence, what must be reserved for toys and small objects, and what can be shared with others or even forced upon them. As this is learned, each sphere is endowed with its own sense of reality and mastery. In later life, this provides the individual with diverse means of recreation: through solitary play, through play with objects, and through play with other human beings. All are needed for a rounded life.

"The playing child advances to new stages of mastery." He masters

[1] Erik Erikson, *Childhood and Society,* W. W. Norton & Company, New York, 1950, p. 194.

toys and people and his own fears. He masters his feelings about some of life's inequalities by playing mother and doctor and school. As a four-year-old, he tries out being a policeman, a driver of cars, a parent; as an adolescent, he tries out, in phantasy and in company with others, all the things he might be or do or own.

By school age, he wants new and real worlds to conquer. What adults call work becomes important to him. He may even think of it as work as long as it is confined to school, but the aim is the same when he "plays" at home or with his Scout troop at building houses and furniture.

The various uses of play that appear in the developmental stages are continued throughout life as recreation. There is recreation that involves the pleasures of sensual perceptions, kinesthetic sensations, and vocalizations. There is recreation that is a means of learning that life has rules. There is recreation through which we give back the blows we have received in real life or work out other aggressions. There is recreation through which cooperation with others is learned and practiced, and recreation that permits us to go off alone. And there is recreation that is work, that carries with it the joys of real accomplishment.

All these things workers in recreation and informal education know, and so does the recreation industry. The task for the profession is to develop the implications of this knowledge more fully so that it can be translated into principles of practice that can be taught and used.

Some Alternative Emphases

Viewing the trends in the way in which the increasing numbers of leisure-time hours are spent by children and adults alike, many thoughtful observers have deplored an apparent tendency toward more and more spectatorship, less and less active participation, whether in play and sport, the making and creating of satisfying things, art or music. These observers are of the well-grounded opinion that the development of the personality is based upon activity, doing and undergoing, trying, succeeding, failing, and growing in the process. Everyone would agree that watching baseball is very different from playing baseball. From the point of view of those who deplore spectatorship, going to a game is a meager experience in comparison with playing a game, and going to see a game that one has never tried to play is thin indeed in potentialities for fostering growth. The same would hold in regard to visiting art museums without having tried one's hand at the visual arts, or any other kind of looking or listening without firsthand experience in similar making and doing.

Without minimizing the values of activity and participation, others now hold that there is growth value also in some standing aside and looking on or listening in. For, they hold, this is not mere standing aside but is a doing and undergoing of another kind. The spectator would not stop to look if he did not find some satisfaction or release in the events he beheld. The baseball or football crowd is clearly not passive, and the emotional values in the theater have been pointed from the time of Aristotle. Full understanding of the psychological processes involved is still lacking, and there are many who fear that it is easier to exploit the emotional life in this way than when overt activity is called for. Yet few would deny the value of vicarious experience of some kind to children and young people, provided this living at secondhand, as it were, does not supplant much good experience at firsthand but rather enriches it, elaborates it, or provides opportunity for healthy emotional release.

Another difference of emphasis in this area centers on the extent to which leisure-time pursuits of children and young people are appropriately carried on in groups rather than alone. Because of a concern with the social development of the child and the cooperation aspects of democracy, there has been a considerable tendency to stress group activities and to try to beguile all children given to singlehanded undertakings into leisure-time group participation—to look upon all desire for solitude as withdrawal, in the more or less technical sense of not liking people, a seeking to escape from the give-and-take of everyday experience. A special facet here is stress on recreation in the family group, as a means of enriching family relationship; work life in most instances now separates family members, but in their leisure hours they can come together in pleasurable pursuits and so create a favorable emotional climate.

All would agree that the child of four or five and older who avoids group life and finds no pleasure in it stands in need of special help. On the other hand, many are beginning to question what they consider to be an overemphasis on group activities for all children at all times. They call attention to the fact that the socialization of the child does not necessarily require unremitting face-to-face interchange with his peers or even with members of his family, and that an activity carried on alone may be as social in background and intent as any group game, discussion, or jointly devised undertaking. At given times and stages of individual growth, any child may require some time and solitude for the resolution of inner conflicts or for the consolidation of advances in emotional growth—time spent in reading, say, or playing solitary games, or even in a certain amount of fantasy. The group makes its demands, and he must be able to enjoy meeting them; he is entitled also to some portion of his life free of these demands to work things out for himself. And whether alone or in groups, he requires opportunity, from school age on, to spend portions of his life in increasing independence of his family.

Whether the leisure-time activities of the young are best carried on always under adult supervision or whether children should more frequently be left to their own devices constitutes still another difference of emphasis. Recognizing the deep dependence of the young on their elders —to guide their spurting energies into rewarding and socially acceptable channels, to curb the impulses to which they frighteningly feel themselves prey, and to lend them unwavering support—many recreation workers stress the importance of adult supervision for all their activities, those in which they have greater freedom of choice and expression no less than those that closely approximate work. Other close observers of child life and development call attention to values in spontaneous activity and in occasional emancipation from the restraints imposed by even the most lenient and insightful adults. As they see the situation, it is only children who are or have been in some large measure deprived who stand in need of such constant surveillance: those who live in an environment that offers little opportunity for wholesome activity appropriate to their years and no inducement to it, or those so bereft of affection and opportunity for healthy growth that, left on their own, they either fall into indolent idleness or seek escape and release in antisocial forms. Other children, given a chance now and again to find their own way through a part of a day, gain in autonomy and initiative and find the later independence of adulthood less difficult to achieve.

All these differences in emphasis—they are not truly issues, since no one would hold to one extreme to the entire exclusion of the other—point to areas where further exploration is called for. For what children, at what stages of development, in which circumstances, how much active participation and how much "standing on the sidelines," and what is the contribution of this to the growth of healthy personality? When is group activity appropriate, and what are the values and limits of working and playing alone? Are adults always necessary or are there definite advantages in some freedom from adults? For whom, and when, and in what circumstances?

As might be anticipated, the answer is not simple. When energies are freer to flow in whatever channels they find most immediately agreeable, the variety of pursuits that may constitute a worthy and rewarding leisure are myriad, and the individual is likely to find what he most seeks sometimes in one and sometimes in another—in achieving and in relaxing, in watching and in doing, alone and in groups, with supervisory help and without it. It is for this reason, among others, that it is impossible to give exhaustive examples of what might be done to further healthy growth through any great variety of all the kinds of recreational and leisure-time facilities for children and young people. Group work and library services are therefore chosen as illustrations merely of relative emphasis in different aspects of this field.

Some Group-work Principles

Recreation and informal-education programs are based on the belief that children and youth need the help of adults to derive greatest benefit from recreational activities. This help may, at certain times and with some groups, be limited to the provision of facilities with only remote guidance. At other times and with other groups, it may consist of service from an adult as an adviser, teacher, coach, or leader.

Service of adults to children and youth in using recreational activities may be spoken of as a professional practice in the field of recreation. The methods upon which this professional practice is based have been developed chiefly by social group workers, although many other educators have made important contributions.

The basic principle underlying social group work is that while the worker individualizes each member of a group, his service is to the group as a whole, through which each individual is helped to meet his unique needs.

There is no set of rules to follow in achieving the purposes for which the social-group-work method is used. The social-group-work method is a process based on the relationship which is established between the worker and the members he serves. It is through his professional use of this relationship that the members and the group as a whole are helped to achieve their personal and corporate purposes. The success of the social-group-work method depends upon the worker's wisdom and discretion in developing the interpersonal relationships within the group and with other groups. The "how" of social group work is therefore discussed in terms of the attitudes and relations of the worker to the members of the group. The first line of a jingle composed by a group of students may be used to describe this process in brief: "Love them and limit them and help them to achieve." [2]

The group worker "loves them" in the sense of having considerate re-

[2] Gertrude Wilson and Gladys Ryland, *Social Group Work Practice,* Houghton Mifflin Company, Boston, 1949, p. 85.

gard for the ideas and feelings of each boy or girl, and in the sense of not demanding love in return. His regard for each individual is stable and dependable. The youngsters can count on him to be understanding (or willing to be told) and interested and free of prejudice. "Unsolicited love," the psychiatrists call it, and a very helpful thing it is for healthy personality development.

To "limit them" is to define the boundaries of the permissible. Most limitations are inherent in the situation. The youngsters may not always like the rules (and they must have the right to say so and to consider ways of changing them), but they like to know what they are. To be left too free is likely to make young people uneasy and somewhat anxious. You never know when the blow will fall or for what reason. It is only within a framework of reasonable and dependable rules that children are free to grow.

"Help them to achieve." A sense of industry, a sense of achievement— this is the personality component that under good conditions develops in the preadolescent years and underpins the adolescent's efforts to establish his identity. To the extent that this personality component does not develop or disappears, the sense of inferiority takes its place. To help young people, through the medium of the group, to make plans and carry them out—their own plans, their own creations—is to further health of personality most significantly.

The three rules work together to enhance each other's benefits. Achievement is best accomplished in an atmosphere of love and in a situation that has limits to it. "Love" makes "limits" more acceptable. "Limits" lessen diffusion of attention and assist concentration on the objective to be accomplished. "Achievement" enhances self-esteem and hence regard for others.

This theoretical formulation social group workers learned from psychiatrists (in real-life terms they had probably earlier discovered it for themselves), and they have worked out some of its implications for the kind of work they do. Recreation workers and those who specialize in informal education will probably also find the formulation valuable, as will all who work closely with children and young people.

Some Aspects of Library Service for Children and Young People

In her book entitled *Literature as Exploration* Louise M. Rosenblatt [3] raises the question, "How can the experience and study of literature foster

---

[3] Louise M. Rosenblatt, *Literature as Exploration,* Appleton-Century-Crofts, Inc., New York, 1938.

a sounder understanding of life and nourish the development of balanced human personalities?" and answers, in part, in such passages as these:

The enjoyment of literature remains as ever the source from which its other values spring.

Through books, the reader may explore his own nature, become aware of potentialities for thought and feeling within himself, acquire a clearer perspective, develop aims and a sense of direction. He may explore the outer world, other personalities, other ways of life. Liberated from the insularity of time and space, he may range through the wide gamut of social and temperamental alternatives that men have created or imagined.

The reader seeks to enter into another's experience, to glimpse the beauty and intensity that the world offers, to fathom the resources of the human spirit, to gain understanding that will make his own experiences more comprehensible, to find moulds into which to pour his own seemingly chaotic experiences.

Literature offers the closest approach to the experience of actual life. It enables the youth to live through much that in abstract terms would be meaningless to him. He comes to know intimately, more intimately perhaps than would be possible in actual life, many personalities. He shares vicariously their struggles and perplexities and achievements. He becomes a part of strange environments, or he sees with new emotions the conditions and the lives about him. And these experiences have at least something of the warmth and color and emotion that life itself possesses. Because the literary experience penetrates to the core of the personality, because it affects both thought and feeling as they are organically intermingled, literature can be an important means of bringing about the linkage between intellectual perception and emotional drive. . . .

The peculiar power of literature resides in the fact that it can exert an influence upon an emotional level, similar to the kind of influence exerted by people and situations in life.

Literary experiences may help the reader gain some objectivity toward his own personality and problems.

These excerpts from a book addressed to teachers set forth eloquently the growth values librarians as well as teachers have long felt to be inherent in reading. Groups in both fields are seeking always better ways of using literature to help children find what they can best respond to, and most require, at different stages of their growth and in the innumerable particular situations in which they find themselves.

The library is not exclusively a recreational institution, even for children of school age, but attention here focuses on its leisure-time work with children. The values that vicarious experience, couched in artistic form, can add to the immediate and "insular" are too movingly expressed in the quotations cited to require further elaboration. And it is to be noted that reading is, on the whole, something that is done alone.

Librarians hold, however, that the selection and reading of a book is less passive than "spectatorship," whether of sports or movies or television. The child participates in the choice of the book and must form his own mental images instead of having them formed for him. He may leave off reading a book and pick it up again, or even reread it when mood and circumstances impel him. He is not bound by the schedule or limited to one chance.

There is also no rigidity about the notion that reading for pleasure is always and of necessity a solitary adventure. Libraries have story hours for groups of young children, some of them too young to be able to read, and do much to encourage reading aloud in the family circle. A child of any age can find natural social contacts in the library, or he can seek relief there from too much rubbing of elbows in a crowded home or with importunate playmates. In recognition of its special requirements of adolescents, some libraries have established special services for them, with specially trained librarians in charge; in such instances, it is not uncommon for an advisory board of young people to help with the organization and planning of youth forums and book-reviewing programs in either broadcast or leaflet form.

Thus it is apparent that for some youngsters the library serves as a kind of leisure-time community center, where, alone and in groups, they pursue such of their special interests and delights as derive from reading. On occasion, it ameliorates an otherwise depressing environment where there is a lack of variety or stimulation; and for some children on the move it is the place where they may find books they have loved, and so provides, by so much, an element of stability.

In terms of adult guidance, the librarian stands always ready, but never obtrusive. His selection of books for the collections may be as far as this guidance goes, or it may extend to intimate acquaintance with individual children and their problems and to supervision of youthful group activities. A child may obtain a library card as soon as he is able to sign his name; from that time on, he is treated as a responsible individual, free to go his own way if he so chooses, sure of a helping hand if he wants help, with the companionship of his peers readily available if it is companionship rather than solitude that he seeks.

With so much to offer (and again it must be noted that only those parts of its work that can be called recreational are noted here, and not all the other ways in which it serves children and their parents, and other agencies concerned with the welfare of both), the library has been described by Dorothy Thompson as "that unique but little noted institution in American life . . . that hands out the magic of thought and rhyme to every snub-nosed urchin with some spark of divine hunger, from Maine to California"—little noted because little publicized and ill supported.

Although all states have state libraries from which both individuals and libraries can borrow books, thirty-three million people in the United States, 90 per cent of them rural, are still without access to a local public library. Twenty-five states furnish financial aid to encourage local service, in amounts that vary from five thousand to three million dollars. Specialized services for children are, of course, even more limited. At least in part because of financial limitations and poor salaries, there is a shortage of professionally trained librarians; in the field of work with children and youth, the shortage is particularly acute. Moreover, training for work with children and adolescents in most library schools continues to stress acquaintance with books and fails to provide sufficiently for opportunity to gain intimate and insightful acquaintance with children and their modes of development.

Personality Components and Leisure-time Service

Knowledge about the various components of the healthy personality and the critical periods in its development would appear to be useful to workers in leisure-time services. Just what this knowledge implies is still not wholly clear. Each profession must adapt knowledge about human psychology to its own professional task, for each has a different job to do and so will put the knowledge to a different use. Only a beginning has been made in the leisure-time field. The following ideas are therefore presented very tentatively.

Most generally stated, the challenge to leisure-time workers is to recognize the outstanding strength and weaknesses of each child being served, and to know what to do with the understanding thus acquired. The sensitive and observing worker notes that one child is fearful and lacking in trust in himself and that another is self-confident. He sees that this one is overdependent or anxious about being dependent, and that that one stands square on his own feet and yet is not afraid to ask for help when he needs it. And so on. The evidence is clear in some cases and dubious in others. The difficulty of identifying individual characteristics is increased when the worker has a large, active, changing membership rather than a small, intimate one that meets frequently and limits its membership. Over-all diagnosis, however, is not called for; rather, the worker must know how to respond to children's feelings and how to sense who is in trouble and, perhaps, why.

A few examples of the kinds of behavior that children may display in connection with leisure-time activities and some attitudes and devices that have been found useful by workers may serve to indicate the value of this sort of knowledge about children. Take first the sense of trust. Without a sense of trust a child is unsure of himself and may have little self-control. He will probably therefore have difficulty in playing with others. He may be a bully or one who tries to domineer or he may be one who withdraws at the slightest disappointment. He may be afraid of rough games, or he may refuse to play unless the worker is near by. He may be the butt of the other children's jokes or be marked as unpopular in other ways. Workers have found that such children are sometimes helped by reassurance and support, and especially by such friendliness and warmth of interest that some of the more secure children can be helped to display toward them.

The sense of autonomy involves the ability and the right to make choices and also the recognition of limits to self-determination. Club work, recreational or informal educational, takes as perhaps its chief objective the development or enhancement of these traits. The worker must be able to permit youngsters to make their own decisions even though failure may ensue (provided it is failure that is endurable), and yet be firm in imposing limitations when the children's self-assertions are dangerous to themselves or too contrary to the mores.

Within any group, children will vary in their ability to make choices easily and constructively and to accept limitations. Sometimes the difficulty stems from cultural sources, from differences in the degree and kind of choice that is permitted in the cultural group to which the child belongs, or from similar differences in the degree of control that is exercised by adults. Sometimes it is traceable to a child's desire to be liked by everybody, or to his inexperience in choosing or in being controlled, or to one or another psychological or social condition that keeps him from acting as maturely as might be expected on the basis of the worker's own cultural norms.

Much self-discipline is required of workers to be firm and yet respectful of a child's wishes and to convey disapproval of conduct without conveying disapproval of the person. Wisdom and flexibility are called for in not allowing one's own ideas about conduct standards to prevail at all times, and especially when conflicting ideas about proper conduct are at issue,

A worker who insists that middle-class American customs be followed at all times may not only be headed for trouble but may miss out on an opportunity to gain greater understanding of the youngsters with whom he is working. The over-all rule is to remember that all behavior has meaning, that the meaning should be discovered before action is taken, and that solutions should be worked out with the group if at all possible.

The sense of initiative and the sense of accomplishment are other personality components that can be both utilized and enhanced through leisure-time activities. Children who have advanced only to the stage at which the first of these components has developed can be distinguished from the others by the fact that they have less interest in finished products and well-executed plans and take more delight in the imaginative play that accompanies their activities. Professional workers must take into account that such children may feel guilty for having undertaken something that did not work out well. They need encouragement in exercising imagination and enterprise, and protection against engaging in tasks that are much beyond their capacity.

For children who are entering into the period in which accomplishment for its own sake is important, rules are of great interest, especially rules that they make for themselves. One of the first items of business in clubs of children seven to ten years old is the drawing up of rules of conduct. The very nature of the rules suggests the struggles the children are engaged in. There are usually rules about telling the truth, about not swearing, about being fair and being polite. Rules about how to play games and how to construct objects are also of great interest at this developmental period.

This desire of young children to be responsible for their own behavior and to be kept within bounds, as well as to know how to do things and do them well, makes club and group recreational activities both possible and useful. The worker, however, must be careful not to be too much taken in by this rule-making interest. Not to be able to live up to the rules, not to be able to do things well is a great threat to children's developing sense of accomplishment. A sense of inferiority can easily result if leisure-time workers utilize children's interest in accomplishment to stress competitive activities and arrange matters so that only a few children can fully succeed.

Much variety in activities is needed if all children are to have a chance to find some things they can do well. Organizations, accordingly, should offer many kinds of programs: classes, interest groups, clubs, athletics, and so on, including an opportunity for children to go off by themselves and engage in solitary activities. Workers should also realize that, in their various capacities as teacher, coach, group adviser, and the like, they have different relations with the group members. They must instruct and lead when the activity calls for learning a skill, and they must stand aside and work through group-appointed leaders when the activity calls for self-direction and democratic action. Activity, passivity on the worker's part: children need both, depending upon what is to be accomplished.

The sense of personal identity—the clear idea of who you are and what you can do—is the fortunate outcome of the struggle of adolescence. In this developmental period, leisure-time activities are of especial importance. Many boys and girls seek their identity by banding together with others of their own age. These groups, spontaneously formed or artificially created, sometimes welcome adult sponsorship and guidance. Workers with adolescents must remember, however, that each boy and girl is trying to discover himself, to establish his own uniqueness. Hence, despite his cliques and his patterned mannerisms, he needs to be known and treated as an individual.

Since adolescents require both group activities and personal attention, the usual community provision of mass recreational facilities is not sufficient. "Canteens," teen-age clubs, recreation halls, and so on, are very useful, but if they are set up without accompanying facilities for small groups and, perhaps, for individual counseling, they may serve only to aggravate the teen-age problems the community thought they would solve.

It is important, too, that recreation centers be under the supervision of adults whom adolescents can trust. Adults who understand and like young people can serve the cause of adolescent well-being in several ways. They can keep boys and girls from using unwisely the freedom that a clubhouse of their own provides, and so can save the youngsters from their own anxiety and from adults' wrath. They can also help boys and girls to see that not all adults are their enemies and that adulthood itself is not something to be feared.

Currently, the idea that all adolescents should belong to clubs is very popular, and many kinds of organizations are offering club facilities. Schools, churches, women's clubs, political organizations, even magazines, newspapers, and radio stations are sponsoring club programs. Professional group workers are of the opinion that the sponsoring of clubs without professional guidance is a dubious undertaking and that adolescents suffer from being too frequently the objects of recruitment. Adolescents, like adults, seek social status. Membership and officeholding in many clubs becomes, to many boys and girls, the "way up." In consequence, interests become diffuse and artificial, energy is depleted, and the real benefits of club participation are lost. For healthy personality development it is the quality rather than the quantity of group experience that counts.

Understanding of the psychology of adolescence suggests, then, that a wide range of leisure-time activities is required if youth is to be well served. The range of adolescent interest is wide, and any one individual finds pleasure and benefit in one kind of activity at one time and another at another. In the rush to provide group activities, the desire of youth for solitary pleasures must not be overlooked. And in the interest in meeting boys' and girls' natural desire for groups that separate them along lines of their own choosing, their idealism and their curiosity about ways that are different from their own must not be so disregarded that they have no opportunity to become acquainted with young people who live "across the tracks" or who come from other parts of the world. In short, not all adolescents are alike, and no one kind of leisure-time program will advance the welfare of all of them.

Availability of Facilities and Services

Leisure-time facilities and services are far from equally available to all children. Generally speaking, children who live in the more prosperous areas of cities are more adequately served than are those who live in run-down, deteriorated sections. In rural areas, the difference between the facilities and services available to higher and lower economic levels may be even greater.

With important exceptions, of which settlement houses are one, privately financed youth-serving organizations tend to favor the middle class. One reason for this lies in the cost of service. For example, an unpublished study made by the Welfare Council of Metropolitan Los Angeles in 1947 showed that the cost of service per child was three or four times as great in the low-income areas of the community as in the others. The higher cost was attributed to the greater difficulty in securing and retaining the services of volunteers, to the larger professional staff required for supervisory activities, and to the greater use of building-centered programs.

Minority groups, especially those of low economic status, are discriminated against in the provision of leisure-time facilities. Not only is there actual segregation by race in some sections of the country but there is also widespread tacit exclusion in most communities. Then, too, girls are less adequately provided for than boys; adolescents, especially those in their late teens, have fewer facilities than do younger children; and out-of-school youths are less favored than those still in school.

The most disfavored groups, probably, are the share croppers' and the migratory workers' children. These children have few of the advantages that rural life is thought to provide. With few, if any, community-recreation services available to them, they are almost completely dependent upon their own resources or upon the cheap commercial amusements of near-by towns. The neglect of these submerged rural groups is the extreme example of uneven distribution of leisure-time services.

That rural youths want more recreational facilities is testified to by a public-opinion poll of young people conducted in Minnesota recently.[4] The replies indicated that going to the movies in the village is the most frequent form of recreation for farm youth, and that village dances rank second. There was much criticism of town people's lack of interest in farm youth's recreation. The boys and girls who answered the questionnaire said they wanted public programs; specifically, youth centers, community centers, and planned recreation.

Both public and private sources can be looked to for the expansion of leisure-time facilities, urban and rural. The amount of money currently spent for such purposes in cities varies considerably, as does the relative proportion that comes from public and private sources. For example, in 1948 the total per-capita expenditure in thirty-one urban areas ranged from $1.30 in Oklahoma City to $4.80 in Baltimore.[5] In Los Angeles, nearly half of the funds came from public sources and in Tulsa, less than three per cent, while the proportion that came from private contributions ranged from 14.5 in Baltimore to 49.9 in Nashville.[6] Comparable studies for rural expenditures are lacking.

Interest in public-financed services in the recreation field has increased greatly in recent years. Only five years ago, North Carolina pioneered in the creation of a State Recreation Commission. Several other states have followed suit since that time, and, at present, proposals for this sort of service are before many state legislatures. Leisure-time services in general, and recreational services in particular, will probably increase markedly in the near future. It is highly important, therefore, that close attention be given to developing the theory and working methods of this newest of professions and to training an adequate number of workers for at least leadership positions, since leisure-time activities, well conducted, are a great aid to the healthy personality development of children and youth.

[4] *Recreational Resources of the People of Minnesota,* "Report of the Governor's Advisory Committee on Recreation," St. Paul, 1950.
[5] *Expenditures for Community Health and Welfare, 1948,* Community Chests and Councils of America, Inc., New York, p. 15.
[6] *Ibid.,* p. 28.

✗ XIII ✗

Vocational Guidance and Employment Services

EVENTUALLY most children will work in some capacity, and as adults they will spend more of their waking time at work than in any other activity. From their work they will receive varying amounts of money, and this in turn will determine their standard of living. But there is more to work than economics. The work they do may determine their social position in a community, may fulfill or thwart their aspirations, and may give or deny them a feeling of successful accomplishment, a sense of being useful. And, because so much of an individual's time and energy are spent in the work he does, the satisfaction he draws from his occupational activities, whether in industry, a profession, or a home, may be a decisive factor in determining how effectively he functions as an individual, a parent, and a citizen.

A person's vocational adjustment is determined not only by the adequacy of his wages and the conditions under which he works but also, to a large extent, by his family and school experiences long before he goes to work. "The child's sense of belonging, which he experiences as a member of the family, the feeling of achievement which should be a part of school and play experience are, in part, preparation for [vocational] satisfaction." [1]

In recent years we have become aware of the fact that the pattern of an individual's personality develops largely out of his early experiences, and therefore the qualities needed for individual happiness and responsible citizenship should be forming long before the individual reaches adulthood. But it is not at all certain that an individual's personality is rigidly set by the time he is five or six years old, however important the early years of childhood are. An individual continues always to encounter experiences, and his development as a person beyond the early years is

---

[1] Katharine F. Lenroot, "Why a Community Program for Youth Needs the Employment Service," *Employment Service Review,* Vol. 15 (1948), pp. 4–5.

affected by the wholesome ones he enjoys and the injurious ones he suffers. Failure to preserve the sound basis laid in childhood may set a pattern for continuing failure, frustration, and maladjustment that is costly both to the individual and to society.

The relation between satisfactory accomplishment and sound personality has long been recognized. The interplay between factors in healthy personality development and the work life—the satisfactions found in it, and the ability to perform adroitly—have, however, seldom been explored, except, perhaps, in the case of individuals with personalities so badly impaired that they could no longer perform their vocational tasks.

Obviously, a good work life grows out of the whole series of events underlying all healthy development. Satisfaction in both the processes and the outcomes of work rests upon a sense of trust—of confidence in one's own capacities and of their acceptability in the eyes of the world. The importance of a sense of autonomy is similarly apparent: the individual must feel that he is an independent human being whose activities nonetheless intermesh with those of other human beings. In our culture, initiative is highly prized, its absence widely deplored. Without a sense of accomplishment, of satisfaction in real tasks brought to completion, and of the knowledges and skills concomitantly acquired, which make for good workmanship, any worker is clearly lost. Further, the individual's sense of identity, of what he is as a person and of the special role he plays, is perhaps most surely defined by his occupational skills, the work group of which he can properly and confidently count himself a member.

It is, perhaps, the very emphasis upon the vocational in our society that has led to some confusion. On the one hand, an individual can scarcely count himself a respect-worthy adult unless he can and does perform remunerative work (this holds specially for men); social status is largely based on type of occupation; and success is generally measured by vocational achievement. On the other hand, the notion of work as harsh and an atonement for evil is still with us: "in the sweat of thy face shalt thou eat bread." The situation is further complicated by an economy that tempts to exploitation and by the division of labor and the high degree of mechanization that have followed upon industrialization, so that much work is indeed dull, repetitive, and in itself meaningless.

Were it not for these factors, the continuity of the work life from the age of five, six, or seven, when the sense of accomplishment emerges (or the child falls into a sense of inadequacy and inferiority) to the end of the years of productivity would be clearer. Child labor would be seen as evil not only because it is exploitation in its most harsh form but also because the nature of the child's labor and its circumstances rob him of the environment he requires for healthy development. No one objects to the child's responsible performance of useful tasks in school or home; this is an essential constituent of the activities through which healthy development is achieved. The problems of employment of young people, too, could be considerably clarified by an analysis of what can be done to offset the drab monotony of most jobs in an industrial civilization, and of the part the remunerativeness of work plays in young people's lives, not only as an economic necessity but also as a psychological factor in a culture that equates economic self-support with independence and that holds nothing of much worth unless there is a money price upon it.

It is difficult even to focus on the role of work in the development of the child, because work has all too often come to mean what an adult does, painfully, of necessity, without zest, without intrinsic reward, and without other goal than to earn his bread. Such activity, it is by now universally agreed, has no place in the life of children, and some have begun to question what it does to adults—whether the seeking of tawdry thrills and dubious escapes in leisure may not be the inevitable counterpart of hours of unsatisfying labor, for example, and whether family life and parental relationships may not be adversely affected by the frustrations of an empty work life. From such work as this, children must without doubt be protected—even if the work is not, as in fact it is, overly arduous for them, exploitative, and preclusive of the schooling to which they are entitled.

But when work is conceived as the accomplishment of foreseen goals, the bringing of accepted tasks to successful conclusion, despite difficulties and distractions, it then becomes apparent that no child can grow up healthily without it. In school, in hours outside of school, and even to a certain extent before the years of schooling, he properly and appropriately works in this sense. Before school age, he wants to learn to tie his shoelace and labors long against his own lack of coordination and the relative recalcitrance of his materials to achieve the desired skill. In school he works both alone and with others to accomplish foreseen ends of rich variety and increasing complexity and difficulty. And, generally speaking, not all of his out-of-school time is spent in aimless, random expenditure of energy; he has things he wants to do, and the doing calls for directed and concentrated effort. Without such work and some success at it, he fails to develop the essential sense of accomplishment and is likely throughout life to feel himself inferior and inadequate.

Moreover, the limitations imposed upon him by his accepted task—the way in which it keeps him from doing other things, for example, and the difficulties he encounters in controlling the medium (paper and pencil, clay, the herd he must bring home from pasture, or whatever it may happen to be)—help him as do the limitations his parents and other adults set for him. They provide a safeguard against what he feels may be the catastrophic results of the untrammeled expression of his impulses. And the task in hand simultaneously provides him with acceptable channels for the expression of both the urge to love—either the thing upon which he labors or those for whose sake it is done—and other, more difficult urges, such as those to dominate and destroy; the latter can now be released by "dominating" difficulties and "destroying" impediments to successful performance or accomplishment.

Work, appropriate in amount and kind, is, accordingly, an essential in healthy development from the age of five or six onward, and even makes its appearance in rudimentary forms, such as learning to dress, wash, eat at the table, before this. It is perhaps important to note that the kind of work that is likely to have beneficial results always falls within the perimeter of the child's own intent and purpose, his capacity for seeing and feeling the meaning of his work to himself and others. Tasks imposed without rhyme or reason real to him, in no aspect of which he can find intrinsic satisfaction, performed under compulsion only, are likely to lead only to frustration and fury, an unrelenting rebelliousness that may take many forms—from pervasive indolence to open defiance of all demands, or the dour compulsion to drive others to work to distraction, for example. The amount of work, no matter how appropriate, varies with the age. The span of attention is short in the early years of childhood, even during the first school years, and children need much opportunity to engage in activities that are under less constraint even than that imposed by a conscious end in view.

For the child who lived in the family household that for many constituted a relatively self-sufficient economic unit two or three generations back, meaningful tasks of economic significance were not difficult to find. The work done in this context was of social significance manifest even to a child, and it provided early opportunity for responsible performance. If the chores were not done, the crops, the animals, the family food supply suffered, and other goods were lacking. Meanwhile, the child, emulating his elders, tried his hand at many kinds of work, became increasingly adept in all, and grew without strain or abrupt transition into economic manhood. The same does not hold even of the farm child of today, for industrialization has gone so far that no farm any longer pretends to anything like self-sufficiency, and agriculture in general has become mechanized, scientific, for the most part remote from the simple manual tasks in which children could participate with their elders, seeing the crops through from the breaking of the ground to the harvesting and processing. Yet the farm child, unlike the urban child, still observes and comprehends just what it is that his parents do, from which they derive their livelihood.

For the urban child in an industrial civilization, the breadwinner's work outside the home is enigma. He can participate to a certain extent in household tasks, but their economic bearings are so abstract as to escape him. It is therefore difficult to find work for him that relates him immediately to the associated life of the family around him, that provides him with genuine responsibility, that heads smoothly into adult vocation and economic participation. Yet he learns early that economic participation and adult status go hand in hand and that men are identified by the work they do. Daddy is not only a parent and a husband but also, perhaps more strikingly, a plumber, or a stevedore, or a clerk, or a doctor.

During adolescence, the establishment of one's identity as a person, as a mate and a prospective parent depends, for boys at least, on one's capacity to establish an identity as a worker and earner. Social status, standard of living, and style of life are seen to rest upon what variety of worker one becomes, and upon how much one may hope to earn in that capacity. Yet the young person, if he has been relatively fortunate, has been engaged all along in tasks which, though meaningful to him, are of no economic value. In more and more instances, he has been protected from work outside the home for many reasons, but perhaps primarily because such work as he could perform in an industrialized community would interfere with his well-rounded growth.

Now the time has come, however, when it is no longer enough to be good at mechanical jobs, or at playing the piano, or at leading group discussions. Even if economic necessity does not press (a circumstance that is relatively rare in the population), for the sake of achieving one's independence of the parental home and one's manhood, one must somehow transmute the work one has done to date into a salable commodity or learn some new skill that pays. The transition in orientation is in most instances perhaps not so abrupt as it here appears, but the fact remains that an urban, industrialized society first makes it difficult for a child to grow gradually into his vocation because the work it has to offer is not suitable for children, then confronts him with a difficult adaptation in the type of task to which he has learned to give himself, and finally plunges him more or less abruptly from a setting contrived, no matter how blunderingly, to help him thrive into one in which the well-being of the worker is only beginning to be conceived as an end in view, and the work itself, or the possibility of profit from it, comes first.

This is the complicated scene in which workers in the vocational guidance and employment field operate, trying to protect children and young people as a whole from the evils of exploitation and of work that burdens rather than facilitates their healthy development, and trying to help them, as individuals, find their way through the maze of modern vocational life to the work that is right and rewarding for each in accordance with his capacities and inclinations, his uniqueness as a person.

Child Labor

Paradoxically and tragically enough, the blight of child labor followed upon the introduction of machine methods of production that were eventually to lighten so greatly the total burden of human labor required for survival in the Western world. The dislocations of the industrial revolution were such as to give rise to extreme poverty on a wide scale. The new processes were such that they could be performed by children, who could be paid less than skilled adults. And the economic and social thought of the times was such as to make the loud outcry on behalf of human values strike hollow against mechanistic theories of the labor market.

It took no new insights into personality development and the conditions necessary for its sound progress to reveal the cruelty and iniquity of working children long hours under unhealthful conditions for the sake of the profit that could be made from it. This was not the work that could help a child to find himself or to learn the discipline involved in achieving an end in view; it was work for starveling earnings only, performed under the dire compulsion of economic necessity. Yet the humanitarian battle to bring it to an end has been long and hard fought. Nor can we yet congratulate ourselves that in our own country in our own time it has been totally and irrevocably won, that child labor has passed beyond the limits of what prevailing morality will tolerate anywhere for any child.

This holds despite the fact that marked progress has been made in recent years. In 1950, the employment of children under fourteen during school hours was probably at its lowest point in our history. To this relatively happy achievement a number of factors have contributed: the mechanization of industry and agriculture; state and Federal minimum-wage laws and other legislation; an increasing tendency among employers to require a high-school diploma of the young people they hire; union insistence on better labor standards.

But though great strides have been made, some continuing exploitation of children, especially in street trades and agriculture, remains as a challenge to the nation's conscience. Working and living conditions among the children of migratory farm workers are a particularly flagrant case in point. With their parents, these children move from state to state, following the crops. They have no stable home life, and poverty, insecurity, minority status, general social ostracism are their constant lot. Local sentiment frequently discourages their attending school. If and when they do attend, they are likely to be shunned; they find a curriculum ill adapted to their needs; and, because of repeated moves and time lost in work, they are almost invariably below the grade level appropriate to their age.

The Federal Fair Labor Standards Act, which became effective during 1950, forbids the employment of children under sixteen years of age in farm work during school hours; it applies to all those farms the products of which move across state lines. Properly enforced, this law would protect many thousands of boys and girls over the country, including the children of migrant farm families. But in some rural sections it is now being voided by the device of closing down the schools when young harvest hands are needed. With no schools in session, a legal loophole is created, and the Federal government is powerless, since the Constitution delegates the enactment and enforcement of school-attendance laws to the states.

Youth Employment

Exclusion from the world of work, from responsible paid employment, can be a serious handicap to adolescents attempting to establish their sense of identity. For boys in particular, working and earning are likely to represent the hallmark of a selfhood independent of the parental family, the key to respect-worthiness as members of the adult community, the assurance of beginning to know at least what they are to be as men. They need regular full-time employment urgently when the time for full-time employment has come (the age varies with the economic status of the family, the characteristics of the individual adolescent, the requirements of the work in which he is going to engage). Before then, almost all are likely to profit by part-time employment as a token of a full-fledged worker identity to come, as an aid in the transition from child work to economic participation, and, concomitantly, as a means to more satisfactory occupational choice.

When the work that they need, whether for these reasons alone or for these reasons combined with stringent economic pressure, is not available for them, their progress toward adulthood is thwarted. They feel rejected and come in time to doubt their worth: they feel there must be something wrong with them if they must continue to hang around like children instead of going out to earn like acceptable grown people. If the situation is not soon resolved, lasting damage may result.

Historically, the accolade of adulthood, in the guise of being wanted for, and trusted with, paid work, has been conferred at earlier and earlier ages in periods of economic expansion, and withheld until later and later when jobs were scarce and the labor market glutted. Thus the fluctuations of the labor market have conditioned opportunity for sound growth at this period. Frequently, a requisite experience is impossible for many to achieve, and unless counteracting steps are taken to help adolescents achieve a sense of independence and identity by some other means, they remain as children overlong.

It is not only during depressions that young people are at a disadvantage in competing for jobs. Even in normal times, unemployment can be a serious problem for them. In the spring of 1947, a special study was made of 411 boys and girls sixteen through nineteen years of age who were out of school and working or who wanted to work in the busy city of Louisville, Kentucky. Eighteen per cent of the eighteen- and nineteen-year-olds and 30 per cent of the sixteen- and seventeen-year-olds were unemployed. Many of them had been idle for months. The January, 1950, figures of the Bureau of the Census indicate that young people seeking jobs in which to get started constituted a large and significant proportion of the nation's unemployed.

In view of the international commitments the nation has assumed, production and employment are likely to remain at unusually high levels for some time to come. This situation should not obscure the basic fact that young people just out of school are at a disadvantage in the labor market, and that protracted unemployment, insidiously harmful for all, is particularly hard on the young, uncertain of themselves, their capacities, and their sure place in the adult world. In immediate connection, attention must be called in blazing letters to the plight of those discriminated against in employment because they are Negroes, Jews, or of recent Southern European immigrant stock.

The current trend toward increased employment of young people, particularly on a part-time basis while they are still of school age, offers both an opportunity and a challenge to those interested in their welfare.[2] They need protection from exploitation and from detrimental working conditions, and help in capitalizing upon the educational values implicit in their occupational activities. Young people lack knowledge of what to expect and, in their eagerness to try anything, frequently accept jobs requiring work late at night, substandard wages, and other substandard working conditions. Present legal enactments lag in prohibiting night work for young people of sixteen and seventeen, in regulating and limiting working hours of all under eighteen, and in providing health protection through mandatory medical examinations.

The relation between education and early work experience is relatively complex. There is, first, the problem of making sure that youngsters do not leave school and enter employment before they are ready to benefit, as developing personalities, from it. Legal regulation of the employment of children and young people and compulsory school-attendance laws are two sides of the shield devised to protect them from going or being sent to work while they are still too young, and from working conditions that are likely to be harmful. No state is now without a compulsory school-attendance law; twenty-three states prohibit the employment of children under sixteen during school hours. Progress has also been made in improving compulsory school-attendance laws, eliminating exemptions, and lengthening the school term. But keeping children from work before they are ready calls for far more than compulsory school-attendance laws and restrictive child-labor legislation. Reduction in the number of children who leave school too early calls, at a minimum, for conditions under

[2] Nearly 7½ million of the almost 13 million young people fourteen through nineteen years of age worked at some time during 1949, either full time or part time. Most of these young workers were in paid employment; a few were self-employed; about one-sixth were unpaid family workers (most of them on the family farm).

During an average school month, about 2 million boys and girls fourteen through seventeen years of age work either on part-time or full-time jobs. This figure, fairly constant since 1946, is lower than the peak wartime level, but twice as high as the prewar figure of a decade ago. In the summer, 1 million to 1½ million additional boys and girls of these ages are at work. Among the eighteen- and nineteen-year-olds, from 2 to 2¼ million are employed in an average month during the school year, about 20 per cent more than before World War II. This represents approximately 60 per cent of the nation's boys and 45 per cent of the girls of these ages, some of whom have already married and assumed home responsibilities.

In 1940, only 1 in every 18 boys and girls fourteen through nineteen years old enrolled in school had outside employment; by October, 1949, the proportion had increased to 1 in 5. In October, 1949, Bureau of the Census estimates show that among fourteen- and fifteen-year-old children, 80 per cent of those working had part-time work while continuing in school. Almost half of those sixteen and seventeen years of age with jobs at that time had part-time work while in school.

which no child need be deprived of schooling because his family cannot afford it, and for enough schools, with enough properly qualified teachers, and programs of instruction designed to provide enticing experience for all pupils, regardless of their eventual vocational destination.

Second, there is the vastly challenging problem of helping fledgling workers to learn as much as possible from their job experience, to grow and develop as a consequence of it, rather than merely to work and earn. Fantastic as any such intent may at first appear, there is reason and background for it. Forward-looking schools everywhere are attempting to make schooling as lifelike as possible, and to bring school and community closer together in order that older children and adolescents may learn responsible participation in community life by participating responsibly in it. Not unrelated to this, the practice of interlarding work experience with schooling is spreading at the secondary level and beyond. There remains much to be studied and learned about making such work experience yield its maximum in educational and developmental value, and the same would hold for the early work experience of those who are at present no longer under the guidance of the school or any other agency.

Occupational Choice as a Process

Optimum vocational guidance, whether of the young worker or of the adolescent still in school, waits upon fuller understanding of how individuals do in fact choose their vocations and about the elements that influence the selection. A recent study [3] both notes the relative neglect of theoretical inquiry in this field and formulates a tentative hypothesis to the effect that occupational choice goes hand in hand with the developmental process.

By this proposal the choice itself is a process, a series of decisions over a period of years, each decision growing out of those which preceded it and to a degree conditioning those which follow. Further, "there is presumptive evidence that major deviations in the occupational choice process are likely to be grounded in basic emotional difficulties." [4]

By the findings of this study, children of about six to eleven make "fantasy choices." Certain adult activities appear pleasurable to them, and they know that certain occupations enable one to engage in these activities. Hence, they choose the occupation which permits an activity that seems attractive at the moment. To the realities of interest, capacity,

[3] Ginsburg, Axelrad and Herman, *Occupational Choice: An Approach to a General Theory,* Columbia University Press, New York, 1951.
[4] *Ibid.,* p. 127.

what it might take to translate dream into fact, and even to the facts of their "chosen" occupations they are entirely oblivious.

Early and late adolescence are characterized as a period of "tentative choice." "Realistic choice" is said to be made, with few exceptions, in early adulthood.

During the period of tentative choice the individual, in the characteristic adolescent way, is concerned with determining upon what kind of a person he is going to be so far as a job is concerned. This decision is rendered difficult by the fact, among others, that he has to think in terms of future rather than present satisfactions and yet has little experience on which to base a judgment.

Analysis of the process adolescents go through during the stage of tentative choice shows that first they think in terms of their interests, next in terms of their capacities, and finally in terms of their values. "Would I find it interesting?" is a natural question, one that arises in connection with even the phantasies of early childhood. To this question is often added, in childhood as well as in adolescence, "Could I do it?" In adolescence, however, the latter question is likely to come after the first tentative explorations along interest lines and becomes formulated as "What am I suited for?" The consideration of this question may help the young person discard occupational desires based on interest only or it may reinforce his earlier choice.

Later in adolescence, the boy or girl begins to think of job choice in relation to other preferences, such as desire to leave or stay in school, desire to earn a large salary, desire to live in the city or the country, and so on. Consideration of these preferences serves, as the authors point out, to "resolve conflicts between incompatible objectives by establishing some kind of order among them."

The process of job choice in adolescence characteristically ends with a "transition period," one that bridges the gap between that of tentative choice and that of reality decision. In this period, a gradual settling down occurs, indicative of the partial resolution of the problem of identity. In the relative calm of this period the individual can take reality factors more seriously into consideration and can usually make his compromise between what he wants and the opportunities that are available to him.[5]

In all this tumultuous searching of the self, the outer world, and the acceptable links that may be forged between the two, the youngster, according to the findings of this study, is left largely without supporting guidance from his family. Parents in the lower-income range are likely

[5] The above is almost entirely a paraphrase of *Ibid.*, pp. 186–189.

to discourage boys from following in their fathers' footsteps but to offer no positive stimulation or help. In upper-income families, parents fail to lend a helping hand out of fear lest they domineer and dominate. The reluctance they exhibit may derive in part from a disinclination to assume responsibility in a decision so important to their children's future happiness, especially when they are unsure of the wisdom of the vocational choices they themselves have made and do not find deep personal satisfaction in their own work.

This does not mean that the family is without influence. It is in the family that the child first learns about jobs in the adult world, and it may be there that he has his first work experience. More important, values and goals, "particularly those which center on economic returns and social status," derive more closely from family experience than any other. The same probably holds of attitudes toward work—whether it is regarded as a source of intrinsic satisfactions or merely a source of income with which to purchase satisfactions elsewhere, to compensate for the doldrums of the job.

Finally, the question of whether parents are confused about their role has to be considered. "If they define their role as one of leadership and do tell their sons which career to follow, they are in fact assuming dictatorial functions and, moreover, are trying to discharge these functions in a world about which they may be poorly informed. But that should not be their role. The youngster who is attempting to determine upon an occupational choice needs help, not in resolving the alternatives which face him, but in clarifying understanding of both himself and of the reality. When he does not receive this help, as is so frequently the case, he misses an essential type of support, and in some cases this may actually be experienced as an emotional deprivation." [6]

What, then, of the school and of vocational counseling and placement services as sources of the help so sorely needed?

Education for Vocational Participation

Federal interest and funds under the Smith-Hughes and George Barden Vocational Educational acts have stimulated a vast increase in vocational-education programs. Under these laws, the Federal government matches state and local funds for vocational education, dollar for dollar. Total expenditures under these programs more than doubled from 1940 ($55,000,000) to 1949 ($115,000,000). More than 3,000,000 students

[6] *Ibid.*, p. 236.

were enrolled during 1949 in such courses as agriculture, home economics, distributive trades, business subjects, and teacher training.

These programs meet, in part, a great need for training youth in specific kinds of work, but it must be remembered that most young people engage in work which calls for little, if any, highly specialized skill. Repeatedly, studies have found that from 75 to 95 per cent of all jobs require little or no training of a specific kind, that such specific skills as are required can be gained in short periods of training, and that for the most part this training is now gained on the job. Some educators hold the view that, wherever possible, technical skills are always best learned on the job, as everything is learned better in a real, as contrasted with an artificial, situation. They suggest, moreover, that specialized trade skills learned out of context in advance are likely to prove useless in the face of rapid technological advances and changes in industrial operations.

Some solutions have been sought in tryout courses in various lines to give young people the "feel" of various general types of work; these serve as a practical basis for vocational choice and in order that the young people may embark on their first job without loss of face or confidence, and so get off to a good start. But even so, it is difficult for the school situation to be sufficiently realistic to save young workers difficult adjustment to repetitive work, time pressure, competition, impersonal supervision, and other similar conditions of the employment world, and this has constituted an additional argument for youth employment on a part-time basis, with the interpretative support and guidance of the school.

One approach to the question of vocational education has been to conceive of all schooling, in at least one of its facets, as vocational in nature. A decade ago, the Educational Policies Commission suggested the following program:

Beginning with the elementary school, and particularly in the early years of secondary education, the foundations of economic understanding and preliminary vocational orientation should be laid. This function is integrally related to general education. It should be clearly recognized in the curriculum and work of the school. All children should know the meaning of work, should come to have respect for all types of honest labor, should learn in school—and, if possible, to some extent out of school—what it feels like to do real work, and should at adolescence begin tentatively to identify themselves with some general idea of future occupational life.

The aim is to educate for the whole of living, with the aspect of life that is called "work" related to all the rest. The various curriculum-content areas, for example, correspond to occupational areas in adult life, and so to a degree constitute a kind of vocational orientation; visits to local firms and plants, designed to acquaint the pupil with the life of his community, perform a similar function.

Surely the school has some strategic role to play if the processes of vocational choice go hand in hand with developmental processes and are successful to the degree that the individual is helped to understand himself (his interests, capacities, values), to become acquainted with the opportunities and limitations in the workaday world, and to relate the two. This responsibility will be more fully discharged as schools become increasingly adept at making their full and special contribution to healthy personality development from the time the child first approaches their doors.

In attempting to provide appropriate experience for all adolescents, it is well to bear in mind that they are largely future oriented, and that vocation looms large both in this future and as buttress for the sense of identity they so urgently seek. This consideration may be profitably pondered by the schools, which, on the rebound from an earlier and now discarded exclusive emphasis on preparation for adult life, now try to concentrate upon the present life of the child as of worth in itself. The well-supported belief that this concentration upon the present constitutes the soundest preparation for the future should not obscure the fact that, for the adolescent, the future is omnipresent, and that he is likely to assess all his activities in its light. It may be wise, therefore, to explore ways of making more explicit for him the relationship between what he does in school and his own goals in the future—his vocational choice and preparation.

Adolescents of the lower-income groups are peculiarly dependent upon the school for stimulation and the broadening of occupational horizons. The words "passive" and "stunted" are used by the authors cited above to characterize the process of occupational choice among them. Only in the school are these boys and girls likely to acquire more than a meager acquaintance with the myriad forms of work; their parents are without suggestion, and they hang on the words of their teachers. Often the level of their vocational expectations is beneath what they could achieve despite the obstacles they confront, and the school is challenged to identify and encourage pupils of promise.

Noting that these youngsters of low-income background will drop out of school as the law permits unless their schoolwork is meaningful to them, these same authors nonetheless raise pointed questions about the practice of shunting them generally and early into vocational courses. The thirteen-year-old is not yet ready to make a vocational decision, and the child of academic aptitude is likely to be lost to further education. Providing shopwork, for example, may keep them off the labor market but does not necessarily further their development; the sound maturation of many might profit more from economic independence at the age of sixteen or thereabouts.

In brief, though general principles are emerging, there remains much to be explored by way of practical implementation before schooling for all groups provides its optimum contribution to that aspect of development which eventuates as a satisfactory and satisfying vocational identity. The problem as a whole is not the school's alone, deriving as it does from many factors, cultural, social, and economic, and deserves study from many angles by many groups in related disciplines.

Guidance and Placement

Guidance programs in the schools have been expanded through funds made available under the George Barden Act of 1946. Ten years ago, 1,300 schools had 2,400 vocational counselors, most of them serving half-time or more. In 1948, about 4000 schools were served by 8000 counselors who gave some guidance service. Vocational-education funds, under certain legal restrictions, can now be used not only for supervision of counseling programs, as was the case prior to that year, but also for training counselors and for necessary travel, salaries, supplies, and equipment. More than forty states now plan to provide for some or all of these services in the schools, and states are encouraged to undertake supervision, counselor training, and research. While Federal funds are insufficient to reimburse local services in most cases, this pattern does have an impact on all local planning. The problem of providing guidance services in many small high schools has not, however, been satisfactorily solved; and, for example, many rural young people who are not interested in farm employment are up against difficult decisions and adjustments as they migrate to the cities in search of wider opportunities.

Assistance in finding appropriate jobs is given by many agencies, chief among which are the 1,800 state employment offices affiliated with the United States Employment Service, through which grants of Federal funds are made. Counseling services to youth are offered as a feature of the program and may include testing and other forms of appraising the young person's abilities and training, giving occupational information, and referral for additional training if necessary, as well as the usual placement interview.

In the employment offices, counseling service is directed primarily toward those who are about to leave school or are already out of school. At the present time, these services reach only about a third of the young people who enter the labor market each year. Services to youth in school have been concentrated chiefly on students seeking summer or part-time jobs. An expansion of the public employment-service facilities and an increase in employment counseling, especially in the smaller employment offices, are desirable in order to help eliminate the wasted resources that result from mismatching worker and job.

Counseling should also be made more widely available to out-of-school youth by state employment services, schools, and community agencies. Adjustment to a first job is difficult for many young people. One day they are students in the protected environment of the school, the next day they are on their own, part of the complicated machine of industrial enterprise which, unlike the school, is not operated for their particular benefit. A poor start can be a damaging experience for a young worker—getting fired soon after he begins, finding himself in a job that is beyond his abilities or for which he is not prepared, or in one that neither utilizes his capacities nor offers him opportunity to develop them, or that presents problems of industrial or personal relations with which he cannot cope. In addition, first jobs are almost always routine. The satisfactions to be drawn from them lie chiefly in the excitement of a new environment, new personal relationships, and the new status they offer. The young worker needs help of many kinds—in maintaining his self-esteem, in selecting training for advancement, or, when his present field of work is unsatisfying, in deciding on a new vocational goal.

For most young people, the step from school to work is a step into the unknown. Counselors find that the young people know little about labor-market conditions or about the kind of jobs they want and for which they are fitted. Asked what kind of job they want, they may say "a steady job." Asked what they can do, many of them say "anything"—which often means "nothing." What the young person actually needs to find is work that is in line with his general interests and abilities; that presents some challenge and at the same time offers him a chance to succeed; that enables him to feel that his present experience, even if the work is only routine, leads to adequately paid, congenial employment—a means to an end, in which he can take some pride. Thus, the young person about to start his working career needs more from the counselor than an analysis of the labor market, a survey of the community's economic resources, and information about seasonality of jobs. Good vocational counseling never loses sight of the many-sided and developing individual seeking help, his health, social and educational circumstances, personality, abilities, and interests.

The correction of a number of prevalent misconceptions would greatly facilitate the counseling process; for example:

That "you can get nowhere without a college education." There are excellent fields which do not require academic training.

That white-collar work is more desirable than a trade or technical work. Skilled work in any field is respect-worthy, and a trade is frequently more remunerative than a white-collar job.

That vocational guidance and vocational training should result in selection of a specific goal that will last throughout life. A young worker should not drift, it is true, but a shift along the way from one type of work to another may be advantageous and may utilize in a different way all his training and experience.

That aptitude testing is the answer to all vocational problems. Although aptitude tests represent a very important aid in counseling, aptitudes alone do not guarantee success. Most people have a variety of abilities—sufficient to succeed in more than one occupation—and the wise counselor knows that great ability in a given area may not prove rewarding when supported by little interest, or at least not so rewarding as even mediocre ability reenforced by great interest. In using tests, he makes certain that they are reliable and that they are properly interpreted, but he uses them only as one source of information about the young person he is counseling.

Interest inventories are subject to even more serious question. It has been pointed out that if a person says he does not know what his interests are, he means either that he can gain no satisfaction from anything or that he is finding it difficult to translate his interests into a vocation compatible with his goals and values (which, incidentally, are seldom explicitly studied by the counselor, probably for want of specific techniques). In fact, some raise a question as to whether the general vagueness of young people seeking vocational guidance is in fact due to the difficulty of finding one's way in the maze of the modern industrial world, or whether it may not be more truly attributed to a breakdown in the developmental process of occupational selection.

This question gives rise to another: whether the resources in the counseling field should not be devoted more to contributing to the long-range developmental-choice process and less to salvaging the individuals who remain with unresolved difficulties when the time to work has come. There is a general trend in this direction in the educational- and vocational-guidance fields, handicapped by lack of resources in personnel, theory, and technique. Gradually, however, parents and teachers, as well as adolescents, are being taken in on the problem—learning that selection begins early and that it involves a strategy of flexibility as capacities develop, interests and values change, and the fluid conditions of life impinge upon the individual. There are signs also that this field is integrating more closely with the child-guidance movement, broadly conceived, in recognition of the basic fact that personality develops as a whole and that no facet of it can be singled out from all the rest.

Much work remains to be done in delving further into the specific factors in the individual's life history that influence vocational choice and attitudes toward work, and into means for bringing these factors to bear constructively. Implementation into practical programs is likely to be rendered difficult, not only by cultural confusion concerning the values of labor but also by the stubborn facts of the nature of much of the work in a highly mechanized civilization, and of the effects of this kind of work upon those who engage in it. The challenge is sufficient to engage the best thinking and concerned efforts of all relevant fields.

⌁ XIV ⌁

Health Services

PHYSICIANS, nurses, dentists, social workers, clinical psychologists, physical therapists, nutritionists, and others professionally concerned with children's health are also concerned with children's personality development. Some of these people work with healthy children, others with the sick or disordered; some work with individual children, others with groups; some are primarily concerned with treatment, others with prevention; some are active in all these aspects. All health workers, however, in their dealings with children and their parents, may influence for better or worse, intentionally or unintentionally, the personality growth and development of children.

As infants and children are brought to physicians' offices, to clinics, to well-child conferences, for school-health examinations or for dental care, their parents come with a great variety of questions about the care of children in sickness and in health. Older children and adolescents may, if they have established a friendly, trusting relationship with the physician or nurse, bring up their own concerns about physical development, illness, or even family problems. It is through the help with these everyday problems given to parents and children that personality development of the children may be assisted or hampered. As the physician or other professional person involved is able to help solve these questions in a way which fits in with the child's general developmental needs and which takes into account the parent's worries, doubts, and fears, he has not only furthered the child's maturational process but has also helped to enlarge the parents' capacity for maturity and improved the emotional atmosphere of the home.

This is the essence of a mode of practice which, without losing anything of the contributions of a specific professional discipline, enriches and adds to them a potential for promoting total health in the child. The general principles involved can conveniently be grouped around the following four topics: (1) supporting of developmental potentials in the child, (2) fostering good parent-child relations and promoting parents' self-confidence, (3) timing elective procedures to avoid critical developmental periods in a child's life, and (4) using the psychology of interpersonal relationships in work with children and parents.

Supporting Developmental Potentials

The human organism grows and develops in all spheres—physical, intellectual, emotional, social, sexual. All these spheres are interrelated. In all of them there is a general human growth pattern; yet each individual follows his own individual pattern, which is in part inherited and in part the product of forces in the environment which impinge on the growing organism from conception through adulthood.

Through their knowledge of growth and development, health personnel can assist parents to adjust their demands on their children to individually unfolding capacities, and to provide opportunities for them to achieve more mature satisfactions. This calls for awareness on the part of health worker and parent not only of the general course of growth and development but also of the capacity of the individual child to tolerate discomfort, to wait for gratification of his needs and easing of his tensions. The mother needs to know, for instance, not only when but how to judge a child's readiness to give up the 2 A.M. feeding or to use the cup or to begin self-feeding. Much of personality development takes place in a balance between frustration and nonfrustration, and success in moving from stage to stage depends upon learning to deal with the attendant anxiety in ways which preclude becoming overwhelmed and disorganized.

A parent who is either frightened and uncertain or overconfident may not be able to gauge a child's developmental readiness, neurophysiological and psychological, to give up an old way of satisfaction and take on a new one. Ability to support a child in meeting frustrations as he takes over new ways is affected by the parent's own maturity and feelings of adequacy in the parental role. If his anxieties are sympathetically and intelligently dealt with during the early months of infant care, if his ordinary questions addressed to physicians, nurses, and other health personnel are answered and his worries allayed, his deftness and sureness as a parent are likely to increase and he is in a favorable position to develop increasingly mature attitudes in his relationships with his child. He is then better able to support the child's developing independence, to establish conditions that help the child accept the limits imposed by training, and to provide the satisfactions he requires in order to move successfully to the next stage of development.

It is much easier to aid parents to this end early in the game than after the child's personality development has gotten off to a poor start and the parents' tensions, doubts, confusions, and anxieties have become a working part of their every move in relation to the child. Skilled health workers are able to avoid mobilizing resistances that lead either to rejection of counsel or to an uncritical, wholesale taking on of any current theory of child care. Parents may lose perspective and, with it, the ability to keep on middle ground between giving the child complete gratification, on the one hand, and either imposing rigid limits upon him or completely neglecting him, on the other. Either way they fail to provide the proper support for the child to meet successfully the frustrations and anxieties necessarily involved in the process of growing up.

"Anticipatory guidance" is a device that has been developed to help parents meet developmental changes in their children with equanimity. It is based on the general notion that what comes out of the blue may be disturbing, that forewarned is forearmed. Physicians, nurses, and others have for some time been discussing with parents what is to be anticipated from their children in various developmental phases. At first, they told parents what to expect by way of changes in the rate of weight gain and in appetite, or about when the child might sit up, or walk, or talk. Later, there was a tendency to emphasize changes in children's hehavior or responsiveness. Currently, various factors which support developmental processes are being given increasing attention.

In addition to helping parents to gain a realistic picture of the developing child and his needs, anticipatory guidance can give them perspective on their own role in their child's progress. Many parents are unaware of the way their feelings affect their children; others are acutely concerned. A realistic perspective on the relative influence that they and other factors exert on the personality development of children goes far toward helping parents deal with their unnecessary anxiety, guilt, and frustration.

Anticipatory guidance can well be given before children are born. Patients frequently confront obstetricians and general practictioners with questions that reflect a variety of anxieties, fears, and worries born of folklore. As these questions are answered directly and honestly in the private office, in the prenatal clinic, or in classes for mothers- and fathers-to-be, the fears of many are assuaged and are replaced by serenity and feelings of competence.

It is not difficult to assist a mother to feel more competent in her job as she cares for her child. There are always some things for which she can be praised in order to counteract her misgivings that she is doing everything wrong. No one ever can be a perfect parent all the time. Also, most experts agree that children, in general, if halfway well guided, develop reasonably well. These things must, of course, be communicated by someone who recognizes how important the mother is to the child, and who accepts her as a parent and as a person trying her best.

Anticipatory guidance is useful, too, in minimizing the possible ill effects of acute illnesses and convalescence on personality development. It can be used to ward off invalid reactions and a chronic concern on the part of both the child and his parents about minor fluctuations in temperature, skin color, and the like. If a physician or nurse or medical social worker senses that a parent feels he "should have" prevented an illness or an accident, a frank discussion of the frequency of such feelings of self-blame in like situations may help to alleviate the feelings and so to obviate their ill effects upon the child's personality development.

Anticipatory guidance can also be used effectively with older children. It is appropriate, for instance, to discuss directly with an adolescent his concerns relative to rapid or slow physical growth, other changes in his body, and changes in sexual awareness and drives.

Fostering Good Parent-child Relations and Promoting Self-confidence

The infant's need for adequate mothering and warm affection has been known in general for some time. Health workers of a half-century ago were aware that sick infants progressed better when they had warm, motherly care. In more recent years, the disastrously disorganizing effects of early and sustained emotional deprivation have been a focus for clinical investigation, and the importance of mother love in child development has been widely popularized.

In their contacts with children and parents, health personnel are concerned with fostering a warm parent-child relationship. This means helping parents to perform effectively in the maternal or paternal role and to gain satisfactions in so doing. It also means helping parents to live with their children from day to day without undue anxiety, tension, or preoccupation, in an atmosphere in which their love can flourish. Most parents have the capacity for mature parenthood; even most of those who seem at times to be overly tense and anxious can be assisted to weather the storm and to develop into mature responsible parents, able to give to their children the experiences requisite for developing satisfying interpersonal relationships.

The recent development of "rooming in" as a part of the care of newborn infants has come out of a concern for continuous, confident, warm relationships. Modern obstetrical hospital procedures have kept mother and infant separated during a period when the mother, especially with her first child, could be developing confidence in her ability to care for him. The mothering process begins early, and tensions are likely to arise in the inexperienced mother when the baby is kept isolated in a nursery and she has no opportunity to get acquainted with him. These tensions are communicated to the infant and upset him; in some instances, both tension and upset persist long after mother and infant have gone home. As the infant's feeding, sleeping, and general disposition are affected, the mother's concept of herself as a good parent is upset, and there are further ill effects on the interaction between them.

"Rooming in" is a good way of helping to establish smooth, satisfying parent-child relationships early. The newborn infant is kept in the room with his mother, who shares in his care from the beginning. The mother develops an increased confidence in her capacity to be a mother as she holds and cuddles him and finds that she is able to feed him when he is hungry, ease and solace him when he is uncomfortable. "Rooming in" is not, however, a magic button which, in and of itself, guarantees the child's normal personality development. Moreover, some mothers are not suited to it and adaptations of the plan have to be devised to facilitate early contacts between mother and child. After several previous pregnancies, many women look forward to the lying-in period as a vacation from their usual cares. Other mothers, emotionally tense and upset, try hard to utilize the rooming-in method, but nevertheless cause disturbance in the child.

Some hospitals serving children are trying to bring other of their practices in line with the general purpose of maintaining the continuity of parent-child relationships. Admissions of a nonemergency nature may be postponed for a short period to provide time in which child and parent may be prepared for the coming separation. If the child is in a developmental phase during which his need for parental emotional support is particularly acute, the separation experience may be postponed for considerable periods when there is no urgency or the procedure is purely elective. Attempts are also being made to increase the frequency of parents' visits to hospitalized children in order to reduce the hiatus in the interchange of emotional responses.

For similar reasons, the routine practice of separating the child from his parents during immunizing injections or dental care is being newly evaluated, with careful attention to the child's needs at different ages and periods of development. At some times, a child badly needs the emotional support of a parent in undergoing a new, difficult, or painful experience; at other times, he gains more by being on his own. The parent's reactions, too, are important. If the parent is tense and apprehensive, his fears are communicated to the child and tend to upset him: in such cases a child usually does better if the parent is excluded.

Good relations between parents and children and self-confidence of parents in the carrying out of their duties can be further promoted by health personnel by various devices for securing and maintaining the active participation of parents and children in health procedures.

Parents always, and children in accordance with their developmental capacity, can benefit by knowing about a health problem, doing something about it, and sharing in the responsibility for getting well or staying well. This requires that the physician, nurse, dentist, or other health worker take the parent and child in on his planning and activities. Parents need knowledge, in simple understandable terms, of what an illness is and of what is to be expected during its course. A mumbo-jumbo of complicated technical lingo may sound impressive but it does not help a parent understand what is the matter with his child and what he can do about it. Blunt orders without explanation may be followed blindly by a dependent parent, but seldom without underlying resentment and irritation.

As a physician or nurse shares the responsibilities of the care of the child with parents, rather than taking the burden of care and credit for success entirely to himself, he helps them to an increasing maturity and competency in parenthood. A physician's awareness of parental anxiety in the stressful situation of a child's illness also helps him to cut through the host of apparently irrelevant questions that are the superficial manifestation of worry and enables him to provide appropriate reassurance.

Information is helpful, no matter how bad the news is. The mother who, on being told that her child had a brain tumor, said, "Thank God! Now we know!" was not being facetious. An unknown danger had changed into a known one. It was a profound relief to learn what the trouble was and what the next steps were to be. This settled, she was able to approach the child and his situation more competently, with less anxiety, and the change for the better in her emotional status was reflected in the child.

Children, too, find a more meaningful way of participating in a therapeutic or prophylactic program when they are acquainted with the facts of a situation in terms they can understand. A three-year-old child permits an examination of his eardrum with less reluctance when he knows it is a way for him to get better. A school-age boy accepts a program of increased rest and inactivity more readily when he knows what its purpose is. Not only is a child's cooperation in a therapeutic or prophylactic program better when he is taken in on it, his feelings and fears about his illness are helped by a clearer understanding, and there may be a beneficial effect on the course of his illness. Many sick children look on illnesses as, at least in part, a punishment for something they have done or thought. A child with rheumatic heart disease, guilty and anxious, is more relaxed after his misconceptions have been cleared up; his tension and pulse rate decrease, and this results in less of a load on his damaged heart.

When parents give the physician information about a child's illness and his early development and background, they are helping him in diagnosis and in planning treatment. Careful attention to what a parent has to say increases the parent's feeling of importance; he is the one who, in a way, knows most about his child and can best help him. Belittling the parent in any way—by interrupting him, listening impatiently when he goes into apparently irrelevant details, questioning the advisability of something that has been done—diminishes his confidence in himself as a parent and heightens his defensiveness. Such feelings make it difficult for the parent either to act upon advice or otherwise to participate in carrying out any suggested program.

A child's capacity to share in the responsibility of getting better is enhanced when he is taken in on giving the history. When the child, rather than the parent, is asked "just where it hurts," and is encouraged to tell how he is sick, he begins to feel that things are being done *with* him and not only *to* or *for* him. (Moreover, the physician may gain valuable diagnostic information.) In the case of one eight-year-old boy, diagnosis of atypical convulsive attacks was delayed for several months because his parents, long overconcerned about bowel functioning, had told only that he had attacks of abdominal pain. It was not until an attack was witnessed that the diagnosis became clear; the boy became mentally confused, put his hands on his abdomen, lost consciousness, and sank to the floor. His parents had interpreted the attacks as pain; no one had asked the boy.

Children can also participate in the physical examination in a variety of ways; all ways encourage his initiative and help him to feel important and respected. A child who can take off his own clothing should be allowed to do so and not be undressed by his mother or a nurse. The two- or three-year-old can handle a stethoscope and grow familiar with it before it is placed on his chest. Somewhat older children can hold throat sticks, the percussion hammer, or other instruments for the doctor until he is ready to use them. The strangeness and awesomeness of a syringe can be dissipated by encouraging the child to help wash it or, if he is younger, to play with it and squirt it. A child in a dental chair can hold a mirror so that he can see his teeth as they are examined, or he can find out about the various instruments.

When hospital admission becomes necessary, the reasons for it can be explained by the doctor directly to the child. This is far preferable to informing the parents and leaving it up to them to tell the child, for being drawn into the process helps the child to preserve a measure of autonomy; it also obviates the possibility that he will hold his parents to blame for his admission. This is particularly important in view of the fact that often enough parents have not contemplated hospital admission before bringing a child for examination; they may even have assured him that he would definitely not be left in the hospital. If the admission is elective or not an emergency, the child may well be permitted to choose to come back on another day, especially if something important to him is coming up in the immediate future. One eleven-year-old girl who rebelled loudly and tearfully when hospitalization was proposed for treatment of laryngeal polyp cooperated cheerfully when admission was delayed so that she could attend a Scout meeting that evening.

In hospital wards, participation can be used to help children become increasingly independent and self-sufficient. They can serve as nurse's helpers in general housekeeping activities like pushing food carts and carrying linen and can help in the care of younger children when the age group is mixed. When children are expected to remain by their beds and not "interfere" with ward routines, their gregariousness and desire to work cooperatively are squelched, whereas active participation not only contributes toward making hospitalization a constructive growth experience but also promotes convalescence.

Permitting parents and children to participate actively in health procedures helps to support children's personality development both directly through utilizing their developmental capacities and needs for mastery, and indirectly through helping their parents to grow in competency and self-confidence as parents. There are, however, one or two possible misconstructions that merit special mention.

When children and parents are taken in on decisions about medical procedures, for example, it must be recognized that the limits within which any given individual is able to participate comfortably (whether in "knowing" or "doing") vary widely. For example, one seven-year-old girl who had to be hospitalized for a day in order to make X-ray studies of her gastrointestinal tract was apprehensive about the experience and tried to postpone it. When she was asked when she would come in for it, she became increasingly tense and anxious; this was a decision which she could not make. But when she was asked whether she would like to come this Wednesday, next Wednesday, or the one after, she could decide without discomfort; choice for her became possible only when these limits were set.

In addition, the physician, dentist, or nurse who tries to support developing independence and initiative through enlisting the child's participation needs to remember that he is in fact an authority and is so looked upon by both the child and his parents. Though advice offered to a parent or child should not be given dogmatically, because active participation grows out of a sharing of responsibility and not out of obeying blindly, it must nevertheless be given in a way to carry conviction of its correctness. Responsibility for decisions first rests primarily upon the physician and involves the parents secondarily, who look to him for authoritative replies and recommendations.

Timing Elective Procedures

During certain periods of a child's life, the number of stimuli he receives from his environment and from within himself is especially high; he is flooded with new ideas and experiences. Clinical observations lead to the belief that the process of integrating experiences, ideas, and other stimuli into the developing personality is readily disturbed by unusual external events at such periods of "flooding." David M. Levy's studies of emotionally disturbed children who had undergone surgical procedures bear out this general thesis; the second and third years were apparently particularly vulnerable points in the children he studied, and he suggests that elective surgery be postponed until after a child has reached three years of age. There is in fact a considerable body of clinical evidence to show that surgical or other traumatic procedures carried out when a child is learning to walk or talk may interfere for some time with the development of these capacities, and that pubescent children are also apt to be emotionally upset by surgery.

Parents should also be advised not to plan elective surgery during the two or three months just before or after the birth of a new child in the family. The period of the mother's lying in is occasionally chosen for the elective hospitalization of a child, with the idea that by so doing—since there will be no one at home to care for him—two birds may be killed with one stone. But the orderly process of the child's personality development may be seriously disturbed by carrying out such a plan.

Most children are inevitably exposed at some time to health procedures that are physically or emotionally painful. A great many must undergo surgery or be separated from their families by hospitalization for study or treatment. Some of these experiences cannot in any circumstances be postponed or delayed.

But many elective surgical procedures can be put off for considerable periods. The "T & A" is probably the one of these most frequently performed, though wholesale removals of tonsils and adenoids is fortunately on the wane, at least in some areas. In many instances, such operations may be safely postponed, and then should not be performed until the child is four and a half or five years of age.

Correction of minimal cosmetic defects, either congenital or acquired, can be postponed until the child is old enough to understand the necessity for it and to assume some degree of responsibility in deciding whether to proceed, and when. Cosmetic defects that either interfere with physical functioning or are so disfiguring as to hamper social adjustment are more urgent; they cannot be postponed indefinitely. Even so, decision as to when to proceed should take into account the child's stage of development and capacity for participation.

Most pediatric centers now tend to operate on congenital hernias in infants rather than to wait until the child is toilet trained or later. As surgeons have become more adept in dealing with the smaller operative field and control of infection has become more effective, the early correction of this condition has become feasible, and there are cogent arguments in its favor. Although separation of infants from their parents is theoretically unwise because it interferes with developing parent-child relationships and jolts the baby's sense of trust in himself and his environment, actually infants seem to be able to withstand surgery relatively well, both physically and emotionally.

The other common elective surgical procedure is circumcision. Although such operations are most commonly performed in early infancy, a number of them are performed on older children. Psychiatrists, in general, believe that the mutilation threat involved is greater than that in other surgical operations and that this threat is a focus out of which many later personality disturbances crystallize. In some instances, circumcision is clearly indicated but rarely is it an emergency procedure.

The enlistment of the child and parents in making decisions about the timing of elective procedures is important. The degree to which a child can share in the responsibility is relative, depending on his developmental readiness. He should not be expected to accept a load too great for him;

neither should he be protected and guarded from any load at all. Each time he succeds in mastering a new and difficult life situation he has gained constructive growth experience.

Using the Psychology of Interpersonal Relations

Thus far, we have been concerned with *what* health personnel can do in their practice to help children to develop into mature, emotionally healthy, happy, and responsible adults. These have been summed up as supporting the children's developmental potentials and aiding parents to perform their roles with competence and satisfaction. We must also consider *how* these principles can be put into operation, how health workers can take into account the intrinsic psychology of interpersonal relations— parents' attitudes and feelings as these influence their capacity to utilize advice effectively, and health workers' attitudes and feelings toward children and parents.

Observant health personnel long ago recognized that some parents are able to use information and advice constructively; others, apparently trying just as hard to be cooperative, succeed only in making matters worse. Still others argue each point or even completely reject any and all recommendations. Some find it relatively easy to act on suggestions about physical care but cannot make use of suggestions about child behavior. Attempts to understand these observations led to clinical investigation and the discovery of much that is now known about the psychodynamics of parent-child relations.

Most disturbances in parent-child relations are not due to stupidity, ignorance, or pure obstinacy but are related to the parents' past experiences and their own personality structure. A parent's earlier relations with his own parents, with his brothers and sisters, and with other people important in his youth, together with the unresolved hostilities and resentments that stemmed from them, have been found to be significant in his present relationship with his child. Patterns in the parents' behavior with a child (such as overmeticulous care, on the one hand, or neglect, on the other; rigid standards of obedience or almost complete lack of any limitations put on the child; preoccupation with feeding, education, and the like) were seen to be related to patterns which had figured conspicuously in the parents' childhood home.

Workers in psychiatric settings began to develop methods of helping parents to free themselves from emotional conflicts that prevented them from using knowledge about child rearing effectively. But the methods they developed called for too many special skills and insights to be directly applicable in more general child-health settings. Attempts to gear the basic therapeutic concepts developed in psychiatry to general medical work with children have yielded results slowly, and knowledge of methods and approaches is still incomplete.

In the meantime, the health worker's job of communicating sound concepts of child rearing to parents became more difficult. The concepts of child rearing considered sound in the first two or three decades of this century underwent marked change. Emphasis shifted from rather rigid rules on "habit conditioning," which were supposed to fit the child into society, to the importance of permissiveness and understanding on the part of parents, who were advised to adapt their demands on the child to his capacities and to adjust themselves to his motives and emotional needs.

Many of the new insights deriving from scientific study of human development have been quite confusing to parents. Concern with the significance of parent-child relationships in the life and growth of the child has contributed to the uneasy self-consciousness of many parents about their influence on their children. Publications, both professional and lay, have overstressed the pathological in parental attitudes, without calling sufficient attention to the great variety of feelings a parent inevitably experiences toward his child, the beneficial effects of natural, spontaneous parent-child relationships, and the child's strong, biologically derived potential for normal growth and development, given halfway decent direction. Many intelligent parents earnestly striving to do a good job are preoccupied with the permanent damage which they must have done. They fear they "reject" their children because at some point during the pregnancy or afterward they wished they had never had them. (By this criterion all children are rejected!) Bewildered by the seeming inconsistency among experts, many parents have become so insecure, jittery, and anxious that they find it next to impossible to function comfortably, confidently, and casually in their relationships with either their children and/or physicians and nurses. Hence they constitute a peculiarly vexing problem to health workers.

It is becoming increasingly recognized by health workers that the job of being a parent cannot be learned as an intellectual exercise. When parents attempt it, the trivia of daily infant and child care are likely to become mere mechanized rituals performed for the child's "good" by the book. Important recommendations made by professional health workers, carried out in routine manner and without emotional conviction, defeat their basic purpose; the notes are played but there is no music.

Take "demand feeding" arrangements, for example. Feeding the infant when he demands food rather than on a schedule decreed by someone else is designed to help develop a feeling of mutual trust between mother and child and to satisfy the infant's important psychological needs for oral activity. Demand feeding applied as an unfeeling technique does not develop in the child trust either in his relationship with his mother or in himself. When every evidence of discomfort is interpreted as a signal for feeding, when an attempt is made to gratify the infant before he expresses discomfort, the child fails to gain any capacity to wait, to store tension, to handle emotional strain. Sleeping problems arise, and clinging to parents is intensified.

The basic fact is that it is not so much what is done as the way it is done that is important. All of us know that there are many ways in which a parent can remove a meal without saying anything, thus carrying out sound advice frequently given for children presenting feeding difficulties. The meal can be taken away in a pleasant manner that implies, "Mealtime is over and it's time to do the dishes." Or it can be snatched off the table in a way that says in effect, "Look what you have done to me by not cleaning everything up!" It can even be removed with an external air of controlled calm that almost snarls, "This is what I am supposed to do, but if the doctor hadn't said so, you know what I'd do to you!" Words are not required to communicate feelings, whether warm and accepting or hostile and resentful, and when words are used, the spirit in which they are spoken is more important, in an emotional sense, than are the words themselves.

As a parent assists his child in developing socially acceptable toilet habits, as sex information is given, as a child is prepared for the birth of a new brother or sister, the *how* it is done is as important, if not more so, as the *what* and *when*. The process of helping a parent to become more competent and effective involves more than fostering either intellectual learning or the capacity to obey orders. Becoming an adequate parent is an emotional growing-learning experience.

Just as what the infant or child gains in his relationship with his parent depends on the satisfactoriness of the emotional interaction between them, what the parent gets by way of advice, direction, information, and the like, from the physician or nurse is useful only when interpersonal relationships are good. This is the keystone of any health program for children that attempts to do a complete job. The way in which the physician or nurse responds to parents' troubled, and often troublesome, questions is as important as the content of the answers he or she gives.

Individualization of Health Services. Good health workers recognize differences among people and respect the dignity of individuals. Parents have a right to feel that they exist as individuals rather than as anonymous members of the patient population in a hospital outpatient department, well-baby clinic, or busy private office. Such small gestures as addressing parents by name instead of calling them "mother" or "father," telling them the name of the physician or nurse with whom they are talking, and expressing interest in their comfort all help.

Any routine that gives a patient a feeling that he is not being considered as an individual detracts from the kind of interpersonal relationship essential to the promotion of total health. Sometimes even a habitual bit of idle chitchat designed to put the parent at east can become so mechanical as to defeat its purpose. For instance, it is usually sound to compliment a mother on her baby, but if one says "What a pretty baby!" when the mother believes that the baby is homely, the device may backfire. Some routine procedures help to eliminate the possibility that important physical details may be overlooked, but even administratively determined routine does not have to be gone through in routine fashion. It is the individual dentist, nurse, social worker, or physician who applies the "routine" in the case of each individual child or parent; the way he goes about it determines whether the child patient or his parent feels that things are being done to him or with him.

Even certain new sensitivities on the part of health workers may be so generalized as to interfere with individualization of services. Not all children are afraid of needles; nor are all parents overanxious, overintense, and insecure. To assume that a child is afraid when he is not may actually induce fear. Parents differ in their capacity to take over sound health principles and make them a working part of their relationships with their children, and even the same parent differs from time to time and in differing circumstances. A mother temporarily separated from her husband, for whatever reason, may respond differently than she would if the family circle were intact. A parent disturbed by the critical illness of his own parents may for a time exhibit less than his usual confidence in his own capacities. A basically dependent parent may need help in coming to feel that his request for advice is legitimate and sensible, whereas another parent with strong feelings of self-sufficiency has to be so guided as not to detract from his feeling of being able to cope with things.

Respect for the parent and belief that he is trying to do a good job, no matter how far short his performance may fall, is necessary. Acceptance of an individual as he is, with no threat, actual or implied, that he is to be changed against his will is fundamental for all professional workers who deal with parents and children.

Respectful listening, with full attention, is essential and serves several purposes. It assures the parent or the child that his problems as he feels them—no matter how irrelevant or inconsequential some of the details may seem to the listener—are important and are receiving due consideration, and that he himself is accepted and respected. Moreover, as the tale unfolds, much about the child's role in his parents' psychic economy may be revealed, information that is often essential and always helpful. Many unrealistically overconcerned parents refuse to be assured, no matter how thoroughly the child is examined or how authoritatively they are told that all is well. But as a worried mother tells her story about her child's obdominal pain, the source of her anxiety may be traced to an earlier family experience with neglected or undiagnosed appendicitis. Once this is known, it is much easier to allay her fears, and so to free the child from the impact of emotions that belong to some other part of his parent's life experience. Careful listening is also of value in helping to work out plans and solutions that lie within the practical living situation of the family.

Referral to another health agency is sometimes necessary and is ordinarily easy when the problem is physical. Acceptance of the referral and full cooperation are far more difficult to come by when psychiatric service is indicated. For many parents, to acknowledge that their child has an emotional problem is tantamount to acknowledging failure. It is, therefore, exceedingly important for the physician or nurse to avoid in any way implying blame—by attitude, tone of voice, or spoken word. Sympathetic understanding, expressed in an interview or two, without threat or pressure of any kind, helps parents to face the issue. Sometimes it even results in immediate changes for the better in the family situation and some relief of the child's symptoms. Always, it is important to remember that no psychiatric therapeutic program is likely to be successfully launched unless parents are motivated to seek psychiatric help out of their own understanding and concern rather than in blind obedience to an order or in meek cooperation with a friendly health worker.

Another aspect of individualizing health services should be mentioned. In outpatient clinics and hospitals where health personnel rotate, the continuity of established relationships with parents and children is often interrupted. While in some instances this seems to make little difference (particularly when the patient participates in the transfer from one worker to another), in other instances it seriously interferes with a treatment program. In some health settings, attempts are being made to preserve the continuity of relationships with patients through appointment systems or other schemes, such as keeping the hospital resident staff in the outpatient department one or more days per week throughout the year. Some criticism is now being voiced about the custom of transferring children from well-baby clinics to other health settings when they become ill. The effects of such shifts on children and parents require further study.

Attitudes and Feelings of Health Workers. The warm accepting attitudes required for work of this kind rest upon real liking for children and interest in them, and on liking for people in general. Clinical health practice has no place for the misanthrope. But though a friendly attitude is required, the relationship should not properly be "social." Many physicians have found that meeting frequently on a social footing with patients and their families puts them at a disadvantage in the more psychological aspects of their practice. Such work makes it imperative that physician and nurse remain objective, in the sense that they avoid getting personally entangled in patients' problems.

The health worker is looked on by parents and children as an authority, and that in effect is what he is. His role is that of an expert; it is not a parental role, or a familial role. If health personnel take over a parental role, the earlier struggles parents have had with their own parents tend to be reactivated. Advice is likely to be either rejected or followed blindly, and as the physician's or nurse's own feelings enter into the picture, their attitudes may be unwittingly influenced to the detriment of their capacity to be of real help.

Irritation at a parent's indecisiveness may betray a health worker into laying down the law in authoritarian fashion. Irritation at a child's clinging to his mother may stir a dentist to remove the mother brusquely from the scene or may light up a hostility that communicates itself to the child. A parent's anxious questioning all too often goads to secret scorn. A challenging parent can make a physician feel insecure, uncertain of the validity of his knowledge, and anxious, and he may, as a result, either respond with a whole series of dogmatically positive assertions or undergo some degree of paralysis of action. Any health worker who is anxious about his own competence may become either overly rigid or overly permissive with children and their parents.

The feelings that health workers experience in relation to the parents and children whom they are trying to help affect the way in which they are able to carry out health procedures, give anticipatory guidance, enlist participation. Like all human beings, these workers are subject to emotional reactions in relationships with other human beings; irritation, resentment, hostility, or anxiety is more or less inevitable from time to time. Some of these untoward feelings tend to diminish in intensity and frequency as a worker develops sympathetic understanding of why particular parents and children behave as they do. Moreover, as he becomes aware of such feelings in himself he is better able to deal with them and to take them into account in his practice. When he understands both why a parent is aggressively challenging and how such a parent makes him feel insecure and anxious by putting him on the spot, his control over the total situation is greatly enhanced.

There are many questions for which current knowledge provides no certain answers. The mature and seasoned health worker feels no need to answer when parents address such questions to him; the insecure worker, however, feels he must reply, even if he has to draw upon unproved conjecture or folklore. The mature worker is able to say, "I don't know," or "We don't have much knowledge about it yet." To say this too often may shake the confidence of parents or children, but when they sense the personal security of a mature individual behind the words, their disturbance is ordinarily not very great.

The degree to which a professional health worker can share his doubts and misgivings with parents is an index of his own personal maturity and sense of professional competence. Unfortunately, anxious health workers occasionally try to protect parents from hard realities just as anxious parents try to protect their children. Though the desire to protect parents is understandable, in certain precarious situations no physician can honestly be very reassuring and will only fail if he tries. The anxiety must be frankly shared, and the parents helped to face the situation as it is. Parents may be quite disturbed for a while but in the end are usually able to share greatly in the responsibility, supported by the knowledge that the physician, nurse, and others are earnestly interested in their child and in them and will do their very best.

Many young mothers with first children, who feel particularly inadequate, look to someone on whom to be dependent. Such a mother may find in the physician or nurse a person who needs to be boosted by such dependency. For a while she leans heavily, and the health worker gains a certain satisfaction from the relationship. But the professional worker may soon begin to resent the numerous telephone calls and other demands on him; he can extricate himself from the relationship without unduly upsetting the parent only if he appreciates his own part in its development.

Overidentifying with the child, to the detriment of relationships both with him and with his parents, is another common pitfall in all child-health settings. The child is, after all, the center of clinical interest, and so the parent can easily come to be regarded as a necessary but baneful appendage. At times, the parent is even regarded as a natural enemy from whom the child must be protected. This is especially apt to occur when the parent-child relationship has gone askew or when a parent says, "I know it is all my fault, please tell me what I am doing wrong." Overtly or implicitly expressed, overidentification with the child detracts from the health worker's respect for the parent and impedes every effort to help him meet the child's needs.

Overidentification with the parent is perhaps less common but is not unknown. Here respect for the individuality of the child suffers. Interpretation of the child's behavior in terms of his own developmental needs tends to be blanketed out by the assumption that only destructive nonconformity can be expected of him. As a health worker is aware of his tendency to overidentify with either parent or child, he is better able to maintain a realistic perspective on the interaction between them and to appreciate his helping role better.

A parent or child may respond in kind to the physician's or nurse's anxieties, whether these are based on a realistic concern over the outcome of a critical illness or on his emotional reactions to the persons involved in a case. This not only impedes health promotion but may also interfere with the treatment of illness. Anxiety on the part of a physician when a child is seriously ill may lead him into a frenzy of illogical therapeutic activity that disturbs both child and parent.

Many physicians and other health workers claim that a busy practice, with its attendant unremitting demands for service, leaves no time for attention to psychological factors. Experience suggests that this plaint derives less from insufficient time and more from the health worker's lack of familiarity with the principles of a psychologically oriented practice and his fear lest he be upset by what parents may reveal if he listens with a sensitive ear. When his training has given him a working knowledge of personality development and parent-child relationships, he seems able to find whatever time is necessary. In actual fact, awareness of the import of parents' and health workers' attitudes takes no extra time at all. Support of growth potentials is an intrinsic part of total health supervision, and ten or fifteen minutes suffice for a lot of listening and understanding.

Health Practices with Well Children

We turn next to a consideration of current practices in total health supervision for children and adolescents which are especially appropriate to fostering healthy personality development. These practices, although they have not been universally adopted, are considered by forward-looking health personnel to be important and worthy of wider application.

It is generally agreed that adequate health supervision of presumably normal children is the means by which preventive health services can most readily be provided and positive health be promoted. Ideally, health supervision includes the following basic elements:

1. Preparation of parents during the prenatal period for the care of the child
2. Periodic medical examination of the child for
   a. evaluation of development
   b. discovery of defects or deviations
   c. correction of any abnormalities, defects, or disease uncovered
3. Protection by initial and booster immunization against those communicable diseases for which there are effective immunizing agents, with passive protection being given when indicated in the individual case
4. Promotion of nutrition
5. Periodic dental examination and treatment, including the use of generally accepted preventive methods
6. Promotion of healthy personality development through attention to parent-child relationships and the guidance of parents concerning the stages of normal personality development and the management of minor personality or behavior disturbances.

The Prenatal and Neonatal Periods

There is much to be learned about the role of emotional factors in the physical conditions of pregnancy and about the effects of emotional stress in the mother on the fetus and infant. Some of the stoppages of labor are known to be related to emotional stress, fearfulness, and subsequent fatigue. There are those who believe that emotional factors in mothers-to-be have a great deal to do with the vomiting of early pregnancy and are related in some measure to the toxemic disorders of later pregnancy, and that anxiety and emotional stress in a mother during pregnancy may have some effect on the developing fetus.

The recognition of the importance of the obstetrical period in the development of healthy parental attitudes toward children has led to experimentation with techniques designed to improve the emotional hygiene of pregnancy. Some physicians, aware that parenthood is a severe test of the emotional maturity and integration of an individual, include some reference to pregnancy and parenthood in their discussions during premarital examinations.

The fears and superstitions of pregnant women may reflect a good deal of folklore but they do give rise to anxiety and are often based on ignorance of physiological and anatomical facts. The insecure, fearful, uninformed parent-to-be is often helped materially by correct information sympathetically and understandingly given. It is not only unkind but unwise to brush off a pregnant woman's anxious questionings with a curt, "You're not going neurotic on me!"

Classes in infant care for mothers-to-be, and in some places for fathers-to-be, have long been a part of the guidance offered by some centers during pregnancy. They are usually conducted by public-health nurses, with nutritionists and physicians participating on occasion. Many anxieties and feelings of inadequacy harbored by parents regarding their capacity to take care of infants are resolved by this device. Instruction in physical care—bathing, diaper changing, feeding, and so on—helps mothers and fathers to be less afraid and tense in handling their babies, and it has been demonstrated that, as fathers are drawn in, they can lend mothers emotional support more effectively during the lying-in period and after the return home. Such classes also offer opportunity to present the normal physiology and anatomy of pregnancy and, by so doing, to dispel many fears.

Occasionally classes for prospective parents take the form of small discussion groups with professional leadership. Active participation on the part of group members and exchange of views and experience among them lead to an easing of tensions and worries about the looming job of being parents. Such results are not easy to achieve in the busy office of the general practitioner or obstetrician. It has been suggested, therefore, that discussion groups be set up, with physicians participating on a rotating basis.

In some programs the pediatrician discusses infant care with the mother during the pregnancy period, with a view to obviating or allaying her anxieties. Those who have tried this scheme believe that it has proved helpful in promoting feelings of maternal competency and in fostering sound parent-child relationships. Others question its advisability on the ground that many women develop a strong emotional tie to the obstetrician, and that he is, therefore, often in a better position than any other professional person to lend counsel and reassurance on the problems of infant care.

The emotional impacts of childbirth on the mother are also worthy of consideration. The importance of the fear factor in childbirth has recently been brought to attention, particularly by Dr. Grantly Dick Read of London, who has devised a technique for dispelling fear and aiding the natural childbirth forces. Though agreement with Dr. Read's explanations of the physiological ways in which fear interferes with childbirth is far from universal, there is widespread acceptance of the importance of the technique. "Childbirth without fear" or, better, Dr. Walser's slogan, "pregnancy without fear" lessens anxiety and tension and reduces both the number of standstills in labor and the chance of resort to excessive anesthesia, which may be directly harmful to the infant. It may also reduce the number of complications of pregnancy, though this is not yet certain.

Another device for fostering the mother's sense of competence in child care is that known as "rooming in"—the keeping of the newborn in the hospital room with the mother.

In brief, rooming-in has been demonstrated to be practicable and valuable for a selected group of mothers. It has been shown to be safe; when the mother is well, the danger of infection in the infant is no greater, and perhaps less, than in the average hospital nursery. Bringing mother and infant closer and more continuously together during the lying-in period need not necessitate expensive hospital reconstruction, as is sometimes claimed. Although rooming-in, rigidly interpreted, is more expensive not only in hospital construction but also in hospital management, effective compromise solutions that bring mother and infant closer together are within ready reach. The success of rooming-in, however, depends on adequate preparation of both mother and hospital staff, and it is here that the chief changes need to be made.

Consideration of the ways in which health services in the neonatal period may be improved calls, also, for discussion of prematurity. This condition is now the most important single cause of infant mortality and it poses certain special problems in early care. Since little is yet known about the specific causes of prematurity, much of the pioneer work thus far has been directed toward keeping premature infants alive. This requires prolonged hospital care—several weeks to two or three months—which disrupts continuity of contact with the mother. With exceedingly small infants the measures necessary to preserve life preclude handling and cuddling, the kind of "mothering" so important to normal infants. The stability of physiological functioning is so precarious that even minimum handling leads to marked respiratory irregularity and sometimes to frightening episodes of stopped respiration.

In addition, the mother of a premature infant is apt to develop feelings of self-blame; she should not have had a baby so soon after the previous one, or should not have worked so hard, or gone shopping, or whatever; or it may all have been her husband's fault. A father may look on the puny baby as evidence of his own inadequacy. Along with this there is realistic anxiety that the baby may not live or may not develop normally, which the physician and nurse cannot honestly deny. The physician and nurses, however, can help keep realistic anxieties from becoming excessive and disproportionate and can help parents resolve their unrealistic feelings of guilt and shame.

Certain practical measures can also be taken to offset the problems in physical care. Most physicians and nurses responsible for the care of premature babies have been impressed by the contribution that good nursing, with a warm personal interest and concern, can make to survival. In some settings, the type of physical care that is at first necessary is changed as the infant grows larger and stronger, and more handling and cuddling are included. Sometimes, too, when the infant has become large enough, the mother is encouraged to come to the premature nursery to take part in his care.

Infancy

The importance of health supervision during infancy is generally accepted. Until recently, however, attention has generally focused on promoting good physical health rather than on total health care. During the past two decades, there has been increasing interest in including mental-health factors in health supervisory practice—especially with infants. Treatment of incipient personality and behavior disorders was the first step, which was followed shortly by efforts at prevention through programs designed to promote total health. This sequence is not surprising since help was originally sought from clinical psychiatric services for children which had been established for the treatment of incipient or already developed disturbances. To begin with, the psychiatrist, psychiatric social worker, or clinical psychologist attached to a service for infant health supervision usually worked in isolation from the rest of the staff, treating individual children whose social and emotional development had already gone astray. Now it is thought far more sound to introduce psychiatric insight into infant health supervision through staff orientation, so that each health worker can better participate in total health supervision.

In the course of experience, certain practicable methods have emerged. The importance of encouraging warm, accepting, understanding parent-child relationships is generally accepted. Warm parental feelings cannot be created by fiat, but the atmosphere in which they flourish can be fostered. As parents are helped to feel more competent and sure of themselves, they begin to gain satisfactions from parenthood and become less irrationally anxious and concerned about problems of day-to-day living with their children, and mutual regulation between them and their infant gradually develops in relation to the child's developmental needs. They are better able to judge when a child is able to give up an earlier mode of satisfaction and take on a new one—when to give up the 2 A.M. feeding and when to move on to a three-meal-a-day schedule, for example. Information about individual rates and rhythms obtained in anticipatory guidance ceases to be merely intellectual and becomes a working part of the parental role. All this presupposes an understanding of patterns of growth and development on the part of the health worker.

The provision of safe, adequate nutrition has long been an important part of infant health supervision, resulting not only in a lowered infant mortality rate but also in the markedly decreased incidence of nutritional disturbances and dietary deficiency disorders. But for some years now, forward-looking pediatricians have been concerned with how an infant is fed as well as with what he is fed. This concern developed in part because it became apparent that, despite the provision of adequate amounts of suitable food, many children refused to take the food in sufficient quantity or developed various other "feeding problems." Interest was also stimulated by new knowledge of the significance of oral activities in infancy for sound emotional development.

Though the notion that a well child's own appetite is the best index of how much food he needs at a particular time was relatively slow to take hold, rigid scheduling and control of amounts of food intake were gradually relaxed in favor of meeting the infant's psychological and physiological needs. Unfortunately, both self-demand schedules and breast feeding—the latter previously neglected in this country, in part because of the ease and safety of bottle feeding—have been enthusiastically seized upon as ready-made through tickets to emotional health.

Although it is generally agreed that breast feeding should be encouraged because it is probably best for the infant both physiologically and psychologically, breast feeding is not a *sine qua non* for healthy personality development. The advantages of breast feeding are many. A good case can be made for nutritional advantages, and some case can be made for psychological advantages. It does bring mother and child closer together, and the more difficult sucking required may be beneficial, though experimental evidence for the latter is still lacking.

Nevertheless, it would seem unwise to assume that a child's whole future personality development hinges on whether or not he is breast fed. The mother does not exist for the young infant only as a flowing or nonflowing breast. She bathes him, dresses him, comforts him, cuddles him and chucks him under the chin, "gooes and gurgles" at him, takes him out to air, and displays him proudly to friends and relatives. Even in early infancy, warm, supporting maternal attitudes involve much more than offering the breast. Overemphasis on the importance of breast feeding may lead the mother who for one reason or another is unable to nurse to think she has caused irreparable damage to her child. This may plunge her into a state of chronic self-blame that is hard on both herself and the child.

Bottle feeding can meet infants' nutritional requirements and it need not necessarily interfere with adequate "mothering" and warm supporting affectional relationships. It is believed desirable to hold the baby in the arms while bottle feeding but even this may not be essential if the mother's basic attitudes are good. And if attitudes are not good, neither breast nor bottle feeding meets the infant's psychological needs which center around feeding.

Whether the baby is bottle or breast fed, both his nutritional needs and his psychological needs are now thought to be best met by letting his appetite be the guide as to times and amounts of feeding. Infants' needs for food intake are rhythmic and regulate themselves into feeding patterns within two or three weeks. If the child's lead is followed, the transitions from many to fewer feedings a day and finally to three meals are easily accomplished. Gradual weaning, in pace with the child's readiness to take over the newer methods, is not traumatic. It is worth noting, however, that solid foods may be beyond the child's neuromotor capacity if introduced too early, and that his "spitting them out" (a reflex action) may be misconstrued as willful refusal, a situation which is likely to lead to strife between parent and child, with attendant emotional disturbance.

In practice, compliance with the self-regulatory feeding patterns of individual infants works out very well, on the whole. Some mothers, however, need definite direction before they are able to accept the relative flexibility and act upon it. The kind of parent who applies a regularly scheduled feeding program overrigidly is ordinarily unable to keep to a self-demand regimen without ritualizing it to the child's detriment. By and large, a permissive attitude which respects the infant's varying needs is important in establishing a sound psychological hygiene of feeding arrangements. But self-demand feeding is only as good as the spirit in which it is applied.

The Preschool Period

As a rule, preschool health supervision, either in private medical practice or in a publicly sponsored well-child clinic, takes place at regular intervals, though not as frequently as during infancy. This period is marked by rapidly developing skills and interests, patterning of behavior, increasing self-sufficiency and ability to do things independently. It begins with relatively marked dependency on parents and ends with capacity to move into school life.

Physicians and nurses become especially aware of the gaps in their training as they try to deal with the ups and downs of personality development during this period. There are fewer ready-made, easy answers now, and it is no longer possible to maintain a more or less purely biological viewpoint, for the child's efforts to find out what he can do impinge upon adults' feelings about right and wrong. Moreover, both parents and professional people are apt to inject into child rearing emotional sets that properly belong elsewhere. A large part of the prophylaxis of this period must, therefore, center on viewing a parent's concern about a child's "problem" objectively, from the angle of the child's developmental status. The situation is frequently so difficult that some health personnel are tempted to duck it by an overpreoccupation with unimportant deviations in physical growth or by spacing health-supervision visits far apart. Then, too, in their own procedures, doctors and nurses must keep in mind the child's developmental stage. For instance, the physician, if he recognizes the strivings for independence, is less apt to feel frustrated during physical examinations when an apparently compliant child does a sudden about-face and refuses to permit some necessary procedure. At such a time it is important that his approach be supportive rather than arbitrarily hostile.

Some of the many questions that parents of preschool children bring to health settings may be answered on the basis of a physical examination, but most need a broad knowledge of growth and personality development. Concerns about feeding and poor appetite reach a peak because during this period appetite falls off as physical growth slows up. Power struggles about eating can disorganize family life and color parent-child relations for a long time. With anticipatory guidance good prophylactic results have been obtained.

The "no, no" stage is easier on all concerned when parents are not taken unaware, when they can see in it the child's struggle toward autonomy rather than plain recalcitrance. They are interested, too, to know that repeating sounds or actions over and over again—standing and sitting, walking and climbing—is part of the way in which a child develops important skills, and that the intense motor activity of the latter part of this period is not dangerous but, rather, necessary to a developing sense of autonomy and initiative. Then as the child begins to display a capacity to use his imagination, parents may need help in viewing his tales in their proper light rather than as evidence of lying.

Parents of preschool children want to know how to reply to queries about sex differences and where babies come from and are frequently concerned about a child's genital manipulations. Pat formulas do not help, because parents who are most anxious about such matters cannot handle them casually or without giving rise to feelings of shame in the child. Such parents need careful discussion and a chance to unburden themselves of some of their own doubts and misgivings before they are ready to use advice with any effectiveness.

Help in preparing a child for the birth of a new baby also requires time and care. If the individual child's total developmental picture and his relationships with his parents are left out of account, the anticipated jealousy is all too readily intensified.

Parents constantly call on health personnel to evaluate the total development of their children during this period of growth. The problems with which they are concerned are often more or less normal parts of personality development and are "problems" only in terms of a parent's emotionally colored, preconceived ideas. Helping a child to pattern his sleeping, eating, and excretory behavior to meet social demands is apt to bring a parent's emotional sets, prejudices, and anxieties into sharp focus. Telling a parent what is normal is not enough; effective help calls for an understanding of why a particular bit of behavior constitutes a problem for the particular parent who asks about it. But viewing the situation only from the angle of the parents' mistakes is not helpful either. There are no absolute rights and wrongs in child rearing. Even coercive methods of enforcing certain behavior patterns may have little effect on a child's over-all personality development if he has a warm, satisfying, and supporting relationship with a secure parent who respects him.

Lateness in the acquisition of usable speech bothers most parents more than lateness in walking or teething, and this problem is frequently presented to physicians during the preschool period. There is great variation in the times of appearance of physical aptitudes, depending on differences in patterns of neural maturation. It can be safely said that most children will eventually talk, and even that a time will come when their parents will wish they would keep quiet. But this kind of reassurance is no substitute for careful examination and evaluation of possible factors involved when a child is belated in starting to talk. Slow mental development, complete or partial deafness, severe emotional disturbance, infantilizing relationships with parents must all be considered before a child is classified as "just a late talker." The early recognition of hearing defects is important in getting appropriate educational measures under way. A mentally retarded child may have a better chance if the situation is recognized early and his parents are given appropriate help and guidance.

Children's behavior during this period may be a severe test of parents' feelings of competence. There is much current confusion about "discipline," and many parents feel uncertain about exerting the firm, supporting, reassuring control that makes a child feel safe in the face of his own drives to be self-sufficient and to do as he wants before he is able to discriminate between what is harmful and anxiety provoking and what is safe and comfort producing. This benevolent and considerate guardianship, by setting reasonable limits, protects the child from his own impulsiveness and from essentially meaningless experiences that lead to doubt in himself and shameful or guilty feelings about what he has done or proposes doing.

Elementary-school Years

The period which extends from the time the child is five or six years old to the time at which he develops secondary sex characteristics is usually regarded as the most healthy of any during childhood. This may account, in part, for the relative infrequency with which parents take well children of elementary-school age for health supervision. It is also true that hospital clinics generally discourage well-child "checkups" because they are swamped with the care of sick or disordered children. For the most part, the health of this age group is supervised, if at all, in school health settings, and many of these are rather inadequate. Ideally, the same health personnel who have supervised the health of children during their infancy and preschool years should continue to do so. Physicians or nurses who have developed good working relationships with individual children and parents are in a better position to influence total development than anyone new who is unaware of all that has gone before.

During these years, physical growth is steady and reflects general health and nutritional status. Where adequate nutrition is already a working part of the family knowledge and habit, nutritional disturbance is infrequent and is usually related to economic insufficiency, physical illness, or emotional disturbance.

The appearance of the secondary dentition makes attention to dental health imperative. But dental care is often inadequate because there are too few dentists, and services are financially out of reach for many families. Orthodontic care in particular is less available than it should be. The newer prophylactic measures for preventing dental caries are, however, being used more and more widely.

In general, supervisory health visits during the school years are geared toward making the child's learning experiences in school as effective as possible. Attention to the visual and hearing status is an essential part of the medical examination. Increasingly effective group screening techniques are being developed for use in school settings to find those children who need more detailed examination, and increasing attention is being paid to ways of getting discovered defects remedied and to providing special educational facilities for children who need them.

Correction of, or allowance for, defects that interfere with meeting the skeletal or neuromuscular demands imposed by any and all aspects of the school situation is a part of any health supervisory program. Evaluation of cardiac status demands careful attention, and the presence of actual heart damage or mere functional murmur has to be dealt with in a way that does not give rise to anxiety. As the child reaches the later years of this period, physical disturbances or defects that interfere with full participation in the school's program of physical education and sports become increasingly important.

In some schools, health examinations have become more than the rapid, perfunctory physical surveys that were once customary. Parents are involved, sitting in during the physical examination, giving the physician pertinent history, and discussing findings with him. This has proved more effective than a dozen letters in gaining parents' cooperation in getting defects corrected. When the health history is obtained by the teacher or school nurse and the results of the examination are later communicated to the parent in a conference with the physician, the results are far less satisfactory, although this procedure is better than working with no health history at all.

In all health supervisory contacts with school-age children, attention should be paid to emotional factors; any examination should include a history of the child's general adaptations and an evaluation of his emotional status. Emotionally disturbed or preoccupied children do not take well to learning. Their capacity to absorb what is taught may be blocked, their relationships with teachers and other children may be disturbed, and their behavior may be such that their presence in the classroom cannot be tolerated. Vague complaints of school-morning stomach-ache or headache may be related to lack of satisfying school activities or progress. The primary seat of the difficulty may be either in the home, when emotional relationships have gone awry, or in the classroom, where the child may be misplaced in terms of his capacities or may be struggling with an unrecognized problem, such as a reading disability.

As the physician discovers remediable or partially remediable physical or emotional defects, the total program for the child usually requires close cooperation on the part of the school. The teacher who is interested in the child's whole development may be a vital factor in the ultimate success of any prescribed regimen. Conferences initiated by the child's physician or the school nurse are important ways of gaining the teacher's participation and cooperation. Cooperative ventures like this lead to increased understanding of the particular child, which may well spread to better understanding of other children.

There are other areas of educational practice in which health personnel may make an indirect contribution to the total health of the child. Health workers may participate in health education in the classroom or may assist educators in planning the content of courses that include material on physical hygiene, nutrition, accident prevention, and the principles of mental hygiene. Courses concerned with family relationships, mental hygiene, and the like, are being introduced more and more widely into secondary schools, and experiments in giving children understanding of human behavior and its motivations are being conducted in some elementary schools. Such collaboration between health workers and educators should prove helpful in devising valid methods of promoting healthy personality development.

By paying close attention to their use of the medical findings, health personnel working in school settings can do much to support and encourage parents in their relationships with their children and to support and encourage the children themselves. There is much possibility of mis-use of recommendations. For instance, the enthusiastic reporting of a cardiac murmur of no clinical significance may lead to marked anxiety and has frequently precipitated overprotective coddling for a heart dis-ease the child never had. Unless discovered defects are communicated to parents very carefully, the parents may feel criminally neglectful and de-velop feelings of self-blame that adversely affect their relations with their children. As another example, children often get the idea that they will not be promoted unless they get the recommended dental work done or some other treatment accomplished. The availability of dental care and the family's capacity to pay for it then affect the child's feelings about his parents and his attitude toward the academic program.

In many forward-looking educational programs, much attention is be-ing paid to emotional health. Guidance counselors, clinical psychologists, and, in some school systems, child psychiatrists are an integral part of the school, though not usually a part of the school's health services. Child psychiatrists and other physicians can be helpful in developing mental-health programs that will aid the teachers and other school personnel. It must be noted, however, that specific techniques developed in clinical psychiatric settings cannot be transferred without adaptation to other settings; psychiatrists should not be looked to for advice about teaching methods and the administration of schools. What psychiatrists have to offer is knowledge about children's feelings and their emotional needs and the ways these are manifested at school and in the community.

Even if there were an adequate number of competently trained child psychiatrists (and there is not and will not be for some time to come) it would be unwise to refer all children with symptoms of maladaptation for psychiatric treatment. The need for psychiatric care cannot be deter-mined by the nuisance value of the symptoms, which may have little rela-tion to the seriousness of underlying factors. Though it is difficult to say categorically when an emotionally disturbed child becomes an emotionally disordered child, a careful evaluation of the child's reactions and milieu often makes it possible to distinguish between the two. If the child is stranded in an earlier stage of development, if he is unable to relinquish earlier satisfactions and turn to more mature ones, he may be a candidate for psychiatric care, but even this may be a relative matter.

Many physicians, oriented in the mental-health aspects of their prac-tice, are able to evaluate the severity of the disturbance and the need for referral. They recognize both their own competence to deal with the common garden variety of behavior disturbances and the limits of their competence, and they know when a child psychiatrist is needed, just as they know when to call in a surgeon in a case of abdominal pain. Health personnel who are trying to carry out sound mental-health principles in their practice with children must remember that all children from time to time display symptoms usually regarded as evidence of emotional disturbance, that all parents from time to time fall short of the ideal of parenthood, and that what sometimes appears to be distorted parental behavior may be a result, rather than a cause, of the child's disturbance.

Adolescence

Adolescence is usually regarded as a period of emotional upheaval, and in health settings these youngsters are likely to reveal their concern about their relationships with people and about their own bodies. The adolescent for the first time begins to regard the physician as *his* and not his family's. If a good working relationship has been previously established, or if it grows out of sympathetic understanding in the present, he frequently feels like asking questions and even seeking personal advice. Feelings of being "different" are particularly disturbing at this time, and many adolescents are concerned about their height, weight, and strength. The growth spurt begins at various ages, and the late starter, two years or so behind his associates, may be much worried. Characteristically, he wants to know whether he will always be short, whether he will be able to compete on equal terms in athletics, when his whiskers will begin to sprout. The undeveloped girl in a group of girls well into physiological puberty may feel exceedingly unhappy; and the converse may also be true. Many times these worries can be greatly relieved by knowledge of the variability in growth curve and assurance from an authoritative source that a late start into physiological maturity in no way is disastrous.

Other adolescents ask about the amount of sleep they need or ways of improving strength and health. A few attribute their lack of group acceptance to acne or some other trivial defect. Simple explanations and emotional support tend to relieve adolescent anxieties. As the young person finds his concerns dealt with seriously and patiently, he is enabled to talk about his sexual preoccupations and his misunderstandings and misapprehensions about the ways in which sexual activity or the lack of it will affect him. Counsel and advice by a sympathetic physician (who is regarded as "knowing about such things" by virtue of his training) can be markedly steadying.

If health advisers are receptive, the adolescent may also bring them his confusions, doubts, and guilts about his struggles to emancipate himself from his parents. Any health worker who is able to function as a "special" friend, a confidant and supporter, can help the child view this problem realistically, keep him from overextending himself in his rebellion against parental standards, and so protect him from compounding his emotional distress.

The extremes of emotional behavior occurring quite normally in adolescents make premature referral for psychiatric treatment a particular hazard for the enthusiastic but unwary health worker. In contrast with younger children, who are usually brought by their parents or other adults for psychiatric help and who do not clearly see their own needs, most adolescents know when they are in difficulty and are likely to accept psychiatric help when it is needed. Here, as always, a clear conception of the emotional aspects of the age period is important in evaluating the seriousness of isolated segments of behavior, and psychiatric diagnostic criteria appropriate for adults are of as little help as they are in earlier childhood.

It is especially important during adolescence that both physical findings and the individual's attitudes about himself be carefully interpreted; undue medical attention to essentially unimportant variations may lead to exaggerated preoccupation with the body on the part of adolescents seeking an "out" for their anxiety about more basic, internal drives. Albuminuria, for instance, is not uncommon and is usually not a sign of kidney disorder. The adolescent thyroid is far from stable but it usually straightens out if it is left alone. Rapid pulse rates and elevated blood pressures are often found transiently in tense, keyed-up youngsters who are unused to physical examinations (some are quite embarrassed at the thought of exposing their changing bodies) or who for some reason are anxious about the findings.

The health worker who is active with adolescents continues to have contacts with parents. If parents can be helped to understand the puzzling behavior of their adolescent children, they tend to develop an increased tolerance toward the frequently unreasonable and irritating behavior of their offspring. Such tolerance circumvents many of the impasses that arise when adolescents and parents lock horns, and smooths the adolescent's path to maturity.

As more is learned about physical maturation and emotional development in adolescence, and this accumulating knowledge becomes a part of their training and experience, health workers will become more secure in tackling total health promotion during this period. There is already great interest, and there are signs that the teen ages are beginning to emerge from the neglect which they once suffered.

In summary, then, health supervisory practice offers opportunity to foster healthy personality development in children of all ages through contacts with the children themselves and through improving parent-child relationships. This is a part of total health supervision. Some workers are already utilizing important mental-health principles in support of children's developmental potentials in their day-to-day practice. Success depends on their recognition of the relevancy of various specific techniques and methods in the over-all picture and on their awareness of interpersonal relationships in their dealings with parents and children.

At the present time, total health supervision is more widely practiced during some age periods than during others; it is relevant and important at all ages, from the prenatal period through adolescence.

Total health supervision is not the prerogative of a few health workers, specially favored by training, but of all health workers active with children in all health settings. More widespread use of such practices depends on orientation during the training period, undergraduate and graduate, of all health personnel. In-service training schemes now being tried would seem to be effective for workers already in practice. Health workers who by training and experience have been most concerned with the promotion of mental health are now ready to impart their experience and developed skills to their colleagues.

Health Practices with Sick or Disordered Children

Illness of varying degrees must be expected in every child's life. From his illness, as from all his experiences, a child learns about himself and the world in which he lives. Any illness, with attendant physical and emotional strains, may complicate his progress toward maturity; on the other hand, as he meets new and difficult life situations successfully, he may gain increased confidence and trust in himself. Given certain conditions, even hospital experience may serve to further a child's emotional growth; it may build his trust in those outside the home by demonstrating that people respect and appreciate him even though they may find it necessary to hurt him.

More research is required for fuller understanding of what the experience of illness means to individual children and for the building of sounder principles of care. But health personnel are presenting evidence that the preparation the child receives in regard to his illness and the kind of care he receives during and after it determine in large measure whether the experience will be emotionally harmful or constructive.

What Parents Can Do

In the young child's early explorations of his environment, he is bound to experience falls, bumps, bruises that pain and surprise him. He touches a hot radiator, and his startled face and his cry of pain and rage indicate that his hurt is not only physical but emotional. This is one of the first opportunities the mother has to start building the child's attitude toward pain.

Similarly, the inevitable experiences of visits to the doctor and the dentist may be used for positive health teaching. The child is very likely to come to feel pretty much the way his parents feel about these contacts; he is very quick in his identifications. Conversation in the home, sometimes not intended for his ears, can condition him in one direction or another. If the parents are themselves emotionally upset by pain, the child will absorb their uneasiness very quickly.

Prior to any new experience of this kind, the child should be told simply, confidently, and truthfully what he may expect and what will be expected of him. He should have a chance to talk freely about it, to express how he feels, to ask questions and get honest answers. Where possible, it is wise to arrange preliminary visits to the doctor's or dentist's office; then the physician, dentist, or nurse, who understands the child's fear of injury and his need to trust, can do a great deal to help him and his parents prepare for the examination or treatment visit.

Although an illness may have a particular meaning for a particular child, some reactions are so universal as to warrant particular attention. Many children, if not most, associate illness and punishment. How often we say, "You didn't wear your rubbers as I told you, and now you are sick." When this is said scoldingly, the child is likely to feel the fault lay in disobeying rather than in getting wet. One boy was quite convinced he had developed rheumatic fever because he had gone wading against the orders of the camp counselor. This association between illness and punishment for wrong-doing is greatly reinforced if the child has been threatened for indulging in forbidden activities. In trying to enforce discipline, parents often use the doctor as a bogey man, and children who masturbate or wet are told, not infrequently, that their genitals will be amputated as a punishment or operated on as a "cure." A child who has been subjected to threats of this sort quite understandably looks at physician, nurse, and hospital through fearful eyes.

Since a known danger is easier to face than an unknown one, fear of injury can be minimized by telling every child—even a two-year-old—in advance exactly what is going to happen to him. Such precautions are particularly important if surgery is contemplated. Children are often told fantastic tales to conceal the real reason for their leaving home when they are headed for the hospital. One boy suffering from acute appendicitis was brought to the hospital in the middle of the night in his pajamas with his sled. His parents had told him that he was going for a sleigh ride, and it was several days before he could react to any of the hospital personnel with anything but suspicion and hostility.

When the child is going to the hospital he should by all means be told so in advance—though not too long in advance, for younger children do not comprehend time very clearly, and older ones sometimes worry if told more than a day or two beforehand. (On the other hand, some children know for weeks that they are going to the hospital for corrective surgery and do not seem to be disturbed by it.) The child should also be told the reason for going, with emphasis upon what good it will do him, and he should be instructed about the general routine he may expect. In addition, he needs opportunity to ask all the questions he wants and to have them simply answered. It is also wise to avoid too pleasant a picture of what will happen and promises of early dismissal. Overly extensive elaboration of details may give rise to the notion that the parent is anxious.

There are times when parents are unable to decide whether or not they should permit their child to undergo surgery. They have a right to ask the doctor as many questions as necessary to allay their fears and feel certain that their decision is good; after that, they may continue to need support as they carry through. In certain instances, it is wise for the child, is he is old enough, to share in this process. When several children in the Children's Hospital in Cincinnati who required surgery for the repair of a congenital heart lesion were taken in on the problem, they were so eager to have the advantages of the correction that they accepted the procedure not only with calm but even with anticipation.

In all circumstances, children react much better to carefully explained truth than they do to the subterfuges to which parents sometimes resort in an unwise attempt to "protect" them. Under the adult's inability to tell a child the truth about what is in store lies his own inability to face it; the child absorbs his parent's anxiety, to which a physician who has failed to respond supportively to the parent's concerns and questions may have contributed. When parents stand solid and calm behind their child, the child reflects their assurance in his own reaction to what confronts him.

What the Physician Can Do

The physician's work is as closely bound up with the home and the family as it is with the hospital. His responsibility in preparing the child for dealing with illness does not begin when admission to the hospital is contemplated but rather when he first sees the child and his parent, begins to establish his personal relationship with them, and to guide the parent-child relationship. Anything he can do to help make these relationships good adds to the contribution he can make to total health. In addition, it is likely to mean fewer hectic afternoons in the office with frightened children and exasperated mothers. Then, too, when, as in the case of an acute emergency, it is too late for guidance in relation to the particular event, both the parents and the doctor can count on the child's previous relationship with them and the other adults who have so far made up his world.

A child can feel that the doctor is his friend, a person who likes and understands him. Even if painful things have to be done, he can sense that the doctor always keeps his word, that he hurts no more than he can help. To scold a frightened or recalcitrant child for expressing his natural feelings in the doctor's office soon convinces the child that the doctor neither likes him nor respects how he feels.

Many children, left in ignorance, brood over their ilnesses and their possible causes and results. A child, who has been voiding yellow urine all his life, experiences some shocked surprise and begins to speculate when he starts to void red urine with acute nephritis, for example, but it is not unusual to find that no adult has thought to explain the change to him in terms he can understand. The sick child worries less if he knows the facts.

The timing of admission to a hospital is often of great importance. In general, separation from home and parents should not be contemplated at a time when a child is going through a period of particular stress, such as the three months before to six months after the arrival of a new baby in the family, or at times of rapid development, such as the period during which he learns to walk or talk. It has also been observed that operations are much more hazardous for one- and two-year-old children than for older ones. Children at this age have a keener response to pain than do older children; they are more dependent on their mothers; they have less experience with people outside the home; and they cannot comprehend what an operation is all about.

What the Hospital Staff Can Do

Admission to a hospital means different things to different children. Its meaning for any particular child is determined by his past experiences and his developmental status. The child who has been loved and accepted by his parents is better prepared to tolerate some separation from them because he feels sure of them and because he expects to find kind, protective care not only in his family but elsewhere. A child who has been unloved, rejected, or threatened with abandonment may interpret admission to the hospital as punishment or as an attempt on the part of his parents to rid themselves of him.

At the time of admission to the hospital, the parents as well as the child need understanding, support, and acceptance. Giving them an opportunity to express their fears, guilt, grief, resentment, or hostility, and accepting their expression of feelings contribute greatly toward giving them peace of mind—and they must have peace of mind if their child is to make a comfortable adjustment to the hospital, to separation from those upon whom he is so dependent, and to his illness. Time spent with the parents is time well spent; much can be done to relieve their anxiety, prepare them for the child's probable reactions, make them feel understood and accepted regardless of how they or the child respond to this difficult situation.

Most of the hospital admission procedures, history taking, and preliminary examinations are essential to adequate medical care, but thoughtful planning for the child and his family leads to a simplification of machinery and to the avoidance of long waiting periods and repetitious conversations with numerous physicians, nurses, clerks, and attendants. Some hospitals serve meals and provide play materials and someone to play with children who must wait while their parents are involved in the details of admission.

In some hospitals, too, the head nurse from the ward in which the child is to stay comes down to the admitting office and talks with the mother and child before they are separated. She inquires about the child's nickname, his eating habits, his place in the family, and anything else that the parent particularly wants her to know. She tries to conduct the conversation so that the child feels her interest, her kindness, and her desire to understand him and make him happy. In addition, she suggests a few simple things that will help the child feel that the links with his home are not broken—that he have one of his old toys, that his mother leave her scarf with him, that he be sent a postal card every day. By this procedure the child not only becomes acquainted with the nurse in the presence of his mother but is also assured of a friendly relationship between his mother and the nurse, which is also very important to his sense of security.

Both the child's and the parents' fear is alleviated when the parents accompany the child from the admitting rooms to the ward, and when his mother stays a while to help with undressing, getting to bed, and perhaps the first meal. If painful and unfamiliar procedures are to be carried out soon after admission, she may remain until they are over, provided she is able and prepared to give the child support.

In some hospitals, parents are encouraged to come into the hospital on the day of operation and stay with their child until he leaves for the operating room. They are usually not allowed to accompany him there, both because physical facilities are not available and because it would call for more psychological preparation than the present staff is able to give, but in both wards and private rooms they are encouraged to be on hand when the child is returning to consciousness.

Evidence of the wisdom of such measures is provided in a study conducted by Dr. David Levy.[1] Children who remained free of emotional difficulties after operation had been told the reason for the operation and how it would be performed. They were taken to the hospital by the mother or father and given sedatives in the bedroom to spare them the experiences of being wheeled down a corridor, suddenly seeing weird instruments and people in white, struggling against the anesthetic. Returned to the bedroom, they woke up where they went to sleep and were greeted first by their parents.

A few hospitals in the United States make arrangements for one of the child's parents to stay with him when there seems to be a particular need for their continued presence. Over a period of years, Dr. J. C. Spence, Professor of Child Health at the University of Durham (England), has developed an arrangement in the hospitals of Newcastle-upon-Tyne by which mothers are admitted to the hospital to care for their own children. This idea is not so revolutionary as it at first sounds, for the greatest amount of children's nursing is done by mothers in their own homes; the mother's nursing unit is merely an extension from the home to the hospital. Not all illnesses can be cared for by this kind of nursing, and the needs of the other children in the home have to be considered, but the majority of children under the age of three seem to derive benefit from it.[2]

Because the hospital scene often shifts rapidly, plans for continuity of care and for avoiding precipitate changes should be made in advance—by assigning a single nurse or group of nurses over a period of time, arrang-

[1] David Levy, "Psychic Trauma of Operations in Children," *American Journal of Diseases of Children*, Vol. 69 (1945), pp. 7–25.

[2] J. C. Spence, "The Care of Children in Hospitals," *British Medical Journal*, Jan. 25, 1947; reprinted by U.S. Children's Bureau.

ing for selected workers to visit regularly, planning a repetitive sequence of activities, and the like.

Whenever possible, mothers should accompany their children when they are transferred from one ward to another, otherwise a child is likely to worry lest his mother not be able to find him when she comes to visit. The child should at least be told his mother knows where he has gone. If it becomes necessary to transfer a child to another hospital for specialized care, one of his parents should accompany him; if the exigencies of the situation do not permit this, immediate visiting at the second hospital is important.

Daily visiting hours may increase the load carried by ward personnel but are sufficiently important to warrant it. Time in the hospital seems endless. The child, who in all probability has never before experienced separation from his parents, needs the reassurance that comes from seeing them every day. Their arrival helps prove to him that he has not been banished for being "bad." The visit may have therapeutic value even when it is followed by tears and seems to have been disturbing rather than comforting. Children are angered at their parents for putting them into an uncomfortable place and for leaving them alone, and daily contact provides opportunity to express and work off some of these strong negative feelings, an opportunity that is very important in the prevention of emotional problems.

On the other hand, the presence of an agitated and anxious parent may not only take up an unreasonable amount of the hospital staff's time but upset the child and even complicate diagnostic and treatment measures. It may also disturb other children in the ward or room. If such a parent is not calmed by reasonable reassurance and explanation, it may be wise to limit the length of his visit to five or ten minutes in order that the acutely ill child may have emotional as well as physical rest. Suitable isolation may lessen the ill effects on other children in the hospital. After the acute phase is over, a parent like this should be helped to see his child's illness in proper perspective, and social workers should try to help him deal with the factors underlying his distress.

Visiting hours should also be used by ward personnel to form relationships with the patient's family and to gain the kind of information that increases understanding of the child—by listening to parents talk about their children and observing them in their relationships. This is important in addition because parents who have felt welcome, understood, and respected in the hospital are in general more receptive to help when the time comes for the child to be cared for at home.

Most children regress to an earlier behavior level when they are ill. This holds especially true when they are in the hospital, separated from mother and home. They tend to demand attention similar to that which they received as babies and need much sympathetic understanding. Recently acquired habits go first; young children may be expected to soil themselves for a while. Usually, as the physical illness subsides and the child comes to accept the new people and routines, his habits are reestablished rather quickly. It requires good judgment to accept and treat regressive behavior as a symptom of illness and to help the child back to his own maturity level gradually as he gets better. Prolonging the regressive period may hamper him in making a good emotional adjustment during his convalescence.

As the child convalesces, it is wise, then, to get him back into normal relationships with other children as quickly as possible, though care must be exercised to proceed gradually, lest the child, too suddenly, be deprived of dependent care, feel rejected, and begin to show signs of increased anxiety. As he demonstrates increasing capacity for independence, it should be recognized, approved, and encouraged. He can be weaned from dependence most easily when he is helped to find satisfactions in experiences with other children. Then his need for dependence lessens and he begins to accept sharing his mother's or nurse's love with others.

Illness, pain, or any new experience may precipitate latent anxieties regarding previous experiences. The hospitalized child needs opportunity to uncover his fears, anxieties, doubts, and questions to a sincerely interested, sympathetic adult—parent, doctor, social worker, or nurse—who will not judge or punish. His anxieties may relate to any of the usual childhood problems or may be specifically associated with the illness or hospital experience. The nurse, in her long-time intimate contact, can set the stage for this kind of uncovering and can help the child cope with his emotions. Since he may fear rejection because he has confessed something he felt was bad, the nurse must not only be discreet about what she has been told but must also demonstrate her continued friendship in every way, otherwise the child is likely to begin to reject her.

The ill child can also be helped to express his emotions through his play. One two-year-old who could not be comforted by anyone soon settled down when a dressing like her own was put on her doll. Doctors' and nurses' kits are popular with children and are helpful to them in working out tension and anxiety. Painting, clay modeling, drawing, dramatization, storytelling are therapeutic and should always be available, particularly when the child is working his way through some emotional problem. While engaged in these activities, the child may reveal much about his inner feelings to the skilled observer. Emotions can also be released through motor activity—a Bingo pounding bed for a young child, a tricycle or table tennis set for an older one. Ambulatory children enjoy helping the hospital staff with regular ward activities, such as setting the table, serving meals, or reading to other patients.

For the majority of children, the mere passing out of toys and other play materials on a hospital ward does not suffice. They need stimulation and help in finding interesting activities, particularly if they have been hospitalized for long periods of time. Some need to be taught how to use materials; some need encouragement before they can express themselves—they have been so inhibited at home that they cannot play spontaneously. Those who are in a hospital that has the services of a recreational therapist are fortunate.

The hospital nursery school for the young child and opportunity to continue regular experiences in play, school, reading, church, and social activities for the school-age child and adolescent are being recognized as essential. As indicated above, the child relinquishes the dependency of acute illness much more easily when he develops interest in group activities. The schoolteacher (often supplied by the local public school system), the librarian, the nutritionist, the occupational therapist, the priest or minister can all enrich the hospitalized older child's life in important ways. Plenty of play and work space, an outdoor play area, and good equipment must be provided if the program is to be fully effective.

Inevitably, the child comes into contact with a rather large number of adults in a hospital. There was a time when a physician, several nurses, perhaps a technician or two, and a teacher represented the total expected number. Now the professional group has increased, and there have been added, as well, more attendant personnel, such as ward maids, porters, orderlies, and other helpers. Though many of these workers have only brief contact with the child, they become a part of his environment and may be of great significance to him.

No mention has thus far been made of health personnel in administrative and policy-setting positions who rarely have direct contact with the child patients but who can create an atmosphere in which professional workers are able to function effectively in support of children's developmental potentials. If an administrative officer is unsympathetic or without understanding, the work of the professional staff is seriously impeded. The administrator's attitudes and those of the professional staff also affect the nonprofessional personnel in the health setting. In a large modern hospital there are many clerical workers, elevator operators, doormen, technicians, housekeepers, and the like, who have contact with children and parents. If their relationships with the professional staff are characterized by considerateness, understanding and appreciation, they are more likely to be warm, understanding, accepting, and supporting rather than impersonal, scornful, or downright callous, and the atmosphere of the institution is much more helpful to the well or sick child.

It becomes increasingly apparent, then, that there should be an over-all plan for giving all personnel, through in-service training and supervision, insight into, and understanding of, children's emotional needs. To be effective, such a plan must include the administrator of the hospital, the chief of the medical staff, the nursing director, every department head, and every worker on the unit staff, and it is important that personal relationships among them be friendly and relaxed, for tension at this level may be as disastrous to the child's sense of security as it is among the members of his family.

What Architects Can Do

Too many hospitals, clinics, health centers, and convalescent homes are built without study of the ways in which their architecture might facilitate the daily work of the staff in promoting the total well-being of children. Though architects often figure importantly in councils planning schools, they are seldom represented on community groups planning child health facilities. With the help of competent architects, communities can get economically built hospitals and convalescent homes that make life easier for management, the doctor, the nurse, and the child, through integration of design and engineering. More than one hospital administrator has secured a better staff by showing them a plant they would "love to work in."

The contribution of the clinic and hospital architect who recognizes the need for flexibility in the use of facilities for a continuously changing group of patients and who brings with him a feeling for children in addition to his technical skill can hardly be overvalued. Today, over half the hospitalized children are cared for in institutions of less than a hundred beds. New scientific developments, improved methods of curative care, and expanded home-care programs may make it difficult to predict how many children in a community are likely to need hospitalization. Yet it is undesirable to place children in adult wards at times when pediatric units are overflowing, and wasteful to maintain a large pediatric unit only partially occupied. Movable partitions, by providing flexibility in allocating floor space and making possible adjustment in the size of units, facilitate both segregation of child patients from adult patients and desirable grouping of children within a unit.

Experience has shown that ideally the following features characterize the architecture of general hospital units and outpatient departments:

1. Special facilities for child patients, segregated from adult patients
2. Space and provision for parents to remain with children whenever necessary, and guest rooms for mothers who wish to stay overnight
3. Easily available conference rooms where doctors, social workers, and nurses may talk privately with parents
4. Means for grouping children of the same age together
5. Playrooms for younger children and social rooms (including library) for adolescents, large enough to permit parents and children to play or talk together during visiting hours or while waiting for outpatient treatment
6. Equipment (such as toilets, washbasins, tables, and chairs) of a size suitable for children
7. X-ray rooms especially for children whenever possible
8. Space for the child's possessions near his bed
9. Means of rolling beds to outdoor porches
10. A dining room for children out of bed

The problem of how to group patients, whether by age or by service, presents some real difficulties. Age grouping has certain advantages: it brings services closer together, it allows for better use of space and equipment, it simplifies ward routine, and it supplies satisfying companionship for the children. It has, however, some definite disadvantages: surgical patients are frequently "clean" from the standpoint of respiratory infection, whereas medical wards have a higher percentage of "dirty" patients. Small units and good technique help to prevent the spread of infection. If the decision is in favor of age groups (which seems to be the prevailing view in this country now), wards should be so planned that patients with respiratory infection can be completely segregated.

Special wards have to be provided for certain specialized types of care. A premature unit is one example of this kind. Such special units are suggested only when the type of care required cannot be given on the general ward.

The size of groups is a question to which there is a variety of answers. The solution may be to provide units of several sizes (one-bed, two-bed, and four-bed) in each section. It is especially important that a number of one-bed rooms be provided. The cubicle is certainly not the answer to air-borne infection; new admissions need to be isolated until their condition is definitely determined; very ill children need to be cared for in a room alone. One-bed and two-bed units are specially adapted to provide for care of children whose parents should stay with them. With changing ways of financing medical care, hospitals in the future will probably find increasing demand for rooms of this size, and the sharp distinction between ward patients and private patients will disappear.

Training of Health Personnel

As health personnel have become more generally aware of their role in promoting healthy personality development in children and youth, they have sought ways of increasing the knowledge and skills they need to perform it adequately. In consequence, the reorientation of both preservice and in-service professional training has, in the past decade, been the subject of considerable thought and, in some centers, experimentation.

There would seem to be general agreement that all health workers need a working knowledge of normal personality development, of behavioral deviations, and of the factors which play into each. They should also have some knowledge of appropriate diagnostic procedures and therapeutic measures, especially those which are applicable within the framework of their own particular type of practice. This entails insight into parent-child relationships and ways of influencing them, based on a broad understanding of human relationships and a firm grasp of the ways in which the health worker's own feelings affect the parents and children with whom he is working.

Psychiatry has been looked to for help in giving all health workers a desirable working knowledge of personality development and functioning. This has been true in medical education, in nursing, in social work, and, to a perhaps somewhat lesser extent, in dental education. In the beginning, psychiatrists tended to teach psychopathology almost exclusively— the general types and causes of well-developed mental disorders. There were many reasons for this. The facts of personality development and human relationships were then less well understood than they now are. For a long time, medicine in general had been more concerned about disease and its correction than in positive health. The psychiatrist, too, was more familiar with this aspect of his field—and, in any case, it is easier to teach about morbid functioning. Even now, many physicians and medical students are more interested in learning about disturbed personality than they are in learning about how to keep personality healthy.

A survey of the teaching of psychiatry in the undergraduate years of medical training points up certain shifts in the content and methods of teaching: [3] (1) Psychiatry is gradually becoming more integrated into medicine in general; (2) it is being presented more as a basic science and less as a specialty; (3) it is being offered earlier in the curriculum (from the first year on), with major emphasis being put on the emotional aspects of health and disease; (4) less reliance is being placed on formal lectures; (5) interest is mounting in the importance of interpersonal relationships, particularly the doctor-patient relationship; (6) psychiatric teaching hours are being increased.

There is wide variation from school to school, however. In some, a definite attempt is made to relate the content of the course to the student's own life experiences—of illnesses, visits to the doctor, hospitalizations, separations from parents, and the like. By beginning students' contact with patients in the preclinical years, a few schools are attempting to obviate the student's more or less complete isolation from patients while he is immersed in study of the basic sciences. In some, instruction in history-taking centers around the development of interviewing techniques that emphasize psychological implications. A few have introduced family case studies early in the curriculum as a way of helping the student become aware of the broad psychological implications of medical practice. In twelve schools, pediatricians trained in child psychiatry teach personality development. Several believe that the best place for such training is on the pediatric service and not in the department of psychiatry, and a few use the collaborative teaching of psychiatrists, pediatricians, clinical psychologists, and social workers to give students orientation in basic psychiatry. Frequently, prenatal clinics, newborn nurseries, well-baby clinics, nursery schools, public schools, courts, or visits to homes are used for teaching child development and behavior.

The efficacy of lectures for training doctors, nurses, and other health workers would seem to depend on the enthusiasm, interest, and ability of the instructor, though there is general agreement that this is not the best teaching method. Clinical demonstrations and discussions, seminars with free-for-all discussions, ward rounds, well-supervised clinical clerkships conducted by qualified instructors who are adept at teaching seem to be more satisfactory. If basic psychiatric principles are to become a part of the student's everyday working knowledge, he must use them in all his contacts with patients and not save them for special situations labeled

[3] M. J. E. Senn and F. L. Stricker, "An Appraisal of Undergraduate Medical Education in the United States with Reference to the Teaching of Medical Psychology," a paper prepared for the Midcentury White House Conference on Children and Youth.

"psychiatric." Experimentation looks toward teaching psychiatry in such a way that the student will be able to use it in whatever type of practice he eventually engages and not as though he were going to be a specialist in psychiatry.

As these developments in teaching and training become more widespread, health workers will be better able to fulfill their role in total health promotion. There are, however, several very real impediments to the realization of such goals on the part of all medical schools. Though available training facilities are for the most part being used to capacity, well-equipped teachers are too few even for the training of psychiatric specialists, not to mention the kind of orientation described above. Psychiatrists with special training in child psychiatry are particularly scarce. Many schools are unable to find teaching personnel with the necessary training and experience even if they have ample funds; others are unable to meet the competition of the greater financial gain in private practice.

Another very real impediment lies in the allocation of curriculum hours. Many believe that the time has come for a reevaluation of the medical curriculum. Only a very small number of schools have made curricular adaptations to provide more time for the aspect of undergraduate experience here under discussion. There is, however, considerable evidence to show that many do not take full advantage of the hours already available to them.

In pediatric internship and residency training, there are now almost twenty centers that are attempting to include some orientation in the psychological aspects of pediatric practice. This trend has characterized the past two decades, with gradually more and more training centers trying to include the contributions from child psychiatry in the training experience they provide. Some of these hospitals utilize the services of a pediatrician with psychiatric training in a consulting and teaching capacity. Others have consultation arrangements with psychiatric services, or rotate interns and residents through a psychiatric clinic for children. The type of setup developed in the various training centers would seem to depend on the training and personality of the leaders involved, on the needs and desires of the pediatric group, on the presence or absence of a psychiatric clinic for children in or near the pediatric hospital, and on other local conditions. Though there is not as yet any clear-cut consensus as to the best methods, there is more or less agreement that the further the resident is taken from his pediatric functioning, the less he integrates into his practice the contributions from child psychiatry. In most of the settings, the goal remains about the same: not to make a psychiatrist out of the pediatrician but to help him become a better physician, capable of practicing "comprehensive pediatrics" successfully.

Graduate courses in child psychiatry or mental-health aspects of pediatric practice have been given in a relatively few places, and not much information is available about them. They have been for the most part short courses of up to a week's duration, which have attempted to provide orientation in the psychiatric aspects of pediatric practice. The reading of papers on this field in general and pediatric medical meetings, round-table discussions at pediatric meetings, and the increasing number of relevant papers in the professional journals point up the interest of the practicing pediatrician in this field and his desire to learn more about it.

Pediatricians, however, care for only a small proportion of the children in this country. Many of them, however, are engaged in part-time teaching and so are in a position to influence the medical student or general intern as he rotates through a pediatric hospital service. But ways and means still have to be worked out for helping the general practitioner at the postgraduate level acquire the clinical tools with which to assist children to healthy personality development.

It is not our purpose to discuss the training for specialists in child psychiatry, though there is no doubt that their contributions to the training of general practitioners and pediatricians are of great importance in the promotion of healthy personality development of children.

Most dental schools include material on children's dentistry, on growth and development, and on the management of children in office practice —directed toward getting children to cooperate in dental procedures. Dental authorities agree, however, that the great majority of dental general practitioners need additional training in this area. This would entail more material about emotional growth and development of children, along with training in the techniques of handling children. Orthodontistry usually is given at the graduate level, and some dental schools have postgraduate courses leading to a master's degree in children's dentistry. A number of short courses, varying in length from a week or two to several months, are also offered. In all dental courses, from the undergraduate on, there would appear to be need for more orientation to the psychological needs of children. The relation of early oral activities in infancy to later difficulties in adaptation is important in any instrumentation involving the mouth.

In most of the accredited schools for dental hygienists, courses in the psychology of childhood are required. Dental authorities believe that this training should include, in addition, material on emotional and physical development.

Graduate nurses today are aware, to a degree greater than ever before, of their responsibilities for performing services to children and families in such a way that they contribute to healthy personality development. Nursing education is now in a period of transition, with a good deal of experimentation going on in the reevaluation of both course content and teaching methods. In many schools, courses are being given to help the student obtain a basic orientation in human relationships before clinical practice starts; such courses may be called "preparation for family living," "interpersonal relationships," or "normal growth and development." Nursery schools are being used, in some places, as field experience. The importance of knowledge about personality development for maternity and pediatric nursing is receiving especial stress.

Various universities are organizing postgraduate programs for the preparation of nurses in such specialties as obstetrics, psychiatry, pediatrics, and mental hygiene. At this level, an extensive study of personality development is usually included. There, in addition to increasing the scope of their experience, the students have an opportunity to develop additional skills in teaching and supervision.

As health workers come into contact with children and their parents in hospitals, well-baby clinics, school health services, or other settings for child health care, they are most apt to function as part of a health team, and this experience can in itself provide invaluable in-service training. When each professional worker contributes the skills and insights of his own discipline, all can add to their clinical tools for helping children and parents in a comprehensive practice. There have been developed thus far but few such programs. Merely to add a psychiatrist, a clinical psychologist, or a psychiatric social worker to the staff of a well-child conference does not help in total staff orientation unless such a worker is carefully protected from being used exclusively as a therapist.

It has been suggested that child-care centers should be developed under public or voluntary auspices where total health supervision could be provided throughout the periods of infancy, childhood, and adolescence. In these centers, physicians, nurses, dentists, social workers, nutritionists, clinical psychologists, and others would come for formal instruction and supervised clinical work and could work together. In this way the principles of total health supervision could be provided for a variety of health personnel, and much valuable data on children could be accumulated.

In summary, there is evidence of considerable thought, planning, and experimentation in providing training experience that will give health personnel the orientation and clinical tools with which to do a better job in promoting healthy personality development. Yet it would seem that we have not been able to formulate definitive programs, covering both content and methods. The time seems ripe for an attempt to determine which of the experimental approaches have proved valid and to use them as guidelines for further development.

✦ XV ✦

Social Services

WHAT is the role of the social services in the promotion of health of personality in children and youth? What are the implications of present knowledge of personality development for the conduct of social work? These questions, which are similar to those already considered for the family, church, school, and health services, are difficult to answer with certainty for the social services because there is so little agreement about the scope and function of social-service activities. Some authorities define "social services" very broadly, including in their scope a wide variety of activities that contribute to the welfare of the public. Others seek to limit the term in ways that show the area of operation that distinguishes the social services from other social institutions. A report to the White House Conference is not the place to attempt to settle intraprofessional disputes. Nevertheless, we cannot discuss the contribution of the social services to the welfare of children without making clear what manner of services we are talking about, so we shall have to start with a description of the nature of the social services as the writer of this chapter sees it.

The Nature of Social Services

To our way of thinking, the difficulty of defining "social services" or "social work" is lessened if the word "social" is given a clear meaning. To comprehend the way "social" is being used in this report, one must visualize society composed of people organized into groups for the further-ance of particular objectives. "Social" refers to this manner of organiza-tion. People are organized into families in order to produce and rear children. They are organized into occupational groups (including the professions) in order to provide goods and services for others and to se-cure income for themselves. They are organized into groups for worship, for recreation, for political and for governmental purposes, and so on. Each individual belongs to many such social groups. The work of each group is carried on according to rules—ethical, legal, customary—that specify the duties, rights, and role of each member. These groups,

357

generically considered, are social institutions. It is through them that the basic needs of children and adults are met, and society itself is maintained.

Now the important point for our purpose is that in any society there are individuals for whom these social arrangements are not available or do not work well. These individuals are accordingly handicapped to a greater or less extent, depending upon which social institution is involved. As a society becomes more complicated, the likelihood of difficulties probably increases, if only because the number of social institutions becomes greater and the job of each institution more specialized. Eventually, a new social institution arises that has as its particular task providing remedies for these social difficulties. The social services constitute that new social institution.

The most obvious kind of social difficulty is that in which an individual is deprived either of membership in a group or of the use of the services of a group that is vitally important to his welfare. There are, for example, children who do not have parents. For them there is no question but that some substitute for a family must be found. And there are heads of families who are jobless. A job or some substitute for employment must be provided, for we live in an economy in which income is essential to survival. Then, too, many people are socially deprived because medical services, recreational services, and so on, are too few in number or too costly.

The providing of remedies for such social difficulties is the work of the social services, broadly conceived. Playgrounds and recreation centers, free or subsidized medical care, subsidized housing, work-relief projects, foster care for children, social insurance—all measures through which the inequalities in our social system are partially compensated for through public or private financing may be regarded as social services if one defines the term broadly. More narrowly conceived, the social services consist of such of these aids as do not merely extend existing social institutions (as do free or subsidized recreational and medical services) but provide substitutes for them. According to this view, foster care for children whose homes are lacking or inadequate is one of the social services, as are the various insurance and assistance measures through which income is maintained when jobs are lacking or parents are incapacitated.

Some of the substitute social arrangements provided by the social services may be regarded as stopgap measures pending the development of new social institutions that will not so much provide a way out of individual difficulty as be a regularly constituted means of meeting a particular kind of need. For example, the agelong problem of how to assure that everybody has enough income to meet at least minimum requirements seems to have been solved in part by the development of the social insurance system. This system, on the way to being all-embracing, is so clearly a part of the regular economic arrangements of our society that it perhaps should not be counted among the social services. Similarly, day-care centers, now largely a means of dealing with problem situations, may in the future become so customary a part of our social structure as to be a social institution in their own right.

Another kind of social difficulty is found in the fact that some people do not operate well in one or another of the institutional groups to which they belong—the family, the occupational group, the armed services, and so on. The prime example here, so far as children's welfare is concerned, is the family. This basic social institution has to operate well if children are to grow up into healthy, happy citizens.

Each person in a family, the parents particularly, has a host of duties and responsibilities and some corresponding rights and privileges. In our society, fathers, generally speaking, are supposed to provide money with which to buy needed goods and services; mothers are supposed to care for children's physical needs; both are supposed to love their children and each other and to teach, train, and guide their children toward responsible adulthood. Children, too, have their duties, including that of honoring their parents, and they have rights, too, in some of which they are legally supported. In all this, many problems arise, variously categorized as parental neglect, nonsupport, unmanageable child, parent-child relationship difficulty, problems of household management or of marital relations, and so on. Courts handle some of these problems, and doctors, clergymen, and lawyers, others. But the profession that takes as its peculiar task the job of helping individuals, one by one or in groups, to deal with the difficulties they encounter in operating in accordance with the requirements of a social institution is social work, a part of the social services.

A third kind of social difficulty consists of inability on the part of some individuals to make good use of what one or another social institution has to offer. For example, some children do not derive the expected benefit from school because, for emotional or cultural reasons, they and the other pupils and the teachers cannot "get together"; similarly with hospitals and other medical services. A host of difficulties—fear of the disease, worry about home matters, dislike of doctors and hospitals, and so on—may stand in the way of an individual, child or adult, making good use of doctors and nurses and benefiting from treatment. Here social work provides individualized or group service to the end that the difficulties that interfere with good social functioning may disappear.

Parenthetically, it may be noted that most of the kinds of difficulty toward which the social services are directed are not peculiar to people who are in financial distress. People of low income may have fewer resources for help in time of trouble, because of lack of funds or of relatives or friends who have funds, or because of lack of knowledge of the resources that the community affords; nevertheless, difficulty in playing one's expected role in family, school, job, etc., or in making good use of social institutions is not confined to any one economic class. This being so, the social services are not limited to people of low income but, in hospitals, marriage-counseling centers, industrial plants, the armed services, and so on, may be made available to anybody who is in need of their help.

It is the task of the social services, then, to provide means whereby gaps between individuals and social institutions are bridged. Since the family is the social institution that is most important to the welfare of individuals and society, the main work of the social services consists of providing aid for family difficulties, economic, psychological, cultural, whatever they may be. Social services, however, are not limited to this one institution; they operate also in conjunction with schools, with health services, with courts, with recreational organizations, with industry, and with the military services, their work, for the most part, being that of aiding both the particular social institution and the individual who does not fit in or for whom the position in which he finds himself creates problems.

The social services work in several ways in behalf of the social adjustment of individuals and the more effective functioning of social institutions. First, through them facilities and material goods are provided to individuals and families who cannot otherwise maintain themselves. Second, through the social services help is given to individuals and families in dealing with the difficulties, practical or psychological, that stand in the way of happy family life, good school relations, effectiveness on the job, and so on. Third, through the social services that operate within social institutions (in schools, for instance, in hospitals, and in the military services), administrators and professional workers are kept informed about the social factors influencing the behavior of those they have in charge and about the social repercussions of their own work in individual cases. Other means used by the social services to aid in the solution of problems of social relationships are those of community organization and social action. Workers in the social services are in a peculiarly advantageous position to see the deficiencies in social institutions as they affect individuals. This being so, they regard as one of their tasks reporting on their observations and joining with other groups in the promotion of measures designed to correct social ills. This work is done to the end that individuals may find in social institutions and in social relationships a means to a more abundant life.

This, then, is the nature of the social services as it is conceived in this report. It is obvious that if the social services have the function here ascribed to them they have a most important role to play in the personality development of many children. A healthy personality is one that finds satisfaction in relations with people, relations that, for the most part, have an institutional character. It has been shown in the early part of this report that extreme poverty, anxiety and tension on the part of parents, lack of understanding and consideration on the part of other persons of emotional importance to children and youth, and the like, adversely affect personality development. In providing financial and other aid to parents in regard to difficulties in family life, in making foster care available to children whose families cannot fulfill their function, in working with children and youth in regard to problems that stand in the way of their benefiting from and enjoying school, play, work, and other social relations, the social services have an opportunity to contribute substantially to the health of personality of many handicapped youngsters.

Whether the social services succeed in this endeavor depends in part upon the reasons for their clients' difficulties and upon the nature of the social institutions involved. Not all difficulties are remediable by social-service efforts nor are the institutions of a society always such that adaptation to them spells health of personality. The success of the social-service effort depends, too, upon the extent of money, facilities, and personnel devoted to the task. For adequacy in this respect the social services of a democracy are dependent upon an informed and sympathetic public. Basically, however, the success of the social services in furthering the personal well-being of children depends upon the accuracy of the ideas about individual and social behavior on which they are founded, upon the soundness of the methods they use in working with people in trouble, and upon the skill with which they put knowledge and method to work. We cannot hope to evaluate adequately the present status of the social services in these respects. In the subsequent sections of this chapter, however, we shall make more explicit the ways in which the social services are currently contributing to the welfare of children and youth and shall note some of the changes that are needed if they are to perform their function better in this respect.

Some Ideas About Children Underlying Social-work Practice

The social services, like all professions, operate on the basis of certain assumptions and ideas about the nature of human behavior. It seems important to list here some of these as they refer to children, even though we shall not be exhaustive or even systematic in doing so. Such a listing will suggest where the social services now stand with respect to utilizing present knowledge about health of personality.

For more than twenty-five years social workers have been assimilating and making practical use of the relevant findings of those psychologies that are concerned with why people do what they do and how they feel about the doing. With their aim of individualizing each person, his hopes, alarms, and strengths, they may at times have exaggerated the force of psychological elements in defining individual personality, and they may overestimate the ambivalence, the dual qualities of readiness and reluctance, of people who seek help. Social workers have yet to assimilate and put to test the findings of cultural anthropology, of modern economics, and of child-development research. When they do so, they may find this new knowledge as revolutionary for their practice as were the ideas of dynamic psychology they began to work with a quarter-century ago.

At present, the following are some of the main ideas about children and their behavior that guide social-work practice. It is assumed that these ideas are universally applicable, but whether this is a correct assumption social workers have not yet determined in a scientific way.

Work with children and young people, in and out of their families, at play, at work, or at school, sick or well, has convinced social workers of the correctness of the psychological dictum that each child is different, that each is a personality in his own right. Whatever his life is or has been, each child is constantly changing and being changed in ways that are characteristic of the person he is and the person he is becoming.

At the same time, social workers find that there are certain feelings, desires, and actions that seem to characterize all the children and young people they know. Consequently, social workers have been able to develop a certain precision in judging what any one child's giggles, collections, or sloppy clothes may mean to him—only a certain precision, however, because of the incredible intricacy of the young person and of his experiences in living.

Parents, social workers see clearly, are the center of a child's sense of safety. What happens to a family happens to a child. These are rather obvious confirmations of the teachings of psychology. More subtle, for both theory and practice, are the emotional overtones in a child's feelings about his parents and the rest of his family. A child's desire to feel wanted and safe is so great that, even with external evidence pitifully proving the opposite, a child is likely to hold on to things and to potent wishes to prove that he really does belong. There need be no discernible connection between a child's miserable experiences with his parents and his efforts to cherish or to glamorize them. The intensity of an adopted child's daydream that his mother gave him up against her will, the intensity of a deserted child's belief that someday his unknown father will turn up and claim him are often as overwhelming to the child as they convincing to the social worker.

Social workers find no child too young nor any young person so separate as to be unaffected by the disappearance of someone he loves, by the tensions of prolonged family worry, or, for that matter, by humiliation of the family through any kind of social indignity. Similarly, when a child leaves what remains of home for another way of life, or is left anchorless by one or the other parent, the acute poignancy of the event is unmistakable. Even to be left psychologically rather than physically stirs children to intensity and variety of response. True, a child may be too young to remember the exact events, or he may be too schooled in reserve or in frosty toughness to discuss their effect upon him. But social-service practice is based on the conviction that feelings about matters such as these persist in ways which help to speed, retard, or prevent pleasure in human relationships, through which development in so many other ways becomes possible.

Glimpsing that children are likely to assume that they are at fault, and unloved, no matter what the nature of the family catastrophe, social workers have devised ways of assisting parents and children to face difficulties of this sort with fortitude and understanding. Inherent in this help is the recognition that hostility is one of the most likely responses of a child to misfortune. In fact, a child's expressed hostility, whether through his temper tantrums or silence, is a reassuring statement to a social worker that the child considers himself enough of a person to resist what he regards as being "pushed around."

Social workers see the same psychological mechanisms at work with respect to extreme and demeaning poverty. Throughout history, humanitarians have known and protested the weakness of body and spirit that results from such poverty. It is to the terrifying effects of poverty on children, in the richest nation the world may have known, that the social services now testify. Nor are there any plus values in an income so inter-

mittent and chancy that a family chronically slides in and out of desperation. The social services long and anxiously have known what it does to
people and their children when lack of cash and lack of a chance or
ability to earn wipe out human warmth and pride and faith in the future.
When parents' total preoccupation is with the fight to exist, children are
likely to be deprived of parental backing for their varied impulses to explore and test, experiment and withdraw. The rare exception notwithstanding.

It is not only poverty and privation and loss of home and parents that
handicap children in their development. Social workers note that many
children suffer because too much pressure is put upon them, because the
"up" in growing up is too much emphasized. For most children, growing
itself is enough. But it is on the "up" that young people and adults are
likely to set their sights and put their values. Were children under twelve
to write a slogan, it might be: "Sufficient unto the day—or the minute."
Were older people so to write, it might be: "As the twig is bent." From
children themselves, from studies in child development, and from many
of the findings of modern psychology, social work has garnered much to
help it fuse the adult pressure for "upness" with what is known about
children's potentials for the fullest possible life within all the "nows" en
route. Social workers appreciate what the father had in mind who asked
whether this particular nursery school for his two-year-old boy would be
credited by Harvard. It now knows, too, what social and physical and
emotional credits a particular child may earn as he lives a fine two-year-
old life, in or out of nursery school.

Any number of other facts about children and their parents are involved in social workers' richly revised, midcentury view of child life.
Anxiety has been dissipated, for instance, about the importance of the
establishment of certain habits in childhood so as to guarantee that they
will be manifested in adulthood. For example, it now seems possible to
trust the feelings and desires of courtship, or of those produced by a
white-collar job, to produce clean fingernails. Some of the incidents of
development, such as a lie under duress, can be treated as incidents rather
than as the looming shadows of an adult life outside the law. Some denial
of the standards of the parents (such as to deny that father always knows
best, or that a good child confides all, or that fun should occur only in
family groups) is, social workers now see, a basic necessity if the outcome
of growth is to be growing up. Yet a child can no more be protected from
the adult view of time and of values than adults can be protected from
a nine-year-old's inability to understand why he may never be president
if he fails in spelling.

Most children are surrounded by incentives to honor, maybe to over-value, the "up" in growing up. Thus, in some children an inner queasi-ness develops because it looks to them as though others think that full belonging comes only at the far end of "up." It is when a child crumples under the "up" pressure in his growth, when he loses his capacity to grow along as he goes along, that the social services offer him a temporary lifeline to connect what he thinks he is not and never can be with what he can be now and may be tomorrow.

Children's psychological canniness is increasingly noted and valued by social workers. A girl of twelve said that her mother preferred her brothers and added, as evidence, that her mother never spanked her but repeatedly spanked the boys: "You see, what the boys do matters." A six-year-old explained why her playmate wanted to live with her: "When Helen is at her real house her mother hears her talk. But at our house people listen to what she says." Social workers try to catch the child's view of the situation and to use that view in understanding the child.

Social workers are, however, less dependent on words to understand what people are like and what they seek than was once the case. They often find it possible to get a better view of a young man of eighteen as he pitches for his team or helps polish off a watermelon than would be possible quickly in any other way. So it is with the very young. The three-year-old, during his first day in a foster home, in his response to toys, to crackers, and to the social worker's departure tells infinitely more about himself than any words of his could tell.

In their feelings about people and events, children have many charac-teristics in common. For instance, social workers have yet to meet a child who has no fear. Serviceable as fear may be when it consists of rational red lanterns against danger, social workers have learned that when a child has no way to share or even to acknowledge his fears, reasonable or silly, his very chance to develop further may be dulled and cramped. More, they know that inner fears can be expressed in myriad ways, some direct, some oblique. And they sense, as does a child, that fear of death or of failure can no more be removed than it can be denied.

So, too, social workers know few children without some readiness to give and to accept love. They have learned, from psychology and from talks with young people themselves, that if a person of ten, say, or even twenty, is unable to love, that person has been badly damaged in his de-velopmental transit. Social workers know, too, from young people the horrors of hate. They have seen young people's hate become locked so tightly onto other people or ideas or symbols as to restrict their flexibility and freedom of choice. For it is a young person's horror when all adults are hated because they are adults; when all age-mates are enemies unless they belong to "our" gang or club.

Lately, social workers have become more aware of the importance of dislikes, big or little. They have learned from psychiatrists that through his aversions a child continuously finds and describes his own self, his similarity to, and differences from, others. The dislike may be of pistachio ice cream or of endearing terms; it may be of bangs or of strangers, depending on the child, his culture, his age, excitements, and loyalties.

As with love and hate, so with dependence and independence. Children at home, in neighborhood centers, in foster homes, and certainly children in courts demonstrate their desire to be on their own, to run their own lives. Yet always, and sometimes at almost the same instant, they indicate by word or deed a deep desire to be cared for. The healthy defiance of "What's it to you, it's my life, isn't it?" runs along with the equally healthy crack, "What's your hurry? It won't hurt you to listen, will it?"

Along the same line, it is also of great significance for the work of the social services that youngsters deeply desire to be like, in order to be liked by, others of their age. Such a desire may develop very early. For example, there was Clara who, when two and a half years old, struck against going to her day nursery. By many she would be considered spoiled or stubborn. Maybe she was. But the social worker, with the help of the teacher, discovered another reason for the child's conduct. Clara was the only child in the day nursery who did not wear one-piece underwear!

So, with older children, social workers have a fresh slant on what uniforms may mean to children living in an institution, what an agency-labeled car may mean at a farmhouse door. They have learned that ways must be found to assist into the community of children the boy who limps, the girl who has brought her European accent to a Midwest high school, the child who has no parents. Otherwise, the odds are that these young people with conspicuous differences will be disliked and feared as something that is "off the beam." The boy whose voice changes late, the girl who dwarfs her classmates, the first-grader who is too hungry to listen—these, too, have differences with which they must cope. The adolescent who believes that he was railroaded into the detention home, the child who was born deaf—they too have their multiple differences to deal with. They are not like everyone else; they want to be and they do not want to be.

As social workers have caught the meanings of these various feelings and desires, they have developed some ability to judge when a child can handle his struggles by himself and when he needs the kind of help the social services can give. Social workers have seen fragile personalities split to bits by pressures and tensions which might have been alleviated. They are convinced that health and happiness lie in coming to grips, throughout childhood and young adulthood, with the unavoidable doubts and shocks and deprivations that life provides, in the constant individual and community struggle toward satisfactions and achievements.

Types and Sources of Support of Social Services

Having identified the function and some of the basic assumptions of the social services as they pertain to children, we must next consider the main types of social services and their sources of financial support, for these are matters that also have bearing on the part the social services play in promoting the welfare of children.

Various useful classifications of types of social services could be made, depending upon the purpose to be served. Here our objective is a classification that will facilitate the consideration of the ways in which the social services may contribute to the healthy personality development of children. For that purpose a classification that follows the lines of social institutions seems best, for children's healthy development greatly depends on the favorable functioning of these organized systems of activities, as well as on children's ability to participate in their activities constructively. In addition, social-work endeavor itself is largely directed along the line of social institutions, as the above analysis of its nature and function has shown.

It is in connection with the family that the social services do their chief work and make their most conspicuous contributions to children's well-being. This is a fortunate circumstance, for, as much of the material presented in the first part of this report indicates, the healthy personality development of children is highly dependent upon well-functioning family life.

The social services contribute in three main ways to family functioning. First, by various devices they try to assure that no family will lack the essentials of life and that, accordingly, no children will be deprived of their parents' care because there is not enough money for at least minimum food, shelter, and clothing. Second, they provide for children who are homeless, temporarily or permanently, or whose homes are judged to be detrimental to their welfare or whose parents decide they would do better elsewhere. They also are a source of day care for young children whose mothers are employed or otherwise unable to supervise them. Third, they give parents and children assistance in meeting other problems of family life, from those of household management to those of strained interpersonal relations, including those of neglect and abuse of children and those of unmarried motherhood.

These three types of aid to family life provide a convenient basis for discussing the social services' contributions to the healthy personality development of children. In addition, a fourth category must be provided to take account of the work of the social services in conjunction with other social institutions—with schools, health services, courts and correctional institutions, and the like—for here, too, social workers have an opportunity of promoting children's well-being.

Within these categories some of the services have an agelong history and others are of recent origin. In general, the services designed to keep children fed, clothed, and housed came first, while those that provide aid and comfort in dealing with difficulties of an emotional nature developed fairly recently.

New or old, social services of all kinds are operated or administered under various auspices and have various sources of financial support. Listed most generally, they are Federal, state, and local governments, churches and fraternal orders, individuals and privately organized groups, philanthropic foundations, endowments for charitable purposes, as well as the numerous organizations such as hospitals, schools, the military services that provide social services for their clientele or members. All these organizations finance or operate various kinds of social services, so that it is incorrect to regard any particular type of service as being wholly under public or wholly under private direction.

The cost of operating social-service programs is met in various ways. Government—Federal, state, and local—pays the largest share of the cost; money raised by private subscription and community chests pays a portion; and the various sponsors listed above contribute a considerable share. In addition, the persons who utilize the services may pay the cost, in part or in full. For example, fees for service are charged by most child-guidance clinics and by some family-welfare agencies. Both voluntary and public adoption agencies may require payments to be made. Camping programs under social-service auspices are usually supported in part by payments from those who attend, and foster-care services of various kinds are only provided without charge if a child's sponsors are unable to pay in whole or in part.

In accounting for the way the cost of social services is met, attention must be paid to the possible overlapping between auspices and source of funds. In many instances the relation between who pays for and who sponsors or administers a program is very tenuous. In most communities, for example, the individuals or formally organized groups that sponsor social-service programs meet only a limited portion of the cost, most of the funds coming from direct solicitations or from the community chest. Sometimes part of the cost of operation is met by a philanthropic foundation or comes from an endowment established for charitable purposes. In some instances part of the cost of operation of a social-service program under private sponsorship may be met out of tax funds; in other instances a public agency may purchase services from an agency that is nonpublic.

Then, too, the particular governmental unit that is responsible for the administrative operation of a social-service program may not meet the costs in full. For example, although it has full or major administrative responsibility, a local public agency may contribute only a small amount or practically none of its locally derived tax funds to the operation of the program. Instead, it may derive full or almost full support from the state, which itself may be aided by the Federal government. Contrariwise, a state-administered program may be partly financed from tax funds that are collected by local governmental units, and the state may also receive a Federal grant. In fact, the grant-in-aid principle has become one of the main devices by which social-service programs are financed.

What stands out, then, in the sponsoring and financing of social services for children is the large load borne by government, the variety of sources of other funds, and the complicated interrelationships involved. Broadly viewed, practically everyone contributes in one way or another. Consequently, everyone ought to be entitled to some participation in determining the way the social services operate and to a share in their benefits in time of need. Unfortunately, two considerations that derive from the way social services are financed and administered make this impossible at present.

First, the way a program is financed tends to be a factor in the way it operates. In consequence, the services of a privately financed program may remain a privilege, to be granted or withheld as the operating agency sees fit. The services of a program financed completely from tax funds and publicly administered tend to become a right. A completely locally financed public program, however, is likely to limit the right and to insist that only those who are residents may use its services. In consequence of these limitations, social services are far from available to all children in need of them.

Second, the funds available for social-service programs do not necessarily meet the most pressing requirements of children. Money may be available, for example, for physically crippled children but not for the emotionally crippled ones. Funds may be available to provide institutional care of a given type but not available for foster-home care. Most important, funds may be available in the part of the country where need is least, and lacking where need is greatest. These are serious limitations to the social services' ability to promote the welfare of children. In the following analysis of particular types of services they must be kept in mind.

Services Aimed at Maintaining Family Income

Historically, the chief concern of the social services has been to assure that nobody, child or adult, has to be without means of subsistence. Today, in spite of the great increase in other kinds of social-service programs, services aimed at maintaining income still account for by far the largest part of the work. Such services make an obvious contribution to the welfare of many children, for without them many families would lack the basic necessities of life. That minimum contribution is not sufficient, however, if the social services' aim is to promote health of personality. If that is the objective, the money available to families in time of need must be sufficient to maintain a reasonable standard of living. It must be available with certainty and regularity, so that worry about income shall not distort family life. It must be given in a way that maintains morale and does not stigmatize. And, in addition to all this, the financial assistance scheme must be such that it does not undermine adults' willingness to work and does not reduce parents' sense of responsibility.

For centuries, keeping people alive was regarded as a sufficient contribution of the social services to human welfare, except that it was usually added that some attention should be given to the education and moral training of paupers' children so that as adults they will be self-supporting. The public's chief concern was not whether poor relief benefited the recipients but whether it undermined their capacity for self-maintenance. That concern is far from absent today. In spite of the fact that centuries of poor-law history have demonstrated that poverty cannot be eliminated by repressive measures,[1] there are still many who think that financial assistance grants should be kept as low as possible lest initiative and work habits be destroyed.

Actually, under modern cultural conditions just the opposite is likely to

---

[1] For an historical account from this angle see Helen L. Witmer, *Social Work: An Analysis of a Social Institution,* Rinehart & Company, New York, pp. 127–182.

be the case. We have an essentially middle-class culture, one in which self-respect is closely linked with self-maintenance, and most clients of public assistance agencies have the same ideas and feelings about these matters as do the rest of the public. They are all too likely to feel disgraced by not being able to be self-supporting. Nothing is gained and much is lost by humiliating and shaming people, as has been pointed out in Chapter I of this report. The result is much more likely to be loss of self-respect and self-control than moral strengthening. And the effects on children when parents do not feel respected and competent are sure to be disastrous.

There are economic reasons, too, for insisting that financial aid be adequate in amount and that the conditions under which it is given not be destructive of standards and values. Our expanding economy requires the maintenance of widespread spending power and makes it unfortunate for the whole society, for all citizens' health of personality, if the income of any segment is markedly reduced. It spells the end to savings as a means of providing adequately for illness, old age, and the next generation. Recognition of this situation has resulted in a gradual reorganization of social arrangements. Devices for assuring that nobody shall be without means of livelihood are now regarded not only as humanitarian measures but also as necessary parts of a well-functioning society, as important to those who contribute as to those who receive. In fact, the distinction between contributor and receiver has largely vanished, for most of the funds are derived from sources to which all make a contribution.

The economic problem, as it is now seen, is one of assuring a steady flow of income to all families at all times, through wages or other means, and of providing the means whereby all incomes shall be sufficient to meet the cost of adequate maintenance. In our industrialized, democratic society, this provision of adequate income is required for many reasons. It is necessary if economic stability and a rising standard of living are to be achieved. It is necessary if people are to be physically capable of doing vigorous, exacting work in the efficient manner that modern industry demands. It is necessary if people are to feel secure, socially and emotionally—self-confident, self-respecting, and worthy of respect.

At present, five categories of governmental measures deal with this problem. First, there is minimum-wage legislation and other measures by which wages are fixed. Second, there is the provision of free or subsidized goods and services whereby family income is made more adequate without being increased in size. Subsidized housing, free meals for school children, free or minimum-charge health services, and public recreation programs are examples of this kind of provision. Third, there are public-works programs and "made-work" schemes of various kinds that are put into action in time of economic depression. Fourth, there are social insurance and pension schemes, devices for enforcing savings and spreading the burden so that there will be income in time of special need. Fifth, there are public assistance measures to fill up the gaps, some directed to certain categories of disadvantaged persons and a "general assistance" scheme, which is the last remaining remnant of the old poor law. These latter two categories—social insurance and public assistance—comprise the country's social security system. Added to these are the private measures, of which financial assistance through social agencies is the one most pertinent to the present inquiry.

Of these various measures we shall discuss only the social security arrangements and the work of private social agencies, for these are most clearly social services according to our definition. Among these, we shall analyze in most detail the pertinent public-assistance program, aid to dependent children. The chief questions we want to answer about this and other social services are what opportunity they present for aiding in the promotion of the healthy personality development of children and what is required if they are to make the most of that opportunity.

The Social Security System

The welfare of children in an industrial society is closely linked with certainty and adequacy of money income. At base, steady income is required in order that children's physical needs be met. It is required in order that fear of loss of income shall not disrupt family harmony and create tension and anxiety that interfere with personality development. Children need it so that they may feel on a par with their friends. Youth needs it for the same reason, and in order to believe in the future and their place in it. Parents need it for their own self-respect and for the sake of their children.

At present in the United States we have only a limited social security system. The various programs operating under the Social Security Act and other laws are, in the words of the *1949 Federal Security Report,* "inadequate and inequitable." In spite of the great advance over earlier measures it represents, social security covers neither all major risks nor all workers and their dependents. What is needed for the well-being of children is a system by which families will be assured of income adequate to maintain a decent standard of living regardless of unemployment, illness or other physical disability, old age, or death of the breadwinner.

Such a system presupposes general economic arrangements that provide adequate wages for all workers; for adversity, apparently, cannot be compensated at a higher rate than employment without producing social dissatisfaction.

The source of funds for such a system is related to the healthy personality development of children in that possible stigma connected with receipt of payments is involved. Our ideas about self-sufficiency being what they are, it is likely that a system to which all make specific contributions is to be preferred. All legally authorized forms of financial assistance are "rights" but, to date at least, many recipients feel more or less inferior at having to exercise these rights and accept aid that is not an insurance payment. Since such feelings on the part of parents often work to children's disadvantage, serious attention should be given to this matter of source of funds.

The present social security program, far from perfect as it is, is a great advance over the pre-1935 situation. Its contribution to the welfare of children is made most obviously in old-age and survivors' insurance and in the aid-to-dependent-children program. Through these two programs many children deprived of parental care by death or other cause are provided for financially, at a minimum level at least. Children benefit from the other social security measures also. Through unemployment insurance the financial worries of some parents are reduced, with consequent benefit to family life; and through the general-assistance program the basic needs of children not otherwise provided for are met to some extent.

It is impossible to present a clear picture of how many and what children are aided by these programs, and in what measure, nor can we say how many are left out. The variation from place to place and from industry to industry is too great, and too many authorities are involved in keeping the figures. Some pertinent facts are available, however, regarding most of the programs. These are sufficient to suggest that, while much has been accomplished, much remains to be done if health of personality is to be promoted.

Old Age and Survivors' Insurance

The social insurance scheme that most clearly has to do with children is the one that provides payments in case of the death of a wage earner—old age and survivors' insurance. In July, 1950, 664,000 children were beneficiaries.[2] The efficacy of this scheme in meeting the financial needs

[2] Figures on OASI and unemployment insurance from *Annual Report of the Federal Security Agency, Social Security Administration*, 1949.

of children whose fathers (or, occasionally, mothers) have died is limited by the extent of its coverage and by the size of its payments. Potentially, however, it is a very important source of assurance to the great majority of children that they will not be wholly without funds if the parent who earns the family living dies.

Until recently OASI was limited largely to workers in commerce and industry. Under the 1950 Amendments to the Social Security Act many more workers are covered. The most important new additions are owners and operators of small businesses, regularly employed domestic servants, and some agricultural workers.

The effectiveness of OASI in furthering the well-being of children is also hampered by the size of the benefits and by the fact that, as in all insurance schemes, the size of the benefit varies with the contributions of the insured. This means that the children of deceased workers get benefits that vary with their fathers' earning capacity. There are good reasons for this arrangement, but in many cases it continues the low income that, with the father alive, may have adversely affected the children's welfare.

In addition to variations in size of benefit, the effectiveness of the scheme is limited at present by the low scale of all benefits. The scale of benefits was increased by the Social Security amendments of 1950 but it is still not in adjustment with the cost of living. The average primary insurance benefit is now about $42 a month, and the maximum total benefit payable monthly is $150. Such payments are seldom sufficient to provide for children adequately. At best, the scheme can do no more than provide a living for a family somewhat below the level of the dead parent's pay. For families in the lowest income group, it seems doubtful that such a scheme would be sufficient to permit a mother to stay home and care for her children.

Such criticism is not directed at the insurance scheme itself or at the insurance scheme alone. What is needed, as was said at the outset, is a general wage level high enough to provide adequately for children, or sufficient supplementation in the form of free or subsidized goods to make high wages unnecessary. Under such conditions OASI might produce high enough returns to keep most eligible families adequately provided for.

Unemployment Insurance

Unemployment insurance, like OASI, is of benefit to children both in providing money for basic needs in time of adversity and also in reducing parents' worry about loss of income, currently or in the future. Also like

OASI, unemployment insurance does not cover all the workers who need it, and its coverage has been especially lacking in the occupations that are the most transient and that bring in the lowest wages. It is estimated, however, that about 45,600,000 workers (the great majority of all workers) earned some wages in covered employment in 1948, and that about 80 per cent of them had sufficient wage credits to qualify for unemployment benefits.

The size of a worker's weekly benefits depends on the size of his wage and on his being engaged in employment that is covered by the scheme a certain length of time.

In absolute amounts, the average weekly payment in June, 1949, varied from $13.80 in Florida to more than $23.00 in Massachusetts, New York, and Utah. The average payment was more than $20 in fifteen states and less than $15 in five. In four of the states that make allowance for dependents, the maximum was above $35.

What does all this add up to in terms of the contribution of unemployment insurance to children's welfare? There is, of course, no exact answer to that question. Strains on family life are doubtless reduced when maximum benefits are received, and in all families it is unquestionably better to get some benefits than none. The real hazard to a child's development probably depends on how long unemployment lasts and how frequently it occurs, as well as upon the attitude of the parents and of the cultural group toward a person who is without a job.

The present unemployment insurance scheme is intended to compensate the worker and his family for only relatively short-time unemployment. Since it is recognized that with rising living costs few workers can set much money aside for even such emergencies, it may be that benefit rates should be increased. Then, too—the welfare of children being the point here at issue—consideration might be given to extending dependents' allowances, to increasing the proportion of the wage rate paid in the unemployment insurance benefit, especially for workers who earn the lowest wages, and to reducing disqualifications that work against family welfare.

As for long-time unemployment (fortunately rare at present), the only refuge now is general public assistance. This scheme, as will be shown below, is both meager in its payments and more or less humiliating to many recipients. These defects can perhaps be remedied somewhat. Even so, in the event of a period of economic depression it is to be hoped that better arrangements than this or than the others worked out in the 1930s can be devised.

Whatever the measures by which families are aided in times of long-continued unemployment, they must be operated in such a way as to give due consideration to the dignity and worth of the people whom they serve and to the special place that the breadwinner has in our family culture. The economic depression of the 1930s taught social workers the dangers to family life and to the personality development of children that long-continued unemployment of the father brings. Interviews with these children as adults reveal even more clearly than was then realized how devastated they were emotionally because their parents lost control. The control Americans prize is control of choice over getting and spending money, over deciding where and how to live, over the use of their time and energy. For years on end, unemployed parents ceased to be in charge in this sense, and it was having their parents not in charge that terrified the youngsters. Many a young adult declares that to this day he is fearful that he, too, as a parent, will lose this kind of control. Choice, it has been said, is an American's *sine qua non,* and confidence in the future his best security. It is most important for the welfare of American children that wide-scale unemployment be avoided and that the few parents who are deprived of work temporarily or for longer periods be assured of an income on conditions that maintain their sense of self-esteem.

Aid to Dependent Children

For the assistance of persons in financial need who are not eligible for, or not sufficiently covered by, the various social insurance schemes or other such measures, public assistance programs are operated. These programs are largely under state or local direction, but the Federal government has a part to play in the administration of three of the four programs by reason of its financial contributions. These Federally aided public assistance programs provide financial aid to old people, to the blind, and to dependent children. All other categories of persons are provided for under "general assistance," to whose funds no Federal contribution is made.

The Aid to Dependent Children program is the one of chief concern to the present analysis. Under the Social Security Act the Federal government will make contributions to states for the financial assistance of children who are deprived of parental support and care because of the death, the continued absence from home, or the physical or mental incapacity of either parent. To qualify for aid a child must live in his own home or in the home of a close relative. States determine the conditions under which assistance is paid and the amount of the payment. The Federal government will contribute three-fourths of the first twelve dollars of the average payment plus one-half of the balance of all payments within the maximums of twenty-seven dollars per month for the caretaker and the first child and eighteen dollars per month for each additional child in the home.

At present writing, all states except Nevada are participating in the program. Since, however, states vary in funds available for assistance and may also specify the conditions for eligibility, there is wide variation in the adequacy of the scheme. Consequently, no over-all conclusions can be drawn as to the effectiveness of ADC in promoting the welfare of children.

The total number of children receiving payments under ADC was 1,660,904 in September, 1950. This compared with a total of about 4,100,000 children living in broken homes, according to the 1950 U.S. Census. Since about two-thirds of the ADC clients live in broken homes, it appears that ADC is helping to meet the financial needs of over a fourth of all such children in the country.

Differences among States. The proportion of children receiving assistance under ADC varies considerably from state to state, due not only to difference in the number of families that are in need but perhaps even more to difference in state laws regarding other eligibility factors. The range was from 11 per 1000 population under eighteen years of age in New Jersey to 78 in Louisiana in December, 1949, the last date at which such an analysis was made. Twelve states assisted over 40 per 1000 persons under eighteen, and nine states assisted 20 or less. The national rate at that time was 33 per 1000.

There were various reasons for this divergence, aside from the obvious one of difference in family income. In industrial states, where many workers are covered by old-age-and-survivors' insurance, many children of widowed parents received social insurance benefits. In July, 1950, the number of such children stood at 664,000. Not all these children would be eligible for Aid to Dependent Children if they did not receive the OASI payment, but a large proportion of them probably would be.

Another reason for difference among the states is the fact that eligibility requirements vary widely. One of the most important of these has to do with the status of the parents. In general, as OASI has come to provide for families in which the father has died, there has been a tendency on the part of states to broaden the conditions that are covered. Rather than being primarily a means of contributing to the support of children whose fathers are dead, ADC has become chiefly a source of aid to children whose fathers have deserted or been divorced, to those with incapacitated parents, and to children of unmarried mothers. According to the most recent count nationally (June, 1948), death of the father accounted for 22.8 per cent of the cases; incapacity of the father, 26.7 per cent; divorce or desertion of the father, 30.4 per cent; and lack of marriage, 14.1 per cent. Incapacity and absence from home are variously defined, however, with the result that the proportion of cases in these various categories varies widely from state to state.

Since ADC was originally regarded as a means of handling long-time need, some states require that a parent be absent from home a considerable length of time (a few states as much as a year) before the children are eligible for aid. Some insist that a mother institute legal action against a deserting husband before eligibility is established; one makes such action an alternative to waiting six months; and one requires that a deserting father be indicted before his children become eligible. As to incapacity, a few states permit only such disabling conditions as prevent any gainful employment, and others are only slightly less limiting.

Other states operate on the assumption that if assistance is granted early the family can more easily work out other ways of managing its financial difficulties. In consequence, some states have removed time limits for establishing eligibility and rely on the public assistance workers to determine case by case whether there is actual absence or incapacity of a parent. Ideas as to kind and degree of incapacity have also changed, with the result that West Virginia, for example, calls a parent incapacitated who is physically, mentally, or socially inadequate to provide the necessities of life for his children; and Oklahoma includes emotional disability in its list of incapacitating conditions. Some states recognize partial incapacity and the unavailability of work within a parent's capabilities, and supplement an incapacitated parent's earnings from part-time or limited employment, in the belief that the maximum economic and personal rehabilitation will thereby be accomplished.

There is also difference among states in attitude toward giving ADC grants to children of unmarried mothers and to those whose mothers are not of "good repute." The Federal act is designed to assure that equal need is given equal treatment, that children are not penalized for the faults of their parents, and that, as long as a child remains in his own home, his parents shall be treated as responsible adults, capable of managing their own lives and those of their children. Nevertheless, there are communities in which, through administrative rule, this policy is more or less abnegated, with the result that in some states, and in some communities within states, children of unmarried mothers find it more than usually difficult to secure assistance.

Variation from state to state in the proportion of children who are aided is also attributable to differences in the standard of living a state will support for its needy people. These standards vary widely, but exactly how much they vary is not known, for, in spite of the Federal requirements, some states do not yet have standards that are mandatory on all localities. Amounts paid, however, are determined in reference to how much supplementation a child's parent or other relative requires to bring his income up to the level that will provide the child with certain specified items—usually food, shelter, heat, clothing, and light; sometimes all these plus an allowance for such personal incidentals as recreation and school supplies. Depending upon how many of these items are allowed and how much it is estimated they will cost, the upper limit of the income qualifying a child for ADC varies considerably.

As a result of these variations in budget standards, ADC payments vary greatly from state to state. The national average of monthly payments was $70.40 per family in September, 1950. That average means little, however, for in fourteen states the average was under $50 a month, and in twenty-one states it was over $75. The extremes were Alabama, Mississippi, and South Carolina, whose average was under $30 a month, and California, Connecticut, Massachusetts, New York, Oregon, and Washington, with averages over $100.

What can be said for this situation? One way of looking at it is to say that $1000 a year (or less) is better than nothing. Somehow or other, it does keep a large number of parents and children together who might otherwise have to be separated. It must mean, however, that the children in many of these families, particularly those who live in cities, are disadvantaged as compared with the other children with whom they associate or whom they meet in school. In many states ADC budgets make no allowance for personal items of any kind. If children are to have the kind of clothing, money for recreation and participation in school activities, and the like that being on a level with the other children requires, mothers must sacrifice food or other essentials or find some other means of satisfying their children's desires. The petty delinquencies of juveniles can spring from such a situation, for children cannot, with equanimity, forego all the pleasures that others enjoy, nor is it to the advantage of health of personality that they do so.

Some Possible Remedies. What, then, might be done to improve matters? One thing might be, of course, to raise ADC payments and to keep them adjusted to changes in the cost of living. By the 1950 amendments to the Social Security Act some increase has been made possible by the fact that the Federal government is now empowered to contribute to the support of mothers or other caretakers as well as children.

Perhaps, in addition to this, poor states should receive a larger proportion of Federal aid than wealthy states, for it is those states that have the largest child population and, probably, the largest proportion of broken homes. The purpose of the grant-in-aid arrangement is to equalize opportunity, so that needy individuals shall not be penalized by reason of residence, and yet retain the advantages of state and local administration and point of view. True equalization, however, is hard to come by. It apparently requires something that looks like unequal treatment so far as Federal grants are concerned.

Another move might be to regard ADC as a temporary rather than long-time kind of help. This is perhaps a radical proposal, for the continuing aim of ADC has been to keep mothers at home. It may be, however, that this is an unrealistic ideal in our present way of life. In recent years there has been a great increase in the number of mothers, even mothers of young children, who work for wages. Current psychological research suggests that this is a poor arrangement for children under four or five years of age. The research, however, has been confined largely to children of the middle class. Nobody really knows how young children of working mothers are cared for and with what effect on their personality development. Careful attention ought to be given to all aspects of this problem. It may be that, if in day-care centers and other such arrangements due regard were paid to children's emotional, as well as physical, needs, many mothers could be employed without great loss to the well-being of their youngsters.

Actually, many mothers eligible for ADC are already handling the situation in this way. Although exact figures are lacking, it is the impression of ADC aministrators that the average family stays on ADC only about three years. Then, too, each increase in employment possibilities for women brings a decrease in ADC rolls, and vice versa.

If ADC were to become, for the most part, a help in temporary trouble, a lift over the period when children are very young or until other arrangements for dealing with a parent's physical or mental incapacity can be made, there would be need for much more casework service on the part of ADC workers than is at present allowed for. Detailed description of what is involved in that kind of service will be given below. Here, what we have in mind is that ADC workers, in addition to paying thoughtful attention to eligibility and handling this question in a way that is consonant with a client's dignity, would have to be able to help mothers make choices among the various alternatives and give them aid in the use of community resources of one kind or another. Such service would involve the worker in many of the problems of family life; it would require much more time per family than under present arrangements and therefore much lower caseloads; it might even lead to making ADC a family-welfare agency.

If that conclusion were arrived at (and it must be emphasized that to date it is only a theoretical proposal), consideration might have to be given to abolishing some of the distinctions between the types of social services that now obtain and to setting up over-all family and children's welfare agencies under public funds. Such a union of forces is not to be lightly undertaken, however, as developments in the field of private philanthropy can testify. The issues are too complicated to permit adequate discussion here. In general, however, it may be said that more casework service to ADC clients, particularly with respect to helping them to use the payments to best advantage and to discontinue them similarly, might be one way of making ADC of greater value to children.

ADC has a higher aim than that of keeping needy children merely alive. As recently stated, its objective is to "strengthen family life and make it possible for all children to live and grow and learn and develop into maturity in a setting that will help them become responsible, contributing members of their community and country." [3] Many parents of children in receipt of ADC do not require special help in this regard. The attainment of this objective with those who do need help will, however, call for much change in current policy and practice in many states, as well as for different attitudes toward ADC on the part of much of the public.

General Assistance

For needy children and their families who are not eligible for ADC, "general assistance" is provided. This program, in contrast to the others so far described, is both financed and administered locally or through the state government. Because of the wide variation among states and within states, it is difficult to make generalizations about it. Even the conditions that bring families containing children to apply for general assistance cannot be specified exactly, for the kind of incapacity of a parent that would make a family eligible for aid to dependent children in one

[3] *Ibid.*, p. 133.

state would require application for general assistance in another, and the same is true of absence from home. The most that can be said is that, in the over-all social security program, general assistance is regarded as the program that provides for all needy persons otherwise not accounted for.

This conception of general assistance is far from accurate, however, for general assistance itself has many limitations on eligibility. Some states and some communities, for example, will not give assistance to an employable person. Most have residence or citizenship requirements, a hangover from the early poor-law days when mobility of labor was regarded as objectionable. Consequently, in spite of the fact that there is a public assistance office in every county in the country, there are an uncounted number of families that cannot receive aid in spite of need. The families of migrant workers are particularly handicapped with respect to general assistance, as well as other social services. That some children of migratory workers in the Southwest starved to death a few years ago is only an extreme example of general deprivation.

Payments under general assistance are much lower on the average than those under ADC. With the average number of persons per "case" being 1.9, general-assistance payments in September, 1950, ranged from $11.05 a month in Mississippi to $70.82 in New York. The next highest was Rhode Island with $57.81. Seven states paid less than $20 a month, and only five more than $50. How many children were included in the families that got these small allotments is not known. The figures, however, make the hue and cry about the squandering of public funds on pampering the poor sound foolish.

The situation might perhaps be improved so far as children are concerned by making ADC available, under certain conditions, to children whose fathers are unemployed. Another suggestion is to provide Federal grants-in-aid to help defray state expenses for the general assistance program as for the other public assistance ones. It has also been proposed that the distinction between categories of need be done away with, and all needy people, adults and children, be treated alike and generously. With full employment, high wages and high productivity, and broad coverage under social insurance, this seemingly reasonable and fair solution might be possible, for under such conditions revenues from taxes would be high and the number of unemployed to be assisted would be small.

Whatever the solution, it is most important that in many communities a change for the better be accomplished, both in size of grants and in conditions of eligibility. Children in families of very low income are greatly disadvantaged in most ways that make for healthy personality development. Not all children aided by general assistance belong to families that chronically have a very low income, but probably most of them belong to that social group. The present general-assistance arrangements are such as are likely to lower further a family's sense of ability to care for its children adequately. General assistance thus contributes less than it might to the maintenance of health of personality.

Financial Assistance under Private Auspices

In addition to these various legally constituted measures for assuring that, come what may, family income is sustained at least at a minimum level, financial assistance is also available to families through numerous private sources. For many years, aid from this source was regarded by applicants and many others as somewhat more "respectable," perhaps because there was less possibility of publicity, perhaps because more attention was paid to the applicant's feelings about being in need. Now, however, with public assistance made a clear-cut right, with administration greatly improved, and with confidentiality safeguarded, this attitude is on the way out, and public and private assistance programs are regarded as complementary rather than competing.

The economic depression of the 1930s demonstrated, once and for all, that private philanthropy could not hope to be the main source of financial assistance. Actually, it never had been the main source but, so far from middle-class consciousness were the local "poor boards" and the other government-sponsored arrangements, that many people thought of private philanthropy in that light. With the depression, however, came government-provided temporary-relief measures and, later, Social Security legislation and the clear assumption of Federal responsibility for a share in income-maintenance provisions.

Ever since that time, privately supported social agencies have been struggling toward the formulation of a clear policy with regard to financial assistance. Most family-welfare agencies have come to the conclusion that the provision of money for basic subsistence needs over a considerable period of time is beyond their resources and is, moreover, the responsibility of the public welfare agency. Probably all such agencies give this kind of help to families in times of disaster, to tide them over until other arrangements can be made. For the most part, however, private social agencies devote their assistance funds to filling in the gaps in public provisions and to aiding needy families who are not eligible for public assistance.

There is some disagreement among family-welfare agencies as to whether financial assistance should be regarded as an aid to a family (or to an individual within a family) in working out other kinds of family difficulties or whether it should be provided without respect to such considerations. The distinction turns upon the conception of the function of the family welfare agency, whether its main job is to help in the solution of family problems or whether, like the public assistance agency, it has a job of aiding people who are in financial need regardless of their desire for help with other problems.

Besides family-welfare agencies, there are numerous other organizations that provide financial assistance to one or another category of individual and family. The American Red Cross, for example, has its program of disaster relief. The Salvation Army gives many kinds of services of a relief nature. Fraternal and religious organizations spend large sums on caring for their own. And so on. The sums of money spent and the number of persons aided are not known with any high degree of accuracy. Of all these organizations, it can be said that they serve a very useful function in supplementing public welfare provisions, especially for the many people who have essential needs that are peculiar to their own situation and cannot be covered by any broad governmental arrangement.

For the welfare of children in a democracy it seems unquestionable that both public and private sources of financial assistance are necessary. The flexibility of the privately financed organization is required in order that the special needs of each individual and family be taken into account. The legally guaranteed right to receive basic maintenance is required so that nobody has to be dependent on a social agency's decision in this important matter. Both kinds of programs need more funds than they have at present if the welfare of children is to be as much advanced by social-service measures as is possible.

Some Principles of Administration

In describing the income-maintenance measures provided under the social services we have talked mainly about the amount of money provided and the conditions which the payments are designed to cover. Scant attention has been paid to the way in which assistance is given, although it was implied at the outset that it is not only lack of money but possible lack of status that troubles the family that is very short of funds. In our society, the individual who has to acknowledge, through request for financial assistance, that he has not been able to provide for himself and his family is likely to feel more or less humiliated. Since a sense of self-respect and self-worth is an essential ingredient of personal well-being and since parents who are lacking in that sense are often hampered in their relations with their children, it is highly important to the healthy personality development of the many children whose families receive financial aid that assistance measures be administered with this in mind.

In this respect the social insurances have the advantage. Not only have applicants themselves contributed to the insurance scheme but the conditions under which they are eligible to receive benefits are clearly stated in the law. Accordingly, it is usually thought that the individualized approach of social work has no pertinence in this program. For the most part, experience proves this true but some OASI administrators report that they find some situations that should perhaps have individualized attention. Here and there guardians dissipate their wards' money. Mothers become ill and cannot provide for their children's care. Occasionally a substandard children's institution, acting in a guardian capacity and receiving the funds, is tempted to keep a child longer than may be desirable. In short, it may be that the social insurances should make some provision for individualized services if they are to carry out fully their objective with respect to children's welfare.

As with the social insurances, public-assistance clients receive their payments as a legal right. The conditions of eligibility, however, are rather vague in the minds of most applicants, though attempts are made in many states to make the conditions of eligibility so clear-cut and predictable that clients can understand their rights and secure enforcement at law if necessary. In contrast with insurance, recipients seldom have the sense of getting something they themselves have helped to pay for. With assistance from private agencies, the situation for the client is still less clear. In asking for help he is putting himself in the position of one who can be refused without recourse to authority, a position which, to Americans at least, is likely to be an uncomfortable one.

The remedying of the disadvantageous position in which the receiver of financial assistance may find himself is not wholly in social-work hands. So long as many people in the community regard recipients of public assistance with suspicion and perhaps envy, and in so far as the children of recipients are treated as different from others, it will be difficult to preserve in public-assistance clients the psychological qualities that foster family and child welfare.

For close to a hundred years, however, social workers have been trying to develop ways of working with relief clients that will foster self-reliance. At one time, when it was thought that poverty was due to individual fault and that it evidenced a moral lack, the cure was sought in friendly exhortation and guidance. Later, attempts were made to diagnose and remedy the social ills from which these people presumably suffered. To-day, under full employment, it is clear that most applicants for public assistance are people who are unable to work, and there is danger that they may feel inferior and incompetent on that account. Accordingly, social workers now take as one of their chief objectives preserving or bolstering the client's belief in himself and in his ability to operate as a self-respecting person.

Various devices for accomplishing this objective have been developed. Privacy is emphasized. Careful attention is paid to giving the applicant a comfortable, dignified part to play in establishing his eligibility for finan-cial aid. The responsibility for procuring the needed evidence is put upon him, for the most part, and his permission is secured when inquiries about his situation must be made of others. Grants are in cash, and no control is exerted over expenditures. Explanations regarding the size of the grant are made in terms of a standard budget. If aid with problems other than financial is offered, care is taken to assure that the continuance of the grant is not thought to be contingent upon accepting other forms of as-sistance. Moreover, the responsibility for planning and action is left with the client, the social worker limiting his activities to facilitating measures. In short, the client is consistently treated as a person whose opinions count, whose right to manage his own affairs is unquestioned, and whose capacity to make decisions is unimpaired. If he proves himself incapable of living up to these expectations and his dependents suffer thereby, there can be recourse to the courts. The social services do not play the role of adjudicator of right and wrong.

It will be noted that all these policies and practices are based upon the prevailing American values. Whatever success they have in contributing to individual and family well-being is to be attributed to the fact that they are in keeping with American ideals. Most Americans cannot feel self-respecting when they are pushed around, bossed, deprived of choice, and kept in the dark. This is not necessarily true of all people every-where. People of some nations feel prized and safe if they are told what to do and if someone acts as guide and protector in their behalf. There may be cultural groups in our own country that have such attitudes. If so, means must be devised to take their values into account in working with them, for the objective of social workers is not the following of a particu-lar set of rules but the creating of conditions that will preserve or foster in clients a genuine sense of self-worth.

Services for Children Away from Home

As old or older historically than financial-assistance measures are those social services through which provision is made for the care of children who are homeless or who, for one reason or another, on their parents' or the court's say-so, are removed from home. Also like the financial-assistance measures, these services were provided for centuries with little attention being paid to their psychological aspects, it being thought sufficient that the recipients be sheltered, clothed, fed, and given a little schooling.

Without attempting to review the history of the change that led to the present facilities and measures, we may note that today it is widely recognized by social workers that children who do not live with their families must be very carefully handled and provided for if their personality development is to be fostered. This is also true of children, especially pre-school children, who spend the daytime in child-care centers or otherwise away from home. This being so, we shall group together for consideration here all the arrangements and facilities by which care for children away from home is provided, including in the listing detention homes and institutions for delinquents,[4] the mentally retarded, and children who are seriously disturbed emotionally, even though these latter present some special problems and may require some services not mentioned below. This grouping is justified by the fact that all children who live away from home, briefly or for a long time, are exposed to the risk to personality development involved in deprivation of parental care. In addition, since few such children are out of their homes solely because of lack of family income, they are likely to be additionally vulnerable by reason of the fact that their prior experience at home was probably more or less unfavorable.

For the well-being of all these children it is most important what kind of foster home they go to, what the school or hospital or other institution is like to which they are sent, what provisions are made for their day care or for their supervision if they are picked up as wanderers or detained as delinquent or neglected. Unless they are infants, children who are to live away from home need a clear understanding of why they have to go away, how long they will have to stay, what conditions, if any, are attached to their return. Their sense of well-being is very much linked with these matters, as well as with the way they are dealt with in the new home, what sort of connection with their own family is maintained, and what happens at home (if they have a home) while they are away. In this aspect of the work of the social services there is, then, continuous possibility of affecting the lives of children for good or ill.

4 These institutions are also discussed in Chapter XVI.

What Good Foster Care Requires

Arranging for and supervising the foster care of children has become a complicated and skilled undertaking. There is need throughout for a careful balancing between attending to the parents' and child's feelings in the matter and numerous practical details. The experience, it has been found, is unlikely to be a helpful one to a child unless it is undertaken with his parents' or relatives' real desire, especially if the occasioning factor has been the child's difficult behavior. In addition, there is need to take into account social, religious, and economic considerations, as well as those of personality, when matching child and new home. Then, too, thoughtful attention has to be given to maintaining a child's links with his own family whenever possible, as well as giving counsel to his own parents and to foster parents as needed. Unless full attention is paid to these and other matters by child-welfare workers, children stand to suffer grave risks.

Actually, there are no packaged answers regarding the best provisions for children who must live away from home. There are general answers, however, on which the social services draw and from which they evolve methods and services specific to their practice. Next in importance to trying to understand each particular child is the enormous value to each child of having some continuing connection with his own family. The connection may be maintained by correspondence, gifts, visits, and in other ways. Unless it exists, even with a third cousin twice removed, the secret desolation of most children is almost unreachable and is likely to fuel an insatiable desire to minimize the present and to seek a never-never past. Of course, many a child comes back home, for a short time or for keeps. And many a child leaves and returns home again and again. Thus the importance of continuing his connection with those at home and of their continued connection with him is of both practical and emotional importance.

Children themselves have provided another clue as to what they require if the spontaneity of their development is not to be crusted with resentment. They seek a conviction, which only experience can give, that nothing is going to happen about their living arrangements without their having a chance for some "say." The "say" for a five-year-old may consist of choosing the toys he wants to take to a foster home. For a fifteen-year-old the "say" may involve his inner mobilization to try to profit from, or to repudiate, the living arrangements made available to him.

By all odds, the most important single element in social-service provisions for children who have to live away from home is the quality of the people recruited as foster parents, in or out of institutions. Child-placing agencies, to do a job that fosters children's development, have to have professional personnel who genuinely understand and love children, for it is on these people that the delicate negotiations and decisions that must go into successful placement of a child devolve. Nevertheless, the heart of service to children away from home depends, and properly depends, on people who neither have nor need professional training. Parents in foster homes, matrons in shelters, detention homes, and institutions, cottage families who supervise group care, workers in child-care centers, parents who adopt a child: these are the people on whom rests success in foster placement. If such adults are child-wise in an unsentimental manner, and if their greatest satisfaction is to provide for a child's development rather than to assert control for control's sake, then most of the children they have in their charge can relax and grow. Innumerable other provisions have to be made in order to assure smooth running of the foster-care plan, but no provision can do more for a child than the support, warmth, and sound sense of the people who are with him the largest part of the time.

What these people ask of children is most important, of course. Most children are ready to try to make a connection with adults and to try to understand what they regard as acceptable behavior. They need time, however, to learn what the regulations are, and how they differ from those they knew earlier. Except for babies and very young children, few of them seem to be ready to regard any adults as genuine substitutes for their parents. They may want mothering, and fathering too, but they are likely to resent adults who try to compete with or displace their memories and phantasies about their own parents.

Another factor in the success of foster-care plans is the kind of living arrangements available and chosen. It used to be said that a foster home is usually preferable for young children, while adolescents are more likely to do well in an institution. At present, professional opinion holds that there is no such easy answer, in part because there are so many different purposes that foster care must serve.

Children whose personality development has been relatively healthy can probably get along well in either a home or an institution, and it is probably to them, if any, that the rule about age applies. For other children a careful choice has to be made, not only between foster home or institution but also as to what kind of home or institution. Some children, regardless of age, need the close association that good family life permits. Some who are not able to get along well with adults may find life easier when, as in a school-like institution, adults are not very much in evidence. Some who have been so riddled emotionally that they cannot enter into any close relationships may need a small institution that is almost hospital-like in its relief from pressures and in its anonymity.

In all forms of foster care, and in group care particularly, the adults in charge must be aware of the strengths and struggles of each child and use all aspects of life to further his personality development. Evidence of a sound group-care program may lie in the small number of children for whom each adult is responsible, in the basis of selection of members for each group, in the plans made for fun, and in the way that individually devised work is chosen for or by each member of the group. But deeper than devices or programs in group care lies the intent that provisions be made for each child to overcome his particular difficulties with people or things or his own feelings, as he finds ways to work himself out of his self-doubts or confusions through activities in which he has full chance to participate and some chance to succeed.

No one of the various possible living arrangements is necessarily the one that will continue to suit a particular child best. If foster care is to play its part in promoting the well-being of children, there will have to be frequent review of each child's progress so that each can move, as his development indicates, from one way of life to another. Time enters into such a decision, and growth and life have their own speeds within each child and within each situation. It may take one child two years to come to grips with himself and his potentials, whereas another child may have accomplished the same knitting together in two months. Growth does occur under foster care, and children do get ready to be more like other children in being able to put some trust in life, in adults, and in themselves. But unless that readiness is turned into action, through direct experience, any number of sad outcomes may occur. A sort of passive contentment with just getting by may develop as one kind of response. A bitter conviction that effort is futile and that adults have again, and always will, let you down is another. Thus the child's ever-latent doubt as to whether either the authority or the affection of adults can be counted on is reactivated, and important phases of maturation cease. Whatever the response, if a child remains under any particular kind of foster-care arrangement after it has fulfilled the particular purposes it can in his life, he suffers. And so does society, later.

The Supply of Foster-care Facilities

Startling as it may appear, it is the considered opinion of many social workers that, for their own well-being and chance for a good future, more children should live away from home than now do. In fact, many more would be living away were there enough foster homes and institutions to go around.

The cry, raised more than a decade ago, continues: the supply of foster homes is drying up. All evidence indicates the accuracy of the cry. The drying up, however, seems related only to problems capable of solution.

One explanation of the shortage is that rates of pay for foster care of children have not kept pace with the increased cost of living. Another is that, at best, social agencies have not been accustomed to paying all that it actually costs a family to add a member to the household. Therefore, only families of fairly adequate means can afford to accept a foster child.

A third explanation why foster homes are difficult to procure is that social agencies have often had to ask foster parents to care for highly distressed and emotionally complicated babies and children about whom the experts would be baffled. Thus the foster parents often have had little chance to see good results from the devoted attention and warmth they tried to offer such bristly young ones. The "study home" (a small institution where children are carefully examined, observed, and perhaps treated before being placed) may be a partial answer to this difficulty, at least in large cities. Psychiatric treatment centers that provide living facilities may be another. Perhaps, during the years ahead, adequate boarding treatment centers will be developed for the relatively small but socially important number of children who, temporarily, are unable to benefit from either group or foster-home care.

Lamentably, too, most communities offer far too little range of choice in possible new ways of life for children away from home. Much that goes into careful selection, based on what is knowable about each child, depends on there being a full range of facilities (foster homes, group-care provisions, short- and long-time boarding homes, etc.) so that children may move from one way of life to another as their development indicates.

All in all, then, there is much knowledge about what children require in order to benefit from life away from home, and there are some fine examples of good services. There is much more that needs to be known, however, especially about how to be of benefit to children whose cultural background is significantly different from that of the majority.[5]

[5] On this point see our discussion of juvenile delinquency, Chapter XVI.

In addition, what is known is often not put to use as fully as might be desired. There are still far too many institutions and foster-home programs that operate without enough regard for children's and parents' psychology and that hinder rather than help personality development. And there is still far too little money spent on providing facilities of any kind. Children who have to live away from home, for short or long periods, for their own good or because there is no other place for them, require society's especial protection and solicitude if they are to grow up into happy, responsible citizens. That, because of color, creed, or place of residence, many of them should be deprived of the best that is presently known is a loss not only to the children but to all of us.

Services Aimed at Resolving Other Social Difficulties

Social difficulties that may interfere with the healthy personality development of children are, of course, not limited to those arising out of inadequate family income or out of removal from home. There are numerous other sorts of problems in family life that may adversely affect children's development, as has been shown in considerable detail in previous chapters. Disharmony between the parents may make children unsure and distrustful and may interfere with the formation of ideas about what kind of adult they want to be. Severe neglect and abuse on the part of parents may be detrimental to children emotionally as well as physically, though not everything that looks like neglect and abuse turns out to be such, psychologically speaking, when closely examined. Unmarried motherhood often brings serious perplexity and distress and may result in a situation detrimental to both mother and child. Then there are disruptions to family life occasioned by illness, mental or physical, by poor living arrangements, by poor management of family income, and so on. Children and young people may themselves create difficulties for the rest of the family; and there are situations outside the home that may create tension in parents or children and interfere with home life and parent-child relations.

Then, too, personality development may be handicapped by difficulties children encounter at school, in neighborhood relations, in recreational pursuits. Hospitalization may mean a setback for them emotionally as well as physically, and may entail serious social difficulties. Enforced military service may create social and psychological problems for some youths.

Toward the remedying of these and other sorts of difficulties in social relations, help is provided under a wide variety of social-service auspices.

The main sources of social-work assistance to families and children with regard to domestic difficulties are state and local child-welfare services (which are financed in part by Federal grants-in-aid),[6] some public-assistance agencies, and privately financed organizations of various kinds: family-welfare societies, child-guidance clinics, services for unmarried mothers, child-protective agencies, and some organizations whose main job is child placement. Day-care centers that provide casework service should be included in the list, as should some organizations engaged in marital counseling.

Clear lines of distinction among these various types of agencies dealing with problems of family life cannot be drawn, though historically most of the privately supported ones were set up to deal with difficulties of specified kinds. Public child-welfare services have a particularly broad scope of activities, of which assistance to parents and children in their own homes is only one. As to the privately supported agencies, there seems to be a tendency to widen in scope and to combine services. Child-protective services, for example, are sometimes provided under family-welfare-agency auspices; family agencies and child-placement agencies have amalgamated in some cities; and work with unmarried mothers is carried on both in separate agencies and in those concerned with general family welfare.

Social-work assistance with problems that are encountered in school, in connection with medical care or recreation, or that come to light when delinquent acts have been committed may be provided through specialized agencies, social-service departments of the organizations concerned, or through the same sorts of agencies that give help with problems of family life. Community centers and settlement houses and other organizations of that general kind are another source of social-work assistance, as are various counseling services set up under religious or fraternal auspices.

In short, in contrast to financial assistance, which is provided in the main through agencies of the government, there is no one large program whose work can be described and analyzed for its contribution to the emotional well-being of children. Instead, there is a welter of agencies and services, and little that could be said about one program would be strictly applicable to the others. Accordingly, rather than attempting to describe programs or even the specialized branches of social-work endeavor (such as school social work, medical social work, and the like), we shall try

[6] In 1946, 15 per cent of the full-time child-welfare case workers were paid in full or part from Federal funds. Most of them worked in rural areas. *Personnel in Public Child Welfare Programs, June 30, 1946,* Federal Security Agency, 1948, p. 5.

to make clear some of the assumptions and working methods of the two chief categories of social workers (case workers and group workers) that deal directly with children and their parents, and to show how their efforts may contribute to the personality development of children.

The Nature of Social Casework

The many concrete ways in which social caseworkers can be of assistance to parents and children are fairly well known: they may help an overcrowded family find a better place to live; they may facilitate the securing of needed medical care; they may place and supervise a "homemaker" in a home in which the mother is incapacitated by illness or the father is trying to care for the children in his wife's absence; they may arrange hospital care for an unmarried mother; they may secure for a child a place in a summer camp or in a day-care center; they may help boys and girls find jobs or recreational facilities; they may facilitate a change of school or help a family to get financial or legal assistance. And so on.

These and the numerous other kinds of tangible assistance that social caseworkers provide are, however, rarely given in isolation. Usually they form a part of a larger service, much of which is of an intangible nature, consisting chiefly of "talk." Currently, the word "counseling" is being used to designate the social-work services that consist of discussions between a social worker and a client. Sometimes much the same sort of service is given a group of clients as part of social group work.

That the concrete services of social caseworkers may help children greatly is well recognized, and, on the assumption that it consists chiefly of good advice, counseling, too, is generally considered worth while. Modern caseworkers, however, are likely to shun giving advice and attempting to manage other people's lives. Just what they do in counseling and how this kind of service can contribute to the well-being of children can be made clear only by describing in some detail casework assumptions and methods.

The aim of social casework, it has often been said, is to help people to help themselves in regard to their difficulties in social relationships and social responsibilities. Accordingly, in responding to an individual's request for assistance or indication of interest in being helped, a caseworker makes certain assumptions about what people—children as well as adults—are like and how he can be of help to them.

The social caseworker assumes that the individual, be he child or adult, has tried various ways of dealing with his problem and has not found them satisfactory. He assumes that if the person has come to ask for help, he is prepared to do something about his trouble. He assumes that the long-time responsibility for the family's affairs, for the child, and for the particular issue rests with the responsible members of the family and not with the social agency. He therefore holds that it is up to the agency to help the family carry that responsibility, not to take it away from them.

The caseworker assumes, too, that, since all activity involves emotions, the individual has feelings about coming to the agency and accepting its help about the problems at stake. He knows that people vary greatly in the way they feel about seeking help and taking it, and that their feelings must be taken into account if they are to be able to make much use of what the agency has to offer. People may feel proud of doing something about their difficulties and yet also be ashamed, thinking that the need to "do something" is in itself evidence of personal failure. They may feel that they have a right to service because, for example, of having paid taxes or being a church member, and yet they may fear that their affairs will be too much inquired into and that they will suffer loss of both privacy and pride. Some people may fear loss of independent self-direction; others, the criticism of neighbors or relatives; and so on and so on. The caseworker knows, too, that just as people vary in their feelings, so do they vary in the plans they have made for solution of their difficulties. Not infrequently, too, their troubles seem so overwhelming that they see no place to begin.

Taking all these things into account, the caseworker recognizes that only as an individual's feelings about asking for help are understood and as his feelings about his troubles are valued and respected will the caseworker be able to know how to be of service to him. The caseworker will try to obtain this needed understanding of his client by sympathetically and perceptively observing and responding to all that he says and does in the interviews.

The caseworker further maintains that he has a right only to such information as is directly relevant to the person's troubles, to the agency's service and decisions, and to the business of locating and spotting the issues on which the agency may be able to help. Thus the caseworker holds that the best source of information is the individual himself. Certain required information (about citizenship, say, or birth records, etc.) can often be given or obtained by the person himself if he is given a chance. In the great majority of instances, the value of other information is thought not worth obtaining unless the individual gives his consent.

As a corollary, the caseworker maintains that, for the most part, historical facts are less important than how a client himself feels about them. Thus, such facts as the age at which the client left school, when his parents died, whether he ever appeared in court, had a crippling accident, was severely disciplined, and so on, are regarded as of relatively little importance in and of themselves so far as helping the client deal with his problems is concerned. What counts for most is how the client feels about such events and which ones he himself considers important. And the same is true of the positives, so-called—a "normal" home, steady employment, adequate recreation, and the like.

The caseworker knows that any person's self-view, as well as his view of others, is in part a product of his immediate human relations and of the opportunities he is having currently to gain some satisfaction in handling himself and his own affairs. Therefore, the caseworker tries to assure that there is the minimum of frustration in his own relationship with his client. Frustrations that result from the client's feeling that he is not being treated as an individual, that he is not being "understood," or that he is being "drained dry" for no reason discernible to him are avoided as much as possible.

The caseworker assumes, too, that he need not help the client clear up all his difficulties. If the client can work on some fraction of his troubles and come through to some conviction that a modification of his difficulty is the result of his own activity, he will probably be able better to meet other and subsequent exigencies on his own.

So much, then, for the caseworker's assumptions. What he actually "does" is dependent on the individual with whom he is dealing, on that person's problem, and on the extent to which the agency is equipped to deal with the kind of trouble the person describes.

Briefly stated, the caseworker helps the client feel as comfortable as he can about asking for help. He helps him to formulate his difficulties in a way that makes them mutually understandable, and to state the kind or kinds of solution he considers desirable. He helps him to understand what kind of assistance the particular agency can offer in relation to the problem. Through that discussion he makes it clear that the individual may take it or leave it, but that if he decides to take it certain stipulations will be involved, such as that additional information must be supplied or that residence be proved, that consecutive appointments be kept, that the spouse be consulted, and so on.

In working on the foregoing matters, the caseworker utilizes evidence of emotional conflict, of lack of information, etc., in such a way as to help the individual break through his preoccupation with his troubles to a readiness to consider the factual (hence, the feeling) issues at stake. This may be done through joint consideration of alternate actions; through considering what might happen if the applicant took no further steps; through discussion of why the individual was referred to the agency, especially if pressure has been applied; through enlisting the individual's help in figuring out the sorest of the sore spots he is up against, etc.

The caseworker makes certain that the speed of the interview, both topically and emotionally, is geared to the individual to whom he is talking and that he and that person are clear about how things are left at the end of the interview. Is the person to "think things over," "get information," return for a continuation of the initial exploration, file an application, bring the child for observation or for examination, etc.?

All these things the caseworker does neither sequentially nor categorically and perhaps never the same way twice.

This way of working characterizes both the initial interview and the later discussions, both in assumptions and in ways of helping. The specific content of the material discussed will vary as the endeavor continues. As feelings and plans and facts continue to bob up around the issue at stake (child placing, probation, plans for maternal care, etc.), the client's feelings and ideas appear in sharper focus, and usually with less distress than at first, because of the dispassionate warmth with which they are met by the caseworker.

Thus the caseworker serves as a form of external reality against which the individual can view his hopes and hates, his view of others and his view of himself, and his size-up of the situation. By responding to that part of the individual that wants to make things better (from his viewpoint), the caseworker helps him to sort out his crisscross of feelings regarding the trouble at hand and to act on the feelings which he is ready to stand by. He helps him to get and try to hold his focus on what would be the plan that would best suit himself and those who are vitally involved, to find ways to channel his total concern (about his child's disobedience, for example, or his physical handicap or his need for foster-home care) onto something that he can do about it. He thus helps the client to sort out, and act independently of, his impetuous total response, his total feelings.

This result is achieved through holding discussion of plans firmly to the facts involved (of cost, time, regulations, etc.) and through utilizing the increasing appreciation of the individuality of the person and his particular patterns of handling his decisions and human relationships in a way that genuinely lets him use the most positive side of himself. In the course of doing this, the caseworker gives the client enough chance to express his hates or grudges or self-pity or blame so that, by the time the client arrives at a definite plan, the plan is relatively unclouded by motivations born of these emotions.

All in all, then, social casework centers around that typically American value, choice. The client is given choice as to whether he will use the service or not and, within its use, he is given choice as to how to work out his difficulties. Regardless of the kind of agency or the kind of service, this is the heart of casework: helping the client to choose his course of action, free of the distorting emotional reactions that have handicapped him previously.

The Nature of Social Group Work

Social group work has the aim of helping people to develop and use their capacities for satisfying social relationships and for making constructive use of the resources in their environment. It is based on the assumption that experiences with people in groups provide psychological-growth ingredients needed by all individuals. According to their stage of development and their individual needs, group relations take different forms and have different meanings for those who participate. For young children and for adolescents, they are of particular importance in providing the emotional security needed to make growth away from the family possible. For all, group experience provides some of the necessary education in getting along with others.

Social group work originated in the "leisure-time" agencies, and most of the professionally trained group workers are still employed there. In such organizations, group workers use the medium of informal educational and recreational pursuits to help the group members find and use in these experiences the ingredients that will aid them in their emotional, intellectual, and physical growth. The underlying premise is that in all groups there are emotional components in the relationships among the members that affect not only the individuals but also the climate and purposefulness of the group itself.

Social group work is beginning to be employed in a wide variety of settings in addition to those in which it originated, and its usefulness to children who are in particular kinds of social difficulty is increasingly being recognized. Many such children can profit more from group measures than from individual ones, in part because group work provides an opportunity for acting out as well as for talking about one's troubles, in part because many of these children find a close relationship with an adult difficult. The scope of group work is also being enlarged by the application of its concepts and theories to the total management of group situations, such as those represented by a home for maladjusted adolescents or for unmarried mothers.

As an example of these recent developments, social group work with children who are patients in a hospital may be cited. In order that their personality development shall not be impeded, special consideration and help are often needed by these children. The use of group work with hospitalized children presents special problems, of course. The various kinds of help social group workers provide for them, however, are sufficiently like those that might be given children in a school for truants, in a detention home, or in a camp that this example may suffice for our purpose.

The significance of group work as an aid to children who are ill and away from home lies in the fact that during illness emotional problems are likely to appear and that these problems may diminish if the child is able to obtain psychological satisfaction through contact with others, especially those who are similarly afflicted. Illness and hospitalization are likely to arouse various anxieties in children: fear of the new and strange; fear of pain, of diagnostic procedures, and of treatment measures; distress at being away from home; concern and perhaps annoyance at the regimentation of a hospital regime and its authoritative ways. These anxieties must be diminished if the child is to respond well to medical care, and positive experiences must be provided if the child is to maintain his desire to progress emotionally and relinquish the infantile satisfactions that illness may provide.

As in much of the rest of his work, the group worker in a hospital relies greatly on recreational devices as a means of developing group relations as well as contributing to the pleasure of the group members. For this, of course, he needs special knowledge and skill. His major contribution, however, derives from his ability to understand children as individuals and to develop a relationship of trust with them, and also from his sensitivity to the relations among the children and between them and the significant staff members. This being so, he keeps recreational activities subordinated to the children's emotional and physical needs and does not let successful achievement become an end in itself.

To children in a hospital the ward is a social world, which shifts in important ways for each child as patients come and go. In one corner of the ward, for instance, three little girls have established a close-knit subgroup that, in spite of occasional quarrels, gives each of them needed support and affection. Between themselves and the others they erect an invisible but impenetrable curtain, from behind which they throw their barbs of ridicule at new patients and test out the nurses to see how far they can go. No child in the ward escapes their scrutiny; within their small world they are both feared and envied.

In another corner, a shy child is fighting a losing battle not only against his tubercular spine but against the hostility of his peers. Across the way from him is a boy who is a natural leader but whose capacities are getting no outlet because he is struggling to adjust to his cardiac condition. Down the row of beds there is a girl with both polio and a severe emotional disorder, in consequence of which she keeps the ward in turmoil.

It is the group worker's task to penetrate into the vital life stream of this ward, to make a place for himself in it, and, through initiating games and conversations and the making of plans for the children's enjoyment, to make of the ward as relaxed, accepting, and satisfying an environment for each patient as possible. To do this he must know how to handle the children's reactions to each other and to himself—hostile at times, enthusiastic at others, indifferent, seductive, suspicious, and accepting by turns. He will at times find himself cast in the role of substitute parent; again he will represent to the children a means of escape from boredom and a source of pleasure. Occasionally he will have to explain to the children the reasons for the hospital rules and for the treatment measures employed. Frequently he will be the unobtrusive guide and counselor who is ever ready to let the group do as much of the leading as it can.

In addition to recreational measures, the group worker may utilize group discussions as a means of diminishing anxiety and promoting group relations. In a hospital ward, such discussions may center about the particular kind of illness there represented or the problems of illness in general. Older boys, for example, may be disturbed about the effects of their illness on normal masculine development. Children with cardiac disorders or diabetes may be upset by the limitations their disabilities impose. Nor is it necessary to limit discussions to illness and its consequences. Any topic of interest to the group may be used, for the aim is not only to relieve specific anxieties but also to keep alive the children's interest in the usual concerns of their peers.

Such group discussions, in which fears can be freely expressed and facts interpreted, have been found very useful in promoting emotional release and in renewing children's self-confidence. Group work of this sort has been carried on with parents as well as children, and with equally good results. The nature of the particular disorder, ways of caring for the child after his return home, methods of dealing with emotional reactions, and the like, may form the subject matter of the meetings. The chief benefits, however, are likely to come from the opportunity such group discussions provide for release of feeling, for discovery of common problems, and for mutual support.

In addition to direct work with children, group workers may contribute in several other ways to the functioning of a hospital or other institution or to particular aspects of its work. They may, for instance, be very helpful when unhealthy group relations develop among the children, difficulties that cannot or should not be handled on an individual basis alone or be repressed by discipline. Such situations call for understanding and use of the existing network of relations among the children—the subgroups and their attachments, the leaders and the followers, the conspiracies against authority, the "isolates" and the heroes, the subtle ebb and flow of morale throughout the group as a whole. Such understanding a group worker should have, both from theoretical study and from experience, and his relationship with the children and with the staff members should enable him to put it to practical use.

Another point at which a group worker may prove helpful is when assignment of a child to a ward in the hospital or to a cottage in an institution for delinquents or the like is under consideration. Age, sex, intelligence, disease—the usual categories of assignment—are not sufficient for the purpose of selecting a place where a child will thrive best. A factor of major importance is how well the child will fit in with the other children in the group in which he is being placed. A misplaced child can ruin a harmonious cottage; a shy, withdrawn child put in with a group of troublemakers may be seriously harmed by the punishment they inflict on him. The importance of skill in grouping children is being increasingly recognized in children's camps and institutions. Hospitals have paid little attention to this aspect of social group work, but it may be that consideration for the sociopsychic factors in the patient's environment will someday be added to the present interest in those that are psychosomatic.

Group workers also have a part to play in the activities that follow upon the realization on the part of administrators that there are group aspects to the functioning of the institution as a whole. It is becoming clear, for example, that certain group and intergroup relations are of major importance in establishing the social climate and tone of the hospital or institution. One of the most important intergroup factors is the relationship among the various professions represented on the staff. While these are in part personal relations, they also have important intergroup aspects, such as the authority and jurisdiction of each profession and the feelings or rivalry or helpfulness that exist between them. A group worker, being trained to sensitivity to group relations, is often able to contribute to better integration and more mutual helpfulness among staff groups and thus to benefit children by improving the environment in which they live.

Scope and Limitations

With their tasks and services so conceived, it is apparent that social casework and social group work have great potentialities for usefulness in helping parents and children overcome their difficulties in social relations, whether or not lack of money is involved. Used in conjunction with income-maintenance services casework may prevent the loss of self-confidence that resort to reliance on outside sources for financial support may entail for parents. Offered as services in their own right—through family-welfare and child-welfare agencies, in schools and hospitals and day-care centers and other organizations where parents and children are served—casework and group work may be of aid in the solution of numerous difficulties of social life that interfere with the healthy personality development of children.

There is much more that could be said, even in as brief a review as this one, about how the social services can contribute to the healthy development of children in or out of their own homes. Attention could be given to the plight of the many children who are held in detention homes that are not equipped to make the most of the opportunity they have for being of help. The role of day-care centers in the lives of children of working mothers could be discussed. There is much to be said about the job of the social services with respect to adoptions. And long chapters could be written about the aid social services can render to children and youth who have difficulty in fitting in at school, on a job, in military service, and elsewhere.

This is not to say, however, that social work is a panacea for all difficulties in social relations that adversely affect children's development. Present-day casework, it has been shown, centers around freedom of choice. For the most part, case workers have found their services beneficial chiefly to people who "want help" and who, by and large, seek it for themselves. In recent years they have had some success in taking the initiative in work with parents who are accused of neglecting and abusing their children, though some agencies are reporting that they can be most helpful in such cases after court action has been taken and parents are thereby in the position where they must make decisions. There are, however, many people with the kind of difficulties that casework and group work are designed to aid who cannot or do not want to use these kinds of help. Emotional immaturity, inadequate intelligence, cultural predisposition may stand in the way, or just a real preference for letting well enough alone.

Social workers have much more to learn about how to help people make use of the kind of service they now have to offer. They need to find new methods of working with the kinds of people who do not now find their service helpful. They may find in the studies of cultural sociologists better understanding of the ideas and values of people who are outside the mainstream of American culture. People of "higher" social levels may get away from the idea that social work is limited to financial problems and characterized by snoopiness, and they may become less reluctant to use what social work has to offer in assistance with problems of family life. Nevertheless, social work will probably remain a limited kind of service and not a wholesale remedy for all the kinds of social-relationship difficulties that impede children's personality development. Within its limits, however, social work with or on behalf of children has a highly useful job to perform. With improvements in public understanding of its capacities and with improvement in its own understanding and techniques, great expansion of its facilities would seem desirable. At present, these facilities are scarce in comparison with need. In spite of the wide variety of agencies, their coverage and distribution throughout the country are inadequate.

The aim of the public child-welfare program, for example, is that all children in need of its services and facilities should have such help available to them, regardless of economic or social status. The primary objectives of the program are to strengthen family life and to preserve the child's own home whenever possible, and to provide substitute care through relatives, foster families, or group-living arrangements for those children who must leave home for one or another reason. To these ends various services and facilities are provided: casework services to parents and children, homemakers when parents are incapacitated or absent, day-care centers, foster-care facilities and supervision of children in foster families, adoption services, and the like. In addition, attempts are made to stimulate the development and improvement of other services that the well-being of children requires, such as those of a medical, psychiatric, or recreational nature and those of law-enforcement agencies.

At the time of the meeting of the Midcentury White House Conference, in December, 1950, the number of children being served by public child-welfare programs was about 246,000. About 40 per cent of these children were receiving care in foster homes. Some were in foster homes because their own homes were broken or inadequate, some because their parents were temporarily or permanently incapacitated, some because their emotional difficulties required care away from home, and some because they were in the process of being adopted by their foster parents. Another 40 per cent were living in their own homes; in many of these cases, the children and their parents were being aided with problems arising out of neglect or delinquency. The remaining children were being aided by child-welfare workers while they were residing in institutions or elsewhere.[7]

States differed considerably in the proportion of children served. The national rate was about 5 per 1000 persons under twenty-one years of age, but state rates ranged (in March, 1950) from 13 per 1000 in Vermont to about 1 per 1000 in Idaho, Michigan, and Tennessee. These differences were attributable to variations among states in children's need for such services, in the availability of privately financed services, and in the ability and willingness of state legislatures to finance public programs of this sort.

The increase in Federal grants to states for "establishing, extending, or strengthening" of child-welfare services made possible by the 1950 amendments to the Social Security Act may improve this situation somewhat. Federal grants for child-welfare services are, however, limited to "payment of part of the cost of district, county or other local child-welfare services in areas predominantly rural" and to "developing State services for the encouragement and assistance of adequate methods of community child-welfare organization" in such areas and in others of "special need." Helpful as these grants are in increasing the number of child-welfare workers and in improving the quality of the work, it is not to be expected that they will enable the child-welfare objectives to be fully carried out.

In some parts of the country there are still few, if any, public child-welfare workers. The total number of social workers giving full time to public child-welfare work in 1950 was 4,100, an increase of about 40 per cent over the number so employed five years earlier. Even so, somewhat more than half of the counties did not have the services of such a worker, though some of them had the part-time services of a general public-welfare worker. Then, too, the caseloads of many workers were too large

---

[7] *Children Receiving Child-welfare Casework Service from Public Welfare Agencies, March 31, 1950,* multigraphed report, Children's Bureau, Federal Security Agency.

to permit them to give to children and their parents the kind of casework service described above. The median caseload in 1950 was 59 children per worker; 15 per cent of the workers served 100 children or more at a time.[8] All in all, the public program is far from adequate, although there has been considerable change for the better in recent years. Much still remains to be done if personality development of children is to be fostered through public services of this nature.

Information on the extent of privately financed services is scarce, but it is known that these services are largely lacking in small towns and rural areas. In 1948, per-capita expenditures for family welfare services in 29 urban areas ranged from 4 cents to about a dollar a year. Expenditures for protective, foster-home, and institutional care for children were higher, ranging from 45 cents to $4.14 in 31 urban areas, while in the same cities expenditures for recreation, informal education, and group-work services ranged from $1.30 to $4.80 per capita.[9] Figures for other kinds of service of the type here under consideration are not available. There is no question, however, but that the number of social workers in schools, hospitals, courts, mental-hygiene clinics, and recreational organizations is ever so much smaller than would be desirable, and that privately financed agencies' services reach only a small proportion of the families and children who might benefit from them.

In addition, there are inadequacies in quality of service as well. The story is more or less the same throughout all types of social service. On the one hand, there is much inadequacy in both quantity and quality of service the country over, and there is much unevenness in distribution from state to state, between city and country, and even within cities with respect to race and religion. On the other hand, there is much knowledge about children and their families and about how to help them that is put to unusually good use here and there in scattered programs throughout the nation, programs that influence the work of the social services generally. Even so, much more knowledge is needed—about how children develop physically, socially, and emotionally, about intergroup and interpersonal relations and about cultural differences, about means of helping children, and about the helping process itself—and much careful research into these and other questions is called for.

There has been considerable discussion about what might be done to remedy matters. All over the country, community chests and councils are

[8] *Personnel in Public Child Welfare Programs,* 1950, Children's Bureau Statistical Series No. 7, 1950.
[9] *Expenditures for Community Health and Welfare in 31 Urban Areas, 1948,* Community Chests and Councils, New York, pp. 12–15.

struggling with the problem of how to secure more funds. Ways of improving the training of social workers are widely discussed. Research on a broad scale is contemplated. The Social Security Administration recommended in its 1949 report that Federal financial participation be extended to cover social-welfare services that are required by large numbers of families and that are usually beyond the capacity of voluntary agencies to finance on a large scale. Such public social services, the Administration maintains, should eventually be provided for all families and individuals requesting them, no matter where they live.

Lack of money, lack of personnel, and lack of knowledge are not the only obstacles, however, in the way of the social services making their fullest contribution to the healthy personality development of children and youth. As with other major social provisions for children and young people in a democracy, the social services are an expression of an informed and demanding public, a public with an opinion and a chance to express that opinion. Specifically, the extent to which young people, children, and their families profit from the provisions now known to be of value depends on the interaction of the social services, the other social institutions, such as school and church, and all citizens whose concern about the welfare of young people extends well beyond their own front door. Even more specifically, there has to be a community commitment, whether the community is a hamlet, a state, or the nation, as to whether our goal is to include all children who might profit from new or revised arrangements or whether we intend to continue to select only certain children for preferential treatment.

We need, too, to turn the ingenuity born of our conviction to new kinds of formal and informal organized activities. Before the next decade is out we may have devised effective ways for parents and neighbors and young adults in the country to work together for the welfare of children. Some parents and neighbors are already attacking that task. These efforts probably will be effective to the extent that the method and pattern of joint work fits local requirements and interests and groups. Whether in country or town or in major cities, children or adolescents will profit from the best of present-day knowledge about their potentials and wishes and strengths and confusions only if citizens who support the social services through study, publicity, consultation, direct action, or money are prepared for ongoing efforts. What is solved, or almost solved, today becomes a new problem tomorrow, in the flux of the social and economic life of a country that is expanding in production and in population.

✗ XVI ✗

Services of Law-enforcement Agencies

IN this chapter we shall consider some implications of the findings about healthy personality development for the work of law-enforcement agencies with juvenile offenders. To state the topic this way is not to overlook the fact that juvenile delinquency is variously defined or to imply that most children who commit unlawful acts come to the attention of the law-enforcement agencies. In line, however, with our plan for the analysis of social institutions, we are concerned here with the work of the police, the courts, and the institutions to which delinquents may be committed, the aim being to consider some of the ways in which they may improve the emotional well-being of the children and youth they have in charge.

Delinquency, sociologically considered, is behavior a society so disapproves of that it insists it shall not occur. In both negative and positive terms, certain aspects of the proper behavior of children are set forth in the law. Children shall obey their parents, otherwise they may be brought before a court as "stubborn," or "incorrigible." They shall attend school regularly; truancy is a legal offense. They shall not take the property of others or damage it; they shall not injure others; they shall not engage in sexual acts of specified kinds. And so on. In other times and in other societies, the list was different. All societies, however, have categories of forbidden acts, and all have numerous means of securing compliance.

In every society, various social institutions are involved in delinquency prevention and control. Usually the responsibility lies chiefly with the family, but the church, the school, medical, social, and recreational services also play a part. In one way or another all of them do something about preventing legally forbidden behavior on the part of children. Which social institution takes major responsibility varies somewhat with the economic and ethnic group to which a child belongs. As a last resort in some groups and as an early resort in others, the police and the juvenile court are involved.

In the preceding chapters of this report we have considered, by implication at least, some of the ways in which the family, the church, and health, recreational, and social services may operate to prevent delinquency and to help children who commit serious offenses or persist in unlawful conduct. In this chapter it is the work of the legal authorities that is under consideration. The kind of behavior in question, however, is not limited to the children the law-enforcement agencies work with. Accordingly, all knowledge about the reasons for such behavior, whether or not officially labeled "delinquent," is pertinent to the present inquiry.

Causes of Delinquency

Over the last fifty years there has been so much talk about juvenile delinquency and so much search for its causes that we have almost lost sight of the fact that legally forbidden behavior cannot be very different from other sorts of forbidden behavior so far as its genesis is concerned. If the question is put, "Why do children and youth do what is not allowed?" much of the mystery disappears, and the findings regarding the personality development of children in general become applicable.

Characteristics of Delinquents

Much of the research into juvenile delinquency is concerned not with the causes or the meaning of delinquent behavior but with the question, "Who are these youngsters who disobey the law and come to the attention of the courts?" (The "and" is important.) It is well established that most of them come from families of low economic status and that, consequently, they live in houses and neighborhoods that are far from the best. Many of them are below average in intelligence. Many are energetic and restless and physically sturdy. Their pleasures are largely street pleasures, and they are likely to shun (and perhaps be shunned by) established recreation centers. Their parents tend to be hostile or indifferent to them, to give them little supervision, and to pay less attention to their training than is thought proper.

The story, along these lines, has been told too often to need repetition in detail. Some aspects of the story, however, have been fairly well discredited by research workers, without being discarded by the general public. For instance, research workers have found that, in and of itself, the broken home is not to blame. Given the same neighborhood and same national background, broken homes are probably only slightly more frequent among delinquents than among nondelinquents.[1] Similarly, low

[1] Clifford Shaw and Henry McKay, "Social Factors in Juvenile Delinquency," *Report on the Causes of Crime,* National Commission on Law Observance and Enforcement, Washington, D.C., 1931, Vol. II, No. 13, p. 276. See Harry M. Shulman, "The Family and Juvenile Delinquency," *Annals of the American Academy of Political and Social Science,* January, 1949, pp. 23–26, for summary of studies.

intelligence has little to do with the case.[2] Poverty is not an adequate explanation, for some impoverished groups produce many juvenile delinquents and others few.[3]

Other traits long since believed to be associated with delinquency have stood the test of recent research, and some new ones have been added. For example, Sheldon and Eleanor Glueck's latest study, a comparison of five hundred delinquents from underprivileged areas who were inmates of a reform school and five hundred nondelinquents whose homes were in approximately the same areas, comes to the following conclusion:

The delinquents as a group are distinguishable from the non-delinquents: (1) *physically,* in being essentially mesomorphic in constitution (solid, closely knit, muscular); (2) *temperamentally,* in being restlessly energetic, impulsive, extroverted, aggressive, destructive (often sadistic)—traits which may be related more or less to the erratic growth pattern and its physiologic correlates or consequences; (3) *in attitude,* by being hostile, defiant, resentful, suspicious, stubborn, socially assertive, adventurous, unconventional, non-submissive to authority; (4) *psychologically,* in tending to direct and concrete, rather than symbolic, intellectual expression, and in being less methodical in their approach to problems; (5) *socio-culturally,* in having been reared to a far greater extent than the control group in homes of little understanding, affection, stability, or moral fibre by parents usually unfit to be effective guides and protectors or, according to psychoanalytic theory, desirable sources for emulation and construction of a consistent, well-balanced, and socially normal superego during the early stages of character development. While in individual cases the stresses contributed by any one of the above pressure-areas of dissocial-behavior tendency may adequately account for persistence in delinquency, in general the high probability of delinquency is dependent upon the interplay of the conditions and forces from all these areas.

In the exciting, stimulating, but little-controlled and culturally inconsistent environment of the underprivileged area, such boys readily give expression to their untamed impulses and their self-centered desires by means of various forms of delinquency behavior. Their tendencies toward uninhibited energy-expression are deeply anchored in soma and psyche and in the malformations of character during the first few years of life.[4]

[2] John Slawson's study showed this twenty-five years ago (*The Delinquent Boy,* Richard G. Badger, Boston, 1926), as did the *Study of Problem Boys and Their Brothers* conducted by Butcher, Hoey, and McGinnis for the New York Crime Commission in 1929. Later research has confirmed these findings.

[3] Sophia Robinson, *Can Delinquency Be Measured?* Columbia University Press, New York, 1936.

[4] Sheldon and Eleanor Glueck, *Unraveling Juvenile Delinquency,* Commonwealth Fund, New York, 1950, pp. 281–282.

These statistical comparisons of delinquents and nondelinquents by individual traits add little to our understanding of why particular children engage in illegal behavior and what can be done to alter matters, although they are useful in locating the problem and, perhaps, in framing social policy. Two other lines of research, which show some signs of converging, seem to offer hope that practically useful formulations may be forthcoming. The one is that pursued by some cultural sociologists, the other, that which stems from dynamic psychology.

Two Sociological Explanations

One sociological explanation of delinquency that seems especially pertinent is that which grows out of observations regarding the class structure of American society. W. Lloyd Warner and his associates maintain that standards, ideals, goals, and ways of behavior differ significantly from class to class in the United States, and that the various social classes have little emotionally significant contact with each other. The result is that children pattern their behavior after the adults of their own class and do not value greatly the ideals or prohibitions of the others.

The class differences that are particularly pertinent to delinquency are those that distinguish the middle classes from the lower. According to Davis, lower-middle-class parents "exert a strenuous and unrelenting push to motivate their children to study their lessons, to repress aggression at school, to inhibit sexual impulses, to avoid lower-class playmates, to attend Sunday School regularly, to avoid cabarets, beer parlors, pool parlors, and gambling houses. They keep steadily before the child, often in the face of economic disaster, the status goals of a 'nice' play group and social clique, a high-school education, skilled or white-collar occupation, and a 'good' middle-class marriage. . . . With regard to sex, education, occupation, recreation, and marriage, the goals which the lower-class family, white or Negro, sets before the child are basically different. This difference is greatest in those areas of behavior which middle-class society strongly controls, i.e., aggression, sex responses, and property rights." [5] Since these are the areas of behavior to which laws defining delinquency chiefly refer, the relevance of this theory to our topic is clear.

The significance of this description lies in the idea that people of the lower class actually have a conception of what is right and proper that

[5] Allison Davis, "American Status Systems and the Socialization of the Child," in *Personality in Nature, Society, and Culture,* ed. by Clyde Kluckhohn and Henry A. Murray, Alfred A. Knopf, Inc., New York, 1949, pp. 467–468.

differs from other classes, and that they reward and punish their children in accordance with that conception. In other words, it "comes as natural" for their children, under certain circumstances, to fight and steal and engage in what other classes call "sex misconduct" as it does for other children to follow the dominant American pattern of politeness and obedience.

Put so bluntly, one wonders whether this theory is wholly true. It has long been known that many delinquents come from families in which there is much quarreling, drunkenness, promiscuity, and in which parents and siblings have court records for offenses against persons and property. That such conduct is actually approved by parents and taught to children and that it characterizes a distinguishable social class into which children are born and which few leave is another story. If it is correct, it is most important that we discover the rules by which conduct in this social class is regulated. Are they the same in all sections of the country, in rural and in urban areas, regardless of ethnic and racial background? The answers to these questions are important for any work with children, but they are of especial importance for work with delinquents, for presumably a considerable proportion of officially delinquent boys and girls come from this stratum of society.

Another sociological explanation is that which notes as characteristic of American society a distinction between family culture and peer·culture.[6] Partly because children are set apart rather than being fully incorporated into family life, with rights and duties clearly defined, American boys and girls from an early age look to their peers for ideas about conduct, dress, standards of right and wrong. The influence of age-mates grows with the years, and parents themselves are often fearful of opposing their children's desire to be like the others and to do what they do.

This "peer culture" takes somewhat different form in the various social classes, though what is involved here has not been studied in detail. In the crowded parts of cities, the desire of youngsters to be like their peers results in youngsters of nine or ten and up wandering about town on their own, "hopping trucks," "sneaking" into movies, throwing stones, pilfering small objects from "dime stores"—in general, pursuing that American ideal of "having a good time." In the delinquency studies, many of these boys and girls show up as "extroverts," "overactive," in "good physical condition," having "many friends," and the like. Many such youngsters give up this delinquent behavior when they are old enough to earn

[6] See Talcott Parsons, "Age and Sex in the Social Structure of the United States," *American Sociological Review*, Vol. VII (1942), pp. 604–616.

money to pay for their pleasures. Others, however, continue to be dissatisfied with what their low financial state entitles them to and take the delinquent path to pleasure through stealing cars for joy riding and joining in other gang activities.

This explanation implies that it may not be wholly lack of home influence that distinguishes delinquents from nondelinquents, as is so often claimed. In a certain sense, it might be said that the home has little influence with either group once the children approach adolescence. More exactly, it appears that in some social classes parents more or less approve of the standards and values of the "youth culture," while in others they do not.

In the middle and upper classes, especially in urban areas, the home follows and supports the "youth culture," with its emphasis on clothes, athletics, social activities with the opposite sex, and general irresponsibility. When it does not do so, parents are labeled, in child-guidance clinics, as dominating, controlling, or overprotective. In the lower classes, not only are youth standards and values considerably different from those of middle-class youth but many parents are remote from their children for ethnic and other reasons. Some parents try to enforce standards that the youth culture rejects; others are too much out of touch to know what is going on. In either case, most youths are on their own, in the characteristic American way, and more influenced by their contemporaries than by their parents. This being so, there arises the possibility that the standards of the lowest class, described above, can, through the children, reach some of the boys and girls of other social groups. This would account for the influence of "bad companions," so frequently mentioned in the delinquency literature.

Two Psychological Explanations

To these two sociological explanations, two psychological ones must be added. If we say that the parental influence is not as great among American young people as among those of some other societies, it is not to deny that character is essentially formed at home and that it derives in large part from early parent-child relations. There are, however, at least two ways in which delinquency may relate to this fact. The relationship that is usually traced is that emotional deprivations in childhood may lead to dissatisfactions and discontents that under certain circumstances, which are as yet not fully understood, may evidence themselves in delinquent conduct. The other relationship is the one that Erikson notes: that in certain ethnic and racial groups the cultural discontinuity between home life and adolescent street life may be very disruptive emotionally, and that delinquency is one form the emotional disturbance takes.

Evidence to the first point is contained in a recently reported study of delinquency prevention. Two hundred and fifty-four boys, largely from lower-middle and lower-class homes, and, for the most part, regarded as "difficult" by their teachers, were studied over a number of years. It was found that many of the boys engaged in minor delinquencies but that less than a fourth of them committed fairly serious offenses or became persistent delinquents. For the most part, these latter boys were of one of two types: those who shunned close relations with adults (at least the kind represented by the study's workers) and found much pleasure in street or gang life, and those who were neurotic products of emotionally destructive homes.[7]

At the beginning and at the end of the study, the boys were rated with respect to type of home, emotionally considered, and to degree of social adjustment. A close relation between the two ratings was found. None of the forty-nine boys rated as well adjusted when the study started, and only about one in fifteen of ninety-four rated as slightly maladjusted, came from homes classified as emotionally unsatisfying, while all but three of the thirty-eight most maladjusted boys came from the least satisfying type of home. The situation was much the same when the study ended, about eight years later. Two-thirds of the boys from the best homes, emotionally considered, were rated as well adjusted. This compared with a fourth of the boys from the homes put in the middle category, and only one boy out of sixty-three whose homes were rated as poorest. Contrariwise, none of the boys from the best homes, about a tenth from those from homes in the middle group, and over a third of those from the poorest homes were rated as very poorly adjusted, being either seriously neurotic or chronically delinquent, or both.[8] These findings suggest that within the social groups in which delinquency is most likely to occur, the boys and girls who become delinquent are largely those whose early home life is emotionally unsatisfying.

The second explanation—that delinquency may sometimes be attributable to a break in cultural values—is one that has not been adequately explored by psychologists, although "culture conflict" is an old conception among sociologists. Erikson is one of the few who has written even briefly on this subject.[9] In the early school years, he notes, children of

---

[7] Edwin Powers and Helen L. Witmer, *An Experiment in the Prevention of Delinquency*, Columbia University Press, New York, 1951, p. 563.

[8] *Ibid.*, pp. 373 and 399.

[9] Erik Erikson, "Growth and Crises of the Healthy Personality," *Problems of Infancy and Childhood*, Suppl. II, Josiah Macy Foundation, New York, 1950, pp. 48–49.

certain minority groups (Mexicans, Indians, some Negroes and Europeans) usually experience a break in their cultural development and, instead of following their parents ways, develop the American traits of self-reliance and enterprise. These traits, however, are socially useful and psychologically healthy only if the rest of the development is to proceed along the same lines. For these youngsters, this development is threatened as adolescence, with its heightened awareness and sensitivity, approaches, for they now are likely to find, from the way they are treated in school and community, that it is the color of their skin, the background of their parents, or the cost of their clothes, rather than their wish and will to learn, that determine their social worth. Consequently, feelings of inadequacy and inferiority may crowd out or prevent the full flowering of the kind of sense of industry that is so important a part of the American personality. Such a development makes the solution of the problems of adolescence unusually difficult.

American adolescence is itself a phenomenon that is something of a shock to all developing personalities, says Erikson, for it is so standardized and so intolerant of differences that only those who are already well molded along the lines of its ideal can take it easily. For these youngsters of minority groups, already somewhat insecure and inadequate, adolescence is indeed a period of storm and stress. Cut off from their parents and the tradition they represent, doubtful of their own worth, they can only band together in zoot-suit manner and aggressively protect their rights or withdraw into such strange and inaccessible moods that they appear to be schizophrenic. Delinquent acts may be committed in either case, though it is the gang activities that are apt to get the headlines. In either event, "recovery" comes only with the establishment of a sense of identity, a clear sense of social role and social destiny.

Conclusions

Viewed dynamically, these sociological and psychological explanations of the causes of delinquency blend into each other and are mutually reenforcing. Nor do they contradict the statistical findings. They only give them depth and meaning.

Current research seems, then, to support the often-expressed idea that there is no single cause for delinquency and that all we know about personality development is pertinent to it. Nevertheless, the field is not wide open. There are identifiable social and economic factors—poverty, discrimination on the basis of color, class, and creed, cultural differentiation, and so on—that favor the development of delinquent behavior in boys and girls who are too energetic to be easily set aside and too lacking in strength of character (chiefly because of unsatisfying parent-child relations) to find a socially approved way out of their dilemma.

There is still much to be learned about how the various factors favoring the development of a delinquent career interrelate and what can be done to make delinquency less frequent. Delinquency prevention, clearly, is a task that involves the whole community and its way of life, as well as many separate social institutions. Police, judges and other court workers, and those in charge of correctional institutions, however, have the daily task of dealing with these boys and girls in ways that will both protect others from their misdeeds and also favor their own social and emotional growth. It is with their part in the solution of the delinquency problem that we are here chiefly concerned.

The Extent of Delinquency

While sociologists and psychiatrists may debate about the definition of delinquency, those who deal with children in courts and institutions have no such leeway. They are bound by the legal definition, and so, too, are we when we would inquire about the extent of the problem.

Most juvenile-court laws define, more or less specifically, the terms "delinquency" or "delinquent child," although a few, as in the Standard Juvenile Court Act,[10] do not use these words but describe instead, in general terms, the circumstances or conduct that brings a child within the jurisdiction of the juvenile court. Every juvenile-court law of the states and territories includes the violation of a law or ordinance in the definition of behavior that may bring a child under the court's jurisdiction. Such acts may range all the way from mischievousness or minor traffic violations to murder. In addition, the juvenile court is given jurisdiction over the acts or conduct of children that seems likely to endanger morals or health, such as running away from home, being beyond the control of parents or guardian, or being found in questionable places or associating with immoral persons.

There is, however, considerable variation from state to state. What constitutes delinquency in one juvenile-court law is included in the definition of neglect in another. Moreover, not every state gives to its juvenile court exclusive jurisdiction over all offenses committed by children. Some exempt from juvenile-court jurisdiction or give to a criminal court concurrent jurisdiction over cases of serious offenses committed by children.

[10] *A Standard Juvenile Court Act*, rev. ed., National Probation and Parole Association, New York, 1949.

Accordingly, any national count of juvenile delinquents, no matter how accurate, is a count of somewhat dissimilar persons.

Far from all children whose acts or conduct are such as to render them liable to an adjudication of juvenile delinquency come to the attention of the juvenile court. Many of the seemingly less serious situations are handled by the law-enforcement officers, and many escape legal notice entirely. Chance, the economic resources of the family, the customs of the ethnic group to which the child belongs, and the social resources of the community determine to a considerable extent whether or not a given child whose behavior violates conduct norms gets into juvenile court.[11]

Even when the question is put in the simplest and most practical terms and we ask how many children the police and courts deal with and how many are in correctional institutions, a correct answer on the national scale cannot be given. There are, however, two sources of statistics about children who come to the attention of juvenile courts and police departments because of delinquent conduct that provide a partial answer to the question. These are described below. A third source of information is the U. S. Children's Bureau's occasional report on the number of children in public institutions for delinquents.[12]

The main source of information about the number of delinquents is the U. S. Children's Bureau. Since 1927, this Bureau has been collecting and publishing juvenile-court statistics. Being dependent upon voluntary co-operation of courts and state agencies, these reports are not nationwide in coverage. At the present time they are based on court jurisdictions which cover about one-third of the population of the United States. Large urban areas located predominantly in the northeast section of the country heavily weight the statistics, and other sections are under-represented. Among the courts that are included, however, are some that have jurisdiction over rural areas.

The basic unit of count in these delinquency statistics of juvenile courts is the case disposed of officially or unofficially. This means that a given child may appear in the count more than once, if during the year more than one complaint about him was filed and dealt with separately. Also

[11] Sophia M. Robinson, *Can Delinquency Be Measured?* Columbia University Press, New York, 1936.

[12] There are three other statistical series that have some bearing on the question: Federal Bureau of Prisons reports on the number of juveniles charged with violation of Federal statutes; Administrative Office of the U. S. Courts' statistics on juveniles charged with violating Federal statutes who elect to be tried under the Federal Juvenile Delinquency Act; and U. S. Office of Education reports on public and private residential schools for delinquent children.

included in the count are cases which the court handles by dismissal or indefinite continuance without adjudication and by unofficial adjustment.

The second source is the Federal Bureau of Investigation, U. S. Department of Justice, in its reports on police arrests. These reports, too, are based on voluntary reporting by state and local police. Moreover, the reports are limited to arrests in which fingerprints have been taken. These statistics, then, incomplete for the country as a whole, are particularly inadequate for children, for in many jurisdictions law or public policy prohibit the fingerprinting of children. Nevertheless, these F.B.I. figures are the only source of national statistics of children arrested by the police.

Because of the limitations of these two statistical series—differences in unit of count, extent of coverage, and geographic representation—our question regarding the size of the delinquency problem (even when limited to the juveniles known to courts and police) cannot be answered accurately. Nevertheless, these figures are useful in indicating the direction of major changes in the incidence of delinquency. For the period 1938 to 1947, the number of delinquency cases disposed of by seventy-eight urban juvenile courts strikingly paralleled the number of police arrests of children under eighteen years of age who were fingerprinted. Changes in the volume of court cases and police arrests were in the same direction throughout the ten-year period. Both increased sharply from 1942 to 1943, both decreased from 1943 to 1944 and increased again in 1945 to a ten-year peak. Both showed sharp decreases in 1946 and 1947.[13]

Apparently, then, we have fairly valid information as to whether juvenile delinquency, as so measured, is increasing or declining, even though we do not know its total amount. Regarding the latter point, it has been estimated that about 275,000 children under eighteen years of age come to the juvenile court as delinquent in the course of a year. As to how many come to the attention of the police, an estimate based on a comparison in communities in which both court and police report statistics suggests that the number is several times that coming before the court.

The number of children in public institutions for juvenile delinquents is more nearly accurately known, but figures are available only for 1933 and 1945.[14] In the latter year, thirty-six states made substantially complete reports and six others reported incompletely. In the first group of states (which included all the states with a large population except

[13] Edward E. Schwartz, "Statistics of Juvenile Delinquency in the United States," *The Annals of the American Academy*, Vol. 261 (1949), pp. 9–20.

[14] For 1933, see *Juvenile Delinquents in Public Institutions, 1933*, U.S. Bureau of the Census; for 1945, see *Children Served by Public Welfare Agencies and Institutions, 1945*, U.S. Children's Bureau, Statistical Series No. 3.

Massachusetts), there were about 16,000 children in institutions for delinquents and nearly 9000 living outside the institution but under its jurisdiction. Hawaii had 19.2 children in such institutions per 10,000 population under twenty-one years of age, while in the states the variation was from 2.2 in Mississippi to 10.2 in Vermont. The total figures represented a decline of 20 per cent as compared with 1933.

In total, then (if one may be so rash as to total the inaccurate figures), legal authorities of one kind or another deal with a million or more children a year. It seems most important for the nation's welfare, therefore, that their work be done in a way that is as helpful as possible to the children and their parents.

Some Basic Ideas About Delinquency Control

To attempt to derive from current theory and experience some guiding ideas for work with delinquents that aim at fostering their social and emotional well-being seems very brash, for there is little solid research on which to rely. Two things seem clear, however. Such work must be based on sound knowledge of the sociology and psychology of delinquency, and it must be carried on in a way that pays due attention to the social role and function of the various participants—police, courts, institutions, on the one hand, and church, school, medical, social, and recreational organizations, on the other.

Causes and Types of Delinquents

With respect to the first point, we have tried to indicate the chief current conceptions regarding delinquency causation. We have noted that there are social classes in which children are encouraged to engage in kinds of behavior that the rest of society disapproves of. Children from these groups may set the tone for "peer culture" in those sections of towns and cities in which incomes are low and parents are overoccupied with earning a living, for these youngsters' aggressiveness and disregard for property rights are in line with most children's native impulses. The timorous and sensitive may avoid their company, but to many active, energetic youngsters their outlook on life and their activities provide a means of achieving pleasure in a world in which pleasure is highly prized but is usually obtained only by those who have money.

Beyond this, street life and street standards offer an "out" for boys and girls of low economic status whose home life is emotionally disturbing. Such youngsters do not have the basis in parental love and control for the renunciation of selfish strivings, and their economic situation does not permit them to find solace in possessions or in activities that require money. Dr. Franz Alexander has commented on this as follows:

To renounce personal freedom for nothing is evidently more difficult than to renounce it in order to get something in exchange. Therefore, the original unadjusted nature of man is more apt to break through and to overthrow social restrictions in the discontented strata of the population. . . . We have found that criminal behavior . . . often originates from the stubborn wish for compensation for previous deprivations, or is the result of a sense of guilt and consequent need for punishment similar to that found in the psychogenesis of neuroses. . . . If the social situation gives justified reason for discontent and anti-social attitude, the early emotional conflicts are more likely to be worked out on the social level, and the earlier discontent with the family situation together with the social discontent are more apt to lead to non-social behavior than to neurotic symptom-formation.[15]

Intertwined with these various explanations of delinquency is the fact that many boys and girls who belong to minority groups suffer from "cultural discontinuity." What they are taught and the way they are treated at home does not develop in them the personality make-up appropriate for full participation in "American" life. Moreover, the attempts of teachers to foster in them values and outlooks different from those of their parents are often stymied at adolescence by the discriminatory treatment such youngsters encounter on every hand. These boys and girls are, therefore, truly on their own, looking neither to parents nor to teachers for guidance and having only their own peers for support in their struggle to define a place in life and a way of life for themselves.

Measures looking to delinquency prevention and delinquency treatment must take these facts and theories into account. It cannot be expected that any one measure will be effective with all delinquents or that every delinquent can be reached by some combination of the presently known devices. It is reasonable to expect, however, that more delinquents than are presently being aided will benefit if work with them is more solidly based on what is already known.

There are doubtless, as the literature points out, some "accidental" delinquents, youngsters who out of temporary discontent or a desire for adventure become involved in more or less serious misdeeds. There are many who find on the street compensations for poverty and meager home life, who truly follow the crowd and act in the way the crowd's code

[15] Franz Alexander, "Contribution to Psychological Factors in Anti-social Behavior," *The Family*, Vol. XIII (1932), pp. 143–146.

demands. These two groups are the "easy cases," the ones who will probably "go straight," sooner or later, with little effort on anybody's part. Even these, however, can probably be aided by friendship and wise counseling and by the provision of recreational and educational opportunities that are in line with their interests.

All who work with delinquents must be able to distinguish such boys and girls from those whose social and personal problems are likely to lead to chronic rebellion against society. The latter, on the one hand, it has been suggested, are the boys and girls who suffer from seriously disturbed parent-child relations, the neurotic delinquents whose stories are told in the psychiatric journals; on the other, they are the discriminated-against children of minority groups, the energetic, willful, striving adolescents who band together for mutual protection and defy regulation by those they distrust.

Helping the Culturally Deprived Delinquent

There are many descriptions in the literature of attempts to assist neurotic delinquents toward more healthy development of personality, and some guiding principles for such work have been set up.[16] Much less is known about how to deal effectively with the boys and girls who are cut off culturally from full participation in American life. The early psychological development of these boys and girls has been healthy for the most part. They have capacity for sensual enjoyment that is greater than that of most Americans, and they are probably less anxious about the expression of aggressive impulses. Some of them, culturally, have a love of beauty and find pleasure in nature and in music and ritual to a degree that is lacking among middle-class Americans. Their delinquencies arise largely out of their defiant refusal to accept second place in American life. They pit themselves against their detractors (the middle-class adolescents who "high-hat" them and all authority that labels them inferior and no-account) and develop a hardy skepticism of adults' good will.

Real help to boys and girls of this type doubtless requires large-scale revision of certain aspects of American life. Our democracy must be made more genuine. Equality of opportunity and equality of treatment must become a fact, so that the expectations aroused in the early school years and the qualities of personality cultivated at that time can find fulfillment in youth and adulthood.

[16] See, for example, August Aichhorn, *Wayward Youth,* The Viking Press, Inc., New York, 1935; Bruno Bettelheim, *Love Is Not Enough,* Free Press, Glencoe, Illinois, 1950.

In the absence of such confirmation of the American dream, case-by-case work with these delinquents, by legal authorities or others, is bound to be hard going. Such work, however, must be carried on, so it is important to note here what little is known about how it can be done.

One hopeful thing is that, basically, these boys and girls are healthy in personality. Specifically, the experience of their earliest years with parents who, by culture as well as personal inclination, give them much affection and impose few restrictions has laid the basis for feelings of both trust and autonomy, and out of their school experiences they have acquired a feeling for the American version of initiative and enterprise. This good start may have been partially undone by later experiences that caused them to feel inferior and unsure of their direction and goal. This being so, it would seem reasonable to assume that effective work with such boys and girls must aim at restoring their sense of trust and self-worth and at cultivating the development of a sense of achievement. Measures and actions that would further humiliate them must be avoided, and great care must be taken to see that they are accorded the respect and consideration for feelings and desires that foster in them a feeling of being people who count. With this accomplished, measures aimed at helping them to achieve—in school, on a job, at play, in personal relationships—will probably be effective if realistically planned.

There is little concrete evidence to cite to this effect, for most studies of delinquency prevention and delinquency control are not sufficiently analytic of either working method or types of youths served to be of much use here. In the Cambridge-Somerville Youth Study there is, however, some indication of the possible efficacy of such a way of work. It was found in that study that in cases in which parents were fond of their children and interested in their welfare but culturally unable to provide for their incorporation into "American" life, the boys benefited from a type of guidance that was based on friendliness, comradeship, and the provision of opportunities for better accomplishment in school and neighborhood.[17] This finding is in line with theoretical expectation and therefore seems doubly to be trusted.

Functions of Professional Workers

It was said above that for successful work with delinquents attention must be paid not only to the causes of the antisocial behavior but also to the social function of the agency that carries on the work. The roles of recreation worker, psychotherapist, police officer, and judge, for example,

[17] Edwin Powers and Helen L. Witmer, *op. cit.*

cannot be combined without doing damage to the interpersonal relationship on which the service of each to the delinquent youth depends. This follows from the fact that each of these workers has a culturally prescribed job to do, and the doing of it involves actions that are inconsistent with the expectations aroused by the playing of another role. For instance, a police officer has the prime duty of detecting and disposing of cases of unlawful conduct. He, therefore, cannot operate effectively as a psychotherapist, who must be able to hear of misdeeds without expressing blame, or as a recreation worker, who may disapprove but not report to the court.

This being so, we must next consider the various jobs that come under the general heading of "law enforcement," and the opportunity that each provides for dealing with delinquents in such a way as to promote their social and emotional well-being. In this account we shall not be able to go into much detail, for there are few facts on which to rely. Instead, we shall have to content ourselves with an analysis of the job to be done and depend largely upon the preceding analysis to suggest ways in which it might be carried out to the benefit of delinquent boys and girls.

The Police

The police have the responsibility of detecting and, if possible, preventing the commission of crime, apprehending offenders, and preserving the public peace and safety. These duties bring them in touch with many children and young people, both those who violate laws or whose conduct threatens the health or welfare of themselves or others and those who merely play on the streets or hang around public places. They also become familiar with conditions that are potentially harmful to safety and morals. By reason of this there has been increasing emphasis during the last few decades on the preventive aspects of police work and on the importance of dealing with children and adolescents in ways that take into account their immaturity and that make the experience a constructive rather than a terrifying or even demoralizing one.

In some police departments, separate units have been set up for work with children. These go by such names as "juvenile division," "juvenile bureau," "crime-prevention bureau," "delinquency-prevention unit," and the like. These units differ considerably in activities, reflecting the differences in the thinking in the police field as to what constitutes appropriate police work with children. Some confine their work strictly to the performance of police functions and try to carry on this work in ways that take into account the psychology and needs of youth. If a child's behavior calls for judicial action or social treatment, the police serve as a referral agency. Other police units undertake to make social adjustments and even to carry on treatment of a kind.

Important as these developments in the law-enforcement field are, it cannot be assumed that throughout the country children coming to the attention of the police are receiving special attention or being dealt with in a manner appropriate to their needs. In many communities, no special provision for juveniles is made, and the way in which children are treated depends chiefly on the individual officer. At worst, this may be in a way that does not increase their respect for law and those who enforce it; at best, children may be dealt with kindly but not always wisely. In addition, merely the creation of a juvenile unit or the assignment of special officers to work with juveniles is no guarantee that boys and girls will receive any better handling than by the regular officers of the department.

Undoubtedly the police have an important contribution to make to the welfare of youth. They are in a strategic position to discover children who are actually or potentially delinquent and to see conditions in the community likely to promote delinquency long before other agencies have knowledge either of the children or the conditions. The way the police use this knowledge in their contacts with children and in their relations with the rest of the community may help to determine the future attitude of these young people toward the law. Police officers' knowledge, or lack of knowledge, of the community's social resources and how to use them may afford or deny some children the opportunity or impetus necessary for wholesome development. The alertness with which they recognize promiscuous activities and demoralizing influences in streets, parks, bus stations, dance halls, skating rinks, motion-picture houses, hotels, night clubs, restaurants, and taverns, and the vigor with which they enforce the laws and regulations provided for dealing with them play an important part in determining whether the community is a good one in which to bring up children.

In the light of these possibilities, police administrators are giving serious thought to what should be the future emphasis and scope of police work in relation to juvenile delinquents. It is clear that the nature and quality of that work depend to a considerable extent on how police are selected and prepared for the job of law enforcement. They are also dependent upon what the community expects of its law-enforcement officers and how much support it gives them. Basically, there is no doubt but that the work of the police must take its start from the fact that the police are responsible for the peace and safety of the community, and that all their activities must be demonstrably related to that function. The real question is what kind of police actions and activities with respect to juveniles enhance the peace and safety of the community and how such work should be carried on.

It is frequently assumed that the welfare of the community and the welfare of the individual delinquent may be in conflict. For example, the following was among the recommendations of the National Conference on Prevention and Control of Delinquency:

The protection of society should be recognized as the first aim and objective of law enforcement organizations. The right of the individual should properly be considered of greatest importance in a democracy, but when an individual's activity comes in conflict with the welfare of the community, the welfare of the community is of paramount importance. This basic concept should be borne in mind so that in the handling of offenders of all ages, first consideration will be given to the interests of the community, and second, but very important, consideration to the welfare of the individual.[18]

Actually, neither the welfare of the delinquent nor the welfare of the community is furthered if an offender is "let off easy" and not handled in a manner calculated to reduce the likelihood of further misconduct. The chief difference between the "tough" point of view regarding delinquents and that of modern psychology lies in the methods that are used to deter and reform. The aims of the "tough" policy are avowedly the same as those of modern psychology but in actual fact they are likely to be more related to punishment, revenge, and the inculcation of fear.

As has been shown above, all work with delinquents, and children in danger of becoming delinquent, should be based on understanding of motivations and social situations. There is no single answer to what the determining factors are, and there is consequently no single approach that works with all boys and girls. The only common element in all good work is the policeman's clear realization that he is acting as an officer of the law (that is, with authority) and that as the law's representative it is his duty to treat every citizen, child as well as adult, with consideration and respect. Over and above this, he must use his judgment case by case in deciding how he can represent law and authority and yet avoid actions, such as shaming or intimidating, that will cause a vigorous youth still further to rebel.

[18] "Role of Police in Juvenile Delinquency," *Summaries of Recommendations for Action,* National Conference on Prevention and Control of Juvenile Delinquency, Government Printing Office, Washington, D.C., 1947.

Just how the findings of science can be used in police work with juveniles and how police can best be trained are subjects of considerable interest at the present time. One experiment along this line is the Delinquency Control Institute of the University of Southern California. This is both a training center for law-enforcement officers who deal with delinquent and neglected children and a research institute. The following extracts from a recent popular article are suggestive of the Institute's point of view:

"When I came to DCI," one trainee said, "I thought there were only two ways to act: nab a kid and lock him up—or let him alone. Now I know there are fifteen to twenty possibilities, depending on circumstances. . . . Most juveniles, no matter how tough they are, need understanding, not punishment. They'll usually respond to an officer who shows genuine interest. . . ."

DCI heads deplore the sense of isolation from which so many patrolmen suffer. As one officer described it, "I'm a cop. I'm different from other people. Nobody likes me."

"What a waste," comments a DCI instructor. "Here's the key man—the patrolman on the beat—who can spot youngsters heading for trouble better than anyone, and spot conditions that get youngsters into trouble. Yet all too often this key man is not accepted by even the most responsible members of the neighborhood. . . ."

DCI trainees are taught how to utilize the resources of professional and civic groups and public welfare agencies. . . . "The patrolman's real job is to use community facilities already available," says DCI Director Dan Pursuit. "He can't run a recreation center, be a minister, probation officer, social case worker and run every youth-serving organization. But he *can* work closely with all of them. . . ."

But don't get the idea that there is any soft sentimentalism about DCI. Psychiatrists spend hours teaching trainees to spot girls and boys who can't be helped just by sympathetic understanding—who need psychiatric treatment. "I know now," a DCI-trained policewoman said, "that there are children beyond help from either me or the courts. The hours I used to waste on these cases I now spend aiding other children. I get results—and I'm not constantly deviled by failures."

When youngsters can't get along with others at all or constantly rebel against authority without seeming cause, DCI trainees see to it they get thorough physical and psychological examinations. Often they prevail upon doctors and psychiatrists to donate their services if parents can't pay. . . .

Before leaving DCI every trainee is familiar with all the specialized services in his neighborhood. He knows whom to approach and what assistance to expect from every youth organization, church, and welfare agency. "It's the first time anyone bothered to tell me where to get help," said one trainee. "All I got before was hell when I failed to do a job." [19]

This, then, is one of the current answers to how policemen can carry on their work in a way that is both helpful to youngsters and protective of the community. They can approach each offender with friendly interest and with respect for his right to be heard. They can make use of all the resources of the community in securing help. They can firmly but kindly take those in charge whose conduct is dangerous to themselves or others. They can, in short, combine authority with consideration and, in so doing, help to demonstrate to doubting youngsters that the law and society are truly concerned with their welfare.

The Juvenile Court

Much the same can be said of the work of juvenile-court judges and probation officers. The court's opportunity to contribute to the well-being of youngsters against whom complaints of delinquency have been entered lies in its role of arbiter and judge. It must pay respectful attention to the views and the rights of both parties, demonstrating in so doing that just and equal treatment is a rule of the society. It must insist that the laws of the society be obeyed.

In carrying out its function, the court thus has the opportunity of showing youth both that there is authority in society and that that authority is not used arbitrarily. Since for many delinquent youngsters one of the chief problems is that of accepting limitations and restraints, this is a very important function, psychologically speaking, but one that must be exercised with great skill if it is to prove helpful to them.

In the training of the lawyer (and, therefore, of the judge) a good basis is laid for this work, in that lawyers are taught to view disputes objectively and to disentangle fact from fantasy and error. They also develop skills in arbitration and conciliation, in standing between two angry parties and working out a basis for agreement. The juvenile-court setting, moreover, is such as to provide opportunity for the exercise of such skills. The procedure is informal; the review is not limited to a particular act; there are no strict rules of evidence to be adhered to.

There are, however, lacks in legal training and possibilities for unwise use of authority in the juvenile-court setup that cause many to question whether too much power has been given to judges. When these courts were first established, more than half a century ago, it was assumed that

---

[19] Miriam Zeller Gross, "He Could Be Your Child's Best Friend," *Woman's Home Companion,* December, 1950, pp. 41 f.

a friendly, unbiased attitude and a good stock of common sense were all that were called for if judges were to do their work well. Now, as a previous section of this chapter has shown, the complex nature of delinquency causation is better known, and it is clear that much special knowledge is required of the individual who has to determine what kind of treatment a delinquent needs.

Several devices are currently used in some states to lessen these difficulties. One of them, of long standing, is that of giving to probation officers the responsibility of securing pertinent information about each child and his situation and of making recommendations to the judge or, in the less serious cases, of effecting adjustments. Another is that of setting up a psychiatric clinic under court auspices, the clinic's job being to examine delinquents and advise the judge in regard to their psychological and social disorders and needs. A third, used in only a few states, is that of giving over to a "youth authority" the responsibility for decisions about the handling of children and youths [20] adjudged delinquent and committed to the care of the state.

It is obvious that the effectiveness of these devices depends in part upon the caliber and training of the persons involved and upon the volume of work they are called upon to do. These devices are not panaceas and not substitutes for the judge's skill and wisdom. The first two are of little value unless the judge is equipped to make good use of the information thus secured; and even the presence of a youth authority does not relieve the judge of the responsibility of making decisions that are of great consequence to the well-being of the children he deals with.

Other proposals looking to the betterment of the juvenile court's work vary between two extremes. One extreme aims at a thoroughly "socialized" court. Such a court would combine legal and social-work philosophy and techniques. It would not only judge and prescribe but also carry out treatment in many cases, and it would include in its jurisdiction children "in danger of becoming delinquent." The other extreme aims at limiting the court to the determination of whether violations of laws or ordinances have occurred, and to the protection of the constitutional rights of the accused, perhaps through the appointment of counsel. Between these extremes there have been such suggestions as that part of the present juvenile-court work regarding delinquents be turned over to social agencies—the collecting of social information, for example, and the supervision of certain delinquents placed on probation—and that the court confine itself to cases in which the use of authority is clearly called for.

[20] The Youth Authority Acts in at least *two* states—California and Minnesota—cover youths above juvenile-court age as well as the younger offenders.

In the discussion of juvenile-court proceedings and what might be done to improve them, we must not, however, lose sight of their purposes, which are, first, to determine whether the child comes within the jurisdiction of the court and, second, what care and treatment would best promote his welfare. Because the charges are not criminal in nature, it has been possible to do away with many of the procedural formalities deemed necessary in criminal proceedings to safeguard the rights of the defendant, such as confrontation and juries and public hearings. Nevertheless, juvenile courts must strive to achieve the objective of these procedural safeguards; that is, to secure all the relevant, trustworthy facts needed to enable the court to arrive at an intelligent determination of the issues before it.

The first issue before the court is whether the child comes within its jurisdiction. Probably there is real dispute about this question (about whether the child committed a delinquent act) in only a small proportion of cases. Nevertheless, where the question is raised, sufficient facts must be presented to the court to form an adequate basis for the judge's decision. What is at stake here is the child's freedom and the parents' right to the unrestricted care, custody, and control of the child. Accordingly, when parents or child contest the basic issue as to delinquency, they must have an opportunity to refute the statements presented and to give their own version of the situation.

With respect to the second issue involved—the care and treatment that would best serve the welfare of the child—it is clear that its intelligent determination requires the fullest possible presentation of the relevant facts. In this connection, the social findings and the medical and psychological evaluations are very important "facts" (even though under customary legal procedures they would be considered "hearsay"), as are the child's and the parents' analyses of the situation. The court, however, does not have to accept all these "facts" without question. Rather, it is the court's duty to ascertain to its own satisfaction the validity of the reports, even as it is the attorney's duty to point out, through questioning or through presenting additional facts, those factors that should be given special consideration by the court in determining not alone the reliability of the facts presented but also what action would be to the child's best interest. In all this, however, care must be taken that the proceedings be kept informal and that the fundamental purpose of the hearing, the development of a sound plan for the child, be maintained.

These being the court's purposes and duties, it seems to us that improvement in the work of the juvenile court is more to be expected from improvement in personnel, both qualitatively and quantitatively, than from changes in structure and function or from delegation of duties to outside organizations. As long as the power of adjudication is left with the court (and there would be no court otherwise), the judge must be able to procure and to use wisely and responsibly the kind of testimony that is pertinent to the causation and prevention of delinquency—testimony about motives and feelings and psychosocial situations as well as about deeds. For such testimony he must rely in part upon well-trained probation officers or other court workers, men and women who know how to interview youngsters and how to evaluate what they learn. No supplement to a juvenile court can compensate adequately for lacks in the court itself, lack of time and staff to do the required job well, and lack of the kind of knowledge about child behavior that can make decisions about the disposition of cases truly constructive.

At present, much stands in the way of this ideal. The training of probation officers is woefully lacking, and salaries are usually too low to make insistence on graduate study feasible. Even the National Probation and Parole Association's standards of selection call only for a bachelor's degree, with courses in the social sciences, and for a year of supervised work in a social agency or its equivalent. As to judges, there is little in the law schools' curricula that prepares students specifically for juvenile-court work.

In many localities, both judges and probation officers secure their jobs through political appointment that pays little attention to qualification for work with juveniles. In many courts, both judges and probation officers have numerous duties in addition to those concerned with juvenile cases. In short, much change is required both in the preparation of court workers and in conditions surrounding the court's work before the juvenile court can be expected to make its best contribution to the welfare of children and youths who commit delinquent acts. Nevertheless, the outlook is more hopeful than in the past, for what is needed to make a court function well is better known now than ever before.

Probation and Institutional Care

Regardless of how effective the police may become in controlling delinquency or the juvenile-court judges in mediating between youngsters and those who complain of their misconduct, there will always be certain boys and girls who must be placed under some sort of restraint if they are not to continue in a delinquent career. Judges have two main courses of action open to them in such cases: they may prescribe either probation or institutional care. In either event, the opportunity and the responsibility for aiding in the personality development of these boys and girls pass into other hands.

Probation and institutional care can be discussed under the same heading only so long as one talks in terms of general principles. Probation officers' contacts with their charges are largely limited to the scheduled times at which they meet to discuss problems and progress. If they do anything in the interim it must be through other people—parents, teachers, social workers, ministers, and the like. Workers in institutions, in contrast, have collectively the opportunity of affecting the boys and girls through almost all aspects of their daily life. Nevertheless, since the objectives of the two groups of workers are the same, the basis of their working methods must have much in common.

One common element in the work of probation officers and institution staff is the philosophical belief that society has the right to restrain individuals whose behavior is injurious to themselves or others but that its representatives exercise that right justly only when they do all in their power to effect the rehabilitation of the individuals in their charge. Another common element is the psychological theory on which, it now appears, such rehabilitative work can profitably be based.

In previous sections of this chapter the chief ideas presently current in regard to the causes and "cures" of delinquency have been described. Here, however, we must be more specific if we are to indicate the main ways in which young offenders may be aided by those to whom authority over them has been entrusted. In the following account we have drawn upon a recent article by Bruno Bettelheim,[21] the head of an institution for delinquent children, whose work is representative of modern thinking and practice. Unfortunately, work of the kind here recommended is far from usual. For a description of the way delinquents are handled in many state training schools and other institutions the reader is referred to Albert Deutsch's *Our Rejected Children.*

Persistent delinquents, the boys and girls who constitute the majority in training schools and perhaps even on probation officers' rolls, engage in misconduct for various reasons, but three main types of motives have been found that provide a basis for treatment planning.

The first kind of motive is that of the immature, uncontrolled boy or girl who does what he pleases with little regard for right, wrong, or consequences. He has seldom found that waiting or renouncing pays, either

---

[21] Bruno Bettelheim, "On the Rehabilitation of Offenders," *Federal Probation,* Vol. XIII (1949), pp. 5–15.

in the desired goods or in the affection and esteem of persons he cares for, so he acts impulsively and with little inhibition. Many of these youngsters come from the economically deprived level of society, have been more or less looked down upon in school and elsewhere, and have little reason to want to do as persons in authority desire.

Such boys and girls are particularly in need of demonstrations that obedience and conformity to society's rules are worth while. They have to be helped, bit by bit, to control their impulses and to discover that such control brings rewards, both in affection and esteem and in achievement of some of their desires. Care must be taken that these youngsters are not subjected to too many and too severe frustrating experiences, for it is only slowly that they learn self-control, and they are easily thrown back into their old ways.

A second type of motive is that of the delinquent who engages in misdeeds in order to get even with society. These boys and girls harbor a deep-laid suspicion of almost everybody. They feel that the world is against them and that, in self-defense, they must strike back. They expect to be punished for their misbehavior but they are not stopped by punishment, only more than ever convinced that the world is against them.

Such youngsters, say modern psychologists, will never change until they are convinced that their belief that everybody is down on them is wrong. It has been found that if those who have them in charge refuse to punish them and, instead, treat them very kindly no matter what they do, the boys and girls will fairly soon be reluctant to misbehave for fear of losing the acquired benefits. Once started on the way to good conduct, these youngsters must increasingly be shown that their old idea about people's attitude toward them is unjustified. If friendship and interest in them are consistently demonstrated, many of them will eventually develop the kind of control by conscience that keeps most people straight, and they will be able to benefit from the rules and restrictions that are normally binding.

A third type of motive for delinquency, encountered rather infrequently, is desire for punishment. Some delinquents engage in misdeeds for the express purpose of being caught. Instead of trying to avoid detection, they actually seek it and, having been punished, they again strive to do something that is wrong. Punishment obviously does not help this kind of neurotic youngster, nor is abstention from punishment helpful either. What is required in these cases is psychiatric treatment, long continued, for the emotional disturbance is too deep-laid to be reached by environmental methods.

There are doubtless other types of motives that lead to persistent delinquency. Each writer is inclined to make his own categories, in line with methods he has found successful. These three, however, are said to account for the majority of cases, and there are some general rules that apply to all of them and probably to most of the others as well.

Basically, most persistent delinquents are lacking in a sense of self-respect, a sense of being people of worth. Since respect for oneself, that prime requirement for personal well-being, depends upon being accorded respect by others, one basic rule in dealing with delinquents (as with all youngsters) is to treat each one as unique and of importance, as one whose interests, desires, and concerns are of worth. Another rule of great importance is that of keeping promises, of making certain that plans decided upon are carried out if at all possible and, if not, that clear explanations be made. Such attitudes and such behavior should characterize all the staff of the institution, for what these boys and girls most require is a demonstration that they are persons of value in an environment that is trustworthy throughout.

Self-respect is further enhanced by successful accomplishment of meaningful tasks. Many of these boys and girls have seldom achieved anything that both they and their parents, teachers, or employers thought worth while. Having little feeling of accomplishment of tasks well done, they have come to adolescence with little on which to base decisions about what kind of adults they can and want to be. Along with measures to restore trust and personal dignity, there must go, therefore, measures aimed at reducing these youngsters' feelings of incompetence and inferiority. School, shop, athletic field, assigned tasks throughout the institution provide endless opportunities of this kind, but great care must be taken that in these various aspects of institutional life the youngsters do not repeat their previous unfortunate experiences of ineptitude and failure.

Since a considerable number of delinquents may have gotten into difficulty because the standards and values of the social class to which they belong differ from those of the majority, advantage can perhaps be taken of the close life an institution affords to introduce such boys and girls to ways of life that are different from their own. Whether the administrators deliberately plan it or not, these ideas and values will underlie the institution's way of life. Nor will they be wholly strange to the delinquent. These delinquents have heard middle-class standards enunciated in school and illustrated in the movies, but they have never experienced them in a setting in which they were actually lived out in all aspects of life, in a life of which they themselves were a respected part. Whether, in such a setting, these boys and girls can learn middle-class ways, whether they can change their ideas and beliefs in so fundamental a way is yet to be ascertained. So far as we know, nobody has observed what goes on in even the best training school or other institution with this question in mind.

These various means by which the staffs of training schools and other institutions can aid delinquents in the development of a more healthy personality are also available to probation officers to a limited extent. Both of these groups of officials operate within a relationship of authority, and both must use that authority in a way that is psychologically sound if they are to achieve their common objective. Probation officers presumably have the younger or the less difficult youngsters to work with. This will perhaps compensate for the fewer contacts they have with their charges and the less frequent opportunity to influence many aspects of their lives. It would seem, however, that in addition to themselves using measures that increase the delinquents' self-respect, probation officers will have to work through other persons to the same end and thereby join forces with all in the community who are interested in the children's welfare.

All of this—all the work that has been described in this chapter—takes time and money and staff and careful training of all persons concerned. In this the work of law enforcement is like the work of all professions concerned with human beings. In addition, there is still much to be learned about how the work can best be done. The basic principles, however, seem unmistakable.

✗ XVII ✗

Next Steps in Research

THE purpose of the Midcentury White House Conference on Children and Youth, a continuing endeavor, is, we said at the outset, "to consider how we can develop in children the mental, emotional, and spiritual qualities essential to individual happiness and responsible citizenship, and what physical, economic, and social conditions are deemed necessary to this development." So far, in this fact-finding report to the Conference, we have been chiefly concerned with setting forth where we now stand with respect to knowledge on these matters and with indicating some of the ways in which the knowledge is being used and might be further used for the benefit of children and youth. The advancement of healthy personality development calls, however, not only for the understanding and utilization of present knowledge but also for continuing research. That there are gaps in knowledge and areas of insufficient knowledge has been noted again and again throughout the report. A general statement on this subject, however, is called for, and also suggestions of ways along which research might profitably proceed. Such a statement was prepared by members of the Technical Committee on Fact Finding.[1] The report of the Committee follows:

The Technical Committee on Fact Finding has examined the Fact Finding materials of the Midcentury White House Conference on Children and Youth with a view to delineating some of the areas in which further knowledge is needed concerning child life and development. What is herewith presented can in no wise be regarded as a "blueprint" for the future, the result of crystal gazing, albeit by scientists. Neither is it intended to imply that we have already utilized in practice all available knowledge. This is far from the case. Much of the material presented in the *Fact-finding Report,* through the work of the technical staff, will appear fresh and stimulating and will open new vistas to many workers

[1] Members of the sub-committee that prepared the statement were Abraham Franzblau, T. Duckett Jones, Otto Klineberg.

in the field. Much additional material undoubtedly exists to which we did not have access for the Conference. New areas beckon nevertheless. The indication of a new opportunity has always spurred a new effort.

Since the pursuit of knowledge is endless, its goals ever receding, it is incumbent upon those who even tentatively propose next steps to identify the context in which the answers will be of value.

Perhaps the knowledge most needed today relates to the development of the kind of personalities required to enjoy, preserve, and enhance the democratic tradition with its potentialities and promise. This becomes especially important in view of the ever-accelerated rate of social, economic, and political change, and the unprecedented advances in science and technology.

Sound Personality and the Maintenance of Democracy

Only individuals whose minds are free and whose personalities have developed to healthy social and emotional maturity are capable of living in accord with the high ideals which democratic society demands of us. The capacity to cooperate with others to common ends—to share and to identify with them in spirit—is to a large degree born of confidence in self.

The intelligence, to be truly free, must be freed of impediments both from within and without. The inquiring mind quests where it may, bringing old facts and facets into new configurations, asking new questions, and finding unforetold solutions. For this it must be liberated both from the silver cord of obsolete custom and tradition and from the iron band of fear. It must be able to step out afresh and anew, enterprisingly, preferably in cooperation with others of like mind, but if necessary, alone.

This is the kind of bold and responsible creative imagination called for by the times. Individuals come by it only through propitious experience. How to engender that experience is the crux of the problem of education in a democracy. The mature, emotionally stable, healthy personality is at once the goal and the guardian of the democratic tradition. Such a personality can meet change with adaptiveness, neither resisting it blindly nor accepting it resignedly, but using and shaping it for human betterment.

How assure the development of such personalities? What life conditions in home, church, school, recreation center, neighborhood, and world are most likely to produce growth in this direction? How may these conditions be achieved?

Some Examples of Needed Research

In attempting to answer such questions as these, the *Fact-finding Report to the Midcentury White House Conference* has surveyed and summarized much of the existing information that is pertinent. It has also come upon certain areas in which no answers, or no sufficiently reliable answers, have yet been found. A few examples chosen from among the hundreds of problems suggested to the Committee will be presented briefly below. It is believed that methods now exist by means of which progress in the solution of these and similar problems could be attained with suitable effort.

The Constitutional and Physiological Basis for Personality

We have some evidence that the foundation for healthy personality is laid long before birth but we have little knowledge as to the process by which this is achieved. Ahead lies the task of identifying the contribution of the various aspects of the prenatal environment, as well as the precise nature of genetic influence.

Such knowledge might prove important in controlling the causes of prematurity, certain types of infant mortality, and faulty mental development. The precise role of nutrition during the early and highly formative phases of pregnancy is also only poorly understood.

The Debilitating or Dissipating Diseases of Childhood

While many hitherto fatal or dangerous childhood diseases have been robbed of their lethal power, there are still others for which we lack economical methods of diagnosis, control, and therapy: notably, cancer, leukemia, tuberculosis, poliomyelitis, and rheumatic fever. Rheumatic fever, and its consequent heart disease, account for the greatest number of deaths and chronic disabilities from childhood diseases. Accidents continue to take their heavy toll, and many of these are preventable.

Still prevalent among children are the common cold and dental caries. There is need for research that will clarify the relation between diet and health, energy levels, and resistance to disease.

Personality and the Psychology of Development

The basic task is to describe dynamically how the growing child relates and interacts with his expanding world, and how much of children's personality develops from their own unique experiences and how much from the contributions of parents, neighborhood, and the wider patterns of culture.

Knowledge of how the child achieves internal security and balance will probably help us reduce mental illness and juvenile delinquency.

We also need to know the relative importance of early stages as contrasted to later stages of growth, and the extent to which one may override the other.

Many unsolved problems center also around individual differences. Why do infants have differing modes and capacities of adjustment to basically the same experiences? How can children become tough, viable, and highly resilient and adaptive, while preserving their sensitivity toward higher human values?

The significance and patterning of sex in child development are incompletely understood and contrastingly interpreted. What is the role of the common childhood experiences in achieving sexual maturity? Psychoanalysis, offering its specific theories of dynamic development, evokes wide disagreement both within its own framework and from without. Not only do these and other dynamic concepts need to be examined but we also need techniques by which to test the validity of so-called "qualitative" theories.

Greater insight is needed into adolescence. Environmental forces on the one hand stimulate early sexual maturation and, on the other, place economic and social taboos in the way of realization. We need answers as to how physiological changes occurring at adolescence interact with the culture pattern in shaping the adolescent personality.

How do children react to being different from others of their age group? How does being developmentally behind or ahead of the group, or being qualitatively different, affect a child's emerging concept of himself or his feeling of belongingness or worthiness?

The Child in the Family

What children will be when they grow up seems largely to originate within the nexus of early family relations, especially between the child and the mother. There still remains a degree of confusion as to the exact relationship between organic developmental needs and emotional needs as a basis for physical and emotional maturity.

We need further insight into the implications of breast versus bottle feeding, of varying types of feeding schedules, of handling and rocking, and of toilet training. Especially lacking is knowledge of the implications for personality development of differing class and cultural group patterns of parent-child relationships.

The Child and His Family through the Social Order

How does the family function as the filter between the child and the modern world? Effective social planning and community action depend upon a knowledge of how our customs and institutions bear upon the individual family. The influence of employment in modern industry—for example, the effects of layoffs, of mechanization and depersonalization in working conditions—must be understood as they affect family vitality and stability.

We need also to determine whether the apparent surrender to other agencies of functions traditionally exercised by the family represents a breakdown in its vitality or an enrichment via the specialized services offered by these agencies.

The Child's Group

Little systematic research has been undertaken on the child's peer group, which plays an important role in the process of growing up. We also lack as yet systematic knowledge of how peer group processes vary within differing cultural or socioeconomic levels.

School and community programs aid the child to achieve satisfying relations with others of his own and other age groups leading him gradually to adult status. To what extent does the peer group within the subculture complement and support (or negate) the home or school?

Still largely unknown are the ways in which the values and codes of children are translated and transmitted to suit the needs of each succeeding age group. Research is needed to identify the sources within the culture from which children draw values and standards.

The School

At the midcentury, the task still remains to evaluate our schools objectively. Most of us are so close to them that objective analysis and appraisal become difficult. Educators endeavor to relate the child to the tasks he faces both at the present time and in the future. Do our schools under- or overemphasize intellectual mastery as a facet of personality development? Is it fostered in fitting context with other phases of learning, such as skills, attitudes, and ideals, or in isolation, to the neglect of the other factors?

Educational research is needed on the problems of preschool children and the extent to which the nursery school meets or may increasingly meet their needs.

There is need, too, for better understanding of the contribution to physical and mental growth and learning among all age groups, as well as in the total educational program, of such factors as architecture, playgrounds, furniture, color and lighting, and other aspects of school environment.

Research can reveal what people want their children's education to consist of and hence may lead to a greater harmony of goals and objectives. The ultimate meaning of the school may come not only from concentration upon the technical processes of education but also from research into the role of the school within the larger social process.

Social Service

There is need to understand social attitudes in their genesis, dynamics, and implications for change, and also their effect on the development of existing programs. To what extent are social services and public and private social-service agencies responsive to, and representative of, the exigencies of our citizenry? To what extent are they required and desired? Social agencies suffer from lack of effective techniques of evaluation and appraisal, both of their results and of their instrumentalities. A systematic and tested body of theory is needed for child-welfare work.

Service agencies are searching, for example, for effective ways of aiding delinquent children, of helping children benefit from foster care, and of reducing the margin of guesswork in child adoption. They want to know how to reach certain groups and classes not amenable to present social-work efforts. This will probably call for more knowledge of both individual and group psychology and for increased understanding of cultural differences. Such agencies also need new and more economical therapeutic techniques for the treatment of behavior disorders.

Clinical and Medical Agencies

Training institutions and personnel departments would profit from the development of effective techniques of selecting and training prospective students or staff members for constructive work with children. This would make possible greater attention to the human factor, which requires emphasis not only in clinical and medical agencies but also in all types of institutions—economic, political, religious—that deal directly or indirectly with children.

Religion

We need greater understanding of the effect of bringing religious values into the life situations of children, and we need to evaluate with greater objectivity the role of religion within the child's world.

The Extended Environment

The problem of tracing personality formation in a relatively simple and static culture is great; infinitely more so to attack a complex, multicultural setting such as exists in the United States. Yet this is a problem from which we cannot escape. We need to know more about the life of children everywhere, whether in some faraway Pacific island or at our own doorstep.

If personal worth and freedom are agreed to be the cornerstones of the democratic way of life, what experiences establish the capacity for the enjoyment and utilization of freedom? What are the experiences from which the child may evolve the courage to be an individual, not afraid to be different? Has the family retreated in this vital area? We need information also about the contributions of the institutionalized and semiorganized aspects of the child's environment in this respect.

Research into the origin and prevention of racial and religious prejudice is called for. Is the problem of combatting prejudice only one of coordinating the efforts of existing agencies, or are techniques for providing some other positive type of experience required? We also need in that field a program of evaluation that will replace theory and conjecture with fact.

What are the effects of prejudice upon the personality of both the prejudiced and the victims of the prejudice? What are the contrasting degrees of adjustment when racial or religious differences are clearly defined or slight, or where the oppressed group receives inconsistent treatment at the hands of the oppressing group?

Relatively little is yet known about the effects of poverty and economic inequality or, for that matter, of wealth upon the child's personality. What is the effect of the many incompatible tendencies in our environment: the universal preachment of tolerance versus the undeniable fact of discrimination; the ideal of equality of opportunity and the many departures from it in fact; the drives toward personal economic success and material satisfaction in conflict with spiritual and social satisfactions and goals?

The above are merely samples of the types of studies that remain to be done in the field covered by the Midcentury White House Conference on Children and Youth. There are many others, of course, in which work will someday reveal new knowledge. Likewise, there is much already done that, if properly applied, would make new studies unnecessary.

Some Methodological Considerations

In addition to a consideration of the gaps in our knowledge of child development, the Fact-finding Committee of the Midcentury White House Conference has given attention to child-development research. Would improved methods of inquiry provide answers backed by greater assurance, or even new answers where no answers were possible before?

Study of the Normal

For example, much of what is known about how personality develops derives, paradoxically, from the effort to cure abnormal or sick individuals. Having tentatively observed that a given factor accounts for illness or immaturity, we have assumed that its absence or the presence of its antithesis must conduce to maturity and health.

Of this, there is, however, no scientific certainty. The absence of typhoid germs and the presence of certain minerals, vitamins, and proteins afford protection against typhoid and the respective deficiency diseases. But whether the same holds true for any given practice in child care, such as bottle feeding or early toilet training, for example, no one can say.

In the future, the mainstream of child-development research will probably give more attention to positive factors rather than limiting itself to drawing deductions from negative factors alone. In character, as in agriculture, perhaps the finest product may be grown not by heeding pathology alone but by the identification of positive factors in soil (mind or spirit) chemistry, climatology (the larger human environment), genetics (the home and family)—all the influences that bear upon the bounty and soundness of the crop.

Clinical and Other Types of Evidence

The fact that research in personality formation took its departure from therapy has given rise to another characteristic: much of the evidence is clinical, the kind of knowledge that comes from seeing case after case and generalizing.

Evidence of this kind certainly represents one important approach; but there is a need for additional means of validation, especially for means by which clinical evidence may be reviewed by others, since the clinical method, for all its limitations, seems destined to remain an important means for investigation in this area.

The laboratory by itself has certain limitations, too. It cannot fully reproduce the effective conditions of associated human living any more than it can create life itself in the test tube. As to the statistical approach, the question remains whether certain significant aspects of human personality are by nature quantifiable and whether some of the variables are not destined to be forever unknown. Experimentation with human beings has its practical limits, and experimentation with animals in an effort to learn about human personality will never give us the complete picture, for animals live without custom, ideals, conscience, or aspirations.

Such considerations are no justification for despair among scientists but rather for renewed and more vigorous efforts. Where knowledge is sorely needed and the trail is but dimly blazed, man somehow manages to bring vast resources to bear and to find alternative routes to the goal.

Influence of Culture—The Comparative Approach

Most of the information now available is derived from study of children in the United States and Western Europe, and of quite limited sectors of these. Because human personality develops after a given fashion here, is it in the very nature of human personality to develop after this same fashion always, everywhere, under all circumstances? For example, among primitive peoples who practice polygamy and polyandry, the widely accepted generalizations about the universality of jealousy do not seem to apply; likewise, among peoples to whom acquisition and property mean nothing, prevalent beliefs about the development of competitiveness and status fail to be substantiated.

Future research in child development in comparative cultures, where customs, values, and beliefs vary greatly, is needed for a fuller understanding of the laws that govern the development of all human personality. They should be carried on not only in cultures very different from our own but also in subcultures within our own society. Such comparative studies of different cultures might provide opportunity to analyze, as in a laboratory setup, what happens when different groups of children are differently reared.

The Interdisciplinary Approach

To explain any behavior—sucking, chewing, and eating, let us say— the biologist, the psychologist, the psychiatrist, the anthropologist, the social psychologist, and perhaps even the economist each study it from a different angle, in a different context, with different purposes, and by different methods. When all that they know is put together, it is better understood as a part of human personality and functioning.

But the specialization of knowledge has created certain difficulties in this "putting together" process. The human being just chews and eats, so to speak. He doesn't do it biologically, psychologically, psychiatrically, anthropologically, sociologically, or to illustrate the economics of food consumption. These are merely ways of studying how and what he eats, in what circumstances, and why.

Putting Humpty Dumpty together again becomes difficult because the biologist studies, thinks, and talks in terms of the oral structures and functions, energy intake and output; the psychiatrist in terms of drives and motives, conscious and unconscious; the anthropologist in terms of customs and taboos; and so on. It is relatively easy to string together what all of them have to say about eating. To put it together in an integrated way is yet another and far more difficult thing. It is infinitely more difficult with such things as delinquency, creativity, or willingness to follow where the evidence points.

In the view of the Committee, to accomplish this may require a new kind of training for research workers to acquaint them with cognate fields as well as their own.

It may also require the joint planning of research projects by persons from all relevant disciplines. This may be difficult and time consuming, for the various disciplines will have to explain their aims, methods, and problems to each other. Ample time for preliminary exploration and allowances for initial awkwardness, perhaps even blundering, may be required before a new kind of composite answer may result from the use of such research methods.

The Longitudinal Approach

It takes human beings longer to achieve mature physical development than any other species, and the personality goes on developing throughout life until senescence. Further, many factors play upon it, some earlier, some later in the life history, all interacting and influencing each other.

Research efforts will need to be channeled into studies of large groups of children over long periods of time in order to study these factors fully. Much more material of this type already exists than has as yet been adequately analyzed. Such studies, although costly, may provide long-sought and sorely needed answers to help man deal effectively with the problems of human personality in a democratic society.

Conclusion

The fact-finding materials prepared as the scientific basis for the Midcentury White House Conference on Children and Youth abound in evidence that, while much progress has been made, we are far from a satisfactory state concerning our knowledge of the problems of human behavior. Our nation at the midcentury has within it many unknowns—processes and patterns—operating beyond our control or in undetermined ways. The frequent appearance of unanswered vital questions and unsolved social problems forcibly stress and attest to this fact.

All social- and medical-science professional personnel with experience in the use of scientific methods place a very high priority on the need to ascertain the influences that determine direction in human behavior, especially those that encourage the attainment of adequacy and maturity. The focus of the Conference recognized this and so stated.

Within the limitations of time and professional resources, we have sought the current general level of knowledge. We clearly recognize the inadequacy of this general level. Good will, good intention, ample funds, and the desires of well-motivated parents, citizens, community leaders, and professional workers can go only so far in increasing the number of well-adjusted, happy individuals unless we also earnestly seek to increase knowledge. We are unable otherwise to progress beyond the application of that which we presently know and assume to be valid and good. That which appears merely to be common sense and seemingly plausible theory constitutes an even more inadequate base.

For our problems there are no simple solutions. Only consistent, intelligent study with constantly increasing scope can yield any appreciable improvement or any dramatic changes. In the modern world, change and interaction seem to increase by geometric proportions. Many find it impossible to live comfortably with themselves; how can we expect them to face with equanimity relations with others—in their own family, the community, state, and other nations?

Many feel that a peaceful world is an impossibility without further study of man and his behavior. If this be true, now is the time to organize for greater effort lest it be too late. This might justify the hope of achieving an increase in happy, productive citizens, whose individual worth is at the heart of the very concept of democracy. We need more knowledge and at a rate greater than our limited efforts have hitherto allowed. Projects of research should be designed and undertaken upon a scale adequate to meet the problems and unknowns we face.

Fortunately opportunities exist that strongly portend success. Methods and tools have recently been developed, and are spreading rapidly, whereby the imponderables and the differing influences of many variables may be brought into clearer focus, tested, and objectively viewed.

Further, existent at present are small groups of scientists working in our universities and research institutions who are competent to serve as the initial nucleus for the development of such research.

These focuses of intellectual activity are one of our most cherished possessions. From such teams of biological and social scientists—all too few and undermanned—have come many of our basic research findings and discoveries. The American people and the world at large owe much to the patient and untiring efforts of these few. From the efforts, for example, of our medical researchers have come breathtaking discoveries in the fields of physical health that have strained the very structure of our methods of applying them.

Increasingly, further progress must be tied to the goal of combining and coordinating inquiry and research along broad fronts. Lack of methods, difficulties in semantics, the imbalance of specialization, poor communication, lack of research personnel, the limitations of students in the field of application have been and still are deterrents to scientific progress. But all these are correctable, hence merely heighten the challenge.

The needs are many. The opportunity to train in considerable numbers carefully selected potential contributors to knowledge should be increased. Following this, full opportunity to use their intellectual abilities is essential. Our present, able investigators require adequate research support providing the stability and continuity essential if ideas are to flourish. Our professional schools, especially, need to be heavily supported.

All research workers are not necessarily good teachers, and certainly all teachers are not necessarily good scientists. But if the intellectual curiosity of the scientist is removed too far from the educator, both suffer. Education, research, and application are an interdependent triad. They call for close association and careful balancing, lest the product be inferior, lest knowledge become static, and the professional worker become a dispenser of equal degrees of fact and fancy. Ignorance—man's greatest enemy—could thus become the order of the day.

The cherishing and expansion of our universities and professional schools, seen in this light, become the key to future progress. Though results be slow in arriving and costly in terms of dollars, this seems little enough when balanced against the objective of human happiness and the improvement of the relations of human beings to one another and to groups. There are no short cuts to progress. We must continue to move forward, or founder on the shoals of retrogression.

The Technical Committee on Fact Finding strongly advises that the seeking out and summarization of all pertinent knowledge coming within the focus of the Midcentury White House Conference on Children and Youth be made a continuing process, thus leading to earlier awareness of gaps and neglected areas and better application of both existent and new knowledge.

MEMBERS OF THE STAFF OF THE MIDCENTURY WHITE HOUSE
CONFERENCE ON CHILDREN AND YOUTH

Melvin A. Glasser, *Executive Director*
Henry F. Helmholz, M.D., *Chief Consultant*
Winifred Wilcox, *Administrative Assistant*

STATE AND LOCAL ACTION

Louis de Boer, *Director*
Juanita Luck, *Assistant Director*
Gertrude Davis, *Consultant*
Lois Gratz, *Consultant*

COMMUNICATIONS

Marvin Beers, *Director*
Margery R. Cunningham, *Assistant Director*

PROGRAM

Gordon Lippitt, *Program Coordinator*
Muriel W. Brown, *Program Consultant*
Harry J. Wiener, *Exhibits Consultant*

NATIONAL ORGANIZATIONS

Elma Phillipson, *Consultant*

FEDERAL GOVERNMENT PARTICIPATION

Edith Rockwood, *Consultant*

YOUTH PARTICIPATION

Juanita Luck, *Consultant*

FACT FINDING

Helen L. Witmer, *Director*
Ruth Kotinsky, *Assistant Director*

Full-time Consultants

Dale C. Cameron, M.D.
Howard Cummings
Dorothy Lee
Elizabeth H. Ross

Part-time or Short-term Consultants

Millie Almy
Herbert W. Beaser
Muriel W. Brown
Kenneth B. Clark
Norris Class
Donald Dukelow, M.D.
Sibylle Escalona
Roma Gans
Regina F. Herzfeld
Eleanor P. Hunt
Alice Scott Hyatt
Mary Alice Jones

Moses Jung
Leonard T. Kurland, M.D.
William S. Langford, M.D.
Sol Markoff
Maryland Y. Pennell
Ruth Reed
Duane Robinson
Sophia Robison
Edward E. Schwartz
Morton A. Seidenfeld
A. Delafield Smith
Ruth Taylor

INDEX

449